MADNESS

WITHDRAWN

MADNESS

An American History of
Mental Illness and Its Treatment

MARY de YOUNG

McFarland & Company, Inc., Publishers
Jefferson, North Carolina, and London

BP45

LIBRARY OF CONGRESS CATALOGUING-IN-PUBLICATION DATA

de Young, Mary, 1949–
    Madness : an American history of mental illness and its
treatment / Mary de Young.
        p.   cm.
    Includes bibliographical references and index.

    ISBN 978-0-7864-3398-8
    softcover : 50# alkaline paper ∞

    1. Mental illness—United States—History.   2. Psychiatric
hospitals—United States—History.   3. Mental illness—
Treatment—United States—History.   I. Title.   II. Title:
American history of mental illness and its treatment.
    [DNLM: 1. Mental Disorders—history—United States.
2. Hospitals, Psychiatric—history—United States.   3. Mental
Disorders—therapy—United States.   WM 11 AA1]
    RC443.D35   2010
    362.196'89—dc22   2010026435

British Library cataloguing data are available

Front cover image ©2010 Shutterstock

Manufactured in the United States of America

*McFarland & Company, Inc., Publishers
    Box 611, Jefferson, North Carolina 28640
    www.mcfarlandpub.com*

3/29/11

To Gabriel—welcome to the family.

Acknowledgments

I WOULD LIKE TO OFFER a sincere thanks to my colleagues and friends who offered advice and support during the writing of this book. I am particularly indebted to Richard Joanisse, Bob Hendersen, Joe Verschaeve and Elizabeth Chapelle, Michael and Mary Louise Ott, Jennifer Stewart, Erika King and Robert Beasecker, Karen and Dan Lorenski, Mark VerStraete, Pam and Terry Roach, and the "Shrieking Sisterhood": Patti Haist, Barbara Corbin and Judy Baars.

Much of the research for this book was conducted during my sabbatical. For supporting that project, I want to thank my colleagues in the Sociology Department of Grand Valley State University, as well as the dean of the College of Liberal Arts and Sciences. The librarians at Grand Valley State were always and forever helpful, as was the staff of the Wellcome Library for the Understanding and Appreciation of Medicine where I spent many a happy hour while in London.

Robert Charles Bogdan, of the Center on Human Policy, Law, and Disability Studies at Syracuse University, gave permission to use the text of several postcards from his extensive collection. The Pickler Memorial Library at Truman State University gave permission to use materials from the Harry Laughlin Collection on eugenics. To both, I offer my thanks.

Contents

List of Tables

Preface

Bring me to the test, and I the matter will reword—which madness would gambol from. —Hamlet

THIS IS A BOOK ABOUT MADNESS. Were it about almost any other topic, that simple declarative sentence very well might suffice as an introduction.

But madness is not like most other topics. "Madness is a veritable Proteus," a scholar once propounded. "How infinite its varieties! How mercurial its qualities! How artfully can lunacy ape sanity! Is there not reason in madness; folly jumbled with reason?" (Porter, 2006, p.1). Indeed, there is— and much more.

As Chapter 1 explains, madness is protean. Like the Greek sea-god Proteus, the oracular old man of the sea and the herdsman of the sea-beasts, madness changes its shape and answers only to those capable of capturing it. Some readers might find that analogy facile, even romantic. They can put down this book and look out their windows and see sidewalk psychotics, unkempt, stinking of piss and talking to themselves, and wonder what is protean about their madness. Agreed. Somewhere between 1 and 3 percent of the U.S. population is psychotic (Torrey & Miller, 2001), that is, out of touch with a consensually agreed upon reality, and often unable to take care of themselves. And although they should engage our compassion and stir our advocacy—much more than they do, sadly—they are not the only people who have borne the burden and the stigma of madness.

Chapter 1, therefore, acknowledges that psychosis has been historically invariant, even while suggesting it is culturally sensitive, and focuses more on the plethora of other nervous, character, affective, behavioral, sexual and

1

identity disorders that have, at one time or the other in U.S. history, been categorized as madness. And here is where the protean nature of madness is evident. Much of what has been understood, treated and represented as madness throughout U.S. history has been socially constructed, that is, it has been contingent upon the prevailing aspects of society at that particular historical moment. As those forces change, categories and diagnoses of madness have changed as well. That concept of social construction may be unfamiliar and, for some readers, hard to take. In contemporary American society we think of madness as a *disease*—mental illness, to be exact—and diseases are biological, not social. But mental illness is a quite recent concept, the product of a steady process of medicalization, that is, of attaching, in this case, psychiatric labels to behaviors, feelings and thoughts that are regarded as socially or morally undesirable. And the very word "undesirable" speaks not to disease, but to *dis-ease*—to behaviors, feelings and thoughts that transgress norms, interests and values—and all of those are both social and, themselves, protean.

Chapter 2 deals with subjective experiences of madness. Using both narrations of madness and first-person accounts, now referred to as "pathographies," the chapter explores what it is like to *be* mad, quite regardless of the diagnosis or the historical moment in which the account is written. Giving voice to the mad, treating them as credible narrators of their own experiences, invites them into a discourse that for too long has been dominated by others. They talk about confusion, anger and betrayal and they reveal humiliation, embarrassment, helplessness and sometimes victory— all of that expected, of course—but what may be surprising to readers is that many of them also recount their personal experiences of madness in relationship not only to others, but also to the social world in which they live.

This book is about madness in the United States. And while the European influence on how madness was seen and treated is acknowledged and discussed, the subject of the book is geographically, and therefore socially, bound. Thus chapter 3 examines madness in the Colonial era. With only a few of notable exceptions (Deutsch, 1937; Eldridge, 1996; Jimenez, 1987), little has been written about this pre-asylum era, and for understandable reason. Until the glorious age of the internet, research into madness during the Colonial era required a willingness to read, cover to cover, musty colonial records, and to delve into published diaries and family histories. These days, many of those records are online, and are even indexed, although more for the convenience of genealogists than sociologists. So these too had to be read, cover to cover, for references to madness, which went by a wide variety of euphemistic terms, such as "distracted" and "crazy-brained." Patience is rewarded, though, with glimpses into what really was a different time in every sense of that term, and for revelations into what colonists believed about madness, as well as into what their small, cohesive, communal, theocratic communities did about it, and for it.

The history of madness is the history of the asylum, and a deeply political history that turns out to be. Chapter 4 sets out that history from the establishment of a ground floor lunatic wing in the Pennsylvania Hospital in 1755, through the zenith of state asylums in the 19th century and their nadir in the first half of the 20th century, through the deinstitutionalization movement of the 1960s and beyond, to the present where some of those still standing house the most intractably mad and others have been converted into condos and upscale shops and cafes.

In many ways the history of madness is also the history of psychiatry as a specialty. And that turns out to be a deeply political history as well. First referred to as "alienists," early psychiatrists learned and plied their trade within the walls of asylums. In the process, they were in an almost continuous struggle for legitimacy within the medical profession, and for control of the mad with competing specialties, especially neurology. All of those are topics in chapter 4 as well.

In its original usage "asylum" meant refuge, sanctuary. For some mad patients they have been that, and continue to be, but certainly that is not true for all patients, or perhaps even for most. Chapter 5 uses published first-person memoirs of asylum patients to enter an environment unfamiliar to most readers. Rather than categorizing or grouping those asylum memoirs according to time or place, the chapter uses as its organizing scheme the concept of "moral career." The term may not be familiar to most readers, and on its face it is quite misleading. But the sociologist Erving Goffman (1961) coined the term to mean the sense of self or of identity of the asylum patient that is slowly and steadily shaped as much by the experience of institutionalization itself as by any real or imputed madness. Despite the changes to, and in, asylums over U.S. history, the concept of moral career remains a viable organizing scheme for capturing the otherwise diverse experiences of mad patients.

The search for the cure for madness is also the search for a reason to be optimistic that the mad can be cured. Chapter 6 details the quest to find the therapeutic intervention that will restore sanity. There are a lot of larger than life personalities profiled in this chapter, psychiatric entrepreneurs who often went to great lengths to sell their version of a cure in what always has been a competitive therapeutic marketplace. There is a lot of trial and a great deal of error discussed in this chapter. Readers may be shocked (no pun intended) by the staggering array of therapeutic interventions devised to whirl, douche, restrain, cut, fever, shock, and dope mad patients into sanity.

All of them came into use with such promise but few lived up to it, and some, it may be convincingly argued, made a mockery of it.

Readers may find it quite tempting to be archly critical of the profiled psychiatric entrepreneurs, perhaps even to wonder aloud if some of them were, themselves, quite mad. But in reading the chapter be mindful of their social and scientific contexts, of the location of each within changing ideas about the relationship between the mind and the body, between madness and sanity, between physician and patient, and between patient and rights, both human and civil.

Chapter 7 concludes the book, or, better stated, *ends* it. Madness resists conclusions; in so many ways an examination of it only raises more question, invites more inquiry, and generates more discourse. And that is just as it should be.

Each chapter of the book is introduced with an epigraph by Shakespeare. No stranger to madness was he. His plays are peopled with mad characters, from Ophelia to Lear to Lady Macbeth, and have introduced into the English language a veritable lexicon of euphemisms and clever turns of phrase to describe their experiences of madness. In the first 30 years of American psychiatry, no fewer than 13 lengthy articles of Shakespeare criticism were penned by the leading alienists of the day and published in the *American Journal of Insanity*, the precursor to the *American Journal of Psychiatry*. Whether their fascination with Shakespeare was a ploy to increase their own cultural authority in a new and mysterious field or a genuine homage to someone whose insights on madness they believed superior to their own is immaterial. The fact remains that early American alienists were self-consciously transforming Shakespearean notions of madness into their own scientific theories (Blumenthal, 1995; Reiss, 2005).

To today's readers, Shakespeare may not be all that familiar, and that actually is the reason for the epigraphs. Although Shakespeare certainly was an astute observer of human nature, maybe even an expert on madness, the use of the epigraphs at the start of each chapter is intended to disturb the familiar, much as madness itself does.

There is a great deal of original source material, often quoted at length, in this book. No attempts have been made to achieve some kind of post hoc political correctness by correcting misspellings, adding [she] to the persistent male pronouns in order to achieve gender equity, or [*sic*] to call attention to an inaccurate expression or an unconventional spelling. These original materials are presented as is, and with the purpose of offering perspectives on madness that are both particular and contrasting.

"Madness" is used throughout the book as a kind of umbrella term for what, throughout American history, has been a stunning array of conditions of being mad. And those who are diagnosed or otherwise imputed to have any of these conditions are referred to as "mad" throughout the book. The term is not particularly politically correct these days, but it is not at all used pejoratively. It is descriptive of the wide range of behaviors, thoughts and emotions that have transgressed the normative and the familiar, required interpretation, and prompted therapeutic intervention or social control. The word "asylum" also is used consistently throughout the book to designate the similarly stunning array of institutions put into place to hold and heal the mad.

Consistent with one of the central tenets of the sociology of knowledge is that to explain why certain diagnoses of madness appeared at certain times in American history, why certain beliefs about madness throughout that history came to be accepted as knowledge and certain therapeutic interventions as de rigueur requires that personal views be bracketed off. That is the obligation of the sociologist as author. Readers are invited to come to their own judgments.

1

What Is Madness?

To define true madness, what is't but to be nothing else but mad? — Hamlet

BASKET CASE. CRACKED. CRAZY. CUCKOO. Daft. Deranged. Insane. Lunatic. Psycho. Out to lunch, lost the plot, not on the ball; not the brightest bulb in the chandelier or the sharpest tool in the box or the roundest marble in the toy chest; one card short of a full deck, one curl short of a perm, one sandwich short of a picnic, one clown short of a circus. Bananas, crackers, nuts, fruitcake, picklepuss. Off the deep end, round the bend, over the edge, in a blue funk, off the rocker. Nervous Nellie, Sad Sack, Gloomy Gus. Addicted, anxious, depressed, delusional, melancholic, manic, neurotic, psychotic. Dementia praecox, drapetomania, hebetude, hysteria, monomania, neurasthenia; bipolar or dissociative identity or obsessive-compulsive or post-traumatic stress disorder; schizophrenia: catatonic, chronic undifferentiated, disorganized, paranoid, residual.

The lexicon of madness is ample: from euphemisms, idioms, descriptive terms to diagnoses, both unfamiliar and familiar, the language for talking about madness is, and always has been, rich and expressive. Even then, the lexicon is far from complete. There is March Madness, Midnight Madness, mad money, and methods to madness; there is madcap fun, and there is mad as in angry or as in love. There is the *Mad Men* television show, *Mad* magazine, more than a few "mad" video games, and a scattering of "mad" rock or punk bands. There are mad heroes and villains in literature, mad scenes in opera and in theatre, mad antiheroes in film, and a fascinating iconography of madness in paintings, drawings, photographs and sculptures.

A Google search of "madness" gets 44 million hits; a search of "mad" gets four times that.

All of these terms and representations suggest that madness is too much of something—nervousness or sadness, as examples—or perhaps too little of something else—sociability or rationality, as other examples. They suggest a differentness, and some hint at a dangerousness. None really speaks to a cause or causes in the plural, thus always inviting speculation that it is a moral flaw, a weakness of character, a defect in the brain, or even a dalliance with whatever passes for that epoch's evil spirits, that produces it. All obscure the relationship between madness and the historical moment, that is, between the definition, representation, control, treatment and even the experience of madness and the larger sociocultural context.

Yet even though the lexicon of madness hides more than it reveals, it always reveals *something*. That something is not just personal, as interesting as that is, or observational/diagnostic/therapeutic, as interesting as that might be; but it often is about larger, more philosophical concerns shared by the mad and the not-mad alike, concerns about "normality and abnormality, imagination and judgment, authenticity and personality, power and oppression, the divided self" (Porter, 1991, p. xv).

Violet Into Orange:
Where Sanity Ends and Madness Begins

Herman Melville was familiar with madness. As a child he had witnessed his father's descent into a wild delirium that lasted two weeks, until his death; his brother's erratic behavior and his untimely death caused his mother to suffer bouts of debilitating depression (McCarthy, 1990). His short stories are peopled with mad characters, and his 1851 masterpiece novel, *Moby Dick*, features not only a peg-legged sea captain who is so single-minded in his pursuit of a great white whale as to be deranged, but also an insane cabin boy who befriends him, and a sailor cum mad prophet who warns him of the dire consequences of his vengeance against the whale that took his leg. But it was in his posthumously published novella, *Billy Budd* (1924), that Melville contemplates not just madness, but its supposed opposite, raising an intriguing question:

> Who in the rainbow can draw a line where the violet tint ends and the orange tint begins? Distinctly we see the differences of the colors, but where exactly does the one first blindingly enter into the other? So with sanity and insanity [76].

If indeed sanity and madness, although perceived as distinct, even as opposites, in truth blend into and around each other, then one of the most persistently vexing questions in the social history of madness is revealed: Who gets to say whether someone is sane or mad? Saying it, after all, is not just a discursive act; it is a label that has profound consequences for how a person is perceived, interacted with, and treated, perhaps for a lifetime.

The "Belle of Amherst," poet Emily Dickinson, knew that. Scholars and followers have debated for years whether her reclusiveness was symptomatic of madness, but as she withdrew further from family, friends and society she was not just mindful of the blurred line between sanity and madness, but also of the power and privilege invested in "the Majority" to declare where that line is:

> Much Madness is divinest Sense
> To a discerning Eye;
> Much Sense the starkest Madness
> 'Tis the Majority
> In this, as All, prevails.
> Assent, and you are sane;
> Demur, you're straightway dangerous,
> And handled with a Chain [1891, p. 24].

Dickinson's poem probably was penned in 1862 but it was not published until years after her death. From today's perspective, 19th century diagnostics were crude, maybe even naïve. Mad people were melancholic or manic, or some variation of either one. To use Melville's imagery, they were orange, but without much in the way of subtle hues that might differentiate one shade of orange from another. That is not so in the 21st century. The *Diagnostic and Statistical Manual of Mental Disorders*, better known as the *DSM-IV*, sets out in detail all of the hues of orange that distinguish one type of madness from another, and that presumably makes it easier to distinguish all types from the "violet tint" of sanity. Has this 886-page, three-pound "psychiatric bible," then, with its precise criteria, multiaxial system and diagnostic codes, rendered Dickinson's indictment of "the Majority" obsolete? No, not really.

Consider the fact that since its first edition published in 1952, the *DSM* has gone through several revisions; it is now in its fourth revised edition, with a fifth soon to come. What is being revised through all of these iterations of the "bible of psychiatry" is the very notion of madness. As a result, diagnoses disappear from one edition to the next. Homosexuality is a good example. Categorized as a sexual deviation, it appears in the first and second editions; in the third, it is a type of madness only if it is "ego-dystonic," that is, if it causes persistent and marked distress (Spitzer, 1981), but in the

1987 revision of the third edition, it disappears completely. Those in charge of revisions had capitulated to the outrage of gays and lesbians both inside their membership and outside of it. Homosexuality does not reappear in the fourth edition, published in 1994, although presumably it could be included in the diagnosis of "Sexual Disorders Not Otherwise Specified," but only if it causes persistent and marked distress, specifically about sexual orientation. Homosexuality as a sexual orientation has not changed over the past half-century, but attitudes about it have. And as "the Majority" opinion, in both the general public and the psychiatric profession, has shifted in recent years, it has lost its diagnostic reliability.

As the result of the continuous negotiation over the boundaries between sanity and madness made necessary by social change, diagnoses also suddenly appear in various editions. The first edition of the *DSM* listed 106 diagnostic categories, the fourth 292, including such categories as Disorder of Written Expression, Caffeine Induced Sleep Disorder, Circadian Rhythm Sleep Disorder, and Developmental Coordination Disorder. As the vices and sins, bumps and grinds, human frailties, and everyday kvetching of previous generations are medicalized by vote of the membership, "the Majority" decides where violet ends and orange begins.

"The Majority" also decides what is left out of the *DSM* altogether. The battle over the inclusion of "Victimization Disorder" ended in defeat, with women psychiatrists and feminists vigorously, and publicly, protesting its inclusion in the *DSM-IV* (Kutchins & Kirk, 1997). "Road Rage" may or may not be included in the *DSM-V* under the title of "Intermittent Explosive Disorder"; ever since the public got wind of the possibility, the proposal has been the subject of considerable ridicule. Obesity and internet addiction as brain disorders are still undergoing debate (Block, 2008; Volkow & O'Brien, 2007). The considerable disagreement over "Psychosis Risk Syndrome," a diagnosis that would label a predilection towards schizophrenia for adolescents (Moran, 2009), and "Post-Traumatic Embitterment Disorder," which labels the persistent feelings of as much as 2 percent of the American population that the world is unjust and unfair (Roan, 2009), may mean that either or both will be left out of the forthcoming edition. As the debates over these and other diagnoses, both new and old, are being waged outside of voting member (let alone public) scrutiny (Spitzer, 2008), only time will tell what "the Majority" will decide.

Perhaps it goes without saying that nowhere in any of the iterations of the *DSM* can a diagnosis of "sane" be found or, for that matter, a description of it. In the *DSM*'s terms, perhaps, sanity is to be understood as nothing more than the absence of everything "the Majority" included in the most recent addition.

"The Majority" Sociologically Reconsidered

There is a different read on Dickinson's oft-quoted poem: "the Majority" refers to males. As a single woman living in 19th century society, Dickinson begrudged the power and privilege of males to impose limits upon the intellectual and creative expressions of females, and she bemoaned those females who assented to that male authority with their own "discerning eye" closed.

This gendered read of the poem raises interesting questions about the biases that might influence not only where the line between sanity and madness is, but also how distinct it is. The social history of madness is replete with accounts of women declared mad by vengeful husbands, unenlightened physicians, or insensitive judges (Caminero-Santangelo, 2003; Geller, 1995; Grobe, 1995; Wood, 1994). It is filled with critical analyses of male control over women's bodies that has sometimes transformed biological functions, such as menstruation and menopause, into psychiatric conditions, and of male control over the gendered self, so that women's emotions, drives and thoughts have also sometimes undergone that same transformation (Caplan, 1985; Chesler, 1972; Showalter, 1987). That history is also crammed with essays describing the battles to wrest women's lives from psychiatric control, by challenging the way women are understood, diagnosed and treated (Astbury, 1996; Cosgrove, 2000; Winters, 2009).

Throughout U.S. history, power and privilege have not been vested in just one gender over the other, but in one race over the others. Whites, in other words, have constituted "the Majority." The most blatant examples of the exercise of white power and privilege in determining the line between sanity and madness occurred during the tumultuous decades before the Civil War when abolitionist sentiment was coalescing into a vigorous social movement, and the decades after when emancipated slaves began settling in towns and cities in the North.

The U.S. census of 1840 will serve as the preface to this account. Conducted by the office of the secretary of state, John Calhoun, this census was the first to count the number of citizens with physical or mental disabilities, including madness. The findings were remarkable: the rate of madness for free blacks in the North was one in every 144.5, a figure six times higher than the rate for whites, while the rate of madness among black slaves in the South was one in every 1,558. Even more remarkable was the finding that the rate of madness among all blacks steadily decreased in a southerly direction, that is, in the direction of slavery, with the highest rate of one in every 14 reported in the most northerly state of Maine, and the lowest rate of one in every 4,310 in the most southerly state of Louisiana (Nobles, 2000).

The conclusion to be drawn from the census appeared unimpeachable: freedom drove blacks mad. For antiabolitionists there was no more compelling proof that blacks were naturally inferior to whites and thus well suited for slavery.

The 1840 census provided the fodder for an unrepentantly racialized discourse about madness that would continue for decades, despite the fact that the findings did not hold up to scrutiny. When two northern physicians, Edward Jarvis of Massachusetts and James McCune Smith of New York, independently analyzed the findings, the gross errors in data collection and reporting were exposed. Jarvis, a skilled statistician who reviewed the census for entertainment while recovering from a broken leg, found that many northern cities were listed as having more mad blacks than they actually had black residents. Other errors were equally egregious. The census, for example, stated 133 mad blacks were institutionalized in the whites-only asylum in Worcester, Massachusetts; this single error multiplied the cited number of mad blacks in the state by three times. On the basis of his meticulous analysis, Jarvis concluded that "here is proof enough to force upon us the lamentable conclusion, that the census has contributed nothing to the statistical nosology of the free blacks, and furnished us with no data whereon we may build any theory respecting the liability of humanity, in its different phases and in various outward circumstances, to loss of reason or of the senses" (Jarvis, 1844, p. 83).

Smith, the first black physician to practice medicine in the United States, was equally painstaking in his analysis of the census, and his findings were consistent with those of Jarvis. In a "Memorial" presented to the U.S. Senate on behalf of other black leaders, he asserted that once the census was corrected for errors not only would it be evident that the rate of madness was no higher for blacks than for whites, but also that any conclusions that blacks were inferior to whites and therefore better off enslaved than free would be proved erroneous (Smith, 1844).

Finally surrendering to critics, elected officials launched a congressional investigation into the census, charging none other than the office of secretary of state John Calhoun to look into its own findings. Not surprisingly, it stood behind them. While that verdict effectively ended the debate over the census, it only egged on the debate over the inferiority of blacks, their peculiar susceptibility to madness, and their enslavement.

Weighing in to that debate was Samuel Cartwright, a Louisiana professor of medicine and expert on the "diseases of the Negro." To Cartwright, slavery was justified on biblical grounds. The Pentateuch, the first five books of the Bible, he asserted, "declares the Creator's will in regard to the negro; it declares him to be the submissive knee-bender. In the anatomical confirmation of his knee, we see '*genu flexit*' written in his physical structure, being more flexed or bent, than any other kind of man" (Cartwright, 1859, p. 331).

He went on to explain that some types of madness were peculiar to blacks, both enslaved and free, and in doing so, he drew a racialized line between sanity and madness. Black slaves, he argued, are prone to drapeto-mania, that is, an urge to abscond from service, or to run away to freedom. This type of madness could be prevented and cured with a good whipping as well as by occasional acts of kindness, both of which reminded black slaves of their biblical destiny of a lifetime of submission to the superiority of whites. Both enslaved and free blacks were prone to another type of racial-ized madness. Dysathesia aethiopica, or hebetude of the mind, not only resulted in dry skin and lesions on the body, but also in "rascality," with its symptoms of insolence, procrastination, and idleness. For black slaves, this type of madness was the consequence of living as if they were free, and it could be cured only by displaying less kindness on the part of the slave owner. For free blacks, it was the result of freedom.

So acrimonious had racial discourse become over the decades before the Civil War that abolitionists themselves often were diagnosed as mad by their pro-slavery opponents, and there was a newly minted diagnosis that was particularly befitting for that purpose. Monomania was considered a derange-ment of one faculty of the brain that resulted in a pathological obsession with, expression of, or concentration on, a single idea. For the self-proclaimed "radical abolitionists" who were declaring slavery unconstitutional and demanding its immediate end, the label of monomania effectively medical-ized abolitionist ideology, casting both it and its adherents as mad. For those who opposed abolition, no better example of its madness could be found than that of John Brown, who had led a failed 1859 raid on the federal armory in Harpers Ferry, Virginia, to secure arms for a slave insurrection. Wounded and captured, Brown was charged with treason. Ironically, in their desperate bid for clemency, many of his defenders as well as his attorney found them-selves siding with their opponents by insisting Brown was indeed in the throes of monomania, a plea regarded as a "ridiculous artifice" by Brown himself. "I may be very insane, and I am so if insane at all," he told the court. "But if that be so, insanity is like a very pleasant dream to me. I am not in the least degree conscious of my ravings, of my fears, of any terrible visions whatever; but fancy myself entirely composed, and that my sleep, in partic-ular, is as sweet as that of a healthy, joyous little infant" (Sanborn, 1885, p. 609). Brown was found guilty of treason and hanged.

And what of the madness of Abigail Folsom who was notorious for try-ing to insert her opinion into antislavery meetings. Her co-abolitionists, though, had no tolerance for the opinions of a woman. Her speeches were dismissed as little more than hysterical rants, and her demands to be heard as nothing more than defiance of male authority. Every attempt was made to ostracize her, from labeling her mad to forcibly removing her from abolitionist meetings. She was briefly jailed in 1842 before being transferred to the Worcester Lunatic Asylum.

Folsom's views on slavery certainly were extreme, but they were in line with those of her more notable male colleagues. It is more likely that it was her bold transgressions of her "proper" role as a woman that prompted her co-abolitionists to turn gendered meanings of madness against one of their own (Morris, 2001).

Flawed though it was, the 1840 census left an indelible impression that for blacks freedom was tantamount to madness. The Emancipation Proclamation, the defeat of the Confederacy, and the eventual passage of the Thirteenth Amendment, which finally abolished slavery altogether, did little to change a nation that was both unprepared and unwilling to accept blacks as equal citizens. In that contentious milieu, "the Majority" continued to exercise its prerogative. Drawing on both the racial prejudices that permeated society and the prevailing scientific discourse that had medicalized those attitudes, asylum physicians drew a distinctly racialized line between sanity and madness. In the words of a superintendent of a Missouri asylum:

> The sudden demand upon sluggish and uncultivated brains [of Blacks] for vigorous and effective action, while competing with dominant and cultivated Caucasians in the struggle for existence; the melancholy that comes like a blight with the sense of failure, and hopelessness of contention; the aspirations for social and political success and recognition, so frequently doomed to disappointment, have borne legitimate fruit in the generating of diseased brains and disordered minds, to a degree vastly disproportionate to the numerical relation of the races [Cited in Hughes, 1993, p. 166].

While "the Majority" agreed that blacks were at a much higher risk for madness than whites, it was far from hegemonic in theorizing the cause. For most, the cause could be found in the essential differences in the character and constitution of blacks. But for others, it was the contingencies on freedom for blacks that were the causes of madness. On that point, E.Y. Williams, professor of psychiatry at Howard University, argued as follows:

> From available statistics ... the incidence of mental disease in Negroes has definitely increased.... The Negro rate has largely been augmented due to the Negro's marginalization, economic safety and migration. This migration has been largely from states where the amount spent on Negro education is about one-third to one-sixth the amount spent on whites in the same area, and about one-tenth to one-fifteenth of that of Northern states. Urbanization of the Negro as seen by shifting of population with all its attendant ills due to economic factors also tends

to increase the rate.... As no scientific criteria have been established as to differences in opportunities, social, political, economic; hospitalization (private and state); educational facilities; rules for admittance; and further due to biased and conflicting statements, this problem must be left "*sub judice.*" The most that may be gleaned from this study is the faith in the ability of the Negro to survive and increase [1937, pp. 391–392].

Blacks, just like homosexuals and women, were hardly passive dupes in the continuing process of gerrymandering the line between sanity and madness. Many protested the prevailing theory that racial inferiority made them more vulnerable to madness; their protests appeared in scholarly literature, court cases, and popular culture performances. But there were two particular times worth noting by way of examples, when blacks did not so much change the line as their position vis-à-vis the line.

The first was in 1946. The Lafargue Psychiatric Clinic had just opened in the basement of a church in Harlem, a major black residential, cultural and business neighborhood in the Manhattan borough of New York City. It was founded by a white psychiatrist, Frederick Wertham, and it charged a fee of just twenty-five cents per session. While one of the city's newspapers heralded the opening with the headline "They're Crazy Anyway" (cited in Eversley, 2001, p. 445), blacks had an antithetical view. Greatly influenced by the "universalist" theory of black intellectuals who posited that everyone, regardless of race, came into the world with the same psychic drives and needs, they argued that it was the social context that indelibly stamped its influence on each person (Doyle, 2008). The famed black novelist Richard Wright, in his commentary about his 1940 novel *Native Son*, put it this way: "I felt and still feel that the environment supplies the instrumentalities through which the organism expresses itself, and if that environment is warped or tranquil, the mode and manner of behavior will be affected toward deadlocking tensions or orderly fulfillment and satisfaction" (Wright, 1991, p. 442).

While agreeing that blacks were experiencing more than their fair share of madness, the founders of the Lafargue Psychiatric Clinic argued that the madness of blacks was nothing more than a "reasonable psychic response to the lunatic obsessions of U.S. white supremacist culture" (Eversley, 2001, p. 447). Thus, by casting "the Majority," that is, whites, as mad for being so blindsided by racial prejudice as to refuse to address, let alone resolve, "the Negro problem" (Myrdal, 1944), i.e., the social conditions in which most blacks were living and the prejudice all were suffering, blacks did not so much move the line between sanity and madness as redefine which side of the line they, as a race, occupied.

The Lafargue Psychiatric Clinic closed in 1959, but the racialized debate over madness resurfaced a short time later. The violence of the Civil Rights era prompted some psychiatrists to bring before the American Psychiatric Association a recommendation that racism be classified as a mental illness. The association rejected the proposal, arguing that because so many white Americans are racist, even the extreme racism that resulted in the murders of Civil Rights workers and leaders could be considered normative—that is, a social problem at best, but not a type of madness. The proposal resurfaced in 2002 when black psychiatrist and Harvard professor Alvin Poussaint renewed the recommendation, this time arguing that "extreme racism" be classified as a type of madness. Specifically, and using the *DSM-IV* diagnostic criteria for delusional disorder, he proposed the following subtype:

> Prejudice Type: a delusion whose theme is that a group of individuals, who share a defining characteristic, in one's environment have a particular and unusual significance. These delusions are usually of a negative or pejorative nature, but also may be grandiose in content. When these delusions are extreme, the person may act out by attempting to harm, even murder, members of the despised groups(s) [Poussaint, 2002, p. 4].

The proposal generated a great deal of debate over a variety of terrains, most prominent of which was the now differently racialized line between sanity and madness. Perhaps one of the more interesting responses to the proposal was offered by Gavin Yamey, the deputy editor of the *Western Journal of Medicine*, and neuropsychiatric researcher Philip Shaw, who reminded debaters about the political firestorm that followed when the American Psychiatric Association was determined to continue to categorize homosexuality as a mental illness:

> Racist beliefs may, of course, be part of an underlying mental illness, but they are not in themselves pathologic. What if we try to classify all racist beliefs as representing some other form of psychological illness? For example, let's try to call racist beliefs "overvalued ideas," the psychiatric term for logically understandable but not acceptable ideas pursued by a person beyond the bounds of reason. We run into trouble when we think of extreme racists who do little more than vote for a quasi-fascist party once every 5 years. This is scarcely acting beyond the bounds of reason; indeed, it is acting within the constraints of a liberal democracy. Let's try saying that racists who commit hate crimes have a "personality disorder." Again, this is problematic, because we return to introducing social policy into a psychologically based diagnostic system. Enforcing such policy is not the proper role of psychiatrists and is beyond their common duty as citizens. Medicalizing [prejudice] is just an easy out. And it takes medicine down the well-trodden path of trying to deal with "dissidents" by calling them patients [Yamey & Shaw, 2002, p. 5].

In a compromise, of sorts, the American Psychiatric Association is considering adding the diagnosis of "Pathological Bias" to the forthcoming *DSM-V.* Hypothesizing that 95 percent to 98 percent of racist behavior is socially, culturally or politically determined, the diagnosis is aimed to discern that "sliver" of racist behavior that is based in madness, and that might possibly be determined by neuroimaging tests (Finn, 2004, p. 32). In the meantime, while the inclusion of this new diagnosis is being hotly debated, the American Psychiatric Association issued a "Resolution Against Racism and Racial Discrimination and Their Adverse Impacts on Mental Health." The position statement recognizes that racism and racial discrimination not only "[diminish] the victim's self-image, confidence and optimal mental functioning [but also] render the perpetrator unprepared for the 21st century society that is becoming increasingly multicultural and global." It also acknowledges that racism and racial discrimination lead to mental health care disparities, and encourages its members to be mindful of their impact "in the lives of patients and their families, in clinical encounters, and in the development of mental health services" (American Psychiatric Association, 2006, p. 1).

There is another "ism" that influences "the Majority's" drawing of the line between sanity and madness. While it could be, and has been, persuasively argued that the contingencies of lower and working-class life also ineradicably stamp their influence on mental health, thus accounting for the historic overrepresentation of poor people institutionalized in the nation's asylums (Hollingshead & Redlich, 1958; Bourdon, Rae, Narrow, Manderschild, & Regier, 1994), a sociological corollary might be entertained as well:

- If psychological discourse has been crucial to the formation of American middle-class and upper-class identities (Pfister, 1997), and

- If that discourse indeed has "performed as an excellent substitute for social and economic motives in explaining social behavior" (Hoffman, 1953, p. 198),

- Then "the Majority," as defined in class terms, will interpret lower class status not as the result of context, but of essential and pathological differences in character, such as laziness, irresponsibility, the desire for immediate gratification, intellectual incompetence or moral weakness, and

- Then, the undesirable and threatening condition of poverty will be seen as the effect, rather than the cause, of these essential and pathological differences in character,

- Thus, "the Majority" will shift the line between sanity and madness to medicalize the social expressions of these essential and pathological characteristics, such as compulsive gambling, sexual addiction, and impulse-control disorders (Furedi, 2004).

This corollary suggests that the label of madness can, and is, used as a tool of social control of the underclass, an argument that has been strenuously made over recent decades by influential social theorists (Foucault, 1965; Goffman, 1961; Scull, 1989). On rare and ironic occasions, though, "the Majority" has used the label of madness to valorize and promote, rather than stigmatize and control, its own constituents. Two examples, a century apart, illustrate this point.

The late 19th century was a time of incredible social, technological and ideological change. The invention of useable electricity, steel and petroleum products produced a second industrial revolution that brought about the telephone, the typewriter, and the expansions of railways and steamship lines. Women were seeking educational opportunities, children were being taken out of the factories and into the schools, immigrants were flooding into the country, Native Americans were being confined to reservations, blacks were seeking equal opportunities; traditional religion was losing its hold while both religious sects and secularism were increasing theirs; sports and leisure activities abounded as did the fine arts; the gap between the rich and the poor became unfathomable, and between the rich and the newly emerging professional class, unbreachable.

In fact, it was this newly emerging professional class, the "brainworkers," as they were called—the white, urban, educated teachers, ministers, clerks, managers, accountants and civil servants—who were thought to be more vulnerable to a particular and, it was ardently believed, uniquely American type of madness known as neurasthenia. It was George Miller Beard, a neurologist, who popularized the diagnosis. Neurasthenia, literally translated as "nerve weakness," he explained, is caused by the very forces of modernization that were so rapidly transforming American society; thus those who were most likely to suffer from it were the movers and shakers who were making these changes possible. Modern civilization, he concluded without a touch of sarcasm, "is paid for by nervousness" (Beard, 1881, p. 76). And the price was high. Neurasthenia produced a stunning array of symptoms, including, but not limited to

> tenderness of the scalp [and] the spine ... teeth and gums; tenderness of the whole body; general or local itching; abnormalities of the secretions; vague pains and flying neuralgias; flushing ... tremulous and variable pulse with palpitation; sudden giving away of general or special functions; special idiosyncrasies in regard to food, medicine, and external irritants; sensitiveness to changes in the weather; a feeling of profound exhaustion unaccompanied by pain; ticklishness; desire for stimulants and narcotics; insomnia; nervous dyspepsia; partial failure of memory; deficient mental control; seminal emissions; spermatorrhea; partial or complete impotence; changes in expression of the eyes and countenance; mental depression and general timidity; morbid fear of special kinds, as agoraphobia

(fear of places), aacraphobia (fear of lightning); sick headache and various forms of headache; disturbances of the nerves and organs of special senses; localized peripheral numbness and hyperesthesia; general and local chills and flashes of heat; local spasms of muscles [Beard, 1879, p. 246].

A rapidly modernizing society could ill afford to stigmatize its movers and shakers. To that end, neurasthenia was understood not just as the price that brainworkers paid for their contributions to society, but as the *privilege* of their cultured and affluent class. This type of madness was a veritable "badge of honor" (Lutz, 1991, p. 275) that not only distinguished brainworkers from their economic and cultural inferiors, the muscleworkers, but also whites from blacks and Native Americans since neither of these minority races was thought to be much bothered, if bothered at all, by the "exciting causes" in modernizing society (Beard, 1881, p. 189). So by vesting neurasthenia with such cachet, Beard and his followers "found a way ... to lend scientific credence to and provide a biological basis for the social position and political ideologies of the white American upper classes" (Campbell, 2007, p. 162). No wonder neurasthenia was so popular with "the Majority": it was an indicator of modernity, a marker of class and racial identity, and a matter of national pride. "Americanitis," as it was sometimes dubbed, was considered one of the nation's "most distinctive and precious pathological possessions" (Dana, 1904, p. 341).

Just as those who "possessed" this pathology avoided stigma, they also avoided institutionalization. The treatment of neurasthenia generally was not carried out in asylums, but in well-appointed sanitaria and rest homes—sometimes referred to as nervine asylums—physicians' offices, and the patients' homes. At the Battle Creek Sanitarium in Michigan, founded by physician John Harvey Kellogg, for example, neurasthenic patients were given frequent enemas, strapped into the vibratory chair to stimulate intestinal peristalsis, dunked in freezing water doused with radium, encouraged to exercise and recreate in the fresh air, and fed a low-fat, high-protein diet that included Kellogg's own brand of cereals, granola and corn flakes (Kellogg, 1908). The treatment regime was aimed not only at curing neurasthenia by strengthening the nervous system, but also at teaching brainworkers to maintain their nervous energy through diet and exercise. Parodied a few years ago in the novel *The Road to Wellville* (Boyle, 1993), and in a later film by the same title, the regime also was the subject of satire decades ago in the O. Henry novella, *Let Me Feel Your Pulse* (1910), in which a physician gives a prospective patient a guided tour of the sanitarium after a nerve-restoring lunch of phosphoglycerate of lime hash, dog-bread, bromoseltzer pancakes, and nux vomica tea:

An hour or so after luncheon he conducted us to the workshop.... "Here," said the physician in charge, "our guests find relaxation from past mental worries by devoting themselves to physical labour—recreation, in reality."

There were turning-lathes, carpenters' outfits, clay-modeling tools, spinning-wheels, weaving-frames, treadmills, bass drums, enlarged-crayon-portrait apparatuses, blacksmith forges, and everything, seemingly, that could interest the paying lunatic guests of a first-rate sanitarium....

"The gentleman pouring water through the funnel," continued the physician, "is a Wall Street broker broken down from overwork...." Others he pointed out were architects playing with Noah's arks, ministers reading Darwin's "Theory of Evolution," lawyers sawing wood, tired-out society ladies talking Ibsen to the blue-sweatered sponge-holder, a neurotic millionaire lying asleep on the floor, and a prominent artist drawing a little red wagon around the room.

"You look pretty strong," said the physician. "I think the best mental relaxation for you would be throwing small boulders over the mountainside and then bringing them up again."

I was a hundred yards away before my doctor overtook me. "What's the matter?" he asked.

"The matter is," said I, "that there are no aeroplanes handy. So I am going to merrily and hastily jog the foot-pathway to yon station and catch the first unlimited-soft-coal express back to town."

"Well," said the doctor, "perhaps you are right. This seems hardly the suitable place for you. But what you need is rest—absolute rest and exercise" [pp. 9–12].

The parody aside, "The San," as the Battle Creek Sanitarium was known, treated—and was visited for consultation by—a veritable who's-who of the nation's movers and shakers. The roster includes industrialist Henry Ford, publisher C.W. Barron, athlete Johnny Weismuller, entertainer Eddie Cantor, educator Booker T. Washington, aviation pioneer Amelia Earhart, and entrepreneur Madame C.J. Walker, who had amassed a fortune from developing and selling body care products for blacks.

Neurasthenic brainworkers also were treated in their physicians' offices, where they were counseled on proper diet, encouraged to get more rest and exercise, and received any one or more of a range of pharmaceuticals, including quinine, arsenic, opium, bromide, zinc, valerian and cannabis (Caplan, 2001). But treating physicians especially favored electrotherapy, as much if not more for its psychological effects, as for its physical effects. Beard described the general faradization procedure that he particularly favored, in the following way:

In this method of treatment the feet of the patient are placed on a sheet of copper to which the negation pole is attached, while the positive, either a large sponge or the hand of the operator, is applied over the head (the hair being previously moistened), on the back of the neck, down the entire length of the spine, down the arms, over the stomach, liver, bowels, down the lower extremities—in short, over the entire surface of the body, from the head to the feet, but with special reference to the head and spine [Beard, 1869, p. 219].

At home, neurasthenics were treated with the rest cure. Created by physician S. Weir Mitchell, the rest cure combined a protein-rich diet heavy in red meat and milk, electrotherapy and massage with several week-long rests in bed and complete isolation from family and friends. Mitchell was no stranger to neurasthenia; he had suffered two debilitating attacks and had successfully treated himself each time with a regime of bed rest followed by outdoor recreation (Earnest, 1950). His own experience aside, he realized the rest cure was not particularly well-suited for male neurasthenics since the dependency and passivity it both produced and required feminized them (Lutz, 1991). Thus, the rest cure became both the bane and the blessing of female neurasthenics.

The rapid changes of the late 19th century had a significant impact on gender relations. While "true women" still were wedded not just to husbands but to families and homes, "new women," educated and ambitious, were finding their ways through, and their places in, society. Yet these "new women" could not free themselves from what most physicians, including Mitchell, believed was their innate emotional oversensitivity, constitutional fragility and nervous delicacy. Thus, the brainwork that they aspired to was considered deleterious to their mental and physical health; the rest cure, then, legitimated "a traditional definition of femininity based on dependency and passivity" (Lutz, 1991, p. 31).

Several notable women were treated with the rest cure. Jane Addams, founder of Hull House, spent three months in bed sans the books she so much enjoyed reading; the novelist Edith Wharton was confined to a hotel room for four months, visited only by her nurses; the poet Winifred Howells spent six months in bed, deprived of the pleasure of reading and writing; the pianist Fannie Bloomfield-Zeisler was confined for several months in a dark room, forbidden to play the piano or to study a musical score. The rest cure did little to cure the neurasthenia with which these women were diagnosed; in fact, with the exception of Edith Wharton, whose imagination was freed during her months in bed, it did more to engender ambition than to stifle it in the name of mental health.

Perhaps there is no one for whom that was more true than Charlotte Perkins Gilman. After a month's rest cure for a "continuous nervous breakdown," she was sent home by Mitchell with the admonition that she "live as domestic a life as possible ... have but two hours intellectual life a day [and] never to touch pen, brush, or pencil again as long as I lived" (Gilman, 1935, p. 96). She followed Mitchell's orders for several months, but became so distressed she could no longer care for her husband or baby. On the verge of what she believed was an irrecoverable nervous breakdown, she sought refuge in work and found herself steadily improving. She divorced her husband and, before she launched her career as a poet, writer, and prominent feminist intellectual, penned "The Yellow Wallpaper" (1899), a short story she hoped, as it turns out in vain, would convince Mitchell of the "error of his ways" (Gilman, 1935, p. 95). The story recounts a woman's descent into madness while confined for a rest cure in the nursery of her home. In her derangement, she sees a figure of a woman trapped behind the yellow wallpaper which she tears off to help her escape. The woman is both her and not her, but she is not alone — there are other faces behind the wallpaper, too:

> As soon as it was moonlight and that poor thing began to crawl and shake the [wallpaper] pattern, I got up and ran to help her. I pulled and she shook, I shook and she pulled, and before morning we had pulled of yards off that paper. A strip about as high as my head and half around the room ... I have locked the door and thrown the key down the front path. I don't want to get out, and I don't want to have anybody come in, till [my husband] comes.... Then I peeled off all the paper I could reach standing on the floor. It sticks horribly and the pattern just enjoys it! All those strangled heads and bulbous eyes and waddling fungus growths just shriek with derision!... I wonder if they all come out of that wallpaper as I did?... Why, there's [my husband] at the door!... Then he said very quietly indeed, "Open the door, my darling." "I can't," said I. "The key is down by the front door under a plantain leaf!" ... [A]nd he got it of course, and came in. He stopped short by the door. "What's the matter?" he cried. "For God's sake, what are you doing?" I kept on creeping just the same, but I looked at him over my shoulder. "I've got out at last," said I, "in spite of you and [my nurse]. And I've pulled off most of the paper, so you can't put me back!" Now why should that man have fainted? But he did, right across my path by the wall, so that I had to creep over him every time! [8–9].

By the 1920s the fashionable madness of neurasthenia had all but disappeared. Perhaps it was in some ways a victim of its own success. It was over-commercialized, "ripe for abuse by doctors and institutions who put profits before patients" (Campbell, 2007, p. 165). It was parodied in novels and short stories, and criticized by prominent physicians as imprecise and unscientific. Its sufferers had come to be seen by the general public as self-indulgent, self-pitying and, for all the pretense of being movers and shakers, remarkably lazy (Haller & Haller, 1974).

In another way, though, neurasthenia disappeared because the times had changed. As a result, the relationship between symptoms and diagnosis, physicians and patients, and madness and culture had changed as well. "Americanitis" had served its purpose: it had plucked the new class of brain-workers out of a rapidly modernizing society and protected and valorized them; in doing so it had cohered both class and racial identity in the face of growing diversity.

Not coincidentally, it was at the end of another century, this one the 20th, that "the Majority" also used the label of madness to valorize and promote, rather than stigmatize and control, its own constituents. In this era it was not a particular diagnosis that serves as the marker, but a complex set of ideologies about the self and the inner life that developed in response to the continuing forces of modernization. This example is rooted in the supposition that the erosion of social solidarity, decline of tradition, weakening of shared moral norms, and blurring of the boundaries between the private and the public created a "therapeutic culture" in which psychological ways of understanding, thinking and interpreting inform most, if not all, aspects of everyday life (Cloud, 1998; Furedi, 2004; Rieff, 1966). Therapeutic culture, it is argued, is perpetuated by the very thing it helped create—a diminished self, that is, not just a view of the self as vulnerable, at-risk, victimizable, but the *experience* of the self as such. This diminished self disempowers people and undermines their subjectivity and sense of human agency. Thus, they are more inclined than ever before to see themselves as distressed and dysfunctional, i.e., *mad,* and to seek comfort and guidance from the staggering array of experts, quasi-experts, amateurs and quacks who make up the continuously expanding therapy and advice industry (Moskowitz, 2001).

Thus, in addition to the estimated 50 million Americans who were suffering from diagnosable mental illnesses in 1999, there were tens of millions more who were struggling with barriers to self-fulfillment. They not only flooded the offices of credentialed experts, they also turned to television and radio talk shows for guidance, as well as to a burgeoning self-help marketplace. At the cusp of the millennium there were (and, by the way, still are) in-person and online self-help groups for more than a thousand different impediments to self-realization, contentment and success (White & Madara, 2009). Whether the problem is agoraphobia, bereavement, body odor, depression, eating, extraterrestrial encounters, gambling, lightning strike survival, messiness, sex addiction, writer's block, or "syndromes without a name," there is a group and a coterie of like-situated people to provide support. The prompt "self-help" on the www.amazon.com website brings up 3800 books, with titles such as *Become a Better You, Self Matters, The Mindful Path to Self-Compassion, The Art of Extreme Self Care, Healing Your Emotional Self, Learning to Love Yourself, Awaken Your Strongest Self, Your Truest Self* and *You: The Owner's Manual.*

In the therapeutic culture of the late 20th century, angst was commodified by the blurring of the boundaries between the discomforts and disappointments of everyday life and symptoms of madness, so both could be easily remedied with medication (Rubin, 2004). Whether the drug is Prozac (peppermint flavored for children) or Zoloft, Wellbutrin or Celexa, the message in the bottle is that drugs can restore selfhood, or, as the Paxil advertisement promises, "Talk to your doctor about Paxil today. So you can see someone you haven't seen in a while—yourself" (cited in Herzberg, 2009, p. 1). This search for the authentic self, prompted by the demands of modern life and guided by the self-help industry as well as by billion dollar advertisement campaigns by pharmaceutical companies, created what a newspaper columnist definitively declared is "a nation of nuts" (Windolf, 1997, p. 6).

As cynically amusing as that aphorism might be, it is not exactly correct. Just as was the case with neurasthenia a century before, the angst over the authentic self of the late 20th century has been appropriated by "the Majority." This was, and continues to be, a largely white, urban, educated, professional and upper class type of madness (Lichterman, 1992; Metzl, 2003). So appropriated, it is generally without stigma and is addressed, if not treated, in private offices, in inperson and online support groups, and in the comforts of the home, but certainly not in asylums. And, perhaps even more tellingly, at least from a sociological point of view, although the demands of society are blamed as its cause these remedies rarely ever require a confrontation with them. Cure, if it can be called that, comes in the form of bolstering self-esteem, getting in touch with the authentic self, not from challenging ideas and certainly not from tackling the vicissitudes, inequities and unfairness of modern life (Ehrenreich, 2009; Kaminer, 1993).

"To Great Wit Allied"

Madness, as has been pointed out, always has been interpreted as a disease; although, of course, what is meant by "disease"—its causes, origins, consequences—has shifted throughout history. And, as has been explained via the discussion of neurasthenia and the enfeebled self of today's therapeutic culture, it occasionally can be appropriated by "the Majority," who relieve it of stigma and transform it into a badge of honor. Consistent with that transformation is another, even more subversive, interpretation of madness that has endured over time, and that is that it is an unlikely gift. Whether bestowed upon the Holy Fool, the mad artist, the wild-eyed prophet or the insane genius, madness sometimes has been seen as a blessing in disguise, as bequeathing the gifts of prophecy, creativity, inspiration, insight, and even love.

Western history in general is peppered with just enough of these well-known tortured souls—Vincent Van Gogh, William Blake, Robert Schumann, to name just a few—to make this proposition that madness is a gift worth considering (Jamison, 1993). The novelist Virginia Woolf, for example, described her madness in terms of a "shower of fireworks," but at the same time she reassured a friend that it was the source of her creativity: "As an experience, madness is terrific I can assure you, and not to be sniffed at; and in its lava I still find most of the things I write about. It shoots out of one everything shaped, final, not in mere driblets, as sanity does" (Nicolson & Trautman, 1975, p. 180).

Stepping away from the scientific debate about whether there indeed is a relationship between madness and creativity and genius—and the debate these days is vigorous—it is more sociologically interesting just to consider the claim that there is. True, that claim has been around since the Greek philosophers. Plato, for example, argued for the existence of a heaven-sent *furor poeticus*, a divine madness that transported poets and artists into the world of divine truth. This claim has achieved mythical status in Western history despite the fact that it is difficult to find many artists, geniuses or visionaries who willingly have "clothe[d] their own selves in the mantle of madness" (Porter, 1987, p. 61).

Perhaps the seductiveness of the claim has to do with the persistent fascination with the reaches of the mind, with that line that demarks the familiar from the unfamiliar, the sane from the mad, the ordinary from the exceptional. Perhaps it also has to do with the need to culturally represent the unfamiliar, whether in literature, poetry, art, music, theatre, film, or other venues of performance. Madness indeed may be represented in those cultural forms. But the forms, in turn, shape the cultural and individual conceptualizations of madness (Gilman, 1991); thus, and only when convenient, the myth is reified. And when the myth is reified, the prevailing way, maybe even the *only* way, to appreciate and appraise the creativity and genius of the author, artist or performer is through the prism of madness.

American history provides a number of examples of this cyclical process that fuses madness and creativity/genius—poet Anne Sexton, artist Jackson Pollack, mathematician John Nash, comic Robin Williams, to name just a few—but one of the more interesting is the example of the artist Martín Rameríz, a Mexican immigrant whose drawings recently were exhibited at the American Folk Museum. Rameríz, who died in 1963, had spent more than half of his life in California asylums and while institutionalized had created a portfolio of 300 drawings on scavenged scraps of paper glued together with mashed potatoes and drawn with melted crayon wax, shoe polish, saliva and charcoal. Diagnosed with catatonic schizophrenia, Rameríz rarely spoke, but his drawings have elevated him to the status of one of the greatest artists of the 20th century—but with certain qualifiers that reveal the inextricable entwining of his madness with his artistic genius.

Rameríz's art is not considered label-free "contemporary art," but is regarded as what is variously referred to as "Outsider Art," "Art Brut," or "Vernacular Art," i.e., a form of *identity* art in which the biography of the artist is as, or even more, important than the formal features of the art, itself

(Fine, 2003). Indeed, when his drawings were first exhibited in the 1950s, they were not even attributed to him by name, but rather only to a "Mexican schizophrenic." Exhibits held a decade later were accompanied by a short, and inaccurate, biography that focused more on his madness than on his life. For patrons and most critics—another version of "the Majority," who are wedded to the idea that "only an artist who is nuts can produce work with guts" (Hall, 1986, p. 58)—it is Rameríz's madness through which his art is appraised and appreciated.

The Fine Line Reconsidered

Emily Dickinson may not have found this sociological read of "the Majority" to be "divinest sense." But the fact remains that throughout history the line between sanity and madness often has been negotiable, and more often than not has been inscribed by gender, race, socioeconomic class and sexual orientation. To say that madness is protean is not to assert the reductio ad absurdum argument made by a number of sociologists and antipsychiatrists (Laing, 1967; Scheff, 1966; Szasz, 1974) that it does not exist outside of the label; but it is to invite an engagement with those who wonder about their own position vis-à-vis the line, even if only whimsically and just every now and then, as a psychiatrist once did:

> At noon I was walking from my parked car to the back door of the Jones Building [of Milledgeville State Hospital] when I heard above me a God-awful cackling. I looked up to the second and third floors. The patients were crowded at the barred windows, slapping their thighs and laughing hysterically. They were pointing at yours truly. Suddenly it dawned on me! I was carrying an open umbrella to keep off the rain, but the rain was stopped and the sun was shining brightly. What they were yelling at me was "Who's crazy?" [Cranford, 1981, p. 131].

It is also to invite an appreciation of those who know which side of this blurred and changing line they are on, but are content to be there, perhaps seeing their madness as what the poet Anne Sexton (1982), herself no stranger to it, once termed a "miraculous sickness" (p. 574). It is an invitation, too, to understand those who protest their location along that line, resisting the label of mad stuck on them by what the poet Bill Nordahl (1994) calls "the conformity monster," or who, like the poet Peter Meinke (1977) wonder if it is normal to be "half-crazy" (p. 54). It is to invite an engagement with those who just question where, in any particular place and time, that line really is:

> 'Tis said there is only one man who is sane
> All the rest of the world have some twist in the brain,
> Would you single the fortunate many from the mass?

Pray turn from the crowd, sir, and look in the glass.
Self-conceit betrays weakness in manifold forms,
Begetting false hopes and delusions in swarms,
Yet we safely pass muster, unless we outrage
Some standards of soundness set up by the age.
Will it always be so—and who shall decide,
If our wisdom is not to much folly allied? ["Poem," 1873, p. 2].

The admonitory poem raises another significant point that counters the argument that madness is nothing more than a label. The "outrage" against "some standards of soundness set up by the age" speaks not only to the inextricable link between madness and the social context or "age," but also to the chaos, the "outrage," that madness so often creates. It was not a poet but a sociologist who made that point: "Mental symptoms are not, by and large, *incidentally* a social infraction. By and large they are specifically and pointedly offensive. It is this havoc that psychiatrists have dismally failed to examine and that sociologists ignore when they treat mental illness merely as a labeling process" (Goffman, 1971, pp. 356–357).

It is also the "havoc" that greases the wheels of the mechanisms of social control. Madness as an outrage against prevailing social norms not only draws attention to itself but also demands that something be done. It is another sociologist who makes that point:

[The havoc of madness creates] the need to develop strategies for limiting and encapsulating the threats, both symbolic and practical, that the [mad] pose to their immediate interactional partners and to the social order more generally — strategies that have clearly varied across time and space, but ways of coping that of necessity must allow for the more or less continuous employment of containment and damage limitation. The lunatic may be seen variously as the embodiment of extravagance and incoherence, incomprehensibility and ungovernable rage, melancholy or menace. The various manifestations of Unreason—the rages of the raving, the dolour of the downcast, the grotesquely denuded life of the demented—pose characteristic and to some extent distinct problems for society. But all of these varieties of craziness serve to create almost unbearable disturbances in the texture of daily existence [Scull, 2004, p. 418].

Because madness disturbs daily existence, transgresses the familiar, and crosses a socially imagined line that separates it from its opposite—normal, sane, healthy, natural, usual—it also begs representation. Throughout history, those who embody the notion of madness have been represented not only in the words, drawings and photographs in medical and psychiatric texts, but also in the fine arts, theatre, opera, literature and poetry, film and television. How they are represented generally reflects, and at the same time reifies, the prevailing notion(s) of madness, thus the representations are as protean as madness itself. The representation of the mad "maintains its own vocabulary of images, and these are linked to the various manifestations of [madness] much in the same way that psychiatric nomenclature relates to that same spectrum. The selection of a specific representational system is related to the entity described, but is not interchangeable with that entity" (Gilman, 1982, p. 224).

Often these representations are accompanied by symbols, that is, arbitrary signs that acquire conventional significance. During the Medieval and Renaissance eras the mad depicted in paintings and drawings often are waving or leaning on the stick or cudgel of madness, as can be seen in Lucas Cranach the Elder's painting *Melancholy* (1532). In opera, the descent into madness typically is symbolized by the color white and by a solo that deconstructs the operatic form with dissonance, high pitch, and quick shifts between major and minor tonalities (Erfurth & Hoff, 2000), as the mad scene in Gaetano Donizetti's 1835 opera, *Lucia di Lammermoor*, exemplifies. In contemporary American B-films, the mad are often masked, otherwise disguised or physically deformed, symbolizing their "otherness," and are carrying weapons of some kind, accentuating their dangerousness (Wahl, 1997), as the film *Halloween* illustrates. The point is that these representations and the symbols that may accompany them are the "means by which observer[s] can order [their] perception of reality" (Gilman, 1982, p. 224). With them, unfamiliar madness becomes more familiar, avoidable and perhaps even controllable.

Interpreting the Cause(s) of Madness

Because of its transgressive nature, madness was feared. It still is. People always have felt vulnerable to it, if only in moments when emotions are running high ("You're driving me mad!") or thoughts are out of line ("I must be crazy to think this way!") or behaviors are out of order ("I think I'm losing it!") or stresses are overbearing ("I just can't take it anymore!"). Lucretia Davidson felt that way, too. A promising 19th century poet, she died at the age of 17, not from the madness she so dreaded, but from tuberculosis. Her unfinished poem, "The Fear of Madness," published posthumously, speaks eloquently to her sense of vulnerability:

> There is a something which I dread;
>   It is a dark, a fearful thing;
> It steals along with withering tread,
>   Or sweeps on wild destruction's wing.
> That thought comes o'er me in the hour
>   Of grief, of sickness, or of sadness;

Tis not the dread of death,—tis more,—
It is the dread of madness.
Oh! may these throbbing pulses pause,
Forgetful of their feverish course;
May this hot brain, which, burning, glows
With all a fiery whirlpool's force,
Be cold, and motionless, and still,
A tenant of its lowly bed;
But let not dark delirium steal—[Unfinished]
[Davidson, 1841, p. 4].

What was the madness that Davidson so much feared? From the Ancient Greeks on, madness always has been interpreted as a disease; but even in saying that, its protean nature is evident (Porter, 1991). What kind of disease is it? Does it originate in the brain, the mind, the body? Is its cause in the ups and downs of all lived lives or, perhaps, in the lifestyles and habits of some, or in the disruptive traumas of a few? Or is it more of a *dis*-ease than a disease, originating in a failure of adaptation, a rejection of conformity, or an unwillingness to accept and move on. If it is, why is that *dis*-ease experienced by some people and not others?

American alienists, the early term for psychiatrists, probably would have had little to say to Davidson to allay her fear. While most of them agreed that madness was a disease of the brain, they were somewhat mystified about its cause(s), and therefore could not relieve anyone of a nagging sense of vulnerability. Davidson's short life was lived between 1808 and 1825 when psychiatric knowledge was in its infancy. If she indeed had become mad during her life, how would the cause of her madness be understood? Alienists at that time generally agreed that madness was the result of an imbalance in the delicate equilibrium between the natural world, the social world and the inner world of the individual. They would have inquired about "moral" sources of that imbalance, i.e., a dissolute lifestyle or excessive strains and stresses, and they would have looked for physical causes, such as a head injury or a somatic illness. Whatever they found, and some alienists would have been content having found nothing, such was the mystery of madness, they would have theorized that the "exciting cause" carved a lesion on her brain which, in turn, sent "false impressions" to her mind. In early 19th century psychiatric thinking, the brain and the mind were inviolably separate. The brain, as an organ, was considered mortal, but the mind was considered the soul; to even entertain the notion that the mind could become diseased was to question the prevailing religious dogma that the soul is immortal (Grob, 1998).

Several decades after Davison's premature death, the influence of religion on psychiatric explanations of madness had weakened and, interest-

ingly enough, religion itself was theorized to be a cause of madness. The
enumerators of the 1860 census were instructed not only to count all of the
institutionalized mad in the United States, but also to list the cause of the
madness for each and every one of them. "As nearly every case of insanity
may be traced to some known cause," the directive stated, "it is earnestly
desired that you will not fail to make your return in this respect as perfect
as possible" (Department of the Interior, 1860). Among the possible causes
were listed intemperance, grief, affliction, heredity, misfortune, and spiritualism, the latter referring to a controversial sectarian belief system that had
challenged traditional religion in the 19th century by positing that the spirit,
soul, or mind survives death and can be contacted through a human medium
or clairvoyant. But clearly spiritualism was not the only religious cause of
madness the enumerators were to consider.

In a long introduction to the topic of insanity included in the published
census report, "religious excitement" is described as one of "the most frequent generative agents of insanity" (Kennedy, 1864, p. xc). Why? Religious
excitement of any kind exhausts the nervous system; generates so much fear
of hellfire and damnation as to depress the vital energy; overcomes reason;
and requires so much solitary reading and meditation as to interfere with
necessary social obligations, thus leaving its adherents vulnerable to attacks
of madness (p. xci). Census enumerators discovered that in 17 asylums, religious excitement was the single cause of madness of a total of 2,258 patients,
i.e., 6.1 percent of asylum patients (p. lxxxix). Religious excitement is not
considered a cause of madness these days, although as late as the 1930s it
still occasionally was cited as such in the case records of asylum patients
(Bainbridge, 1984). But as one of the prevailing interpretations of what causes
madness, it gradually lost its relevance, beaten back by a growing agnosti-
cism and host of newer interpretations that were more germane to the changing times.

Now, take a more contemporary interpretation of the cause of madness.
Elyn Saks (2007), a professor of law, feared madness as well. The voices in
her head, the suicidal fantasies, the lapses in personal care all pointed to a
particular type of madness—schizophrenia—but it took years for her to
accept the diagnosis. Saks's understanding of the cause of her madness
reflects the prevailing understanding post–"The Decade of the Brain," as
declared in 1990 by the National Institute of Mental Health, and that is that
schizophrenia, a result of genetics and neurochemicals, is a disorder of the
brain. The human brain "comprises about 2 percent of a person's body weight
... and it controls 100 percent of that body's activities," Saks writes. "So in
terms of how much territory the brain occupies vs. how much power it
wields—well, it is mightily powerful indeed" (p. 317).

Had Saks been diagnosed decades before, say in the 1950s just as an example, it is unlikely that a brain disorder would have been proposed as the cause of her schizophrenia. In that post–World War II era, with its pro-family, child-centered focus and its ethos of innocence and consensus (Coontz, 1992) the cause of schizophrenia was found in the family. Whether it was the "double-bind" that parents put their children in by creating intolerable stress with contradictory demands (Bateson, Jackson, Haley, & Weakland, 1956), the "scapegoating" they used to force their children to bear responsibility for their own problems (Ackerman, 1958), the "pseudomutuality" they created by maintaining a façade of family harmony by denying family problems (Wynne, Ryckoff, Day, & Hirsh, 1958), or the "schizophrenogenic" parenting of mothers who rejected and alienated their children (Fromm-Reichmann, 1948), the cause of schizophrenia was anchored deep within the family, not within the brain.

Had Saks been diagnosed even earlier, say the 1920s, the cause of her schizophrenia would have been anchored deep within her gut, not within her family. In that era, as psychiatry struggled to enhance its status in medicine and moor itself to medical science, the specialty was going through its first biological revolution. The origin of madness was to be found in the body. And schizophrenia—the quintessential type of madness, with its disordered thinking, delusions, hallucinations, and often bizarre behaviors—it was being argued, originated in the colon where, if not promptly and efficiently evacuated, ingested food would ferment, creating focal sepsis and spreading toxicity to the brain (Cotton, 1923; Holmes, 1916).

Perhaps this retrospective approach does little more than affirm the impression that Saks was very fortunate, indeed, to have been diagnosed in this era; there are, after all, drugs available to ameliorate her worst symptoms, and others to prevent their reoccurrence. But the fact is that she would have been considered just as fortunate in each of the other eras where intensive psychotherapy would have been thought, and perhaps even experienced as, an effective remedy for her madness in the 1950s, as would a colectomy in the 1920s. Or maybe this retrospective approach only affirms the impression that each era enjoys a little more evolution of medical thinking in the ongoing march towards a complete understanding of the causes of madness. Holmes would have disagreed: "The truth is, that medicine, professedly founded on observation, is as sensitive to outside influences, political, religious, philosophical, imaginative, as is the barometer to the changes of atmospheric density" (1911, p. 177).

In that regard, there is no question that medical advancements have played a significant role in determining the causes of madness. But medicine itself is a social enterprise, conducted as it is by people—working within and influenced by a particular social context—who bring into the enterprise and in their interactions with the mad, their own knowledge, values, beliefs and prejudices that may influence them in a variety of ways, from what interests them to how they talk about what interests them (Jordanova, 1995; Lachmund & Stollberg 1992; Turner & Sampson, 1995). In other words, the *meanings* of medical innovations and insights—in this case about the causes of madness—are not fixed over time. These days there still are rejecting mothers, but only in bad jokes are they thought of as schizophrenogenic; and there are, of course, still colons, but no one is recommending their removal to cure schizophrenia.

2

The Experience of Madness

O! let me not be mad, not mad, sweet heaven; Keep me in temper; I would not be mad! — King Lear

IN 1841 A RETIRED BUSINESSMAN referred to as "A.B." was admitted to the Bloomingdale Asylum in New York City. Intelligent, chivalrous and strikingly handsome at age 50, he had made a fortune in business before retiring to live a genteel life in the country. The paroxysms of madness that had plagued him before his retirement—the short periods of frenetic activity, incredible generosity and buoyant spirits that had alternated with longer periods of suspicion and despondency—haunted him in his retirement. On a visit to the city, and in a state of "delightful exhilaration," he encountered a prostitute upon whom he took pity. He escorted her home, offered to pay her rent if she would discontinue her dishonorable profession, hired a physician to treat her syphilis, and wrote a long letter to her mother, assuring her that her wayward daughter soon would be reformed. These and other extravagances during his visit to the city prompted his friends to once again consider the possibility that he was mad and would benefit from institutionalization. He concurred, however reluctantly, but struck a compromise: he would admit himself to an asylum if a physician of his choice would visit him regularly in preparation for testifying on his behalf in a future judicial hearing on his sanity.

Once admitted, A.B. calmed considerably and was granted liberty to wander about the asylum grounds. What limits were placed on him he then ignored and the liberties were revoked, sending him into state of angry excitement. His mental state is then briefly but meticulously documented over the subsequent months of his institutionalization:

December 1. Spoke of having attained the 30th degree in masonry (but one removed from divinity), but immediately fearing he had committed himself, turned round and said to me, "this is not official, and you must not make use of it." He soon got excited and went on talking about masonry, heraldry and religion....

December 6. Exceedingly anxious to visit the city; mind much yet disordered. In a conversation with me today, said that if we lived twenty years we should see Napoleon on the earth again; that there will be a resurrection of him as well as of Alexander, Washington, and all good and great men, but not of such rascals as Caesar, Ben Franklin, Tom Jefferson, &c. Now being prevented from going to town, he became excessively enraged.... [I]t was proposed that he should remain here a week longer ... [and] at the expiration of this period ... he was to go home.

December 23. Released.

December 30. Brought back by an officer in a wretched plight, his clothes torn and dirty.... Said he, with great self-complacency, "Do you know whom you have been treating so long? I am St. George, sir, and have received many communications from on high since I left here."... Among other times, he revealed, with great gravity, that "the devil is white." Considerable physical excitement.

January 1. Still great mental disorder. Seems to live entirely on the productions of his imagination....

January 4. Still under considerable excitement, and various delusions....

January 8. Mind considerably sobered; says he begins to think he has been extravagant, but if listened to, soon runs into his usual vagaries about masonry, &c.

January 15. Continued ... to keep his mind under control.

After a jury finds him sane, apparently persuaded by his eloquent defense of himself, A.B. is discharged from the asylum, only to return two days later in a "depressed state," admitting he was mad and regretting the foolish behaviors in which he had once again engaged. He was taken again before a sheriff's jury, offered no defense, and was found insane and returned to the asylum. The documentation continues:

February 13. Mind in a very tranquil state; says he has never been so rational since he has been here.

February 20. Allowed to go to the city to spend a few days.

February 24. Returns to the asylum in a composed and pretty correct state of mind.

February 26. Discharged much improved ... [but] he was not considered quite sane, because, from being unduly excited, he had sunk into the opposite extreme, [the] depressed state of his feelings gave a somber hue to everything brought before him. In this state he returned home, and continued in that frame of mind which for several months usually succeeds a paroxysm of excitement ["Dr. Mac-Donald's Case," 1841, pp. 23 & 25].

Contemporary readers of this case study very well might immediately conclude that A.B. was in the throes of bipolar disorder, now understood as a brain disease in which episodes of manic mood alternate with episodes of depressive mood. Actually, he had been diagnosed with monomania, a diagnosis new to 19th century American alienists that labeled what was understood to be a derangement of just one faculty of the mind, in A.B.'s case the emotions, and that was detected more by observing conduct than by listening to conversation. In bipolar disorder's historical pedigree, monomania occupies a small, quite flimsy, branch (Healy, 2008). But the rush to diagnose in the first place, made so much easier and more facile by the psychological literacy of today's populace, occludes one significant fact: A.B.'s experience of madness was narrated by someone else. While narrations like these can be, and indeed have been, rich and insightful, they are always deficient in capturing subjectivity. And when subjectivity is attended to, it becomes evident that for the mad, madness is often experienced as a protean site for disputes about, and negotiations over, reality, identity, meaning and memory (Estroff, 2004), as well as for the exercise of agency.

Subjective Experiences of Madness

The experience of Lori Schiller is instructive on this point. As an adolescent, she was left by the love of her life for another woman; despondent, she was haunted by memories that she had never had before of her brief summer fling—memories of a sexual encounter that was both desired and feared. Then, in the middle of the memory, "a huge Voice boomed out through the darkness. 'You must die!' Other Voices joined in. 'You must die! You will die!'" (Schiller & Bennett, 1994, pp. 5–6). From that point on, the Voices, so intrusive in Schiller's life that they collectively require a capital "V," as if "Voices" was their name, hector her almost constantly. After a suicide attempt, Schiller was institutionalized and diagnosed with bipolar disorder, then with schizophrenia, then with schizoaffective disorder, but the reliability of any of these diagnoses is less revealing than the fact that each of them divests the Voices of their bona fides by relegating them to auditory hallucinations. More directly to the point, when Schiller's madness is narrated by others, the Voices are not real. Consider that narration:

[*Nurse's Notes:*] Patient had episode of severe auditory hallucinations coupled with intense psychomotor agitation. She was writhing, forcefully grimacing, holding her hands to her ears.... This episode lasted about ten minutes. [She] later did admit to feeling she must "fight" the voices when they occur, and that discussing them makes it more difficult to "fight" [51].

[*Schiller's Mother:*] Anyone could see she was hallucinating. Once the doctors ... told us about it, I began to see it clearly.... Sometimes when I would visit, she was able to carry on a conversation.... She would be very coherent and aware of what was going on. Then all of a sudden—boom!—she was gone. Suddenly the disease would take over.... She was listening to something else" [81].

Madness, at least of the type that Schiller experienced, long has been thought to be a loss of touch with reality (Foucault, 1965); auditory hallucinations, then, are thought of as nothing more than or different from perceptions of voices that are not real. But Schiller's own understanding of the Voices is more complex than the various narrators of her madness can appreciate:

> Hallucinations meant that you were seeing something or hearing something that didn't really exist. But when I heard the Voices screaming at me, they were real. When the doctors and nurses challenged me, told me that I was out of reality, and hallucinating, I hated them.... What made them the experts? ... The doctors and nursing staff told me repeatedly that the Voices weren't real. But if they weren't real, then how did the staff know they were there? ... My tormenters were real. I didn't want people telling me they were false or unreal [90].

Even years later, after repeated institutionalizations and a long-term stay in a halfway house, after older medications were replaced with newer medications, and a new job was secured teaching patients and their families about madness at the same hospital where she had spent so much time, Schiller remained conflicted over the reality of the Voices and their place in her own subjectivity:

> For as the Voices began to recede, something startling happened within me. After years of begging them to go, to leave me in peace with my own thoughts, when they finally did leave, I found to my surprise that I missed them ... I should have been happy. Instead, I felt like there was a neon vacancy sign flashing. My head felt so empty. Without them, I felt lonely.... Now that they were mostly gone, I wanted them back. So I brought them back: I willed them back into my life ... I welcomed them like lost friends. They were horrible, cruel and profane, but at least they were familiar [263].

It is as much the exercise of agency here—the willing back of the Voices that had been silenced by medication and therapy—as the reasons for doing so, that is a potent reminder that madness is

> not some rather stereotyped disease process stamped onto some shadowy "every-person," but processes of disorder that interact with a very important and differentiated person—a person who is goal-directed, a person whose feelings and interpretations influence actions that in turn affect phases of disorder or recovery, and a person who uses regulatory mechanisms consciously and unconsciously as ways of making both continuity and change possible [Strauss, 1989, p. 185].

For Schiller, the drive to get well, to live normally, and the expectations adhering to what is taken to be the antithesis of madness, i.e., being in touch with reality, also required the exercise of agency. She realized she had to control the Voices, and she did so by relegating them to the not real. "I have taught myself to use a little mantra when they reappear: *'These Voices are not real,'*" she writes. "When I hear the Voices, *I shake myself back to reality* by using all my senses" (Schiller & Bennett, 1994, p. 269, emphasis added).

The kind of agency Schiller exercised to control the Voices is not uncommon, but may be overlooked or, more likely, misinterpreted by narrators. The sidewalk psychotic who is mumbling to himself may be arguing with voices only he can hear; the emergency room patient who overdosed on her antipsychotic medications may be silencing voices only she can hear (Farhall, Greenwood & Jackson, 2007). To those who observe these experiences of severe madness, and for those who will narrate them, these exercises of agency often are interpreted as more and different symptoms.

Experiencing the Onset

Madness is transition—from sane to mad, real to unreal, powerful to helpless, significant to insignificant, subject to object, perhaps even from loved to hated, accepted to feared. Narrators often look intently for the causes of this transition, searching for reasons that are, perhaps, as jarring as the transition itself. And there have been reasons aplenty throughout history to choose—from God's will, moral failings, dysfunctional families, social stresses, genetics, to neurochemistry, with dozens more in between, and more than a few in combination.

Privileged by a certain ontological distance, the narrator of another person's madness often finds multiple or otherwise complex causes of it. The life of the author Jane Bowles, for example, reveals a plethora of reasons for the madness that finally led to her institutionalization: a childhood in a dysfunctional family and in a patriarchal society that discouraged female initiative and imagination; a deeply suppressed sexual interest in other women; a persistent struggle in reconciling the roles of wife and writer (Fernández, 2001). While all of these, and other factors, are woven together by the narrator to make sense of her madness, Bowles herself had a slightly, but significantly different, take on the reason why she was mad. She personalized the social: in her reasoning, she had failed to be a good child, a true woman, and a faithful wife. God, she concluded, was making her mad as punishment for her sins (Dillon, 1981).

In his "journey into a family secret," journalist Steve Luxenberg (2009) investigates the fate of an aunt he had not know he had, a woman named Annie who had spent all of her adult life in various mental hospitals in Michigan. Luxenberg's mother never spoke of her sister. In fact, she even denied she had a sister, but after her death a series of events revealed the long-buried family secret. Luxenberg's investigation uncovered any number of compelling reasons why his mother had denied her sister's existence—shame, dread that the family taint of madness would decrease her own marriageability—and just as many — shame again, unquestioning trust in physicians, fear of stigma, impoverished circumstances — why his immigrant grandparents had committed Annie to an asylum. But he also was determined to find out the reasons why Annie became mad in the first place. And he found them, if not in abundance then at least to his satisfaction: an intellectual impairment that limited her ability to conform and adjust, a deformed leg that made her the target of mockery, a consanguineous parentage, a mother who for unexplained reasons hated her, the trauma of a sexual assault no one believed she had endured.

Luxenberg's recreation of Annie's experience of madness, though, is limited by the memories of a few distant family members and the sparse official case records he finally was able to secure. The 1940 application for her commitment to the Eloise Asylum states the following: "Patient imagines that someone wants to do her bodily harm. She talks to herself, She laughs and cries for no apparent reason. She cannot carry on a coherent conversation. She assumes one position for long periods" (p. 94). But it is Luxenberg's sense that Annie's madness had snuck up on her, that she had become "increasingly bizarre" (p. 94) over the years, finally taxing her family's limited resources and their patience to the point where institutionalization was their only option. The course of what he imagines to be her slow but steady descent into madness — the insidious transition from good to bad to worse — however, eludes and haunts him.

And that same progression eludes Marsha Hunt (1996), who attempts to trace the reasons why her grandmother Ernestine spent more than a half-century in a Tennessee asylum. Like Annie, the fate of Ernestine had been a well-kept family secret. Hunt had always believed her grandmother was dead and only began her quest to uncover her life when she learned that Ernestine was a resident of a run-down nursing home in Memphis. Nearly 100 years old, Ernestine provides little insight into the reason for her institutionalization; but Hunt thinks she knows the reason: colorism, the "crazy aunt in the attic of racism" (Brown, 2009). Ernestine was a light-skinned, blonde-haired, blue-eyed black, the daughter of a dark-skinned black mother who herself had come from a large family of light-skinned, blue-eyed siblings. Throughout American history color has conferred privilege; light-skinned slaves were afforded more favors, such as working in the house rather than the field; and from emancipation to this very day light-skinned blacks have had better access to employment, housing, education, and social opportunities (Hunter, 2007). Ernestine may have internalized this aesthetic, believing herself white, especially in the face of the abusive treatment she endured from her jealous mother. On that point, Hunt recollects her conversation with her stepmother:

"Color has made so many people crazy," [she said]. "You know, we're the most prejudiced people in the world." She was referring to African-Americans and the caste system we had inherited through slavery, which made us value any resemblance to those who had such complete power over us. As we move further away from slavery, we try to forget certain factors imposed on us. But obviously a slave's trade value was affected by how the slave appealed to the buyer; and how handsome the slave appeared was based on the buyer's beauty standards. Thus Ernestine would have been seen as more beautiful and more socially acceptable than [her mother], and [her mother] would have been less valuable than her sisters and brothers [Hunt, 1996, p. 193].

Delusional about her own racial identity, labeled retarded despite the fact that she had graduated from high school, no small feat for a Southern black female in the early 1900s, Ernestine was institutionalized, rarely ever visited and relegated to a family secret. All that, in Hunt's reckoning, was the consequence of the insidious effects of race politics, not so much between whites and blacks, as among blacks.

For many other narrators, the transition from sanity to madness often seems so abrupt that there is a lingering certainty that the mad person must have known it was coming, must have felt something that signaled its onset. Especially for narrators who have an intimate relationship with the mad persons whose story they are telling, in retrospect the clues are everywhere.

Journalist Pete Early, who chronicled (2006) his frustrating altercations with the mental health system in his desperate attempts to find help for his son, a university student who, in the throes of a manic episode, broke into a neighbor's house and took a bath in her tub, underwent his own transition when he finally realized his son was mad:

Mike's first psychotic breakdown occurred during his senior year at a university in Brooklyn. I have since learned that this not an uncommon time for mental illness to strike young men and women, because of stress. He had been about to graduate and was having a difficult time finding a job. I had never suspected that he might have a mental illness.... Now, looking back, I should have known better. There'd been lots of clues ... [but] I wanted to believe that Mike was just nervous about graduating.... And then his mind broke [10–11].

For those who recount their own experiences of madness, the "breaking of the mind" can happen slowly or quickly, with their awareness that something—although something perhaps not readily identified as madness—is wrong, or without any real awareness at all. Susanna Kaysen (1993), who as an 18-year-old, had admitted herself into McLean Hospital in Belmont, Massachusetts, where she stayed for years, describes the variable "viscosity and velocity" of madness in the following way:

Insanity comes in two basic varieties: slow and fast.... The predominant quality of the slow form is viscosity. Experience is thick. Perceptions are thickened and dull. Time is slow, dripping slowly away through the clogged filter of thickened perception. The body temperature is low. The pulse is sluggish. The immune system is half-asleep. The organism is torpid and brackish. Even the reflexes are diminished.... In contrast to viscosity's cellular coma, velocity endows every platelet and muscle fiber with a mind of its own, a means of knowing and commenting on its own behavior. There is too much perception, and beyond the plethora of perceptions, a plethora of thought about the perceptions and about the fact of having perceptions.... Viscosity and velocity are opposites, yet they can look the same. Viscosity causes the stillness of disinclination; velocity causes the stillness of fascination. An observer can't tell if a person is silent and still because inner life has stalled or because inner life is transfixingly busy [75, 77].

The inner life of author William Styron (1990) had become stalled. The viscous flow of his madness over the years had been so steady that in many ways its final arrival was welcomed. The malaise, restlessness and vague anxiety he had experienced for years now had a name—depression—and once named he not only could identify its cause—a devastating loss during childhood—but anticipate its cure. Before he admitted himself into an asylum, though, Styron was overcome by the torpidity and brackishness of his depression:

> I had now reached that phase of the disorder where all sense of hope had vanished, along with the idea of a futurity; my brain, in thrall to its outlaw hormones, had become less an organ of thought than an instrument registering, minute by minute, varying degrees of its own suffering. The mornings themselves were becoming bad now as I wandered about lethargic, following my synthetic sleep, but afternoons were still the worst, beginning at about three o'clock, when I'd feel the horror, like some poisonous fogbank, roll in upon my mind, forcing me into bed. There I would lie as long as six hours, stuporous and virtually paralyzed, gazing at the ceiling and waiting for that moment of evening when, mysteriously, the crucifixion would ease up just enough to allow me to force down some food and then, like an automaton, seek an hour or two of sleep again [58–59].

That viscous experience of the onset of madness was true for Meri Nana-Ama Danquah (1998) as well. For most of her life she had "nurtured a consistent, low-grade melancholy" (p. 15) that finally took the form of debilitating depression. But as a black woman the onset of her depression, indeed the very intersubjectivity of it, as madness began to intertwine with her gender and her race, consumes her much more than its origin:

> Stereotypes and clichés about mental illness are as pervasive as those about race. I have noticed that the mental illness that affects white men is often characterized, if not glamorized, as a sign of genius, a burden of cerebral superiority, artistic eccentricity—as if their depression is somehow heroic. White women who suffer from mental illness are depicted as idle, spoiled, or just plain hysterical. Black men are demonized and pathologized. Black women with psychological problems are certainly not seen as geniuses; we are generally not labeled "hysterical" or "eccentric" or even "pathological." When a black woman suffers from

mental disorder, the overwhelming opinion is that she is weak. And weakness in black women is intolerable [p. 20].

Danquah's struggle with the intolerable weakness of madness is exacerbated by her struggle with how the metaphors and euphemisms for depression further intertwine with those for race. As a black woman she can find no rhetorical distance from her own madness; it becomes entangled with her racial identity in ways that to her are intolerable since she has always held on to the "one myth" of her life—that of her "supposed birth-right to strength" in a world that "completely undervalues the lives of black people and regards all women as second-class citizens" (p. 19):

> You've heard descriptions of depression before: A black hole; an enveloping darkness; a dismal existence through which no light shines; the black dog; darkness, and more darkness. But what does darkness mean to me, a woman who has spent her life surrounded by it? The darkness of my skin; the darkness of my friends and family. I have never been afraid of the dark. It poses no harm to me. What is the color of my depression? [p. 22].

For Lisa Wiley (1955), in contrast, the color of her madness was of much less concern than the terrifying velocity of its onset. Over five short weeks, the madness seemed to crack her brain and cave in her mind:

> Every day brought more physical suffering and mental torment.... [A] feeling of deadness came over me, for I found I was losing my emotion little by little.... I was emotionally dying inch by inch until by the end of five weeks I had no feeling at all.... Although I could still think and knew what I was doing, my thoughts were lifeless.... Even in respect to time I was dead. There was no future and no past. Everything was just an endless black nothingness [pp. 46, 48–49].

Even though Marya Hornbacher (2008) had been taunted all through her childhood for being "different," and even though she feared, even as a child, that her difference was madness, when madness finally hit it was with such velocity that it left her "scrabbling on the floor of [her] brain for the snatches and snippets of what happened, what was said, and when" (p. 175). To Hornbacher, madness is an uninvited guest that takes over as soon as it arrives:

> You wake up one morning and there it is, sitting in an old plaid bathrobe in your kitchen, unpleasant and unshaved. You look at it, heart sinking. Madness is a rotten guest. You can tell it to leave till you're blue in the face. You follow it around the house, explaining that it's come at a bad time, and could it come back another day. Eventually you give up and go back to bed, shutting the door. But of course it barges in and demands to be entertained.... Soon, your life revolves around it. You do everything you can to keep it comfortable, because you don't want to upset it. You tiptoe around the house and wait for it to leave.... Soon madness has worn you down. It's easier to do what it says than to argue. In this way, it takes over your mind. You no longer know where it ends and you begin. You believe anything it says. You do what it tells you, no matter how extreme or absurd [p. 226].

Whether viscously or with velocity, madness's arrival so colonizes subjectivity that it sometimes has to be personified to be described. So for Hornbacher, madness was an unnamed, uninvited guest that "lounges all day in front of the TV, watching *Oprah* and munching on a bag of chips, drinking milk from the carton, getting crumbs between the cushions of the couch" (p. 226). For Jane Hillyer (1926), it was "the thing" that not only took over her mind but her identity, so that she could no longer recognize herself in the mirror, nor remember with clarity her own name. Madness was "It" to Russell Hampton (1975), a force that battled with "me" for dominance, and for Tracy Thompson (1995) it was "the Beast" that chewed up her self and her will to live.

For the Confessional movement poet and writer Sylvia Plath (1952), madness had a name: "Johnny Panic." In a short story that is a thinly veiled autobiographical account, Plath introduces a young assistant in the psychiatric clinic of a hospital who obsessively transcribes the patients' dreams into her "bible of dreams" where Johnny Panic is the god. Unlike the clinic's psychiatrists who try to "win Johnny Panic's converts by hook, crook, and talk, talk, talk" (p. 165) the assistant savors the patients' dreams, but she also has a terrifying one of her own: a dream of being suspended in a glass-bellied helicopter over an expansive lake filled with dragons, snakes, dead bodies and the detritus of mechanical life—knives, pistons, automobile parts and nutcrackers. The narrator knows that this dream of being suspended over the "Bog of Madness," just like those of the patients whose dreams she is transcribing, is being spun by Johnny Panic. And the narrator knows that just like the patients, she is mad. She is then subjected to a course of electroconvulsive shock treatments that are meant to obliterate her madness and almost does until Johnny Panic's face appears in the overhead lights. In the end, the "masked priests" in surgical gowns, despite all of their knowledge and technology, have not been able to unseat Johnny Panic from his throne.

Being Mad

There are plenty of reasons why, throughout history, the experience of madness has been more often narrated than told. For one, its verbal expression sometimes is incomprehensible by prevailing linguistic conventions; thus it seems unable to stand on its own without interpretation. An interesting 1847 article in the *Knickerbocker,* a literary magazine, makes that point. In it, Pliny Earle, the esteemed medical superintendent of the Bloomingdale Asylum in New York City, offers a verbatim transcript of his interview with a 25-year-old black patient, who because of his orderliness and punctuality was known around the asylum as "The General":

PHYSICIAN. What is your name?

PATIENT. My name is Judge Hamilton Hambleton Hambelton. I am mayor of the city, and my father was Judge and Sheriff Hambleton, Agrippa, King of Damasker, and he gave me this house.

PHYSICIAN. Where were you born?

PATIENT. I was not born; I growed up in Deevah Foolah, in the furthest part of the South Fenterie. All the people there is Irish, and all the children is Spanish. I grew on to Maraziana, where I was planted again. Then I grew to Morypalet, and lived in the city of Calvary a thousand years, and more too, off and on, for I was sometimes in England. I am general to the Heatherens, State of Big Ranger, in Regyptia.

PHYSICIAN. How old are you?

PATIENT. I'm a Thusalem nation years old. I am in the United States of Reguzza. My home is in Bandanna, in Galgotha. If I should lose that, I should never have another. Massachusetts is in Galgotha, and so is China and Boston and Pennsylvania. Baltimore is a diamond State. I go to steal Delaware, opposite Jerusalem. Jerusalem is a gold nation, and Delaware is not. It is in sight of Jericho, and Judea is a thousand miles south.,.,

PHYSICIAN. Have you learned any trade?

PATIENT. Yes, I am a forge-man, a ship carpenter, a plattender—to make plates, china of all kinds; gold tumblers and gold wires; a tanner, a burn-smith and gold-smith, and a shoe-maker....

PHYSICIAN. How many dollars worth of money have you?

PATIENT. Thusalem, Thusalem States of dollars; that money I'm worth. I'm a laborer; I've got the arms in the fogus skies; in the fogus regions.

PHYSICIAN. That's nonsense.

PATIENT. It isn't nonsense. I'm a general.... I've been in a hundred thousand ninety-nine battles; and separate devils makes a hundred million of battles, and more....

PHYSICIAN. What do you expect to do when you leave this place?

PATIENT. I'm going into Jersey shore and going to be drowned, take a new frame, a white man, a large, big lord, and then I'm going home and have that island across the river sent to Massachusetts, into the Island of St. Gorah. [Patient then describes the asylum he himself will head.] I shall have a hundred nurses. I've seen them all; they're good looking people. The patients all lisp, like the French. God almighty wants them broke of this.... I shall have four doctors. It's a very big house; will hold fifty thousand; that's the big part will hold so many.... It has a steeple on it.... It's a little town, twenty-four miles round, a wall running round twelve feet high, and more too, with iron pickets on the top as big as your arm ["Leaf," 1847, pp. 452–453].

In this excerpt Earle is uncharacteristically restrained, content to play the role of interrogator by prompting the story from the unnamed patient without directing its telling. On its face, this transgressive account, which breaks all of the rules of personal disclosure, is incoherent and incomprehensible. Unable to stand on its own, it has to be interpreted and then narrated by someone else. Earle does just that, not by giving a line-by-line translation of the rambling account of this mad patient, but by directing his readers' attention to what might be thought of as the meta-narrative, i.e., the story about the story the patient has told. This account, he reminds the readers, is not really about the patient's bizarre life history nor about his fantastical plan to build and staff his own asylum, but about the fact that even an incoherent and delusional mad patient has a sense of identity and is capable of planning and exercising judgment, all of this, of course, within the constraints of delusion.

But there is another meta-narrative that can be teased out of the patient's account — a meta-narrative about the influence of culture on the subjectivity of the mad. The patient whose account Earle translates is a Gullah, a black native of the Low Country region of South Carolina and Georgia. Because of their geographic isolation in small fishing villages along the Sea of Islands that run parallel to the coast, the Gullah have held on to more of their African cultural heritage than any other group of blacks in the United States. Their culture was, and continues to be, rooted in the oral tradition of storytelling in an English-based Creole language, sometimes known as Geechee, that has an Afrocentric grammar and rhythm, and an altered pronunciation of English words (Politzer, 2005).

While Earle does acknowledge the racial and cultural background of his unnamed patient, his interpretation of the patient's narrative is not influenced by it. This is not to suggest that had Earle a more anthropological interest in his patient he would not have found him mad, nor is it to suggest that the patient was not mad after all; but it is to raise the question about the extent to which culture influences the subjective experience of madness, its expression and, for that matter, its interpretation.

Auditory and visual hallucinations have been considered the hallmark symptoms of severe madness for centuries (Leudar & Thomas, 2000), but it is only quite recently that the influence of culture on their content and interpretation has been considered. Latinos with severe madness, for example, are more likely than any other racial or ethnic group to experience religious content in their hallucinations. The cultural syntonicity of the hallucinations, i.e., their coherence with everyday life and cultural worldview, diminishes the distress that hearing voices often creates for the severely mad (Yamada, Barrio, Morrison, Sewell, & Jeste, 2006). A Puerto Rican woman, diagnosed with schizophrenia, explains: "They [the angels] talk nice to me and help me a lot. I talk back to them and they talk back to me. I like them very much because they tell me beautiful things. They live in my room and protect me from evil. Four angels live with me, including Diamante, Quarubin, and Safiro. If they leave, I'll feel lost. They are always in my room. They are beautiful, big wings, and big" (cited in Loue & Sajatovic, 2008, pp. 602–603).

Latinos also report hearing more unidentifiable voices than do the severely mad in other racial or ethnic groups. The fact that these strange voices often issue what are known as advisory commands that tell the hearers what to do may reflect the marginalization and helplessness so often associated with minority status, as well as with madness (Whaley & Geler, 2003).

Severely mad blacks also report religious content in their auditory and visual hallucinations, but are more likely than other racial or ethnic groups to describe race-related themes in their delusions, i.e., their erroneous beliefs. Persecutory delusions are common and most certainly reflect both the experience and the legacy of oppression and inequality for blacks in the United States (Whaley & Hall, 2009).

There is another way to appreciate the influence of culture on the experience of severe madness, and that is to contextualize it within historical periods. When the records of patients institutionalized in the 1930s are compared with those who were institutionalized in the 1980s, the subtle influence of culture on the content of their reported hallucinations and delusions is revealed. The 1930s was a decade of contradictions, anchored on one end by the depths of the Great Depression, and on the other by the rise of Modernism. Patients institutionalized during that decade reported more hallucinations and delusions about wealth, status, and special powers than did asylum patients a half-century later. The decade of the 1980s was politically and economically tumultuous, with the restructuring of American industry and the unprecedented competition for wealth, status and power. The hallucinations and delusions of severely mad patients institutionalized during that decade were influenced by the zeitgeist. They reported more hectoring command hallucinations and more hostile and persecutory delusions than did the asylum patients a half-century before (Mitchell & Vierkant, 1989).

Another historical comparison reveals how culture, in the broadest sense of that term, actually can form around delusion, and then influence its experience and expression. "Patient 0" in the psychiatric canon, i.e., the first mad patient who was ever made the subject of a book-length study, was a London tea-broker by the name of James Tilly Matthews. Committed in 1797 to the Royal Bethlem Hospital, better known as Bedlam, his delusion is described in the following terms: "Mr. M. insists that in some apartment near the London Wall, there is a gang of villains profoundly skilled in Pneumatic Chemistry, who assail him by means of an Air Loom. A description of this formidable instrument will be given hereafter.... The assailing gang consists of seven members ... [who] hire themselves out as spies, and discover the secrets of government to the enemy, or confederate to work events of the most atrocious nature" (Haslam, 1810, pp. 20–21).

Matthews believed that a magnet had been implanted in his head that was sensitive to the gasses and vapors—seminal fluid, nightshade, hellebore, stinking human breath and gas, nauseating Egyptian snuff—released by the

Air Loom. These fumes would lock the fibers at the root of his tongue, rendering him speechless; drop a veil between his soul and his senses, preventing the sentiments of his heart to communicate with his intellect; stick stones in his bladder; talk to his thigh; "kite" unwanted ideas into his brain; stagnate his circulation and breath, a procedure much akin to "lobster-cracking"; violently force fluid into his head; elongate his brain, thus distorting his ideas; screw up the muscles of his face into a grin and pump his stomach full of explosive gas. The Air Loom gang was filling his head with their nonsense, but he was not their only target. According to Matthews, the gang was doing the same to government officials and prominent politicians who, unaware of how they were being influenced, were being brought to the very verge of national and international chaos (Jay, 2004).

There is much more to Matthews' story—his strong political beliefs, his attempts to broker a peaceful accord between warring Great Britain and France, his years in a French prison, accused of being an double agent, his legal battles to be released from Bedlam—but in the psychiatric canon, Matthews is presented as the first fully documented case of paranoid schizophrenia. His delusion certainly was influenced by the political instability of Great Britain at the time. But it also was influenced by the technological advances in these early years of the Industrial Revolution. The Air Loom, according to Matthews, was a massive machine, standing more than 20 feet tall, constructed of oak with brass fittings, keys and levers. It operated according to the recently discovered principles of gas chemistry, as well as the mysterious principles of human magnetism, at that time being demonstrated throughout Europe by the flamboyant physician Franz Mesmer.

In recent years Matthews' Air Loom machine has been featured in the novels *Bedlam* (Hollingshead, 2004) and *The Influencing Machine* (Hayden, 1996), the unpublished play "Haslam's Key" in which Matthews is reimagined as the originator of the science fiction genre (O'Brien, 1993), and in a feature song of the British band Lowland Hundred. At the time, however, Matthews' delusion of mind control was more the subject of psychiatric, as opposed to cultural, interest. Little could Matthews have known that as technology advanced—telegraph, telephone, television, computers, wireless technology—mind control delusions would keep pace. And he never could have imagined that far from isolating and marginalizing the deluded, the delusions actually would create a culture, of sorts, that ironically would end up calling into question whether those who have them are really mad after all.

This contemporary spin on mind control delusions begins with the authoritative text, *Diagnostic and Statistical Manual of Mental Disorders (DSM)*, which in its most recent iteration states that the criteria for delusion should not include any beliefs held by the person's "culture or subculture."

The World Wide Web is rife with self-published Web pages authored by those who believe their minds are being controlled for political purposes by the sophisticated technology of nefarious groups and individuals. Analyses that examine the hyperlinks between these websites reveal a complex and highly structured social network, an online community of believers who not only share the belief in mind control, but also exchange information and provide support and guidance for each other. If the belief in mind control indeed is held by the person's culture, virtual in this case, then it cannot be a delusion according to the *DSM*. Therefore, without other evidence of psychopathology, the person who believes that his or her mind is being controlled by advanced technology cannot be considered mad (Bell, Maiden, Muñoz-Solomando, & Reddy, 2006). James Tilly Matthews, who had always insisted he was sane, would have been amused by this modern paradox.

Having Madness/Being Mad

If a person is physically ill, say with cancer, there is a prevailing understanding that for the time being the body is out of order, but the self is not. If a person is mad, however, the prevailing understanding is that the self is out of order, perhaps forever. More directly put: a person *has* cancer, but a person *is* mad.

A narrator of another's experiences with madness can reveal a great deal about how that person suffers from being mad. In her Pulitzer Prize winning book, *Is There No Place on Earth for Me?* (1983), journalist Susan Sheehan details the daily struggles with delusions and hallucinations, stigma and rejection, bureaucratic indifferences and trial-and-error therapeutic interventions of the pseudonymous "Sylvia Frumkin." Loquacious, brilliant, flamboyant, at times wildly and violently out of control, Sylvia moves from one self-created crisis to another, and into one asylum after another. "Mental illness is worse than cancer," she tells her narrator. "The suffering doesn't have an end point" (p. 350). Her suffering from schizophrenia is palpable. But what remains somewhat elusive in the narrative is who Sylvia Frumkin really is—not her true identity, but her true self. Biographical details are provided, of course, as are descriptions of her as a "heavy, ungainly young woman" (p. 3), but the narrative reads as if Sylvia Frumkin does not have madness as much as madness has her. Yet there are hints throughout the narrative that such is not always the case. "I do crazy things when I'm sick," she tells her narrator, "and then I don't know why when I'm well" (p. 88). On occasion, she is able to remember and reflect on her behavior and even on her delusions, especially the one about marrying a movie star. Her reflection reveals an interesting subjectivity that, were it not cited in her own words, would have lost something deeply personal in the narration:

> You know, it was fun believing some of those things and in a way I hate to give up those beliefs. There's a charm to being sick. I like to be in the twilight zone of the real world. Absolutely real is getting up every day and going to work. I once thought, when I was about to finish medical-secretarial school, before I had my first breakdown on the last day of school, that I'd graduate and get a job. I was looking forward to earning my own money ... to being a grown woman in my own right. If you can work and earn money, you can spend money.... You can have fun. But if you can't have any of those things ... [w]hen you know all those things exist for other people but not for you, sometimes it's very hard to endure the not having [p. 112].

A narrator of another's experiences with madness can reveal a great deal about how those who care about the mad person also suffer, whether from shame, guilt, frustration, anger, or, sometimes, more plaintively, from grief and loneliness. National Public Radio reporter Jacki Lyden (1999) recollects her childhood with a manic-depressive mother whom she could not always understand and could not always love. Lyden's subjectivity, eloquently stated, is nonetheless raw; her mother's, however, remains elusive:

> I longed to know my mother's secret language when she went mad. I yearned to know its passwords and frames of reference. In the last and most desperate stages of mania, my mother's speech falls to pure sound. A gutteral like Urdu, rhythmic and completely foreign. Often I can make out words, but they have no context. At such times I cannot help but go a little crazy myself. I talk to the ghosts, to the people in our lives thirty years ago, to the small girls in long grass. I mean I talk to my mother and to me. I ask us why we cannot grow up, what has happened to make the past so vexing for us both. I torture myself that she is suffering now for all the longings then, longing I helped inflict in my child life. I have become obsessed with finding her in a chiaroscuro world where, despite every act of intimacy I have ever learned, I am in high seas. She is lost. And I cannot follow [p. 19].

Whether written by psychiatrists, biographers, or family members, narratives *about* the experience of madness often drown out the voice of the mad, whose subjectivity is muted, if not silenced altogether, by a set of narrative strategies put into place to create coherent, understandable and engaging accounts. Narratives *of* the experience of madness written by the mad themselves also tend to conform to these conventions. After all, experiences do not automatically assume narrative form. It is only by reflecting on them that coherent, understandable and engaging accounts can be written, not to mention published. Thus, most first-person accounts of madness are written from some distance from the actual experiences of madness.

Accounts of the experience of madness vary in structure, form and purpose. Regardless of that, each can be mined for its descriptions of the subjective experience of madness—descriptions, once again, that would have lost their self-consciousness if narrated by others. There are no rules for reading a first-person account, but to appreciate the subjectivity of madness the following questions have a great deal of probative value (Adame & Hornstein, 2006; Estroff, 1989):

- How does the person describe the onset of the experience of madness?
- How does the person explain the cause(s) of the madness?
- Does the person describe the experience of madness in terms different from that of prevailing medical and psychiatric terminology?
- Does the person experience madness as something separate from the self, or as part of it? Does that relation change during the account, and if so, why?
- How does the person deal with conflicts between his or her sense of self and the reactions of others to a self they perceive has been changed by madness?
- How does the person struggle to reclaim the pre-madness self, and how does he or she know the struggle has been successful?
- How does the person negotiate and manage a spoiled identity, both during the experience of madness and after?

With those questions in mind, even short passages from first-person accounts of madness take on new meaning. Meri Nana-Ama Danquah (1998) describes the onset of her depressive experiences in much more subjectively nuanced terms than either the prevailing psychiatric terminology or the skilled writing of a seasoned narrator would ever allow:

Depression offers layers, textures, noises. At times depression is as flimsy as a feather, barely penetrating the surface of my life, hovering like a slight halo of pessimism. Other times it comes on gradually like a common cold or a storm, each day presenting new signals and symptoms until finally I am drowning in it. Most times, in its most superficial and seductive sense, it is rich and enticing. A field of velvet waiting to embrace me. It is loud and dizzying, inviting the tenors and screeching sopranos of thoughts, unrelenting sadness, and the sense of impending doom. Depression is all of these things to me—but darkness it is not [p. 22].

Although his "invisible disease" of bipolar disorder (manic depression) was repeatedly misdiagnosed and ineffectively treated for years, Andy Behrman (2002) is less worried about its cause—he is content to know that it often runs in families—than he is eager to describe his experience of it. And he does so in terms that introduce a certain ambiguity that the prevailing medical and psychiatric description certainly would not tolerate:

I'll admit it: there's a great deal of pleasure to mental illness, especially to the mania associated with manic depression. It's an emotional state similar to Oz, full of excitement, color, noise, and speed—an overload of sensory stimulation— whereas the state of Kansas is flat and simple, black and white, boring and flat. Mania has such a dreamlike quality that I often confuse my manic episodes with dreams I've had.... Mania is about desperately seeking to live life at a more passionate level, taking second and sometimes third helpings on food, alcohol, drugs, sex, and money, trying to live a whole life in one day. Pure mania is as close to death as I think I have ever come. The euphoria is both pleasurable and frightening [p. xix].

Diagnosed with obsessive-compulsive disorder when he was 11 years old, Jared Kant (2008) finds his "adventures in daily living" with madness to be nothing short of daunting, and he is keenly aware of the effect his bizarre thoughts and behaviors have had on his family and his friends. For some time after his diagnosis, he *was* obsessive-compulsive, unable to separate his madness from his self. His madness was his identity. But as the effects of therapy and medication took hold, and as he became more skilled in managing his own thoughts and behaviors, the madness gradually loosened its hold on his self, with consequences not only for his identity, but for his evaluation of the madness: "OCD can be simultaneously your worst enemy and your best friend. Every time I overcame obsessive-compulsive thoughts and behaviors, I learned more about myself and took greater charge of my life. As a result, I'm of the sincerely peculiar opinion that some good has come from my illness. I can't honestly say that I'm grateful for OCD, but I do think it has made me a stronger, better person" (p. 107).

It could be argued that when madness loosens it grip on the self, whether as a result of therapeutic intervention or successful coping, self-awareness increases. And while the received wisdom is that enhanced self-awareness is good for rehabilitation and recovery, that may not always be so. Kurt Snyder (2007) was diagnosed with paranoid schizophrenia when he was in his late twenties, although he had experienced a slow and steady slide away from reality over the decade preceding the diagnosis. When his madness was florid, he was convinced that his life was manufactured by a virtual reality machine operated by aliens, that shadowy government agents had him under constant surveillance, and that he was on the brink of discovering a new mathematical principle that would transform scientific understanding of the universe. Just as in the case of Jared Kant (2008), therapeutic and pharmaceutical interventions, periods of institutionalization, and the support of family and friends separated his madness from his self. But the self-awareness that developed as a result was for Snyder a "double-edged sword": "Lack of awareness insulates a person from what's happening, and when that insulation is stripped away, the shock and fear can be intense. It may be alternately frightening and confusing to believe that you're the subject of a stealthy investigation by the CIA. But there's nothing compared to the shattering realization that it's your own mind that is tricking you and your own senses that are not be trusted" (p. 48).

Snyder is able now to distinguish himself from what he still refers to as "them"—the auditory hallucinations and the delusions that had once colonized his consciousness. For him there was no single moment when he was finally able to exercise that control, but for Lauren Slater (1996) there was a moment of great insight that vested her with some power over the obsessive-compulsive disorder that had made her life miserable for years, leaving her, in her own eyes, as someone without the right to talk or ask or wonder, as something less than human. She had been in psychotherapy for some time and had been prescribed the antidepressant Prozac, but had not felt any progress in reclaiming her pre-mad self until one late evening when she wandered around the countryside and saw swans floating on a lake. In the darkness they appeared black, jut like the madness that had enveloped her. But she realized in that moment of reflexivity that her mind had been quieted by the sight of them, and that she was in wonder of their elegance. Madness finally separated from her sense of self—she had it, it no longer had her:

> The thought calmed me. I was not completely claimed by illness, nor a prisoner of Prozac, entirely dependent on the medication to function. Part of me was still free, a private space not absolutely permeated by pain. A space I could learn to cultivate. Over the next few days, I noticed that even in the thicket of obsessions, my mind sometimes swam into the world, if only for brief forays. There, while I struggled to take a step, was the sun on a green plate. *Remember that* I said to myself.... And so a part of me began to learn about living outside the disease, cultivating appreciation for a few free moments. It was nothing I would have wished for myself, nothing to noisily celebrate. But it was something, and I could choose it, even while mourning the paralyzed parts of me [p. 45].

Mental Pathographies

From time immemorial, others, whether parents, priests, physicians or psychiatrists, have had charge of the mad. Their epistemic gaze has been privileged in the published literature, so privileged, in fact, that first-person accounts of the experience of madness often have been politely dismissed as the "lay-perspective"—not the "mad person's perspective," but the "lay-perspective," almost as if they could have been written by anyone. But written they have been, and over recent years these mental pathographies, as they might be referred to, have been increasingly recognized as invitations to consider the fact that people have a relationship, of sorts, with their madness, that self and madness are not always and forever inextricably intertwined. That separation of self and madness, however miniscule it may be, allows for both the consideration and the appreciation of how people perceive and represent their madness, cope with it, struggle against it, compare it if not to some notion or reality then at least to some memory of the familiar, and sometimes, triumphantly, win over it.

Not every mad person writes his or her account, of course, so the published first-person narratives not only offer a small glimpse into a much larger problem, but are penned by a highly selective group of authors who have enough skill to write an account, enough social capital to get it published, and enough ontological distance from their madness to make it insightful. Madness may be the scarlet thread that thematically links these various first-person accounts, but the accounts themselves vary in type, i.e., in their expressed relationship between author, narrative and madness (Hydén, 1997).

Quite regardless of type, however, *all* of them are archly political. They position the authors vis-à-vis others, whether families and friends or acquaintances and strangers; locate their lives in relation to formal institutions of social control, albeit asylums, courts or jails; and position them in attitudes of deference or defiance to those who are charged with exercising that control, and to the tools they have at hand for doing so, whether pharmaceuticals, talk therapies, lobotomies, or venesections that drip blood, drop by drop, into pewter porringers. All of the first-person accounts also position their authors in relation to what are so often glibly referred to as "reality," "rationality," "normality," and "sanity." Since these are socially constructed terms, these accounts also place the authors within the particular vortexes of social, political and ideological forces of their historical contexts.

To treat the mad as authentic narrators of their own experiences is not to privilege their discourse above all others, neither is it to elevate them to folk hero status. Rather, it is to invite them into a discourse that for too long has been dominated by "the Majority." The contents of the first-person accounts by the mad may be enlightening, heartbreaking, outraging, befuddling, or inspiring; but if the covers of their accounts were reflective, like glass, they would invite "the Majority" to look at itself, to reflect and take a gander at its own subjectivity. Gazing in the glass, "the Majority" will be able to see "how much sense the voices of the mad commonly made, in the desperate attempts of isolated, troubled and confused people to grasp their actual situations, their own urges, impulses, memories. They form the struggles of the despairing and powerless to exercise some control over those—devils, spooks, mad-doctors, priests—who had them in their power. The logic is there for those who look" (Porter, 1989, pp. 5–6).

3

Distracted in the Colonies

*So it is, besieged with sable-colored melancholy, I did commend
the black oppressing humour to the most wholesome physic of
thy health.* —Love's Labour's Lost

In 1759 BENAJAH HUMPHRY MADE a plea before the Assembly of Simsbury,
Connecticut, for the release of his son from jail. His son was mad. He had
become "delerious and distracted" while serving in the army and, upon
returning home, had murdered his mother. At his trial the court took notice
of his mental state and acquitted him of the crime, but because he was without the financial resources to pay the cost of prosecution he was committed
to jail where, at the time of his father's plea, he had been languishing for
several months, "still distracted." The assembly ordered the chief judge of
the superior court to release the young man into the custody of his father
and also ordered Humphry to "take and safely keep" his son and granted him
£40 towards his care (Connecticut Colonial Records, Vol. 11, p. 313).

Two years later Humphry again appealed to the assembly, "shewing that
he is labouring under very melancholy and chargeable circumstances on
account of supporting and taking care of his unhappy, unfortunate and distracted son." He had used the generous grant of £40 to pay the charges of
his son's trial and imprisonment, and to "erect a small place to confine him
at home." Now, without the means to continue to care for him, he requested
additional funds. The assembly resolved that Humphry "shall receive out of
the treasury of this Colony the sum of twenty pounds lawful money" (pp.
590–591).

The Humphry case reveals something about the colonial legal obligation in regard to the mad, or the "distracted," as they more commonly were referred to. The thirteen original colonies—Connecticut, Virginia, Massachusetts, New York, Maryland, Delaware, Rhode Island, New Hampshire, New Jersey, Pennsylvania, North Carolina, South Carolina and Georgia—were juridical extensions of Great Britain. As separate, sparsely populated, though strongly cohesive societies facing unique challenges to survival, however, the colonies "selected from the English corpus [of law] those sections that they found most consistent with their own attitudes and most relevant to their own needs, and in doing so they gave a discernibly American quality to the result" (Rothman, 1990, p. 20).

One of those sections had to do with the care of the needy. English Poor Law dictated that the care of the indigent be the public duty of the local parish, and because the mad so often were impecunious and, if not, vulnerable to financial exploitation by others, they, too, became a public charge. Their care, as the Humphry case illustrates, was put into the hands of families and sometimes of friends, often with financial assistance from the local assembly. In their absence, communities were legally bound to intercede, first by declaring the mad non compos mentis, i.e., incapable of handling their affairs (a legal term, incidentally, from which the euphemism "nincompoop" is derived), and then by appointing guardians or town officials, known as a selectmen, to manage their affairs, using local treasury funds to do so.

Each of the original thirteen colonies passed legislation that so empowered its local communities to care for their mad as well as to remove any mad who were not local "inhabitants," i.e., those who met what increasingly became complicated settlement law requirements. Massachusetts Colony was the first to enact its own version of this section of English Poor Law in 1694. It was this version, replicated with slight variation in Connecticut, as it was throughout the rest of the colonies, that directed the decision of the Simsbury Assembly to charge Benajah Humphry with the care of his mad son, and to grant him funds for doing so:

AN ACT FOR THE RELIEVING OF IDEOTS AND DISTRACTED PERSONS (1699)

It is ordered and enacted by the Governor, Councill, and Representatives, in General court assembled, and by the authority of the same: That when and so often as it shall happen any person to be naturally wanting of understanding, so as to be uncapable to provide for him or her selfe, or by the providence of God shall fall into distraction and become non compos mentis, and no relations appear that will undertake the care of providing for them, or that stand in so near a degree, as that by law they may be compelled thereto; in every such case the select-men or over-seers of the poor of the town or peculiar where such person was born or is by law an inhabitant, be and hereby are impowred and enioyned to take effectuall care and make necessary provision, for the relief, support and safety of such impotent, or distracted person at the charge of the town or place whereto he or she of right belongs; if the partie hath no estate of his or her own the incomes whereof shall be sufficient to defray the same. And the justices of the peace within the same countie at their countie courts may order and dispose the estate of such impotent or distracted persons to the best improvement and advantage towards his or her support, as also the person to any proper work or service he or she may be capable to be imployed in, at the discretion of the selectmen or overseers of the poor. And where the estate of any such person consists of housing or land, in every such case the Generall Court upon application to them may license and authorize, the selectmen or overseers of the town or place whereto such person belongs or such others as the said court shall thinke fit, to make sale of such housing or land, the product thereof upon sale to be secured, improved, and imployed, to and for the use, relief and safety of such impotent or distracted person (as the Court shall direct) as long as such person shall live, or untill he or she be restored to be of sound mind, and the overplus (if any be) to and for the use of the next and right heirs of such partie. And the like power and authority is hereby granted unto the aforesaid Court with reference to any person or persons now under distraction or non compos mentis, as well as for the satisfying the charges already past for what may be future for the support, relief and safety of any such person [Connecticut Colonial Records, Vol. 4, pp. 285–286].

Colonial records are peppered with cases that reveal the fidelity of local communities to the legal mandate to care for their own as well as to tight-fisted fiscal responsibility. In 1648 the Braintree, Massachusetts, assembly answered the petition of John Heydon "for some reliefe in respect to his distracted or possessed child," and granted him £5 "out of the revenues that cometh from the imposition layd vpon wines" (Shurtleff, 1853–1854, p. 157). When Heydon again petitioned the assembly for assistance three years later, he was granted £5 per annum to be paid out of the town levy until the court "so cause to withdraw theire benevolence" (p. 298). In 1664 an Essex County, Massachusetts, widow was judged "not capable, owing to her present distemper of head, to look after herself." Her modest estate, comprising a dwelling house with an acre of upland, a feather bed, a few pillows and an old rug and blanket, was sold, with the proceeds to remain in the hands of local officials "to be used for her necessary expenses" (Dow, 1913, p. 176). In 1768 the Guilford, Connecticut, assembly had spent £100 in its oversight of the affairs of Thankful Dudley, who had "fallen into distraction" and had been declared non compos mentis. Because this was "a much larger sum than the whole value of her estate," the assembly resolved that a selectman be "fully authorized and impowered, to make sale of said right of land belonging to said Thankful and to account to the selectmen of the said town of the avails thereof, that the same may be improved for her relief and benefit" (Hoadly, 1885, p. 110).

While these cases reveal something about the colonial legal obligation to the mad, they reveal little about *how* the mad were treated by family, friends, guardians or caretakers. The fact that Benajah Humphry was "labouring under very melancholy and chargeable circumstances" two years into his caretaking hints at the weariness and frustration that so often attend that role. A few cases cited here and there in colonial public records and diaries suggest just how onerous and precarious the demands of caring for the mad must have been. In 1690 in Essex County, Massachusetts, the grand jury summoned siblings Nathaniell and Abigail Somes "for frequently absenting themselves from the public ordinances of God," only to learn that Abigail "hath been in a distracted condition for this 2 months and her brother has been forced to make it his wholl Imployment to Loake after her" (Dow, 1921, p. 237). In that same year the quarterly court of that county took testimony from Mary Ivory that her mother "is deprived of her senses and had been an extraordinary care and trouble. Only for natural affection," the record continues, "she could not have undergone such care for twice as much as her husband demanded, for she is as helpless as a child" (Dow, 1921, p. 290). In 1719 the Puritan minister and would-be physician Cotton Mather, whose third marriage was to a woman he himself had diagnosed as either distracted or possessed, wrote in his diary: "I have lived for near a Year in a continual Anguish of expectations, that my poor Wife, by exposing her Madness, would bring Ruine on my Ministry" (Ford, 1957, p. 586). In 1751 in Charleston, South Carolina, a distracted shopkeeper named Peter Calvett, who was given to firing pistols out of his window at night, was boarded in the home of the Rev. Francis Guichard, who came to fear that the shopkeeper would "would greatly Embarrass and obstruct him in the Discharge of his ministerial function" (Gregorie, 1950, p. 460). Local authorities removed Calvett from the pastor's care; the records say nothing, however, about his subsequent placement. And in 1778 the New London, Connecticut, assembly heard a petition from Caleb Comstock, who was suffering a "heavy burthen and distress" taking care of his six children and his wife, who had been distracted for seven years. Because "all attention has and is daily paid to her by him and them for her support and comfort," Comstock found himself "reduced to abject circumstances." The assembly resolved that he should be allowed to sell several acres of land that had been deeded to his wife "to improve the produce thereof for the support of his distressed family" (Hoadly, 1895, p. 149).

The Social Contract

Local communities also had fidelity to the social contract to protect the greater good. Thus the mad who posed a threat to themselves or to others, such as Benajah Humphry's son, were to be kept confined. Even as late as 1790 there were only six communities with more than 8,000 inhabitants and these held only 3.3 percent of the total population (Grob, 1994, p. 13), thus there was no compelling need for the creation of formal institutions to confine the threatening mad. Instead, informal solutions were relied upon. In 1676 Jan Vorelissen of Amesland, Pennsylvania, complained to the court that his son "is bereft of his naturall Senses and is turned quyt madd and yet, he being a poore man is not able to maintaine him." The court ordered that "three or four persons bee hired to build a little block-house at Amesland for to putt in the said madman" and then levied a small tax on the community for its construction (cited in Deutsch, 1937, p. 42). In 1689 Braintree, Massachusetts, residents voted "that Samuel Speere should build a little house 7 foote long and 5 foote wide & set by his house to secure his Sister good wife Witty being distracted and provide for her" (Bates, 1886, p. 26).

Local jails were used in larger communities for the confinement of the mad. In 1689 the sheriff of York County, Virginia, was ordered to provide a "close Roome" for the confinement of John Stock, "whoe keepes running about the neighborhood day and night in a sad Distracted condition to the great Disturbance of the people" (Blanton, 1930, p. 131). The 1712 case of David Robinson is particularly interesting because it suggests that when the mad were threatening—or "unruly" and a risk for "damnifying others," in the parlance of the day—official intervention seemed to be quite self-consciously calibrated to an assessment of the degree of harm posed. Although long considered distracted, Robinson lived with his family in Durham, Connecticut, for years before the local assembly concluded that "he grows outrageous in his words and actions, and cannot, with great hazard to himself and others, be suffered to go at large." For his own protection and that of the community, the assembly ordered that three selectmen "do agree with some skilful physician, (if any such can be had), to take the said Robinson into his care and cure ... also by leasing or otherwise to take care that the estate of the said Robinson be improved for his support and the support of his family" (Hoadly, 1870, p. 358). Six years later, and apparently none the better for care by a physician or for financial support, Robinson was behaving "in a very evil, and oftentimes in an outrageous manner, to the disturbance of the quiet of his Majesties subjects in the said town, divers of whom are very much terryfied with his threatnings, and are in danger of suffering great harm by him, and, as is apprehended, are in peril of their lives" (Hoadly, 1872, p. 90). The assembly then ordered that Robinson be confined in jail.

The threatening mad, as well as the pauper mad, sometimes also were held in almshouses and workhouses in those communities large enough to have such houses. Although they confined a veritable rogues' gallery of inmates—from vagabonds and beggars, to common drunks and stubborn servants, to medical quacks and fortune-tellers, to pipers and fiddlers—neither of these institutions was intended for the care of the mad, and the presence of the mad inevitably was problematic. Often kept in attics and cellars, they were left alone to suffer (Rothman, 1990).

Confinement in jails, almshouses, workhouses or, for that matter, purpose-built structures, was, however, a last resort in early colonial communities, although it grew increasingly necessary as the communal bonds that held together Puritan communities weakened over the years. As long as they were not "unruly," the mad usually were allowed to carry on their lives and wander about at will. The few among them who had at one time in their lives enjoyed good reputations before "by the Providence of God" they became mad remained quite well integrated into their communities.

Such was the case of Joseph Moody. A Harvard graduate, he served the community of York, Maine, with distinction as a town clerk, register of deeds, and a judge of the county court for more than a decade after his graduation. Pressured by his father, a passionate preacher and patriot, to go into the ministry, he took over the Second Church of York in 1732. But Moody struggled in reconciling the fact that as a boy he had accidentally shot and killed his best friend and allowed his death to be attributed to Indians, with his new position of trust and esteem as a moral leader in the community. He resolved to "wear a veil for the remainder of his life [and] ever after wore a silk handkerchief drawn over his face, and was generally known, in the way of distinction, by the name of *Handkerchief Moody*" (Moody, 1847, p. 96). Although he continued to preach to appreciative congregants from behind the handkerchief—even though he was no longer allowed by them to officiate at weddings—Moody grew increasingly distracted after the death of his wife and the fostering out of his children and stepped down from the pulpit in 1738. His congregation and community prayed for his recovery from his "nervous disorder," but declaring himself "nothing but a shadow" (p. 97), he was relieved of his duties a few years later.

Still wearing the black silk handkerchief, Moody became a lodger in the home of a church deacon, but continued to participate in the daily life of the community. When he dined at the invitation of others, "he sat at a side table, with his face turned away from the company, toward the wall, when he removed the handkerchief from his face" (p. 102). When invited into conversation with others, he sometimes "let his friends see his face, by shutting his eyes when he raised the handkerchief" (p. 102). And when preaching the occasional sermon as a locum for his father, "he would turn his back to the people, and turn *up* his handkerchief; and then face them, turning it *down* when he prayed" (p. 102).

Moody's prayers, eloquent and long—sometimes hours in length—and delivered with an aura of moral innocence sometimes attributed to the mad, assured his place in the community. He would daily visit several different families needing intercession, and would "be their mouth to them," i.e., pray on their behalf (p. 102), a practice he continued until his death in 1753. At his request, he was buried wearing the black silk handkerchief over his face.

While Moody's case illustrates how some mad, although certainly not all, were not only tolerated by colonial communities but integrated into them, it also demonstrates how madness solicits cultural representation. The madness of Joseph "Handkerchief" Moody was the inspiration for Nathaniel Hawthorne's short story "The Minister's Black Veil," in which the handkerchief transforms the pastor into a "man of awful power over souls that were in agony for sin" (1837, p. 69). It was dramatized on episode 220 of *Ripley's Believe or Not* radio show of the 1930s and is featured in Ghostly Tours, a walking, candlelit tour through contemporary York, Maine. Rick Moody, a writer and distant relative whose own battle with depression, paranoia, drug abuse and alcoholism is recounted in his book *The Black Veil: A Memoir with Digressions* (Moody, 2003), contemplated a familial legacy of madness. He went so far as to wear a handkerchief himself, as he describes in his book (pp. 236–237): "The prospect was a lonely one, in ways that I couldn't have known at first, so it was something that required labor and philosophy, but it also had a lot of practical issues associated with it, and so like a lot of sad things, it was also *funny*. Would I, for example, wear the veil to lunch with the guys I usually met at noontime at the Star Burger Deli on 46th Street? ... And what about the gym? Would I wear shorts, T-shirt, running shoes, and *a veil*?"

Although the mad were allowed to meander through their own communities, the mad who wandered from one community to the next, harmless though they may have been, did threaten colonial social order and control. Rather like the fabled Tom O'Bedlam of English folklore—personified by the character of Edgar in William Shakespeare's *King Lear*—who feigned madness and roamed the country begging for food and shelter, there were indigent and quite genuinely mad colonists who, because of demographic pressures on local resources, were forced to do the same. Their presence in communities whose often scarce resources already were stretched in the care of indigent local citizens raised problems for poor relief; their sheer visibility as destitute and mad outsiders defied the communal traditions of colonial society. To rectify the situation local authorities, using English Poor Law as precedent, increasingly relied on the legal statute of "warning out."

Warning out had more to do with the economic development of the colonies than with any change in attitude about madness. Complex settlement and inhabitancy requirements that set qualifications for residence, employment, land ownership and land transfer, enforced the distinction between town residents and outsiders (Benton, 1911). And mad outsiders, posing as they did a financial burden to the town in question, were not welcomed.

The colonies continuously refined their laws about warning out by attaching fines and complicated fee schedules. Those who housed a mad outsider without first getting the approval of town officials, for example, were heftily fined, and mad outsiders were to be returned to their town of residence at the expense of that town. Such was the case of Mary Hall, who was allowed by the friends who were obliged to care for her to "stroll about from town to town and place to place, to the great disquiet of many people where she goes by reasons of her ill behavior." The Wallingford, Connecticut, assembly resolved in 1758 that if she is found again outside of the limits of the town, she shall be "forthwith apprehended" and returned. The assembly agreed to reimburse any constable who returned her "four pence per mile for every mile he shall transport her, with allowance for one man and horse tendance if such he had for his assistance and 4 pence a mile for such tendance" (Connecticut Colonial Records, Vol. 11, pp. 111–112).

Nash (2004) finds that the number of transients warned out of the city of Boston increased tenfold between 1720 and 1750. Most were destitute, some were otherwise respectable, only a few were mad. One notable example of the latter was Samuel Coolidge, Harvard graduate, teacher, author and chaplain who in 1742 wandered half-naked in a distracted condition from his Waterford community to the neighboring city of Boston. Over the years, he had been boarded out to different Waterford families, confined in jail and locked in a schoolhouse where, interestingly enough, he also was ordered to teach. But expressing a concern that while he was in Boston he was "very likely to be a Town Charge," the selectmen voted to "warn him out of Town according to the Law" (Record Commissioners, 1887, p. 366).

Black Slaves

The thirteen original colonies were far from static; rather, each was continually developing in response to economic, demographic, political and ideological forces and, in doing so, developing its own unique culture. Broadly speaking, though, there were quite distinct regional differences. With its cold climate, the New England colonies—New Hampshire, Massachusetts, Rhode Island and Connecticut—relied primarily on fishing, shipping, lumbering and fur trading, rather than agriculture, as their economic base. With the exception of the city of Boston, most of the communities in this colonial region were small and government was organized around town councils. The Puritan religion predominated and its influence on family and social life was considerable throughout the region. The Middle colonies—New York, New

Jersey, Pennsylvania and Delaware—combined agriculture and industry as their economic base. Its settlers, most of whom were from non–English speaking countries such as the Netherlands, Germany, France and Sweden, congregated in larger cities, vesting that whole region with a greater degree of ethnic, cultural and religious diversity than what could be found in the neighboring New England colonies. Situated on rich farm land in a temperate climate, the Southern colonies—Maryland, Virginia, Georgia, North Carolina and South Carolina—grew their own food as well as profitable cash crops. The plantation system that put acres of valuable land between colonists inhibited the growth of large cities, thus local government was organized on a county level. Each colonial region had a different and changing relationship with the Indians who were native to it, and each had free black residents and many more black slaves. It is in regards to slavery that "Southern distinctiveness" (McCandless, 1996, p. 4) is most evident.

Although slaves were brought to the colonies in the early 17th century, it was several decades before the colonies began participating in the lucrative international slave trade. Most of the slaves brought to the colonies were from the western coast of Africa and represented an array of ethnic groups, each with its own language and customs. Their nightmarish journey through the Middle Passage, on crowded ships under the command of what often were brutal captains and crew, reduced some of them to madness. A ship's doctor gave this account: "I saw a young negroe woman chained to the deck, who had lost her senses soon after she was purchased and taken on board. In a former voyage, on board a ship to which I belonged, we were obliged to confine a female negroe, of about twenty-three years of age, on her becoming a lunatic. She was afterwards sold during one of her lucid intervals" (Falconbridge, 1788, p. 32). Another ship's doctor coined the term "fixed melancholy" to describe the loss of the will to live that resulted in the deaths of so many slaves during the weeks and even months of the horrific Middle Passage journey (Mannix, 1962).

Slaves brought to the New England and Middle colonies most often were purchased by well-to-do colonists to become house servants, cooks and nannies. Some even cared for mad family members of their masters. Such was the case of Mumbet, who after suing for freedom took the name Elizabeth Freeman. Her nursing skills allowed her master's mad wife to remain comfortably at home until her death (Swan, 1990). Those brought to the southern colonies were purchased to work on the farms and plantations where the demand for slave labor increased as rapidly as the regional economy. By 1790, more than 85 percent of all of the slaves in the country were working in the southern colonies (Schneider & Schneider, 2007, p. 50).

There was much about slavery that could induce madness. The deculturation, loss of identity, breakup of families, brutal treatment and poor living conditions that were the sine qua non of the very institution of slavery undoubtedly affected the mental health of some slaves, but just how many, and to what extent, is apparently lost to history. What is inscribed in colonial records, however, was the fear that slaves, always considered duplicitous and lazy by racial nature, could feign madness in attempts to alter their working or living conditions, thus costing their masters both time and money. And, of course, there was the concomitant fear that unscrupulous owners could sell genuinely mad slaves to gullible buyers by insisting they were only feigning madness. As the domestic slave trade became increasingly regulated by law, the question of deception often found its way into courtrooms. This interrogatory, directed to a buyer who had brought a breach of warranty suit against the seller of an allegedly mad slave named Lawson, illustrates this point:

> What are the symptoms of insanity, if any, which you discovered about the negro Lawson? Were they constantly on him, or did they return only occasionally? Was not the said Lawson an artful designing fellow and do you not believe he *affected* to be deranged? Do you not remember that he pretended to be in love, and did he not state *that* as the cause of his derangement, and did not the plaintiff order him to be whipped saying he pretended only to be deranged, and that he would whip him out of his love fit, or words to that effect? [cited in Gross, 2000, p. 67].

Throughout the colonies it was the masters' legal obligation to provide in manners they saw fit for slaves whose symptoms of madness were considered incompatible with trickery. In this pre-asylum era in which care often was more inconvenience than it was worth, masters usually were content to allow slave healers to treat mad slaves. These healers, variously known as root workers, root doctors, and conjurers, occupied positions of esteem among slaves, in the same way it can be said that the diviners, priests and shamans were revered among Native Americans.

Traditional medicine was one of the Africanisms, i.e., cultural practices, that survived the Middle Passage. Symptoms of madness were understood within an Afrocentric system of beliefs that viewed both physical and mental health as the consequences of harmony with the natural, spiritual and social world. Madness, then, could result from conflicts with the environment, deviation from religious principles and faith, or discord with others (Byrd & Clayton, 2000). Root doctors had a broad knowledge of folk remedies, most of them herbal concoctions, and administered them within social rituals and ceremonies. If the symptoms of madness were unrelieved, however, they were believed to be the result of "working the root," that is, of spells or curses. In that case, either the root doctors themselves or the conjurers in the slave communities used magic, conjuring and divination to ease mental suffering (Chireau, 2006). This belief that madness can be caused by spells and curses, and cured by conjuring, persisted long past the abolition of slavery, its longevity measured by its representation over the centuries and into contemporary times in the poetry, blues music, art and literature of African Americans (Anderson, 2005). The short story "Root Worker" is an example from contemporary literature (Jones, 2006). In this story, Alberta is an elderly black who lives with her daughter, a successful psychiatrist. For years, the "witches had been riding" Alberta, coming to her in the night, lying on her body and filling her mind with fears that her family would be killed. A psychiatric hospital stay did nothing for her; neither did medication. At her insistence, her daughter takes her to "Dr." Imogene, a North Carolina root worker who administers a regime of herbal concoctions, including the "Purple Mess." Weeks later, the witches stop visiting Alberta. Her daughter takes her home and, while planting an herb garden for the treatment of her own black patients, remembers that as a child she had wished a neighbor dead. She wonders if the neighbor had told a root worker who scrounged a lock of her mother's hair and her fingernail clippings from the trash and cursed her with madness and revenge.

Native Americans

In his travels through the colony of North Carolina in the 1730s, James Brickell had many opportunities to observe the traditions and customs of the Cherokee Indians. So unfamiliar were these people to him that he found it necessary to describe them by analogizing them to something the readers of the massive account of his travels, published in 1737, would understand — madness. He observed, for example, that the Cherokee wore feathers "which make them appear more frightful than Ornamental, and more like People distracted than in their senses" (p. 313). And he wrote that at the burial ceremonies of their elders, they cried, lamented and howled "like distracted People in *Bedlam*" (p. 386), a reference to London's Royal Bethlem Hospital, better known as Bedlam, one of the oldest asylums for the mad in the world.

The "Indians" early colonists encountered were from diverse tribal nations with distinct languages, social organizations, material cultures and traditions. Like Brickell, some explorers, missionaries and traders who traveled through or conducted business in any of the thirteen original colonies similarly analogized Native American customs and traditions to madness (Sayre, 1997), but few observed how mad Indians were treated within their respective tribe. The Cherokee whom Brickell encountered, for example, had an extensive knowledge of herbal and plant remedies, and had innovative methods of administering them to their mad, including palatable infusions, "injections" through the use of a scratching comb that abraded the skin, and cutaneous applications by blowing the remedy onto the skin through a narrow blowing tube. For nervous problems alone, the Cherokee administered aniscented goldenrod, Appalachian gooseberry, beetleweed, blue cohosh, canada lettuce, chicory, common dandelion, devil's darning needles, field sowthistle, hoary skullcap, ladyslipper, sourwood, Virginia strawberry, and yellowroot (Hamel & Chiltoskey, 1975).

The Native American worldview in many ways resembled that of the colonial African slaves. Madness was seen as an imbalance between spirituality, community, environment and the self (Portman & Garrett, 2006) that stemmed from breaking a tribal taboo. This complex view was reflected in healing ceremonies and rituals that used confession, atonement and purification rites to restore harmony for the mad, as well as for the tribal communities who bore the burden of caring for them (Gamwell & Tomes, 1995).

Like the colonial African slaves, Native Americans also believed in the malevolence of witches and their power to steal the souls of others by inducing madness. Both groups used material objects such as red pepper, St. John's wort, stones and crystals to protect themselves from evil conjure (Anderson, 2005). If witchcraft, rather than taboo violation, was suspected to be the cause of madness, shamans were called upon. In a trance state and in elaborate rituals, they engaged witches in battle in an attempt to recover the lost souls of the mad (Smoak, 2006).

The roles and specializations of the Native American healers also resemble that of the root doctors and conjurors so revered and feared by the colonial African slaves. It was the task of the diviners to diagnose madness through divination and dream analysis, and that of the shamans, priests or "medicine men" to administer the herbal remedies, conduct the healing ceremonies, and battle the malevolent power of witches. Like the colonial African slave healers, these Native American healers, whose physical or mental differences often were associated with the gift of supernatural powers, underwent long and complex initiation rites. Among the Muskogee or Creek Indians who were indigenous to the southern colonies, prospective shamans secluded themselves from the tribal community and fasted for long periods before receiving days of instruction in magic from elder shamans. Then they were buried under the earth and left to breath through tubes while the elder shamans burned leaves around them; once released from their makeshift graves, they were ready to assume the role of shaman (Hudson, 1976).

As is the case with blacks, the persistence of supernatural beliefs about the origin and the cure of madness can be traced into contemporary times in the art, poetry, songs and stories of Native Americans. The practice of the traditional healing of madness is still being performed in tribal communities and, given all of the reasons for the historic distrust of the systems and institutions of the predominate white culture, shamanistic healing increasingly is being incorporated into, or supplementing, mainstream therapeutic interventions and hospital programs for Native Americans suffering from madness (Grandbois, 2005).

Madness as a Medical Problem

It was not madness, per se, nor any particular symptom or manifestation of it, that concerned the early colonists; rather, it was the dependency it created. The mad drew attention and required intervention not so much for their suffering as their inability to work, engage in daily commerce and manage their own affairs, as well as for their vulnerability to financial manipulation and exploitation. Although their management and control were formalized in law and statute—from the appointment of selectmen to oversee their affairs to warning out—madness was far from a social problem in early colonial America.

It was not much of a medical problem, either. Madness generally was perceived as an impermanent condition, occurring "by the providence of God." Whatever other agents—biological, cultural, environmental, social— that might be generative only occasionally prompted some naïve theorizing on the parts of early colonists. Traumas, both physical and emotional, social stresses, family troubles, intemperate use of alcohol and religious conflicts are occasionally mentioned as the causes of specific cases of madness in colonial public records, diaries and family histories. In colonial society, communality required conformity, and straying from prevailing norms or role expectations was sometimes taken not only as a symptom but a cause of madness. John Winthrop, the first governor of the colony of Massachusetts and a dabbler in medicine and the "practice of physick," described the madness of Ann Yale Hopkins, the wife of the governor of Connecticut, in those very terms:

> Mr. Hopkins, the governour of Hartford upon Connecticut, came to Boston [in 1645], and brought his wife with him, (a godly young woman, and of special parts,) who has fallen into a sad infirmity, the loss of her understanding and reason, which had been growing upon her divers years, by occasion of her giving herself wholly to reading and writing, and had written many books. Her husband, being very loving and tender of her, was loathe to grieve her; but he saw his errour, when it was too late. For if she had attended her household affairs, and

such things as belong to women, and not gone out of her way and calling to med-
dle for such things as are proper for men, whose minds are stronger &c, she had
kept her wits, and might have improved them usefully and honourably in the
place God had set her. He brought her to Boston, and left her with her brother,
one Mr. Yale, a merchant, to try what means might be had here for her. But no
help could be had [Winthrop, 1825/1826, p. 216].

Perhaps the lack of speculation about the causes of madness by early
colonists had more to do with the dearth of medical discourse on the topic
than incuriosity. Before the American Revolution there were fewer than three
hundred qualified physicians in the thirteen colonies. All had graduated from
European medical schools; in fact, there was no medical school in the colonies
until 1765. There were, however, many more "doctors" who tended the
colonists, some of whom had learned their trade through apprenticeship, others who were self-taught "empirics," and others still who, in the role of pastor, ministered to the mind as well as to the spirit (Viets, 1935). Unlike Great
Britain, where a vigorous "trade in lunacy" already had created a network
of public and private asylums and madhouses, medical and lay practitioners
and proprietors, a corpus of conflicting theories about the causes, dynamics
and cures of madness, and a language for talking about them (Parry-Jones,
1972), the treatment of madness in the early colonies was neither institutionalized nor specialized, and neither were the language and ideas for specu-
lating about it.

"Diagnostic" Distinction

While madness was not much of a medical problem in the thirteen
colonies, colonists did struggle to diagnostically distinguish it from one other
condition. Diagnosis constitutes "an indispensable point of articulation
between the general and the particular, between agreed-upon knowledge and
its application" (Rosenberg, 2002, p. 240). Even if naïve and untutored, diagnosis is crucial to how a condition is perceived, defined and managed. Thus
for colonists, particularly those in the New England colonies, making a diagnostic distinction between distraction and "affliction," i.e., control by demonic
forces either through possession by the devil or bewitchment by a witch or
warlock in league with the devil (Weisman, 1984), was crucial for shoring
up the Calvinist theocracy of the Puritans and for maintaining social order
and control.

Making that diagnostic distinction was no easy task, especially since
affliction was thought to present itself in much the same way as distraction.
The 1671 case of Elizabeth Knap (sometimes also spelled "Knapp") of Groton, Massachusetts, is instructive on that point. An illiterate 16-year-old, she

was a servant in the home of the Rev. Samuel Willard, who, in a long and detailed letter to Puritan minister Cotton Mather—who also dabbled in medicine—described her symptoms:

THIS poore & miserable object, about a fortnight before shee was taken, wee observed to carry herselfe in a strange & unwonted manner, sometimes shee would give sudden shriekes, & if wee enquired a Reason, would alwayes put it off with some excuse, & then would burst forth into immoderate & extravagant laughter, in such wise, as some times shee fell onto the ground with it: I my selfe observed oftentimes a strange change in her countenance, but could not suspect the true reason, but conceived shee might bee ill, & therefore divers times enquired how shee did, & shee alwayes answered well; which made mee wonder.... In the evening, a little before shee went to bed, sitting by the fire, shee cryed out, oh my legs! & clapt her hand on them, immediately oh my breast! & removed her hands thither; & forthwith, oh I am strangled, & put her hands on her throat: those that observed her could not see what to make of it; whither shee was in earnest or dissembled, & in this manner they left her (excepting the person that lay with her) complaining of her breath being stopt: The next day shee was in a strange frame, (as was observed by divers) sometimes weeping, sometimes laughing, & many foolish & apish gestures. Afterwards (the same evening,) the rest of the family being in bed, shee was (as one lying in the roome saw, & shee herselfe also afterwards related) suddenly throwne downe into the midst of the floore with violence, & taken with a violent fit, whereupon the whole family was raised, & with much adoe was shee kept out of the fire from destroying herselfe after which time she was followed with fits from thence till the sabbath day; in which shee was violent in bodily motions, leapings, strainings & strange agitations, scarce to bee held in bounds by the strength of 3 or 4: violent alsoe in roarings & screamings [Willard, 1883, pp. 7–8].

This initial "fit" was followed after a short time of respite with several more long periods of increasingly dramatic fits. During one, she was examined by a "physician" of undisclosed qualifications, who concluded the cause of her distress was " naturall," the result of the "foulnesse of her stomacke, & corruptnesse of her blood, occasioning fumes in her braine, & strange fansyes" (p. 11). He administered a physic, and she enjoyed a brief period of respite and the hope of a full recovery. More fits followed, however, and they gave good reason for Willard's diagnostic confusion. During them she variously confided that her unhappy station in life was the reason for her fits, claimed she had consorted with the Devil, insisted she had been "deluded" by the Devil, asserted and then denied she had been bewitched by a local woman, and declared she was possessed by the Devil.

Diagnosis always serves as a courier of extant cultural norms. In the 17th century New England colonies, affliction was as real as distraction, and the possibilities of deceit—of faking either affliction or distraction—and of mischief were as well. Although Willard believed her symptoms were indicative of having been tormented by the devil, rather than having been possessed or bewitched, doubts remained. Thus he concluded his letter with several diagnostically probative questions (pp. 20–21):

1. Whither her distemper be reale or counterfiet: I shall say no more to that but this, the great strength appearing in them, & great weaknesse after them, will disclaime the contrary opinion: for tho a person may counterfiet much yet such a strength is beyond the force of dissimulation:

2. Whither her distemper bee naturall or Diabolicall, I suppose the premises will strongly enough conclude the latter, yet I will adde these 2 further arguments:

    1. the actings of convulsion, which these come nearest to, are (as persons acquainted with them observe) in many, yea the most essentiall parts of them quite contrary to these actings:

    2. Shee hath no wayes wasted in body, or strength by all these fits, though soe dreadfulle, but gathered flesh exceedinglye, & hath her naturall strength when her fits are off, for the most part:

3. Whither the Devill did really speake in her: to that point which some have much doubted of, thus much I will say to countermand this apprehension:

    1. The manner of expression I diligently observed, & could not perceive any organ, any instrument of speech ... to have any motion at all, yea her mouth was sometimes shut without opening sometimes open without shutting or moving, & then both I & others saw her tongue (as it used to bee when shee was in some fits, when speechlesse) turned up circularly to the roofe of her mouth.

    2. the labial letters, divers of which were used by her, viz. B.M.P. which cannot bee naturally expressed without motion of the lips ... were uttered without any such motion:

    3. the reviling termes then used, were such as shee never used before nor since, in all this time of her being thus taken:

    4. they were expressions which the devill (by her confession) aspersed mee, & others withall, in the houre of temptation, particularly shee had freely acknowledged that the Devill was wont to appear to her in the house of God & divert her mind, & charge her shee should not give eare to what the Blacke coated roage spake:

    5. wee observed when the voice spake, her throat was swelled formidably as big at least as ones fist;

4. Whither shee have covenanted with the Devill or noe: I thinke this is a case unanswerable, her declarations have been soe contradictorye, one to another, that wee know not what to make of them & her condition is such as administers many doubts.

Cotton Mather, to whom the letter was addressed, concluded this was a case of diabolic possession. Yet whether through prayer, physic or the tincture of time, Knap recovered. She later married and raised six children. Willard, however, remained conflicted. As a signatory of the "Return of the Several Ministers," a letter advising the newly elected governor on the handling of the witch trials that were going on in nearby Salem, he urged caution in distinguishing between inquiry, presumption and guilt. Although he, himself believed the Salem outbreak indeed was demonic in nature, he feared the community's uncritical acceptance of that premise might lead to the convictions of innocent, perhaps even mad, people (Robbins, 1987).

The witchcraft outbreak in Salem, Massachusetts, in 1692 reveals the potency of that very premise and the readiness to act upon it. A number of young girls had begun behaving as if they had suddenly become distracted. When no physical cause for their trances, seizures and hallucinations could be determined, town officials feared they had been bewitched by someone in league with the devil—a witch, if female; a warlock, if male. At the request of a concerned neighbor, a South American Indian slave who, as a child, had been sold into slavery in Barbados before coming to Salem to serve the household of the Rev. Samuel Parris was solicited for help. Tituba baked a "witch cake," a mixture of rye and the urine of Parris's own daughter, who was one of the afflicted girls, and fed it to a dog in an attempt to counteract the demonic spell. When that provided no relief, Parris's daughter and the other girls were pressured by town officials to name who had bewitched them. They named Tituba, who confessed and named other town women as her coconspirators with the devil (Demos, 1982).

The confirmation of the premise that the cause of the girls' distraction was supernatural set off the same behavior in other girls who, in turn, accused other citizens of Salem of being witches and warlocks. In the end, more than one hundred people were accused. Many stood trial where spectral evidence, i.e., testimony that the accused witch's or warlock's spirit or spectral shape appeared to the witness in a dream at the time the accused person's physical body was at another location, was admitted as evidence (Boyer & Nissenbaum, 1977). Nineteen of the convicted women and men were hanged on Gallows Hill in 1692. One man, Giles Corey, was pressed to death when he refused to answer the charges against him. Longfellow (1902, p. 496) wrote of Corey in *Giles Corey of the Salem Farms* and added a caution:

> Something of this our scene tonight will show;
> And ye who listen to the Tale of Woe,
> Be not too swift in casting the first stone,
> Nor think New England bears the guilt alone,
> This sudden burst of wickedness and crime
> Was but the common madness of the time,
> When in all lands, that lie within the sound
> Of Sabbath bells, a Witch was burned or drowned.

Those imprisoned eventually were released when the spectral evidence that had been the basis of their convictions was discredited. In 1702 the general court took a further step and declared the Salem witch trials unlawful, and in 1711 a legislative bill was passed to restore the good names of those accused and to grant their heirs £600 in restitution (Demos, 1982).

In the demon-haunted world of the early New England colonies, a diagnostic distinction between distraction and affliction was crucial for two reasons. First, it acted as a strong link between ambient cultural beliefs and action. Distraction was believed to be a result of the providence of God and was no fault of the sufferers. While it did not always elicit compassion, it certainly provoked an occasionally uneasy tolerance and it always required management that not only served the interests of the distracted, but also of the communities in which they resided. Affliction, on the other hand, was more complicated. If it was thought to be the result of diabolic possession, exorcizing battles for the souls of the possessed had to be fought between religious leaders and the devil on the terrains of the bodies and minds of those afflicted. Only when the devil had been driven out and denounced could the afflicted be considered cured and welcomed back into communities of believers. If the affliction was thought to be the result of bewitchment then the naming and punishing of the witches or warlocks responsible was believed to break their grip on the afflicted, who, with some additional care and religious tutelage, could be considered relieved of the spell.

Second, the diagnostic distinction was necessary to protect genuinely distracted persons from being named as witches and warlocks. The historiography of the early New England colonies suggests that those who were so named often were the nonconformists who had been relegated to the margins of the tightly cohesive communities in question long before they were identified and treated as agents of the devil. And while the oddity and strangeness of nonconformity, on its face, could be confused with the madness of distraction, the crude diagnostic distinction between the two meant it rarely was.

For the early New England colonists, witchcraft involved volition, not the "providence of God" that was the source of distraction. The deliberate choice to enter into a pact with the devil was believed to leave its traces on the body. The devil's mark—a mole, skin tag, or blemish—usually was found in a "secret" place on the body, such as under the eyelid or in body cavities, and was insensitive to the prick of a pin. It was thought to be a teat through which the witches nourished their familiars, or evil spirits. Unlike the distracted, witches and warlocks were thought to be incapable of reciting the Lord's Prayer. The specters or spirits of witches and warlocks also were believed to be able to harass and harangue in attempts to trick or threaten others into entering into a pact with the devil; they were thought to cause accidents, sickness and other maladies, a power that the merely distracted were never assumed to share (Goodheart, 2002, p. 437). This diagnostic distinction was critical for action: the distracted were to be cared for and managed, the witches and warlocks to be named and put to death.

Treatment of the Mad

No help in the treatment of madness was to be expected in these early years. Physicians and doctors by trade, however, sometimes were called upon to treat the distracted, although their remedies often were of no help, either. The prevailing medical approach to madness was informed by the humoural doctrine established by Hippocrates in the 4th century B.C. The doctrine holds that four "humours," or "vital spirits," are produced by the digestive process, and then are circulated by the heat generated by that process to the heart and the brain, thus determining physical and mental health. Each humour, in turn, was associated with a season, temperature, element and, as the doctrine expanded, with a time of day, color of complexion, taste, bodily organ, tutelary planet and astrological sign. The result was a cosmological doctrine of health and illness that influenced medicine for centuries past the time it was scientifically discredited (Porter, 2006).

Blood, not to be confused with the visible venous blood that circulates through the body, was one of the four humours. Warm and moist, it was thought to be produced in the liver and was associated with the spring season and childhood. It determined a sanguine temperament and when plentiful and in a balance with the other humours was thought to cause serenity, optimism, sensuousness and emotional stability. Black bile was thought to be stored in the spleen and was linked with autumn and maturity. Cold and dry, this blue-colored humour was associated with introspection, sentimentality and melancholy, thus the euphemisms "the blues," "blue devils" and "blue funk," among other descriptors, always have been associated with a melancholic or depressed state of mind. Phlegm could be found in any part of the body. A cold, moist and colorless humour associated with winter and old age, it determined a phlegmatic temperament, and many common illnesses, such as head colds, were attributed to it. The humour choler or yellow bile was warm and dry and thought to be produced in the gallbladder. It was associated with summer and youth, and with the temperamental characteristics of argumentativeness, envy and quick-temperedness (Arikha, 2007), as this late colonial era essay explains:

> A Choleric Man is one that stands for madman.... [H]e has more full moons in a week than a Lunatic has in a year. His passion is like tinder, soon set on fire, and as soon out again.—The smallest occasion imaginable puts him in his fit, and then he has no respect of persons.... He is, like a foul chimney, easily set on fire.... [H]is temper is like that of a meteor, an imperfect mixture, that sparkles

and flames until it has spent itself. His gall is too big for his liver. His spleen makes others laugh at him, and as soon as his anger is over with others he begins to be angry with himself [Anonymous, 1793, p. 2].

In the humoural doctrine, madness was a result of an imbalance between the four humours, and treatment necessitated the restoration of that balance. Doctors, whether qualified, apprenticed or self-taught, often bled distracted colonists in an attempt to reduce the amount of noxious humours. These bloodlettings were performed by nicking a vein with a lancet, fleam stick or scarificator and then collecting the blood either in small pewter bowls called porringers or in cupping glasses with heated rims that drew the blood to the surface by vacuum action. Leeches also were used. With sharp teeth, suckers on both ends of their bodies and secreting hiudin, an anticoagulant, leeches could suck out ten times their body weight in blood before they released themselves. Stored in what often were elaborately decorated glass or porcelain leech jars, they could be used again days later. To a lesser extent, early colonial doctors also sweated and blistered their distracted patients to draw out toxic humours, administered potent emetics to induce vomiting, diuretics to sluice the bladder, and laxatives to purge the bowels, in efforts to restore humoural balance (Jackson, 2001).

The reliance, indeed over-reliance, on what were believed to be these tried and true remedies for distraction was parodied in a poem by Samuel Thomson (1834, p. 2), a self-taught herbalist who built a lucrative business around selling herbal remedies and exposing the "learned quacks" who practiced medicine in the 18th and 19th centuries:

"Receipt to Cure a Crazy Man"

SOON as the man is growing mad,
Send for the doctor, have him bled;
Take from his arm two quarts at least,
Nearly as much as kills a beast.
But if symptoms yet remain,
He then must tap another vein;
Soon as the doctor has him bled.
Then draw a blister on his head.

Next time he comes, as it is said
The blister'd skin takes from his head;
Then laud'num give to ease his pain,
Till he can visit him again.

The doctor says he's so insane.
It must be dropsy of the brain;
To lay in heat while yet in bed,
A cap of ice lays on his head.

Thomson's mockery aside, bleeding, vomiting and purging were not the only remedies for distraction used by early colonial doctors. Each had a variety of botanical and herbal preparations that was a composite of several European traditions, favorite "kitchen physics" that were the folk medicines of the era, and *materia medica* borrowed from the Native Americans. Especially for the educated doctors, whether university or European medical school graduates, the availability of European medical publications added to their medicaments for the treatment of distraction. One of the most popular of those publications was *Primitive Physick* by John Wesley. Originally published in his native England in 1747, the book was reprinted several times in the colonies and the prescriptions in it were copied, usually without attribution, in many American medical self-help books. A theologian and founder of the Methodist movement, Wesley believed madness, like other diseases and disorders, was a product of original sin, but that God also provided primitive remedies in the familiar environs of those who were distracted. His cure for madness is as follows (1843, p. 74):

> Give decoction of agrimony four times a-day. Or, rub the head several times a-day with vinegar in which ground ivy leaves have been infused. Or, take daily an ounce of distilled vinegar. Or, boil the juice of ground-ivy with sweet oil and white wine into an ointment. Shave the head, anoint it therewith, and chafe it every other day for three weeks. Bruise also the leaves and bind them on the head, and give three spoonsful of the juice, warm, every morning.
>
> ☞ This generally cures melancholy. The juice alone taken twice a day will cure.

For "raging madness" Wesley provided a different remedy, coupled with a stern warning against the use of restraints and the heroic treatment of blistering (1843, p. 74):

> Apply to the head cloths dipt in cold water. Or, set the patient with his head under a great waterfall as long as his strength will bear, or pour cold water on his head out a tea-kettle. Or, let him eat nothing but apples for a month. Or, nothing but bread and milk.
>
> ☞ It is a sure rule that all madmen are cowards, and may be conquered by binding only, without beating.—(Dr. Mead.) He also observes, that blistering the head does more harm than good. Keep the head close shaved and frequently wash it with vinegar.

The opportunities to communicate via personal visits or letters with European colleagues also informed the treatments of colonial doctors. Dr. Edward Stafford of London sent a pharmacopeia for the treatment of a variety of diseases and disorders, including distraction, to John Winthrop, scientist and governor of the Massachusetts Bay colony, who had taken it upon himself to collect and disseminate information about medical treatments throughout the early colonies (Massachusetts Historical Society, 1862, pp. 379–180):

> For my Worthy Friend Mr. Winthrop:
>
> For Madness: Take ye herbe Hypericon (in English St. John's Wort) and boile it in Water or drink, until it be strong of it, and redd in colour; or else, putt a bundle of it in new drinke to Worke, and give it ye patient to drinke, permitting him to drinke nothing else. First purge him well with 2 or 3 seeds (: or more, according to ye strengthe of the partie;) of Spurge. Let them not eat much, but keep dyet, and you shall see Wondrous effects in fewe dayes. I have known it to cure perfectly to administration in five dayes.

No better example of the wide-armed embrace of all of these otherwise disparate remedies can be found than in Cotton Mather's *The Angel of Bethesda*. Written in 1724, although not published until the 20th century, the book's single chapter on madness weaves humoural doctrine, European medical advice, kitchen physics and Native American remedies with supernatural, natural, biological and folk theories to produce both remedies for the treatment of madness and a glimpse at the irreconcilably contradictory perspectives on it in early colonial America (1972, pp. 131–132):

> Both the *Meats* and the *Drinks* of the *Mad* should be very *Cooling. Vina grievant animos faciuntque furoribus aptos* ["Wines affect the mind and make it prone to rage"] A Decoction of *Swallows* [swallow-wort is a perennial that acts as an emetic] with *Lapis Prunellae* [a perennial known as "self-heal" in Native American herbal medicine] has been found very good for them. *Bleeding* often Repeted, has done Something to Extinguish the Fury of the *Animal Spirits;* Yett it must be but a little at a time, Lest it cause *Dropsy* [accumulation of fluids]. If any *Excretions* of the *Mad* are stop'd, they must by all means again be opened. A famous Physician cries up, the Decoction of Purple-flowered *Pimpernel* as also the Tops of *St. Johns Wort* [primary remedy in Native American herbal medicine] as specific for *Madness.* The Use of *Hellebore* [Christmas Rose acts as a laxative] for the *Mad* has been considered, Even to a Proverb. *Chalybeates* [iron tartrates in wine] are sometimes Potent remedies, for *Madness. Opiates* have been Significant; But when Anadynes [pain-relievers or soothers] are used for the *Mad.* Some have preferr'd *Camphere* [camphor is a powerful irritant] unto *Opium.* What say you, to *Meconium* [poppy juice] fermented with the Juice of *Quinces? Madmen* have sometimes been perfectly Cured by *Salivation.* The Blood of an *Ass* drawn from behind his Ear, has a Singular and Wonderful Vertue, in destroying the *Volatil Acid* which is the Cause of *Madness.* The *Mad* allow'd no Drink, but what has an Infusion of *Ground-Ivy* in it; would probably find a good and great Effect in it. To be shutt up in a Press, where the scent of *Musk* is too strong for Ordinary Constitutions, has been found a very powerful Cure for *Madness.* One cured many *Madmen* with the Juice of a Young *Swallows* given to the Quantity of an Ounce, twice or thrice, in the water of *Pimpernel* [plants in the primrose family]. Living *Swallows* cut in two, and laid reeking hott unto the shaved Head, have been prescribed, as a Cure for *Madness.* Concerning the Root of *Mymphaea* the *Water-Lilly* dug up in the Month of May, the great *Sennertus* [contemporary German physician] has this Remark; *Specifica proprietate Maniaerisistere Creditur.*

The gentler sort of Acids, and the Cinnabarine Powders [mercuric sulfide], with Emulsions, are the Chief internal remedies in a *Phrensy. Willis* [contemporary English physician] prescribes; Take boyling *Whey* [watery part of milk that separates from the curds]; pour it upon Flowres of *Violets* and *Water-Lillies.* After two Hours Infusion, the mad Person is to drink plentifully of it. *Borellus* [contemporary French physician to King Louis XIV, whose real name was Borel] tells of Woman that was under *Madness* of an *uterine Original* which was cured only with wearing a *Loadstone* [magnet] on her Stomach.

The Influence of the Enlightment

From their founding, the thirteen colonies were in states of almost continuous evolution as they responded to the social, economic, demographic, political and ideological forces impinging on them. As the market expanded and contracted, cities grew and diversified, political loyalties extended, familial and community ties weakened, colonists could no longer rely on the provincial control of the mad among them, nor on what had been the shared tolerant attitudes that from the start had made that possible (McGovern, 1985).

One of the most potent forces that infused colonial life and that helped shape new attitudes and reactions to the mad was the Enlightenment. This 18th century intellectual movement, originating in Europe, emphasized the primacy of human reason and its power to improve society and the conditions of life by overcoming irrationality, superstition and tyranny. Under the influence of Enlightenment thinking, colonial leaders set aside what had become their considerable differences in order to engage in a war of independence from the tyrannical control of Great Britain. The first shots of the American Revolution were fired in 1775; eight years later Great Britain acknowledged defeat and King George III recognized the United States of America as a new and independent country. Interestingly, King George III battled his own madness during the latter years of his reign (Macalpine & Hunter, 1969), a fact that Thomas Jefferson, the principle author of the colonies' Declaration of Independence, commented upon in Enlightenment terms in a 1788 letter:

> [I]t turned out that the king of England's original disease was a lunacy; that all they published about dropsical and hydrocephalic symptoms were lies, that the real disease of lunacy has come on with as little bodily indisposition as usually accompanies the first development of that disorder. There is reason to suspect his is of the dangerous species of madness, I mean that which disposes the subject to do mischief, and will render it necessary for him to be confined as the furious maniacs are [Jefferson, 1932, p. 146].

The Enlightenment's emphasis on reason, i.e., the uniquely human capacity for logic, rationalization, judgment and analysis, increasingly became equated with normality and sanity. The loss of reason, it was consequently argued, produced madness, and madness, in turn, diminished the very humanity of those suffering from it. For colonists who found their inherited understanding and reactions to madness no longer fitting for a developing society, Enlightenment thinking provided the ideas and concepts for a change in both. Over the late 18th and early 19th centuries, madness was transformed from an unfortunate yet manageable and tolerable annoyance into an irrational and threatening medical condition.

That change in attitude is illustrated by a 1794 dissertation written by Edward Cutbush in partial fulfillment of the degree of doctor of medicine (M.D.) from the University of Pennsylvania, which had founded the first medical school in the country nearly thirty years before. In it, he defines madness as "a false perception of truth; with conversation and actions contrary to right reason, established maxim, and order" (p. 13). He goes on to describe how the loss of reason reduces the mad to little more than wild beasts: "Madmen, if suffered to have their liberty, resemble beasts, rather than men; they tear their cloaths, besmear their faces with their excrement, and fly from human society; they ramble and with wonderful rapidity from one object to another, with shouting, singing, and laughing.... Insane persons endure hunger, cold, nakedness, and want of sleep with astonishing degree of impunity" (p. 14).

The treatment of madness, as it was now being reimagined, no longer could be left to the colonial "doctors" who had learned their trade by apprenticeship, or to the self-taught "empirics," or to the minister-physicians. The Enlightenment emphasis on science as the primary means for the mastery of both the natural and social world, and on medical science as the most promising tool for the improvement of human life, meant that the treatment of the mad came under the purview of the newly minted medical doctors. So medicalized, madness became another form of disease, and by the end of the 18th century the mad were considerably less likely to be free to live their lives under the management and guidance of family members and town officials than had the previous generations of the distracted.

The process of medicalization assured that medical theories about madness gained prominence over folk and spiritual beliefs. Although there was disagreement among medical doctors as to exactly what caused loss of reason, the prevailing theories were somatic in nature. Most medical doctors concurred that an imbalance in what they variously theorized were the humours, ethers, animal spirits or "electroid fluids," as Cutbush (1794, p. 33) posited in his dissertation, acted on the brain and other organs of the body to cause madness. These imbalances, in turn, were imagined to be the result of excesses in consumption, accumulation, study, play, prayer, physical effort and passion—in other words, in the activities that were beginning to define a unique "American character" at the beginning of independent nationhood.

This emphasis on the dangers of excess shifted the responsibility to individuals to monitor and regulate their own thoughts, behaviors and emotions. And it shifted the blame to them if they failed to do so. Thus, the attitude towards madness hardened over the post–Revolution years. Viewed as irrational, the mad increasingly were socially isolated; viewed as blameworthy, they increasingly were stigmatized. And viewed as threatening, they increasingly were vulnerable to formal mechanisms of social control within the walls of "the new world of the asylum" (Rothman, 1990, p. 130).

4

Asylums

Fetter strong madness in a silken thread. —Much Ado About
Nothing

In 1750, PHILADELPHIA WAS THE largest city in the colonies. It was a proudly
progressive city that claimed some of the most enlightened colonial leaders
and revolutionary thinkers as residents. Although their political influence had
waned since the establishment of the city, the Quakers continued to spearhead charitable and philanthropic initiatives aimed at reducing the social
problems and relieving the social ills of the 15,000 economically and socially
diverse residents of the city.

The idea of establishing a hospital for the poor, the first of its kind in
the colonies, originated with Thomas Bond, cofounder of the American
Philosophical Society and a surgeon with a thriving practice in Philadelphia.
A formal institution for curing the sick and caring for the mad appealed to
him for several reasons. First, the relief of the suffering of the most needy
segment of the population was a moral mandate that reflected the Quaker
beliefs he still deeply held, despite having been disowned by the Society of
Friends a few years earlier for having taken an oath. Second, by removing
the ill and the mad from the charity rolls, the community's financial burden
for their care would be reduced, an initiative that seemed to be proving successful in Europe where he had received his medical education. And third,
by hospitalizing the ill and the mad, patients would become subjects for the
practice of the kind of scientific medicine that reflected the principles of the
Enlightenment and that also was foundational to the American Philosophical Society (Tomes, 1994).

Unsuccessful in raising the requisite funding himself, Bond solicited the assistance of Benjamin Franklin, arguably the most prominent intellectual, scientific and political figure in colonial America. In 1751, in language that combined Enlightenment thinking about madness and optimism about its medical cure with pragmatic concerns about the cost of supporting citizens who offered the growing community nothing in return, Franklin and thirty-two other prominent citizens petitioned the assembly for a charter and a grant of £2000 to found a hospital:

> That with the Numbers of People the Number of Lunaticks, or Persons distemper'd in Mind, and deprived of their rational Faculties, hath greatly encreased in this Province.
>
> That some of them going at large, are a Terror to their Neighbors, who are daily apprehensive of the Violences they may commit; and others are continually wasting their Substance, to the great Injury of themselves and Families, ill disposed Persons wickedly taking Advantage of their unhappy Condition, and drawing them into unreasonable bargains, &c.
>
> That few or none of them are so sensible of their Condition as to submit voluntarily to the Treatment their respective Cases require, and therefore continue in the same deplorable State during their Lives; whereas it has been found, by the Experience of many Years, that above two Thirds of the mad People received into *Bethlehem* Hospital, and there treated properly, have been perfectly cured.
>
> YOUR Petitioners beg Leave farther to represent, that tho' the good Laws of this Province have made many compassionate and charitable Provisions for the Relief of the Poor, yet something farther seems wanting in Favour of such whose Poverty is made more miserable by the additional Weight of a grievous Disease, from which they might easily be relieved, if they were not situated at too great a Distance from regular Advice and Assistance, whereby many languish out their Lives, totur'd perhaps with the Stone, devour'd by the Cancer, depriv'd of Sight by Cataracts, or gradually decaying by loathsome Distempers; who, if the Experience in the present Manner of nursing and attending them separately when they come to Town, were not so discouraging, might again, by the judicious Assistance of Physick and Surgery, be enabled to taste the Blesings of Health, and be made in a few Weeks useful Members of the Community, able to provide for themselves and Families [Franklin, 1754, p. 4].

The assembly supported the petition and a year later the Pennsylvania Hospital opened in a small rented house to receive its first six patients, four of whom were mad. Just a few years later, Franklin and his colleagues had raised sufficient funds to move the hospital to a three-storey brick building. The ground floor of each wing housed its mad patients.

Enlightenment thinking had created some optimism that madness could be medically cured, a confidence buoyed by the inflated cure-rates published by European asylums, including the Royal Bethlem Hospital in London to which Franklin's petition makes reference. Yet there was little evidence of that optimism in the care of the mad at the Pennsylvania Hospital. Although they were visited briefly twice weekly by a physician and were adequately fed, they were confined to barred cells; and the use of straight-jackets, leg chains and manacles was not uncommon. On fair weather days their cell-keeper, as their lone attendant was referred to, allowed a recreation period in the hospital's "crazy yard," a small fenced-in enclosure; but no other efforts were made to entertain or employ them (Morton & Woodbury, 1973).

Consistent with the intent of the hospital's founders, about half of the mad patients were penniless and had been admitted by town officials in the role of overseers of the poor. The fact that they were being cared for with public funds partially accounts for their austere surroundings and indifferent care. But what also must be factored in is that these patients embodied the Enlightenment notion of madness: they were irrational, unmanageable, often violent to themselves and others, and in need of hospitalization for confinement as much, if not more, than for care. Among the earliest admitted mad patients were a woman who had murdered her infant, a farmer who had burned down his own barn to rid it of rats, a vagrant who had desecrated the Jewish cemetery, a furniture maker who had terrorized and threatened his family and neighbors, and a merchant who had harassed parishioners in their places of worship (Tomes, 1994, p. 26).

The remaining mad patients at the Pennsylvania Hospital were private patients. While some of them most likely were as irrational and threatening as the impoverished mad patients chained in the ground floor cells, not all were. Rather, they required the kind of care their families not only could afford but also believed was superior to what they themselves could provide. The financial resources of these private patients—who included the daughter of colonial portraitist Charles Wilson Peale, the son of Pennsylvania Hospital's own leading physician, Benjamin Rush, and Mary Girard, the wife of the wealthiest resident in the city and patron of the hospital—afforded them better accommodations and better care on the main floors of the hospital, a fact satirized in modern times in *The Insanity of Mary Girard: A Drama in One Act*:

> *Mary:* But I'm not crazy. You must know that I'm not.
> *Furies:* You must be! Mr. Girard had you admitted. As a lunatic, paying patient. The doctors have agreed. To keep you here. As long as Mr. Girard. Continues to pay. Your bills. And quite a lucrative account. You'll prove to be. For a lunatic, Mary [Robertson, 1979, p. 11].

Over the following years, as the nature of family life was being transformed by the rise of capitalism and the wage labor system, families found it necessary to relinquish some of their caring functions to public institutions. In that they document the steady increase in the number of mad patients admitted, the annual reports of the Pennsylvania Hospital are, in many ways, barometers of these larger economic and social changes. But they also are harbingers of a looming crisis. Because only a few of the hospitalized mad patients were released as cured each year, and a few more either were taken back into care by their families or "eloped," i.e., escaped, the new admissions cumulatively added to the mad patient census. Overcrowding meant that several unruly mad patients were forced to share a single barred cell, thus increasing problems in daily management, while those who were more biddable were reluctantly placed among the physically ill in the wards of the upper floors.

To address this overcrowding crisis, a "West Wing" was opened in 1796 in a separate building which could accommodate eighty mad patients. The physical separation of the mad from the sick, proclaimed in a newspaper editorial as "absolutely necessary in order to cure them" ("Pennsylvania Hospital," 1796, p. 3), effectively transformed the West Wing into a lunatic asylum.

The specter of overcrowding even in this new and larger facility also revived the therapeutic optimism that had waned since the founding of the Pennsylvania Hospital. Determined to increase the cure rates, and confident they could, the attending physicians tightened their grasp on the medicalization of madness by experimenting with a variety of treatment techniques. Under the leadership of Benjamin Rush, whose thirty year tenure at the hospital earned him the sobriquet of "the father of American psychiatry," physicians still bled, purged, vomited, blistered and sweated their mad patients, filled them with physics and, only when necessary, restrained them in straightjackets. But they also twirled them in gyrating chairs to increase the flow of blood to the brain and confined them in tranquilizing chairs to decrease it, talked with them, pleaded, cajoled and sometimes threatened them, encouraged them to engage in manual labor and recreation, and to dabble in the genteel arts. The milieu of the West Wing was remarkably different from the barred cells on the ground floor of the original hospital, and so were the mad patients' responses to it. As a result, the medical view of both madness and those suffering from it started a dramatic shift. Loss of reason no longer seemed a sufficient explanation for the madness of those who were responding favorably to being reasoned with; and if a spark of reason indeed could be therapeutically engaged in the mad, they no longer could or should be seen and treated as wild beasts to be confined and controlled.

Epistemic Rupture

There were other factors contributing to this "epistemic rupture" (Foucault, 1965, p. 66) that ushered in changed perceptions of madness and different practices for dealing with it. Developments in the treatment of the mad in Europe had a profound influence on American physicians. Two examples are particularly noteworthy. As medical director of the Asylum de Bicêtre and later of the Salpêtriêre Hospital, both in Paris, France, Philippe Pinel ordered that the chains be struck off the mad patients. His carefully conducted analytic observations showed that restraint and brutal treatment did nothing to restore the minds of the mad, so in their place he introduced *le traitement moral*, or moral treatment, that included work, recreation, and intellectual and religious activities to occupy the minds of the patients and to prepare them for return to a society that had been disrupted by the French Revolution and the Restoration government (Goldstein, 1987). The success of moral treatment in curing, rather than just managing, madness was described in his book, *Traite Medico-Philosophique sur L'alienation Mentale*, which was translated into English as the *Treatise on Insanity* in 1806 and was widely read and discussed by American physicians who were treating the mad. In it, he wrote as follows:

> Few subjects in medicine are so intimately connected with the history and philosophy of the human mind as insanity. There are still fewer, where there are so many errors to rectify, and so many prejudices to remove.... Public asylums for maniacs have been regarded as places of confinement for such of its members as are become dangerous to the peace of society. The managers of these institutions, who are frequently men of little knowledge and less humanity, have been permitted to exercise towards their innocent prisoners a most arbitrary system of cruelty and violence; while experience affords ample and daily proofs of the happy effects of a mild, conciliating treatment, rendered effective by steady and dispassionate firmness.... Attention to these principles [of moral treatment] alone will, frequently, not only lay the foundation of, but complete a cure: while neglect of them may exasperate each succeeding paroxysm, till, at length, the disease becomes established, continued in its form, and incurable [pp. 3–4, 5].

At the same time in England, coffee and tea merchant William Tuke established the York Retreat for the humane treatment of mad Quakers. Convinced that conventional medicine was inadequate to the task of relieving the suffering of the mad, he, too, developed a moral treatment approach. Reasoning that if inhumane treatment makes the *wise* mad, then it surely will not make the mad wise, but instead will only "exasperate [their] disease and excite [their] resentment" (Tuke, 1813, p. 92), he offered in its place a highly structured approach that sought to transform the mad into rational citizens by treating them as if they were rational. American visitors, physicians and laypersons alike were witnesses to the workings of the benevolence, tact and artful manipulation of moral treatment in both managing and treating the mad at the York Retreat; and the published annual reports documented its achievement in returning both the acutely and chronically mad to the community (Digby, 1985). The communication between English and American Quakers and the American publication of Samuel Tuke's (1813) book on his grandfather's principles of moral treatment assured that those most intimately involved with the care of the mad knew of its success.

The epistemic rupture in perception and practice also was influenced by the founding of several small corporate asylums in the Northeast, all of them devoted to the principles of moral treatment, and all of them boasting success in curing the mad. The Friends Asylum opened in 1817 in Frankford, a few miles north of Philadelphia. Like the York Retreat, upon which it was modeled, the asylum was dedicated to the moral treatment of mad Quakers and it quickly demonstrated its success: nearly one-third of the sixty-six patients admitted in the first three years, most of them chronically mad and long considered untreatable, were discharged as "much improved" ("Friends Hospital," 2007). In Massachusetts, the McLean Asylum for the Insane, funded largely by wealthy Congregationalists, opened in 1818. As part of its regime of moral treatment, its patients picnicked on the expansive lawns, rowed boats down the Charles River, and took long carriage rides through the countryside (Bean, 2001). In New York, Quaker activist Thomas Eddy successfully lobbied the state for the funding of a new two hundred bed asylum to be modeled on the York Retreat. Opened in 1821 on the Upper West Side of New York City, the Bloomingdale Asylum's moral treatment regime was hailed as "one of the noblest triumphs of pure and enlightened benevolence" ("Address," 1821, p. 2). And in Connecticut, a survey conducted by the state medical society revealed that one thousand mad residents, some of them transient but most of them cared for by family members or friends, would benefit from institutionalization. To address that need, the Hartford Retreat opened in 1824. Its humane routine of moral treatment impressed an English visitor who wrote:

> No kind of deception, and if possible, no restraint, is exercised upon the patients, who are allowed every indulgence and gratification that are not incompatible with the object for which they are sent hither. They are informed, on their first arrival, that they are laboring under some disease, which has affected their minds, and requires peculiar treatment.... With the aid of soothing language, occupation suited to their inclinations, proper exercise, and appropriate medicines, an alleviation, if not a cure, of the malady is affected.... No one is confined, no matter how violent or intractable, in irons or in solitude. No breach in promise, no attempt to mislead, is ever permitted. The little glimmering of reason, that remains even in the worst cases, is skillfully employed by the keepers and assistants to lead the sufferer into feelings and habits, that at last conduct him to a clearer sky, if not into open day. "Let gentleness my strong enforcement be," seems to be the guiding rule to all who are to co-operate in carrying this principle into practice [Abdy, 1835, pp. 98–99].

Unlike the other new asylums, however, the Hartford Retreat did not rely solely on the kinds of moral treatment that had so impressed its visitor.

Its superintendent, Eli Todd, was firmly committed to a combination of moral and medical treatment. Although Todd had apprenticed with a physician and had been in medical practice for some time before assuming the role of superintendent of the Hartford Retreat, the superintendents of the Friends, McLean and Bloomingdale Asylums were laypersons and they were reluctant, at first, to surrender their control of moral treatment to the visiting and attending physicians who were determined to add medical interventions to the therapeutic routine. Within a short period of time, however, the momentum of the medicalization of madness that had begun years earlier overtook resistance; medical treatments, including the administration of opium and morphine, were not only added to the daily treatment regimes of all of the new asylums, but came to be seen as constitutive of moral treatment itself. Moral treatment, then, "came to be defined as the physicians' responsibility, and its administration was inextricably bound up with the employment of conventional medical therapeutics," thus laying out the ground rules by which future asylums would operate (Scull, 1989, p. 109).

The epistemic rupture in the perception of madness and the treatment of the mad also was influenced by the historical moment in which it was occurring; after all, "the ways [people] look at the world are conditioned by their activity in it" (Scull, 1989, p. 91). As people, by necessity, began assuming active roles in what was becoming an increasingly industrialized society, transforming the raw materials of nature into functional or consumable goods, and competing with each other for jobs, wealth and status, they experienced a shift in worldview. They developed a growing appreciation of the individual capacity for purposive activity and self-determination, and the individual need for self-restraint and self-discipline in a rapidly changing society that offered opportunities and temptations in equal measure. No longer seen as the hapless victim of fate or nature, or the subject of a mysterious God or a menacing devil, the individual was now looked upon as the manager of his or her own destiny, capable not just of charting a course, but of learning, adapting, changing and coping with anything that interfered with the journey.

This new view of human nature encouraged a different view of madness. If, indeed, each individual is agentic by nature, then madness is not a loss of reason, but an illness or even a disease that diminishes the skill to live up to potential. Thus treatment had to be aimed at restoring that capacity through the benevolence, tact and artful manipulation of moral treatment, combined with the pharmaceuticals and interventions of conventional medicine. And because the very notion of agency inspires confidence in the individual knack for self-transformation, this new regime of moral treatment buoyed therapeutic optimism that even the most intractably mad individual could be "restored from the class of mere consumers to the class of producers of the necessities for human sustenance" (Earle, 1887, p. 64).

Kirkbride Plan

By 1841 a total of 16 asylums, all dedicated to the principles of moral treatment, had opened in the Northeast. None better embodied those principles than the Pennsylvania Hospital for the Insane. Overcrowding and lack of space for the demands of moral treatment at the West Wing had made the construction of a new asylum an urgent endeavor. Built on a hundred acres of lush farm land, the hospital opened in 1841 with accommodations for 160 mad patients.

Within its walls physicians continued to treat the mad but did so in a remarkably different social context than had the physicians at the West Wing, and with an optimism sustained by the early successes of moral treatment. The economic and demographic shifts of the late 18th and early 19th centuries had transformed Philadelphia into a major urban center with a racially, ethnically and economically diverse population of 100,000 native-born, immigrant and transient residents. The city's buoyant spirit was expressed in its rowdy politics, embraced in its rich cultural life, expounded in its institutions of higher learning, engendered in its philanthropic initiatives and welfare reforms, and enacted in the Pennsylvania Hospital for the Insane. Imbued with the optimistic spirit of the city and of the era, physicians had an unwavering conviction that madness could and would be cured by a moral treatment regime aimed at transforming the mad into productive citizens (Tomes, 1994).

Thomas Story Kirkbride, an Orthodox Quaker, was appointed the first superintendent of the hospital, and his forty year career is co-extensive with the vogue of moral treatment in U.S. asylums. Insisting that "the insane are really 'the wards of the State,' and ... every State is bound by all the dictates of humanity, expediency, and economy, to make proper provision for those not able to provide for themselves" (Kirkbride, 1880, p. 80), he set about creating a comprehensive program of moral treatment that became synonymous with his name:

> Early hours are always desirable in a hospital for the insane,—early hours for retiring at night, and early hours for rising in the morning. To many this is a radical change in their habits, and this change itself is often of very marked advantage.... By six, it is intended the patients should be getting ready for breakfast, which meal, during the whole year, is taken at half past six o'clock, and previous to which, medicine is given to those for whom it may be deemed desirable in the different wards.... Immediately after breakfast, the rooms and wards are put in order.... [A]rrangements are made for driving, walking, visiting interesting places, and for the special occupations and amusements of the patients during the day....

After the outdoor exercise, the usual indoor resources are at command—reading, writing, conversation, games of nearly every kind, and whatever work is likely to be interesting to individual patients.... At noon, medicine is again administered to those who are taking it regularly, and preparations are made for dinner, which is on the table at half past twelve. Early in the afternoon, the hour depending somewhat on the season, all are expected to be again in the open air, and securing, as much as possible, the advantages which result from it, sunshine, exercise, and whatever else can be combined with these valuable agents for preserving as well as restoring health.... Tea is ready at six o'clock in winter, and at half past six in summer; after which, except in very warm weather, few go outside of the yards connected with the wards. Then begin the special arrangements for making the evenings pass pleasantly. Preparations are made for the lectures and other entertainments in the lecture room, or gymnastic halls, or for the officers' tea parties.... After leaving the lecture rooms, the patients frequently assemble in the parlors, and have music, games, and other diversions, filling up the time to half past nine, between which and ten o'clock, all persons are expected to retire for the night [Kirkbride, 1880, pp. 276–280].

For Kirkbride, the highly structured routine of moral treatment was necessary for breaking the careless habits that simultaneously were the cause and the result of madness. Mad patients who responded favorably to the moral treatment regime were rewarded with improved ward assignments. The best-behaved patients were placed in the upper wards, the problematic in the middle wards, and the worst-behaved in the lower wards. In an institutional setting where diagnosis usurps identity, and individuality is absorbed by similitude, the ward hierarchy system not only was a powerful tool of moral management, but a viable opportunity for mad patients to achieve and maintain status.

As a physician, Kirkbride was not at all opposed to using the *materia medica* of his profession as an adjunct to moral treatment. Morphine, conium, a mixture of iron and quinine, succus hyocamus or black henbane, a concoction of psychotria ipecacuanha, opium and potassium sulphate known as Dovers Powders, and chloral hydrate were routinely administered to mad patients. Nor was Kirkbride adverse to using somewhat modified versions of the "heroic treatments" of his predecessors. Mad patients were blistered, purged to counteract the constipating effect of morphine, wrapped in wet blankets, doused with buckets of cold water, given mustard foot-baths and camphor rubs. And, although he was opposed to restraint, violent or self-injuring mad patients were wrapped in "the sleeves," a partial straightjacket that immobilized the arms, placed in mittens that confined only the hands, strapped to the bed, or placed in a "canvas suit." Those who refused food were force fed. When tact and persuasion failed, their nostrils were pinched, forcing them to swallow; as a last resort, they were fed through a stomach tube to prevent starvation (Tomes, 1984).

All of that said, it was moral treatment with which Kirkbride was most intimately associated. And moral treatment for Kirkbride was not only to be built into the daily regime of asylums, but into the very buildings. Kirkbride was an impassioned advocate for "moral architecture," the idea that handsome buildings on cheerful grounds not only made moral treatment within their walls possible but created in their very brick and mortar a moral order that facilitated treatment. Although he himself had not designed the Pennsylvania Hospital for the Insane, he saw in its simple pattern of a central hall with two wings the template for the kind of moral architecture he advocated.

Over the years of his tenure as superintendent, Kirkbride developed an asylum plan that also came to be synonymous with his name. The Kirkbride Plan was a congregate plan, with all of the 250 patients living under the roof of a single linear building that was comprised of small, connected pavilions, and arranged in the shape of a shallow "V." While Kirkbride discouraged the building of expensive and ornate asylums, he insisted that

> [they] should have a cheerful and comfortable appearance, every thing repulsive and prison-like should be carefully avoided, and even the means of effecting the proper degree of security should be masked, as far as possible, by arrangements of a pleasant and attractive description. For the same reason, the grounds about the building should be highly improved and tastefully ornamented; a variety of interest should be collected around it, and trees and shrubs, flowering plants, summer-houses, and other pleasing objects, should add to its attractiveness. No one can tell how important all these may prove in the treatment of patients, nor what good effects may result from first impressions thus made upon an invalid on reaching a hospital [Kirkbride, 1880, pp. 52–53].

No detail of asylum construction escaped Kirkbride's attention. The Kirkbride Plan specifies the sizes of every room and the height of their ceilings, the dimensions of windows, doors and staircases, the preferred wall and flooring materials, the kind of heating and ventilation system, the lighting, style of furniture and type of decorations. It elaborates on the arrangement of space for outdoor recreation activities, the placement of out-buildings around the grounds, the design of the landscape, and the uses of native flora and fauna.

In many ways, the plan reflected the artistic and intellectual traditions of the American Romanticism movement of the mid–1800s (Johnson, 2001). Whether in the poetry of Walt Whitman or Ralph Waldo Emerson, the essays of Henry Thoreau, the landscape paintings of Thomas Cole or Albert Bierstadt, or the musical compositions of Louis Moreau Gottschalk or Arthur William Foote, American Romanticism emphasized the restorative qualities of nature and the uplifting impressions that beauty and order leave on the mind. In the words of Kirkbride, "It should never be forgotten, that every object of interest that is placed in or about a hospital for the insane, that even every tree that buds, or every flower that blooms, may contribute in its small measure to excite a new train of thought, and perhaps be the first step towards bringing to reason, the morbid wanderings of a disordered mind" (Kirkbride, 1842, p. 47).

In 1844 Kirkbride played an instrumental role in the formation of the Association of Medical Superintendents of the American Institutions for the Insane (AMSAII), the nation's first medical organization and publisher of the *American Journal of Insanity*. Although there was some disagreement among his twelve cofounders as to the most efficacious design of asylums for the mad, and the *American Journal of Insanity* encouraged contributions to the debate from its readers, the Kirkbride Plan prevailed, not only because of the alleged curative effects of its moral architecture, but also because of its investment of trust in the medical superintendent to orchestrate every facet of an asylum's therapeutic environment. The AMSAII published the architectural guidelines for the Kirkbride Plan in 1851. Kirkbride himself published an elaborately detailed guide under the title of *On the Construction Organization and General Arrangements of Hospitals for the Insane* in 1854; and in the flurry of asylum building that followed, the linear arrangement of the Kirkbride Plan could be found in many state asylums across the nation.

Intact Kirkbride Plan Buildings as of 2008
("Kirkbride Buildings," 2008)

Alabama (Bryce) State Hospital (1852): Alabama

Athens State Hospital (1874): Ohio

Buffalo State Hospital (1895): New York

Cherokee State Hospital (1902): Iowa

Clarinda State Hospital (1895): Iowa

Danvers State Hospital (1878): Massachusetts

Fergus Falls State Hospital (1906): Minnesota

Greystone Park Hospital (1876): New Jersey

Hudson River State Hospital (1871): New York

Independence State Hospital (1873): Iowa

Taunton State Hospital (1854): Massachusetts

Traverse City State Hospital (1885): Michigan

Weston State Hospital (1880): West Virginia

Worcester State Hospital (1877): Massachusetts

Disappearance of the Kirkbride Plan
and Moral Treatment and the Emergence
of Scientific Psychiatry

By the time the second edition of Kirkbride's influential book was published in 1880, both the Kirkbride Plan for asylums and moral treatment had fallen out of vogue. While the inspiration for both was the simple principle that "beauty is therapy," as was the motto of the Traverse City State Hospital in northern Michigan (Steele & Hains, 2001), the reasons for their disappearance were far more complex.

Adverse Publicity

While behind closed doors asylum superintendents and physicians debated the finer points of moral treatment, the well known writer Edgar Allan Poe satirized it in a story titled "The System of Dr. Tarr and Prof. Fether," which was published in *Graham's* magazine in 1845. Poe's familiarity with moral treatment was likely the result of his perusal of asylum annual reports published in the popular press that extolled the success of moral treatment in curing the mad. But he also was acquainted with Pliny Earle, who, as superintendent of the Friends Asylum and later the Bloomingdale Asylum, was one of moral treatment's most prominent promoters (Harrison, 1902, p. 230).

Poe's story is of a physician traveling through the south of France who visits the Maison de Sante, a private asylum renowned for its use of the "soothing system." Upon arrival, he is greeted by the flamboyant superintendent, Monsieur Maillard, who describes the soothing system this way:

> One in which the patients were ménages-humored. We contradicted no fancies which entered the brains of the mad. On the contrary, we not only indulged but encouraged them; and many of our most permanent cures have thus been affected. There is no argument which so touches the feeble reason of the madman as the argument ad absurdum. We have had men, for example, who fancied themselves chickens. The cure was, to insist upon the thing as fact.... In this manner, a little corn and gravel were made to perform wonders [Poe, 1845].

Maillard then goes on to renounce the soothing system as dangerous in that it failed to account for the "caprices of madmen" and their ability to "counterfeit insanity." He explains why: recently, the asylum's mad patients, appearing to have been effectively soothed into complacency, carried out their secret plan to take over the asylum and locked the superintendent and his staff in their cells, dressed in their clothes and ate and drank from the asylum's well-stocked larder and wine cellar. Maillard confesses that he found the cavalier treatment of the superintendent and his staff by the mad patients neater and less troublesome than the soothing system, so borrowing from it and from the insights of a Dr. Tarr and Professor Fether, both unfamiliar to the visiting physician, he created a new system that is "incomparably the most effectual yet devised." Maillard's revelation, offered during a sumptuous dinner party attended by a large number of guests, is then interrupted by the asylum's mad patients who have escaped from their locked cells. Tarred and feathered, they appear to the visiting physician to be "Chimpanzees, Ourang-Outangs, or big black baboons" as they fight, stamp, scratch and howl their way through the dining room. Maillard takes cover under a table while his guests, whom the visiting physician had thought were rather eccentric "people of rank," variously orate from the top of the table, pop like a champagne cork, spin like a top, croak like a bullfrog, bray like a donkey, and crow like a rooster.

Poe's story works as a double-edged satire. He lampoons the soothing system of moral treatment for its faith in the curative power of indulgence and amusement, and its naivety about the cunning of the mad. But he also makes fun of the empty-headedness of the visiting physician who has to undergo a beating during the melee to realize that Maillard and his guests are the very mad patients who had taken over the asylum, and that the tarred and feather mad patients are, in reality, the superintendent and his staff. In doing so, Poe raises the question of whether even the trained eye of a physician can discern the difference between sanity and madness.

That question also was raised in published autobiographical accounts. Although commitment policies varied from one asylum to another, all required at the very least medical certificates of lunacy, signed by physicians, before taking into their care persons who were believed to be mad. The certificates could be initiated by the physicians themselves, public officials, or more likely by family members, friends or guardians. The specter of false commitment—of incompetent physicians, unethical public officials, vindictive family members, avaricious friends, or ignorant guardians—initiating procedures that would consign otherwise perfectly sane people to months, years or even lifetimes in asylums, was more the stuff of fiction than fact. But in a few high profile cases, allegedly mad patients contested their commitment or their care, and in doing so brought to public attention the cracks in the façades of the Kirkbride Plan for asylum management and moral treatment.

One of those protesting mad patients was Isaac Hunt, who spent three years in the Maine Insane Hospital. A Kirkbride Plan asylum, the "Maine Insane," as it was known at the time, was devoted to the principles of moral treatment and operated under the superintendency of the eminent physician

Isaac Ray. Hunt's book, *Astounding Disclosures!: Three Years in a Mad House* (1851), details the "confinement, treatment, torture of body and mind, and ... malpractice" that not only prolonged his recovery, but that also worsened the "wild mania" that caused his friends to commit him in the first place (p. 10). From the forced ingestion of stupefying drugs, the drudgery of demeaning labor, the cruelty of staff who jeered at his delusions and threatened him with beatings and restraint, to the alleged machinations of Ray himself, to keep him in the asylum once he had recovered to prevent him from going public with his complaints, Hunt reveals that moral treatment was more rhetoric than reality. After appealing to the board of trustees, the governor and even the president of the United States, Hunt finally secured his release through the intervention of an old friend, a physician newly elected as a city selectman, who threatened legal action against the asylum. Written months after the Maine Insane Hospital burned to the ground in 1850, Hunt concludes his memoir with an appeal for better care of the mad than anything moral treatment had to offer:

> As I have said, I suppose the institution will be rebuilt, and if it must be, I hope that for their strong cells, they will take as a model the new jail at Boston, and as an act of humanity let them be for the wild, noisy patients, at a distance from the peaceable and quiet ones sufficient not to disturb them, and under no circumstances should the shower bath or cold bath be permitted to be used, as it has been used, as an instrument of torture, under penalties which would consign those who thus abuse their power to the State prison. Let the people see to it that none are abused, for the insane, of all human beings, are the most to be pitied, and they should be protected from abuse, as much as the public should be protected from their violence. If the people knew that institution as I know it, they would abandon it forever, for all the good that it could accomplish in a thousand years of the very best treatment, could never repay the horrid atrocities that have been practiced there in the ten years that it has been in operation; and it should be abandoned forever, and its ground enclosed and planted with weeping willows, and its walls allowed to crumble with time, and remain as a monument to designate it as the field of blood, and the curse of an avenging God [p. 355].

Analogizing the involuntary commitment procedures to the signed and sealed "Lettres de Cachet" that the ancien régime French monarchy used to authorize imprisonment without trial in the Bastille, an article in the popular magazine *Atlantic Monthly* laid bare the iron fist in the velvet glove of moral treatment. Anonymously authored, but later attributed to L. Clarke Davis, the noted editor of the *Philadelphia Inquirer* and later of the *Public Ledger* the article asserts that because moral treatment vests asylum superintendents with "the *sole* direction of medical, moral and dietetic treatment of the patients, and *the selection of all persons employed in their care*," as Kirkbride, himself, once wrote, then for these reasons the "capacity for evil" is always present:

The rules of all these institutions, whether public or private, are mostly excellent in their design and in theory; but if they should depend for their execution upon either a wicked, weak or indolent superintendent, they would, instead, of being a safeguard, become a pregnant means of wrong, for their existence only being known, would simply serve to allay suspicion of mismanagement and cruelty, and give more certain opportunities to oppression and evil practices. Rules, however well considered, cannot execute themselves [1868, p. 592].

In an angry rejoinder, Isaac Ray, then retired, disputed the facts in every case of false commitment that Davis details in his lengthy article, but it is for Davis' suggestion that contained within the very philosophy of moral treatment is the potential for its abuse that he saves his most pointed response: "The writer labors under the mistaken notion that the rare, exceptional abuse of a thing can be remedied only by the total abolition of the thing itself" (Ray, 1868, p. 228). Dismissing Davis as nothing more than an "amateur reformer" (p. 242), Ray assures readers that whatever asylum reform is needed will come from "the counsel and aid of those who have personal knowledge of their management and affairs, of the nature of insanity, and of the ways of the insane" (p. 242). Ray concludes the rejoinder with a defense of both moral treatment and the Kirkbride Plan for asylums and their management:

To gain an adequate conception of what the good [asylums] accomplish, let one traverse their halls and grounds, witness the order, peace, and freedom that prevail—the admirable arrangements for promoting the physical and mental comfort of their inmates by means of good food, pure air, abundant recreation, and employment out of doors, books, papers, pictures, amusements within—and learn something of the unceasing, unwearied effort to prevent abuses and render the law of kindness paramount to every other influence [p. 242].

That "law of kindness," the sine qua non of moral treatment, also was the subject of a series of highly publicized attacks by Ebenezer Haskell. The prominent carriagemaker claimed he had been falsely committed for "breach of the peace" to the Pennsylvania Hospital for the Insane in 1866 by family members who owed him money. Over the next two years, he escaped from the asylum four times, the last time fracturing his leg while scaling the wall. While recovering in a hospital he learned that his attorney had filed a writ of habeas corpus securing his release from the asylum and paving the way for an inquest of lunacy before the court of common pleas. A parade of witnesses, from family members, servants and neighbors, to physicians and asylum psychiatrists, testified over the eleven day hearing. In his charge to the jury, the judge instructed them to decide whether Haskell's excitability, irritability, quick temper and talkativeness had changed in quality and quantity from "peculiarities" to madness, as a result of a failed business venture several years before, as had been alleged in court, and whether he was, as a result, deprived of reason and understanding and therefore unable to manage his own affairs. After an hour's deliberation, the jury returned a verdict that declared Haskell was, and always had been, sane.

The reportage of the newspapers that covered the Haskell hearing was mixed; the older established press generally slanted coverage in favor of moral treatment, the newer yellow press against it. But whether for or against, the press printed the allegations made by Haskell and some of the witnesses in his defense that patients in the Pennsylvania Hospital for the Insane, the very paragon of moral treatment, were choked, doused with buckets of cold water, strapped to their beds, confined in bare dungeons, berated, humiliated and even beaten by attendants and physicians, and lied to and about by Kirkbride himself.

Haskell published a scathing account of his time in the Pennsylvania Hospital for the Insane in 1869, and spent the next several years in a vigorous and public anti-asylum campaign that was widely covered by the popular and penny press. In 1891 at the age of 87, he slit his own throat in a failed suicide attempt. The man the press described as "eccentric" and "idiosyncratic" died a few years later ("Eccentric Man," 1891).

Internal Dissent

As the Kirkbride Plan era waned, the majority of members of the AMSAII, which later would become the American Psychiatric Association, were physicians employed in the state asylums that had been cropping up across the country, largely as a result of the advocatory activities of Dorothea Lynde Dix, a former schoolmistress. Dix's recuperative journey to Italy had been interrupted by another serious bout of ill health in 1836. Cared for by English family friends who, in turn, were friends with the Tuke family, she had the opportunity to spend time with Samuel Tuke, the grandson of the founder of the York Retreat, and to learn its principles of the moral treatment of the mad. It was with those principles in mind that Dix had visited the basement dungeon of the East Cambridge, Massachusetts, jail in 1841 after teaching a Sunday School lesson to the female inmates. There she found mad women and men, barely clothed, chained in unheated, foul-smelling cells. Appalled by the site, she began a vigorous campaign to provide clothes for them and warming stoves for their cells. Buoyed by the success of her modest campaign, she embarked on a more ambitious plan to study the treatment of the mad across the country, traveling thousands of miles over the next several years, systematically visiting the jails, prisons, almshouses, workhouses, private homes and asylums that housed the mad, and then drafting memorials to state legislatures to appeal for the building of state-funded public asylums for their care and treatment (Brown, 1998).

The culmination of her campaign was this 1848 memorial to the U.S. Congress that appealed for granting states the right to sell millions of acres of federal land, with the proceeds to be used exclusively for the care of the indigent mad:

> It is a fact, not less certainly substantiated than it is deplorable, that insanity has increased in an advanced ratio with the fast increasing population in all the United States. This terrible malady, the source of indescribable miseries, does increase, and must continue fearfully to increase, in this country, whose free, civil, and religious institutions create constantly various and multiplying sources of mental excitement. There are twenty State hospitals, besides several incorporated hospitals, for the treatment of the insane, in nineteen States of the Union, Virginia alone having two government institutions of State and also incorporated hospitals. Well organized hospitals are the only fit places of residence of the insane of all classes; ill-conducted institutions are worse than none at all. It may be suggested that though hospital treatment is expedient, perhaps it may not be absolutely necessary, especially for vast numbers whose condition may be considered irrecoverable, and in whom the right exercise of the reasoning faculties may be looked upon as past hope. I have myself seen more than nine thousand idiots, epileptics, and insane, in these United States, destitute of appropriate care and protection; and of this vast and most miserable company, sought out in jails, in poorhouses, and in private dwellings, there have been hundreds, nay, rather thousands, bound with galling chains, bowed beneath fetters and heavy iron balls, attached to drag-chains, lacerated with ropes, scourged with rods, and terrified beneath storms of profane execrations and cruel blows; now subject to gibes, and scorn, and torturing tricks—now abandoned to the most loathsome necessities, or subject to the vilest and most outrageous violations.... Humanity requires that every insane person should receive the care appropriate to his condition, in which the integrity of the judgment is destroyed, and the reasoning faculties confused or prostrated. Hardly second to this consideration is the civil and social obligation to consult and secure the public welfare: first in affording protection against the frequently manifested dangerous propensities of the insane; and second, by assuring reasonable and skilful remedial cares, procuring their restoration to usefulness as citizens of the republic, and as members of communities. Insanity prevails, in proportion to numbers, most among the educated, and, according to mere conventional distinctions, in the highest classes of society. But those who possess riches and a liberal competency are few, compared with the toiling millions; therefore the insane who are in necessitous circumstances greatly outnumber those whose individual wealth protects them usually from the grossest exposures and most cruel sufferings ... I ask of the Senate and House of Representatives of the United States, with respectful but earnest importunity, assistance to the several States of the Union in providing appropriate care and support for the curable and incurable indigent insane. I ask, for the thirty States of the Union, 5,000,000 acres of land, of the many hundreds of millions of public lands, appropriated in such manner as shall assure the greatest benefits to all who are in circumstances of extreme necessity, and who, through the providence of God, are wards of the nation, claimants on the sympathy and care of the public, through the miseries and dis-

qualifications brought upon them by the sorest afflictions with which humanity can be viewed ["Memorial," 1848].

When the bill that resulted from Dix's memorial failed to garner political support, she traded on public enthusiasm for the proposal and resubmitted the memorial, this time audaciously asking for ten million acres of federal land. The resulting bill passed both Houses but was vetoed by President Franklin Pierce, who argued that if the federal government were to make a provision for the indigent mad, it would have to do the same for all indigent people, thus usurping the power of individual states.

Years later, in failing health and living in an apartment on the grounds of the New Jersey State Asylum, her "first born child," i.e., the first state asylum funded and built thought her efforts, Dix could boast that despite the failure of her memorial, two federal asylums and 75 state asylums for the indigent mad had been built across the country, 32 of which could be considered the direct results of her advocatory efforts. She died in 1887, eulogized as "the most useful and distinguished woman America has yet produced (cited in Deutsch, 1936, p. 185).

In spite of Dix's efforts, problems caring for the mad persisted, as evidenced by an account of Hiawatha Asylum for Insane Indians (Spaulding, 1986; Stawicki, 1997). Established in 1903 in Canton, South Dakota, the 90-bed Hiawatha Asylum was the first federal asylum for an ethnic group. The 1929 and 1931 inspection reports documented systematic neglect and abuse and concluded that nearly one-half of its patients either could be treated more effectively in their communities, or were not mad at all, but had been institutionalized for conflicts with white persons or agencies. The asylum was closed in 1933, and razed in 1946. Each year Native Americans gather on what is now a golf course to commemorate the 121 patients buried there, most of whom died from medical neglect.

Internal Dissenters

As the influence of state asylum superintendents in the AMSAII grew, the feasibility of the standards of asylum design and practice that had been ratified decades before by the organization came under question. The standards had operationalized the Kirkbride Plan, but critics among the state asylum superintendents argued that they needed much larger and more complexly organized asylums for the care of their ballooning populations of indigent mad patients, and much less expensive asylums to operate given the vagaries of state funding.

One of the dissenters, Dr. John Galt, superintendent of the Eastern State Lunatic Asylum in Williamsburg, Virginia, the first state asylum in the country, proposed that the AMSAII endorse a plan modeled on two innovative European approaches to madness. His plan called for attaching to every asylum a farm and a farmhouse, such as the Farm of St. Anne in Paris, France, in which chronically mad male patients would live and work within the "family circle" of the farmer and his family (Galt, 1855, p. 352). Other mad patients, whose madness seemed only to be exacerbated by the stultifying effects of institutionalization, would experience the restorative effects of a change in environment by living in cottages and working in the community under the general supervision of community residents, an experiment that was proving remarkably successful in the village of Gheel, Belgium.

Galt's proposal was roundly criticized by those AMSAII members who upheld the orthodoxy of the Kirkbride Plan. But it was Galt's veiled references to the plan, itself, as well as to its supporters, that reflected the growing dissent within the organization. Stating that he was satisfied that mad patients can tolerate much more liberty than they currently were allowed, he criticized unnamed Kirkbride Plan asylums, which had "few equals anywhere," for being "much more prison-houses, notwithstanding their many internal attributes of comfort and elegance" (p. 353). He went on to warn that no advancement in the care of the mad could be made as long as "those at the head of the most richly endowed asylums shall deem the true interests of their afflicted charge not to consist in ought on their part but tinkering gas-pipes and studying architecture, in order merely to erect costly and the same time most unsightly edifices" (p. 354).

Galt's charge was taken up by a number of dissenting members of the ASAII. In 1866 the organization voted on a series of new rules for asylum design. After heated debate, the majority of members voted to support the rule that all state asylums must continue to follow the original Kirkbride Plan, and that a district system of asylums should be put into place to address overcrowding. By a slim majority, members supported the rule that raised the maximum capacity of asylums from 250 to 600 patients (Tomes, 1984). The orthodoxy of the Kirkbride Plan prevailed, but so did the criticism of it. The next volley from dissenting members of the ASAII was directed not at the form of the plan, but at its function—moral treatment.

State asylum superintendents always found it more difficult to carry out moral treatment than did the superintendents of corporate asylums. At the mercies of state legislatures, they often were forced by budgetary bottom lines to cut back, or eliminate entirely, the recreational, occupational and educational programs associated with moral treatment, decisions perhaps made somewhat easier by the fact that a significant proportion of their mad patients were immigrants whose diverse cultural, religious and political heritages often created a resistance to, even an antagonism against, the socializing forces of moral treatment. At any rate, budgetary bottom lines also meant that state asylum superintendents often were forced to hire staff, including attending physicians, who were ill-trained or ill-suited to civil and curative interactions with mad patients in the first place (Luchins, 1988).

It stood to reason that AMSAII members who were state asylum super-intendents would be less than enthusiastic about moral treatment, but the most devastating criticism of it came from someone who once had been its most ardent practitioner. Pliny Earle, former physician at the Friends and Bloom-ingdale asylums and later superintendent of the Northampton Asylum in Massachusetts, was, like Galt, one of the thirteen original brethren who had formed the AMSAII. A prolific writer, gifted teacher and skilled physician, he had extolled the virtues of moral treatment. His 1848 description of the moral treatment regime at the Bloomingdale Asylum was canonical: "[E]very practicable effort is made to pursue that system, at once gentle, philosoph-ical and practical, which has resulted from the active and strenuous efforts of many philanthropists, in the course of the last century, to meliorate the condition of the insane. The primary object is to treat the patients, so far as their condition will possibly admit, as if they were still in the enjoyment of the healthy exercise of their mental faculties.... The courtesies of civilized and social life are not to be forgotten" (p. 26). And while Earle never defended moral treatment as the cure for every case of madness, he did assert that it not only interrupted the monotony of asylum life and promoted the content-ment of patients, but also effected "much towards the accomplishment of the great object of the institution — the installment of reason upon the seat from which it has been dethroned" (p. 38). His own carefully collected and ana-lyzed data showed that 62 percent of all Bloomingdale Asylum patients had been cured, improved or relieved of their madness through a regime of moral treatment (p. 108). These data, according to Earle, point to the fact that mad-ness, with exceptions of course, is indeed curable, and that moral treatment is the most efficacious regime for effecting that cure.

Nearly thirty years later, however, Earle had changed his mind. After carefully studying the annual reports of twenty corporate and state asylums, he concluded that the cure rate had been inflated by the counting of multi-ple recoveries of patients whose recurring madness saw them admitted and released many times over a given period of time. Analogizing this finding to a theatrical production in which actors march across a stage, disappear into the wings, and then march across the stage again, thus creating an illusion of large numbers, so too in asylums a small number of patients who experi-enced temporary and repeated restorations created the illusion of an impres-sive number of statistical cures. That the cure rate was an illusion is also because madness itself is elusive. Earle goes on to assert that the cure rate was also influenced, even strongly so, by "the temperament of the reporter; each man having his own standards, or criterion, of insanity" (Earle, 1887, p. 56). It was also influenced by politics. Earle states that some asylum superintendents "cooked statistics" to create both political and public support for their own asylums and, in general, for asylum medicine (p. 226).

These caveats aside, the annual reports of the asylums reveal that the cure rate had declined, often dramatically so. Contrasting cure rates from the second five years of each asylum's existence with the five years previous to the last annual report, he found an average decline of 11.82 percent in the reported cure rate for the twenty asylums whose annual reports he had analyzed (Table 1).

While still proclaiming asylums to be a "beneficent blessing" (p. 62), Earle punctured the therapeutic optimism of moral treatment: "In brief, then, it appears that it may be fairly asserted, first, that all estimates based on the

Table 1: Patient Cure Rate in Twenty Asylums			
Asylum	*Patient Total 2nd 5 Years (% Cured)*	*Patient Total Last 5 Years (% Cured)*	*% Difference in Cure Rate*
Augusta, ME	587 (48.55%)	953 (36.62%)	-11.93%
Concord, NH	471 (46.92%)	746 (32.97%)	-13.95%
Brattleboro, VT	798 (43.50%)	667 (30.43%)	-13.07%
McLean, MA	290 (40.69%)	420 (21.66%)	-19.03%
Worcester, MA	922 (48.59%)	2060 (29.75%)	-18.84%
Taunton, MA	1132 (48.46%)	2189 (28.11)	-20.35%
Butler, RI	279 (39.78%)	520 (35.57)	-4.21%
Hartford, CT	324 (57.40%)	533 (39.21%)	-18.19%
Bloomingdale, NY	635 (47.55%)	602 (32.55%)	-15.00%
Utica, NY	1890 (43.17%)	2125 (32.33%)	-10.84%
Flatbush, NY	1072 (41.88%)	1700 (33.11%)	-8.77%
Trenton, NJ	715 (42.79%)	996 (31.32%)	-11.47%
Pennsylvania, PA	1037 (51.10%)	1871 (42.80%)	-8.30%
Dixmont, PA	479 (37.78%)	1156 (30.01%)	-7.77%
Catonsville, MD	876 (51.59%)	671 (40.88%)	-10.71%
Newburgh, OH	579 (46.63%)	1352 (30.03%)	-16.60%
Dayton, OH	492 (60.16%)	1787 (45.25%)	-14.91%
Indianapolis, IN	826 (57.26%)	1932 (52.48%)	-4.78%
Jacksonville, IL	937 (46.53%)	1818 (31.96%)	-14.57%
Mendota, WI	680 (33.82%)	835 (25.86%)	-7.96%
(Adapted from Earle, 1887, pp. 55–56)			

assumption that either seventy-five, or seventy, or sixty, or even fifty percent of the *persons* attacked with insanity can, at the time of admission to the [asylums], be cured ... are necessarily false, and consequently are both a 'delusion and a snare'" (p. 61). His summary of his statistical study further damaged the considerable reputation the Kirkbride Plan and moral treatment had enjoyed for several decades: "The most important general conclusions to be derived from the statistics included in this Study, are, first, that the old claim of curability in a very large majority of recent cases is not sustained, and that the failure to sustain it is more apparent and more striking than at any antecedent time; and, secondly, that the percentage of reported recoveries of all cases received at the [asylums] in this country still continues to diminish" (p. 226).

External Criticism

It was not just the consequences of adverse publicity or the activities of Dorothea Dix or even the statistical analysis of Pliny Earle that tolled the bell on the Kirkbride Plan and moral treatment. To oversee what was becoming a vast network of costly welfare programs and institutions, states followed the 1863 lead of Massachusetts and created Boards of Charity whose responsibility, in part, was to investigate the conditions of state asylums, examine the management of their mad patients, and publish annual reports of their findings. Originally comprising politically appointed philanthropists and lay social leaders who very well may have been sympathetic to both the Kirkbride Plan and moral treatment, the nature of board appointments changed over the years. Increasingly, professional social workers were appointed, and their education and training in the social sciences led to their dismissal of the Kirkbride Plan as naïve, and of moral treatment as unscientific.

That view was shared by physicians practicing the emerging specialty of neurology. With their focus on the pathology of the nervous system, neurologists were engaged in the profitable outpatient practice of treating mildly anxious and depressed patients with tonics, diets, rest cures and mild electrical stimulation (Tomes, 1994). But to examine the relationship between the nervous system and intractable madness, they needed not just access to asylum patients, but also long-term medical supervision over them. In the battle over the medical control of mad patients, neurologists criticized asylum superintendents for having more interest in utopian building design than in the gritty reality of madness, and in the metaphysical abstraction of moral treatment than in science. Neurologist Edward Spitzka speaks for this specialty in an article published in 1887 in *The Journal of Nervous and Mental Disease*:

> If we look at [asylum superintendents'] annual reports, we find that some of them wax enthusiastic over the prizes gained by their hogs and strawberries at agricultural fairs, while others give you the benefit of their historical ideas on insanity. Beginning with David and Solomon, they pass from Scripture to Homer, thence to Bedlam, and tracing the development of humanitarian sentiments to the present day, when unlucky legislatures were induced, through the expansive views of the superintendents regarding the insane millennium, to appropriate extravagant sums to the erections of an insane paradise, they kindly permit their trustees to publish such "historical" documents accompanied by caricatures of morbid brain tissue in the illustrated monthly magazines. Judging by the average asylum reports, we are inclined to believe that certain superintendents are experts in gardening and farming (although the farm account frequently comes out on the wrong side of the ledger), tin roofing (although the roof and cupola is usually leaky), drain pipe laying (although the grounds are often moist and unhealthy), engineering (though the wards are either too hot or too cold), history (though their facts are incorrect, and their inferences beyond all measure so); in short, experts at everything except the diagnosis, pathology and treatment of insanity [pp. 208–209].

Spitzka goes on to criticize asylum superintendents and physicians for avoiding even the pretense of scientific interest in madness. Rather than performing autopsies on their deceased mad patients to determine brain pathology, he offers as an example of a scientific inquiry that the superintendents got "lost in the contemplation of [the] belittling routine activities" of moral treatment, such as fussing about the "facings of the uniforms worn by attendants, or the recognition of a dramatical or musical entertainment gotten up by some friends ... in the avowed interest of the patients, [but] in reality for the amusement of a select circle of visitors, liberally invited in such occasions" (p. 215). Their resistance to even bringing their practice of treating the mad into mainstream general medicine, he goes on to assert, is exemplified by the initial refusal of the AMSAII to join with the newly formed American Medical Association.

Concluding that because asylum superintendents are "not appointed on the strength of general and scientific culture, [and are] deficient in anatomical and pathological training, without a genuine interest in their noble specialty, untrustworthy as to their reported results, and not in that communion with the general medical profession which every liberal and broad-minded physician naturally seeks, [they] are the *last* individuals in the world to whom the responsible duty of training the embryo practitioner an important specialty should be entrusted" (p. 218). Thus, speaking for his specialty, he recommends that psychiatry be united with neurology in medical school courses, and that neurologists serve as physicians in asylums, with these anticipated results:

> Such appointments would immediately raise the whole tone of asylums; sluggish and incompetent superintendents would be weeded out; the suggestions of experienced and impartial men of high professional standing would lead to many ameliorations in the condition of asylum patients; the assistant physicians would

receive a stimulus to study and research, and as from them would in the end be recruited the coming generation of superintendents, professional ability would at last become a question in the competition for asylum positions [pp. 218–219].

The neurologists' critique of asylum superintendents and moral management was compounded by the 1894 invited address of noted neurologist S. Weir Mitchell on the occasion of the fiftieth anniversary of the founding of the American Medico-Psychological Association, formerly the AMSAII. Reminding the asylum superintendents in attendance that in 1889 they had responsibility for more than 91,000 mad patients in 160 asylums at a cost of nearly $11,000,000, over and above the more than $2,000,000 spent on building construction, he went on to declare that their insistence that they alone should, and could, treat the mad had "done us and you and many of our patients wrong" (p. 414). Mitchell criticized virtually every aspect of asylum management and life, from the asylum boards, the published annual reports, the educational qualifications of attending physicians, assistants and nurses, and the monotony of diet, to the locked doors and barred windows. But it is the very asylum superintendents attending his address whom he most pointedly criticized:

We, neurologists, think you have fallen behind us, and this opinion is gaining ground outside of our own ranks, and is, in part at least, your own fault. You quietly submit to having hospitals called asylums; you are labeled as medical superintendents, and some of you allow your managers to think you can be farmers, stewards, caterers, treasurers, business managers and physicians. You should urge in every report the stupid folly of this.... You may be fair general practitioners in insanity, but productive neurologists of high class regarding disease of the mind organs as but a part of your work? No—I think not. That, you cannot be if you are also in business. It is a grave injustice to insist that you shall conduct a huge boarding house—what has been called a monastery of the mad—and keep yourselves honestly able to move with the growth of medicine, and to study your cases, or add anything of value to our store of knowledge [p. 429].

Mitchell's address provoked little reaction from the state asylum superintendents, who for years had been quietly debating the very points he had raised. They appreciated the fact that as state employees they had little psychiatric autonomy and their work was subject to the vagaries of partisan politics. The failure to toe the political line always impacted finances and sometimes resulted in dismissal. The case of S.V. Clevenger illustrates this point. As a well-known neurologist, activist and scholar, he was appointed superintendent of the 2000-bed Illinois Eastern Hospital for the Insane in Kankakee by the governor in 1893. Upon assuming the position, he was approached by a state legislator with a request that he appoint certain persons to responsible positions at the asylum. Clevenger conceded. However, when he terminated the employment of a physician and several attendants, he immediately came into conflict with his own board of trustees, who were concerned that his decision would negatively impact forthcoming state appropriations. Forced to take a vacation, Clevenger wrote an article for the *Times and Register* that explained his attempt to create a civil service institution, free from political influence and the machinations of "boodlers"—that is, politicos and political appointees involved in graft, bribery and thievery— to thwart him. Upon his return to the asylum, Clevenger himself was dismissed:

> I had determined to make the place a civil service institution, and to that end had discharged no one, until, in April, an attendant was corrected for beating a patient. Gradually I got behind the scenes and found among the *dramatis personae* of the play, a gentleman who performed religious antics ... [and] who allowed attendants to dose patients, at their sweet will, on poisonous drugs ... a lecherous rascal who made free with female attendants ... [and] a brainy scoundrel [who] was the main boodler tool and covered up the tracks of the big thieves. About $350,000 per annum is "used" here to more or less advantage *by somebody* and when I prowled and hunted and investigated, and was up night after night, baffled by intrigues, but finding only rottenness everywhere and incessantly, I foolishly overstepped the requirements of health and was prostrated, to the intense delight of the boodlers, who conspired with some of the more recently employed and corrupted to make it appear that I was insane. This libel was telegraphed and published widely in boodle newspapers, and many of my friends were deceived by the report. It was a fight to the finish.... I discharged several conspirators ... no one without convincing proof, so there are many rascals remaining, who will be ousted soon, upon my return from the vacation my broken down condition necessitated; but worst of all, some of the very persons I had reason to rely upon (but never did), to assist me in wresting this hospital from politics and boodlers, generally, are the least to be trusted. As I fully expected, and prepared for, a new gang of political knaves has formed and blackmailed into fusion with the old gang. Both shall be crushed, whether I remain at the head of the hospital or not, and in my next I propose to give names, dates, letter and details, in full [pp. 656–657].

While Clevenger's case might have been atypical, the point remains that asylum superintendents were keenly aware of the politicization of the care of the mad in state asylums, and they recognized their marginal status in the field of medicine and in public opinion. In a somewhat self-conscious attempt to address the latter, they opened membership in the AMSAII to assistant physicians, thus signaling a resolve to demonstrate greater concern with the treatment of madness than with administrative functions. While they also refused to either endorse or reject the guiding principles that had been drafted by Kirkbride and others of the founding "brethren" of the AMSAII, and that had been so instrumental in establishing the Kirkbride Plan as the model for asylums and moral treatment as the raison d'etre, they did change the organization's name to the American Medico-Psychological Association and adopted a new constitution that set out the goal of the organization as the study of madness, its care and its treatment (Grob, 1983). In his presidential address to the newly named organization, Edward Cowles, superintendent of the McLean Asylum, lauded the Kirkbride Plan for asylum construction, but asserted that the "age of construction," i.e., of providing for the material care of the mad, was over decades before (Cowles, 1896, p. 380). He then set out the expectations for the new asylum psychiatry and the nature of the madness it was to treat in terms that would have been unfamiliar to Kirkbride and others who were committed to the tactful persuasion of moral architecture and of moral treatment:

> The alienist, as a psychologist, is a general physician who is a student of neurology, and uses its anatomy and physiology; but he does a great deal more, for he must include all the bodily organs. He must study all the functions of nutrition and exercise. He is being aided by the more promising contributions from organic chemistry; and bacteriology, in the wonderful advancement it is bringing to the whole science of medicine, is explaining the analogy between the toxic influences without our bodies and those within them.... Thus it is that psychiatry is shown, more than ever before, to be dependent upon general medicine. The best definition of insanity is that it is a symptom of bodily disease; in its initial, acute and curable forms it is a condition due to nutritional changes until consequent damage accrues to the nervous system and the mental organ itself [p. 376].

Cowles' remarks signaled the emergence of a new scientific psychiatry. This new psychiatry would forge often uneasy partnerships with up-and-coming mental health professions, especially clinical psychology and psychiatric social work (Grob, 1985). It would also encourage experimentation with electrical shocks, tonsillectomies, bowel resections, appendectomies, ovariotomies, teeth extractions, thyroid extract injections, malarial and other types of fever inductions, seizure productions, psychotropic drugs, and brain surgeries (Scull, 1994); and it would be practiced in asylums that were many times larger and more bureaucratically complex than the proponents of the Kirkbride Plan and moral treatment could ever have imagined.

Out of Sight/Out of Mind

The Kirkbride era of asylum design, management and moral treatment effectively ended by the turn of the century. Over the next fifty years and through half a dozen name changes—from lunatic asylums, to insane asylums, to state hospitals, to mental institutions, to mental hospitals, to psychiatric hospitals—asylums would earn a public reputation as bleak and hopeless places. Much of that reputation can be attributed to their increasing custodial care function over those decades. Between 1903 and 1950, the number of patients in state asylums increased from 150,000 to 490,000, i.e., from 1.86 to 3.26 per 1,000 of the population (Grob, 1983; Kramer, 1953). This remarkable surge in patients overwhelmed asylum facilities and resources, and effectively shifted their shared goal from cure to custodial care.

What accounts for this significant increase? During the early decades of the 20th century a noteworthy proportion of the increase was due to the transfer of the mad inmates in poorhouses, almshouses or workhouses, as they variously were known, to state asylums in response to the State Care Act of 1890. As undifferentiated welfare institutions, poorhouses always had housed an assortment of dependent persons, including the mad (Grob, 1983). The Huntington County Almshouse in rural Indiana, for instance, lodged eighteen inmates; the range of the dependency of thirteen of them, named and indecorously described, is evident from a local newspaper article:

> We know of no subject that would be so generally interesting to the people of this county as that describing the condition of the institution which is maintained at their expense for the care of the poor and unfortunate who are without homes, and by reason of age and decrepitude, or incurable mental aberration, unable to provide for themselves.... The number of pauper inmates, at this period, is eighteen, of whom we present below some statistical information:
>
> Adeline Cook, a young woman of 18 years ... slightly idiotic, has been an inmate for five years. Adeline holds the post of honor in the institution. That is, she is head cook and chief waitress, a peafowl was ever prouder of its gay plumage than is she of her exalted position. From the savory odors of the kitchen and the nature of her affection—she hasn't a care in the world, and is ten times happier than a big sunflower—she is becoming inordinately fat. Adeline is quite a help, and her services could not well be dispensed with.
>
> Annie Mason, a cleanly and intelligent-looking child of eight years ... has been on the farm six years. She is, also, of considerable help in the kitchen and dining room. A modest little girl that some respectable and kind family should have the caring of.
>
> Margaret Ferber, a young woman of infirm mind; about twenty-three years of age; went to the farm to lie in.... Margaret ... enjoys her *otium sine dignitate* [ease without dignity] as if she were the mistress of an East Indian nabob.
>
> Hester Fletcher, a sprightly, gossipy, and rather prepossessing woman of about twenty-seven years of age ... has been an inmate eight months. She has two children—one a boy three years old; the other a girl, age [?] months. She went to the farm to lie in, and insists that her two children have the same father, which is not altogether improbable, yet considerably mixed.
>
> Morris Lynch, a native of county Kerry, Ireland; sixty-nine years old; has been on and off the farm six years.
>
> Joseph Trovinger ... sixty years of age, and five on the farm; earns all he gets from the county.
>
> Solomon Kast, twenty-seven years of age; blind; has been at the farm two years.
>
> Joseph Nedrow, 71 years of age; ... three years an inmate of the asylum.
>
> Daniel Ellers, of unsound mind; age supposed to be about seventy years; an inmate since last July.

Tommy Karns ... eighty six years old, and five years an inmate; a native of county Clare, Ireland, and twelve years a citizen of the United States.

Jonas Hartsel ... an inmate four years; seventy-three years of age.

Willie Jackson, 3½ years old; born on the farm.... The superintendent is anxious to find a good home for this bright and intelligent little fellow.

Annie Ward, about thirty years of age, hopelessly insane; an inmate since last August last; perfectly harmless, and has not been heard to utter a word.... Her alienation is of a remarkable type. The wild, vacant stare, and utterly woebegone expression of countenance, excite both fear and pity. When, after considerable effort, she can be made to fix her eyes upon the visitor, and to comprehend that there is a human object before her, her lips move as if she were expressing something to which the vocal powers refuse sound. This is a most pitiable case ["County Alms-House," 1871, p. 1].

As states began adopting responsibility for dependent residents, and as political and public resistance to outdoor relief, i.e., the provision of food, money and shelter outside of an institutional environment, remained obdurate, local and county officials began closing down poorhouses and transferring their mad inmates to extant state asylums or to new asylums purpose-built for their reception. It is estimated that on any given day in 1904 there were in excess of 8,000 mad poorhouse inmates across the country; by 1923 the transfer to state asylums had reduced the number to 2,000, most of whom subsequently were transferred as well (Grob, 1983, p. 181).

It was not only mad poorhouse inmates who were relocated to state asylums. Seizing the opportunity to take advantage of the increasing state control over dependency, local and county officials redefined senility in psychiatric terms and also transferred elderly poorhouse inmates to state asylums. Although national figures are not available, a survey of individual states reveals the impact of this transfer. In New York, for example, 18 percent of all first admissions to state asylums in 1920 were for psychosis due to senility or cerebral arteriosclerosis; by 1940 that figure had almost doubled (Grob, 1983, p. 182). Even as late as 1960, long after the last poorhouse had been shut down, state asylums across the country were still taking on the function of old-age homes, in part because of the paucity of alternative facilities for the care of the aged, as this Associated Press investigative report reveals:

One of the profound tragedies of America's mental hospital system is that thousands upon thousands of old folks are being dumped into psychiatric wards along with the chronic insane. In ward after ward at three huge mental institutions, I saw gentle, mild-mannered old people—apparently quite normal except for minor eccentricities—sitting in meek resignation among babbling schizophrenics and brooding manic depressives. Many of them are simply old, with no place else to go, no family willing to give them shelter and care for their simple needs. Some of them had a mild stroke or their minds are confused by the effects of senility. But do they belong in a mental institution?... Many old people are now being classified as psychotic who actually need nothing more than attention to their physical needs, their food, cleanliness, and so on. They will cause nobody much trouble, so they can be cared for quite easily in a facility other than a state hospital [Greene, 1960, p. 12].

The commitment of neurosyphilitics to state asylums also contributed to the significant increase in the asylum population. Caused by the spirochetal bacterium *Treponema pallidum* syphilis is a sexually transmitted disease that reached epidemic proportions before penicillin was commercially produced for its treatment in the 1940s. Approximately 15–20 percent of untreated syphilitics develop neurosyphilis, the tertiary stage of the disease. While neurosyphilis can take several different forms, it was the most common type known as general paresis that resulted in the mood disturbances, personality changes, progressive dementia and, in some cases, hallucinations and delusions that resembled other types of debilitating madness.

Given the incapacitating nature of the disease, and the stigma of having it, there was little that families could, or would, do to care for neurosyphilitic relatives, and because general hospitals lacked separate facilities for their care, they usually were committed to state asylums. It was not unusual, in fact, for syphilitics to voluntarily commit themselves since many asylums offered a course of treatment that could arrest the steady progression of the disease. At the Kalamazoo State Asylum in Michigan, as an example, mercury and bismuth were administered to syphilitic patients, as was the "magic bullet" of Salvarsan, an arsenical compound that checked the advance of the disease in as many as 90 percent of the patients. When it later was discovered that *Treponema pallidum* could be killed by high temperatures, syphilitic patients were placed in the Burdick Cabinet, a box into which hot moist air was infused, injected with malarial blood to cause high fevers and then given a rigorous course of chemotherapy, or injected with typhoid fever vaccine to induce fevers up to 106 degrees (Decker, 2008).

It is estimated that the number of first admissions to state asylums for syphilis rose from less than 1 percent at the turn of the century to more than 20 percent by mid-century (Grob, 1983). While it is true that the development of diagnostic tests, such as the Wasserman and the Lange Colloidal Gold tests, allowed asylum physicians to differentially diagnose syphilis and therefore increase its reporting, it is unlikely that the significant increase in syphilitic patients was only a reporting artifact. Rather, epidemic syphilis had increased the risk of madness during the first half of the 20th century and, in the absence of alternatives and with the promise of treatment, state asylums had become the preferred institutions for the care of syphilitics.

They also became the institutions of choice for persons whose madness was the result of any one of a number of different somatic or neurological disorders, such as pellagra, a niacin deficiency that causes dementia and was common among the southern poor who subsisted on a staple diet of corn; Huntington's chorea, a degenerative neurological disorder that results in bizarre movements, memory loss and dementia; brain tumors that can produce changes in mood, personality and memory; epilepsy, a chronic neurological disorder that, depending upon its type, causes seizures, or involuntary changes in sensation, awareness, or behavior; as well as alcoholism and drug addiction. Approximately 33 percent of all first admissions to state asylums in 1922 for psychosis, i.e., a loss of contact with reality, were of a recognized somatic or neurological origin; by 1940, that figure had risen to 42 percent (Grob, 1983, p. 190).

The Great Debate

The transfer of mad inmates from poorhouses to state asylums, and the commitment of the elderly and the chronically ill to their custodial care were only the proximate causes of the dramatic increase in the asylum population. The question, therefore, remains: did madness increase during the first half of the 20th century? The question continues to engender vigorous debate. At one extreme are those who argue that madness is a "disease of civilization" and that it indeed had increased with the risks inherent in a rapidly modernizing society. At the other extreme are those who contend that madness per se had not escalated much, but the definition of it most certainly had.

Risk Perspective

The risk perspective interprets the significant increase in the state asylum census as the result of changing patterns of psychiatric disease. The perspective posits that the alterations in lifestyles, habits, diets and customs that rapid social change necessitated, as well as the increased risks social change created, had increased madness during the first half of the 20th century.

The escalating incidence of schizophrenia illustrates this point. Although the term "schizophrenia" was not coined until 1908, the thought disturbances, hallucinations and delusions that are among its symptoms have been described in medical treatises dating back to antiquity (Turner, 1992). The risk perspective proposes that it was a "slow epidemic" of schizophrenia that swelled the state asylum patient population (Hare, 1983, p. 451). From an epidemiological perspective, though, the origin of this slow epidemic, i.e., the determinative interplay between nature and nurture, remains a matter of scientific inquiry which ranges over these, among other, categories (Fuller & Miller, 2001; Green, 2003; Susser, Cannon, & Jones, 2002):

- *Social Causes:* poverty, urbanicity, migration, immigration, racism, inequality, social isolation; high "hazard ratios," i.e., indicators of socioeconomic position that include single-parent households, low socioeconomic status, unemployment, rental accommodations and receipt of welfare benefits.

- *Genetic Causes:* flaws in brain-related genes; spontaneous genetic mutations in the sperm of older fathers; epigenetic imprinting; maternal-fetal HLA-B genotype match.

- *Prenatal Causes:* exposure to influenza, Rubella, lead or cats that carry the *Toxoplasma gondii* parasite; genital/reproductive infections, including sexually transmitted diseases; maternal/fetal Rh blood incompatibility; second trimester exposure to analgesics; excess body weight; Celiac disease; folic acid deficiency; exposure to x-ray radiation; pregnancy, obstetrical delivery and perinatal complications such as preeclampsia, hypoxia and low birth weight.

- *Childhood Causes:* vaccinations; maltreatment; head injuries; exposure to X-ray radiation; exposure to cats that carry the *Toxoplasma gondii* parasite; vitamin D deficiency; abuse of cannabis/marijuana.

- *Lifestyle Causes:* increased dietary consumption of wheat gluten, alcohol, and glycoalkaloid; contact with organophosphate toxins and infectious agents; exposure to life stressors such as bereavement, unemployment, and divorce; substance abuse.

Sociological Perspective

The sociological perspective provides an alternative interpretation. It refutes the notion that the dramatic increase in state asylum patients during the first half of the 20th century was due to an epidemic of madness caused by modernizing forces, and argues instead that the increase was the result of the definition of madness being inflated by modernizing forces.

This perspective is predicated on the assumption that the growing capitalist market economy created an urgency to distinguish between those who could contribute their labor from those who could not. Asylums were handy and culturally acceptable institutions for the reception of unproductive individuals. Because the definition of madness is, and always has been, protean, i.e., expanding and contracting in response to cultural forces, asylums have never identified their target population, thus a whole variety of unproductive individuals—from the mad, the poor, the homeless, the senile, the physically and the developmentally disabled, the aged, the syphilitic, the alcoholic, the drug addicted, the seizure disordered, the neurologically impaired, to the eccentric, defiant and non-conforming—were committed to their custody, thus swelling the asylum population during the first half of the 20th century and creating the illusion that madness had increased (Scull, 1989; Sutton, 1991). Further perspectives on this position propose that the elastic definition of madness caught in its net individuals who

> experience *severe problem of living* that involve difficulties with family, friends, and employers. Many also experience life under conditions of extensive deprivation, both economic and emotional.... They begin life, therefore, as victims of a system of inequality of resources and life chances that places them at the bottom of society with little prospect for improvement.... Commitment to a mental hospital has less to do with having a disease called "mental illness" than with being without sufficient resources to deal with problems that are experienced by many people, most of whom do not become mental patients. Mental illness is therefore best understood as a social process than as a medical one [Perrucci, 1974, pp. 161–162].

Hiding behind the public façade of benevolence, according to the sociological perspective, is the true purpose of state asylums: social control. To that end, and just like other "total institutions" (Goffman, 1961) such as prisons and jails, the very existence of state asylums, let alone their endurance over time, is dependent upon their willingness to identify, categorize and sanction an otherwise unwieldy portion of the population. Thus the dramatic increase in the number of asylum patients during the first half of the 20th century cannot be attributed to an increase in madness per se, but to an ever expanding notion of what madness is, and a concomitantly expanding receptivity of state asylums to uncritically commit society's castoffs.

Common Ground

The risk and the sociological perspectives are irreconcilable, and thus leave unanswered the question as to whether madness significantly increased between 1900 and 1950. The opposing perspectives, however, find common ground on one point: the upsurge of such a wide variety of differently ill and disordered patients not only exceeded the capacities of state asylums, lengthened the average institutional stay by years, and raised the mortality rate (Grob, 1983; Malzberg, 1934), but it also fundamentally transformed state asylums into bleak and hopeless custodial institutions. "Treatment can scarcely be said to exist for the majority [of state asylum patients]," said Kenneth Appel, in his 1953 presidential address to the American Psychiatric Society. "It is mostly care and custody. Mass methods, herding and regimentation are the rule.... Individual treatment, personal contact, and conference, the keystone of modern psychiatric treatment ... are absent except in the rarest instances.... Rehabilitation and follow-up care to prevent recurrence of over

100,000 readmissions each year are about nil.... Out of sight is out of mind"
(Appel, 1954, p. 3).

Asylums in Sight, Asylum Insights

It was the stretch between two national traumatic events—the Great
Depression and World II—that not only brought asylums back into sight, but
that generated insights into the human costs of fiscal neglect, institutional
decline, and mass custodial care of the mad. While flashes of insight came
from the occasional scandal or tragedy, it was from an unexpected source
that the first of a series of devastating exposés revealed the snake pits that
so many state asylums had become.

In 1930 the American Psychiatric Association, concerned about stan-
dardizing education and training in psychiatry as well as in increasing the
prestige of the specialty, considered requiring of its practitioners a board
certification in psychiatry. Because any specialty board would be overseen
by the American Medical Association, it was that organization that ordered
its own Council on Medical Education and Hospitals to conduct a thorough
investigation of all asylums as a step towards developing an official policy
on the psychiatric care of the institutionalized mad. Over the strenuous objec-
tions of the American Psychiatric Association, which considered asylums and
mad patients their own "sacred territory," the responsibility of carrying out
that investigation was given to John Maurice Grimes, a young physician with
no psychiatric training.

In an ambitious attempt to collect data, Grimes and three colleagues visited a total of 353 asylums, in every state in the nation, with the notable
exception of Massachusetts, which had refused to participate in the fact-
finding mission. Data not only were collected from observations made during the visits of Dr. Grimes and his colleagues, but also from detailed
questionnaires returned to them by 75 percent of the state asylum directors.
Submitted in 1933 to the American Medical Association's Council on Medical Education and Hospitals, Grimes' preliminary report looked behind the
handsome facades of state asylums, with their park-like grounds, "rustic
bridges, pavilions, walks, baseball diamonds, miniature golf links, and tennis
and croquet courts" (Grimes, 1934, xiv) to reveal the overcrowding that had
mad patients sleeping in hallways, dining rooms and even two to a bed.
Grimes pointed to the oppressive atmosphere created by locked wards, barred
windows, inadequate diets, and attendants who acted more like prison guards
than minders. State asylums, he concluded, served no other purpose than to

confine those whom society had neglected or rejected; as such, their function was more legal than it was medical.

Grimes' preliminary report was heavily edited before it was presented to the delegates at the annual meeting of the American Medical Association. The revised report, made bland and descriptive by the editing, was accepted by the delegates and filed, but because Grimes was then summarily fired, he never had the opportunity to submit a final report. The American Medical Association showed no further interest in the investigation.

As furious as he was certain that the report had been quashed by prominent psychiatrists who, in doing so, "ignored an opportunity to plead the case of America's most neglected and most helpless group of hospital patients" (Grimes, 1934, p. viii), Grimes self-published a book-length version of what would have been his final report. In it, he called for a wave of reform that would bring about a policy of deinstitutionalization, the development of a parole system under medical supervision, the expansion of acute services at state asylums, reform in the care of chronic patients, and the cultivation of a strong working relationship between state asylums and community hospitals.

Although Grimes' book was ignored by both the American Medical Association and the American Psychiatric Association, and was received with little real interest by the public, his insight into state asylums was keen and his calls for reform prescient. A new generation of investigators, free from internecine forces and armed with cameras, would take up Grimes' mission immediately after World War II, and would find much more receptive audiences.

The Conchie Connection

During World War II, approximately 3,000 conscientious objectors were assigned alternative service as ward attendants in state asylums. The job of ward attendant was as low in pay as it was in prestige, but it offered the conchies, as they often were referred to, unprecedented access to the back wards, dayrooms and treatment rooms of 56 state asylums across the country. The majority of the conchies were Quakers, Mennonites, Brethren and other religious dissenters; the remainder refused to fight on the basis of philosophical, political or ethical principles. Quite regardless of whether they were religious or secular objectors, the conchies were appalled by the overcrowding, abuse and neglect of the mad patients they encountered in the state asylums.

Determined to rectify the problem, they established a clearinghouse for information on nonviolent strategies for handling mad patients, descriptions of innovative asylum programs, reports on asylum conditions, and eyewitness accounts of patient abuse and staff incompetence. These were disseminated through the conchie network via a monthly periodical, the *Attendant,* that proved such popular reading that by the end of its first year of publication it could be found in the libraries of every medical school in the country (Sareyan, 1994).

It was the 1400 eyewitness accounts, collected and stored in the clearinghouse, that became invaluable resources for crusading journalists who were eager to spearhead a state asylum reform movement. The first exposés had both local targets and local consequences. In 1943, for example, Walter Lerch of the *Cleveland Press* published a series of articles about the conditions of the Cleveland (Ohio) State Hospital. With headlines such as "Mental Patients Here Beaten and Shackled" (Lerch, 1943, p. 1), and "Food for Mental Patients Revolting" (Lerch, 1943, p. 1), the series sparked such outrage among local leaders and citizens that a grand jury was impaneled to investigate. Their presentment was not just an indictment of the asylum, but also of "Our Governor, the State Legislature, the Welfare Director, the Commissioner of Mental Diseases, the hospital superintendent, the least attendant, and we the people" (cited in Sareyan, 1994, p. 70). Changes were slow in coming, but the series was credited with initiating a reform movement that eventually resulted in a $17 million allocation for the construction of small treatment-intensive hospitals for the treatment of acute cases of madness, the training of personnel, and the modernization of the state's existing asylums.

The conchie affidavits informed a number of other local newspaper exposés as well. In Virginia, for example, the affidavits initiated an investigation into acts of brutality against patients at the Eastern State Hospital that resulted in the resignations of the superintendent and most of his administrative staff (Saeyan, 1994). In Oklahoma, a series of blistering exposés on the state's asylums by fledgling reporter Mike Gorman (1946) led to wide-sweeping reforms and catapulted Gorman into national prominence when he assumed the role of director of the National Committee Against Mental Illness, a Washington publicity and lobbying group.

While the network of conchie ward attendants was pleased with local changes, it was not content with them. It defined the treatment of the mad in state asylums as a national problem, and it needed journalists who could reach a national audience.

Bedlam 1946

One of the journalists who responded to that agenda was Alfred Q. Maisel, a respected reporter and author of several books on military medicine. Maisel wrote searing exposés of two state asylums, Cleveland State Hospital and Philadelphia State Hospital, also known as Byberry. Titled "Bedlam 1946," the expose was published in the popular *Life* magazine; a condensed version was published later in *Reader's Digest*. Replete with disturbing black and white photographs of patients strapped to their beds, wandering aimlessly along dark and dingy hallways, lying naked under wooden benches, and staring hopelessly out of filthy barred windows, the exposé compared state asylums to the Nazi concentration camps with which the horrified post World War II public only recently had become aware. Maisel spared the readers few details:

> Through public neglect and legislative penny-pinching, state after state has allowed its institutions for the care and cure of the mentally sick to degenerate into little more than concentration camps on the Belsen pattern.
>
> Court and grand-jury records document scores of deaths of patients following beatings by attendants. Hundreds of instances of abuse, falling just short of manslaughter, are similarly documented. Yet beatings and murders are hardly the most significant of the indignities we have heaped upon most of the 400,000 guiltless patient-prisoners of over 180 state metal institutions.
>
> We feed thousands a starvation diet, often dragged further below the low-budget standard by the withdrawal of the best food for the staff dining rooms. We jam-pack men, women and sometimes even children into hundred-year-old firetraps in wards so crowded that the floors cannot be seen between the rickety cots, while thousands more sleep on ticks, on blankets, or on the bare floors. We give them little and shoddy clothing at best. Hundreds ... spend twenty-four hours a day in stark and filthy nakedness. Those who are well enough to work slave away in many institutions for 12 hours a day, often without a day's rest for years on end.... Thousands spend their days—often for weeks at a stretch—locked in devices euphemistically called "restraints": thick leather handcuffs, great canvas camisoles, "muffs," "mitts," wristlets, locks and straps and restraining sheets. Hundreds are confined in "lodges"—bare bedless, rooms reeking with filth and feces—by day lit only through half-inch holes through steel-plated windows, by night merely black tombs in which the cries of the insane echo unheard from the peeling plaster of the walls. Worst of all, for these wards of society we provide physicians, nurses and attendants in numbers far below even the minimum standards set by state rules. Institutions that would be seriously unmanned even if not overcrowded find themselves swamped with 30 percent, 50 percent and even 100 percent more patients than they were built to hold. These are not wartime conditions but have existed for decades. Restraints, seclusion and constant drugging of patients become essential in wards where one attendant must herd as many as 400 mentally deranged charges.... The vast majority of our state institutions are dreary, dilapidated excuses for hospitals, costly monuments to the states' betrayal of the duty they have assumed to their most helpless wards [pp. 102–103].

Maisel ends the long litany of horrors in his photo-essay on a strikingly optimistic note. He insists that if the public were informed of the conditions of state asylums, and if civic and political leaders would spearhead schemes to improve the treatment of the mad, "the people of any state will rally ... to put an end to concentration camps that masquerade as hospitals and to make cure rather than incarceration the goal of mental institutions" (p. 118). In fact, Maisel would prove to be prescient in that remark. But reforms took time, money and a public and political will that had to be constantly prodded with fresh exposés.

Shame of the States

One of those exposés was by Albert Deutsch. Although autodidactic, he already had earned an enviable reputation as a scholar on the history of the treatment of the mentally ill when he began a several year investigation into state asylums just after World War II. His findings were published in dozens of caustic reports, illustrated with shocking black and white photographs in *PM* the leftist New York City daily newspaper for which he was a columnist. But the culmination of Deutsch's investigations was the 1948 publication of his book, *The Shame of the States*. Widely read and well received, the book documents his visits to forty state asylums in twelve states, often at the invitation of their superintendents, who, impatient for reform, had become increasingly aware that "only an enlightened public opinion could move state administrators and legislators to take the measures needed to stave off complete institutional collapse" (p. 12).

And "complete institutional collapse" indeed seemed imminent in Deutsch's investigation. In 1946 there were more than 500,000 patients in the nation's 190 state asylums, and despite an annual expenditure of more than $200,000,000 to operate them, state asylums were woefully inadequate to the task of caring for, let alone treating, the mad (p. 31). Not a single state asylum in the country even met the minimum standards of staffing and daily per capita expenditure on patients set out by the American Psychiatric Association. What Deutsch found, which he documented in detail and illustrated with photographs, was a system wracked by overcrowding, understaffing, underfunding, and a disturbing indifference to the care of its mad patients, as these vignettes illustrate:

- As I passed through some of Byberry's [Philadelphia State Hospital for Mental Disease] wards, I was reminded of the pictures of the Nazi concentration camps at Belsen and Buchenwald. I entered buildings swarming with naked humans herded like cattle and treated with less concern, pervaded by a fetid odor so heavy, so nauseating, that the stench seemed to have an almost physical existence of its own. I saw hundreds of patients living under leaking roofs, surrounded by moldy, decaying walls, and sprawling on rotting floors for want of seats or benches [pp. 40–41].

- The average doctor at Manhattan State Hospital ... spends about half his time in paper work—checking patients in and out, making up requisition orders in triplicate and quadruplicate, counting clothes, bed sheets, towels, writing up case reports, accident reports, death certificates, etc. On Sundays only one physician was left in charge of a total of 2500 patients spread over 32 wards. Besides the impossible task of making rounds on all these wards, the Sunday physician had to see visitors and attend to necessary paper work.... The official state regulation requires that each hospital patient has to be interviewed at least twice a year. Yet Manhattan State doctors told of many cases that had not been interviewed for as long as five years [pp. 67–68].

- Dr. Y. Henry Yarbrough, superintendent of the Milledgeville [Georgia] hospital was frank, expressing "shame" at the "scandalous" conditions we encountered, especially in the colored sections. At one point, he turned to me with bitterness and said: "I've never seen anything worse than this anywhere, and you can quote me on that. I've tried hard and mostly in vain for many years to work up enough interest in the legislature and the public to get decent care and modern medical treatment for these poor people. But what can you expect with an appropriation of 76 cents a day per patient? Why, we spend more than that for prisoners" [pp. 90–91].

- No American city would knowingly tolerate, without shame, Ward 7 [of Bellevue Psychiatric Hospital in New York City] ... the "disturbed" women's ward.... You passed through the dimly lit, dingy, ill-ventilated ward swarming with sick humans, many strapped in camisoles or straightjackets, others rendered immovable in their beds by restraining sheets. Cots and beds jammed the narrow corridor where most of the patients spent 24 hours a day, awake and sleeping. Ward N7 has a normal capacity of 22 patients. There were 60 patients milling about when I visited it. On some days 70 patients were herded into that ward, built to hold only 22! Try to imagine this Bedlam on a hot summer's night. Talk about the Black Hole of Calcutta! [pp. 103–104].

Just as Maisel had done two years before, Deutsch ended *The Shame of the States* on an unexpectedly optimistic note. He sets out his vision of an Ideal State Hospital. It would be located near a large city and would have a capacity of 1,000 patients, most of whom would be admitted on a voluntary basis. Its potential for prompt and proper curative treatment would be recognized by the legislature that would fund it on a par with a good general hospital. The Ideal State Hospital would be affiliated with a nearby medical school, and its staff would be encouraged to engage in scientific research and keep current with recent developments in the specialties of psychiatry and neurology. It would operate as a therapeutic community and employees and patients alike would know that "the hospital is intended for the sick, not the sick for the hospital" (p. 184). To transform the Ideal State Hospital from a vision to a reality, Deutsch called on readers to confront their own ignorance and prejudices about madness by acquainting themselves with the conditions of their state asylums, joining organized advocacy groups, and supporting reform initiatives spearheaded by civic and political leaders. Is the Ideal State Hospital a dream? he asks his readers. "Yes. Unrealized at present? Yes. Unattainable? No," he emphatically asserts, "decidedly no" (p. 187).

Reforms

The clarion calls for state asylum reform by local investigators, Maisel and Deutsch increasingly were heeded by the public and politicians alike. Significant changes began occurring on a state level. In Pennsylvania, for example, where the conchie network had been particularly active, the governor engaged in brick and mortar reform by allocating $80 million for the construction of new asylums; in California the legislature allocated $18 million for upgrading state asylum buildings. In Minnesota, as another example, Governor Luther Youngdahl established a Citizens Mental Health Committee to spearhead reform initiatives that included abolishing the use of restraints on mad patients; increasing staff recruitment, training and support; and increasing research into the treatment and cure of madness (Freeman, 1949). On Halloween Eve 1949, Governor Youngdahl lit a bonfire that signified his state's break with the superstitions of the past, proclaiming:

> It is just a little more than 250 years ago since the mentally ill and other citizens were burned at the stake at Salem as witches. Tonight—Hallowe'en Eve—we employ the stake and fire for another purpose—to destroy the straightjackets, shackles, and manacles which were our heritage from the Salem era. As little as eighteen months ago all but one of our mental hospitals used mechanical restraints. Today, most are restraint free. The bonfire which I am lighting tonight consists of 359 straightjackets, 196 cuffs, 91 straps, and 25 canvas mittens.... By this action we say more than that we have liberated patients from barbarous devices.... By this action we have liberated ourselves from witchcraft—that by taking mechanical restraints from the patients, we are taking off intellectual restraints from ourselves.... By this action we say to patients that we will not rest until every possible thing is done to help them get well and return to their families ["Statement," 1949].

In a 1951 follow-up to his exposé, Maisel estimated that two-thirds of the nation's state asylums had made significant progress in upgrading their buildings and in improving their treatment of mad patients (Maisel, 1951).

Deinstitutionalization

Although the overcrowding of state asylums was always a matter of concern to both the conscientious objectors and the investigative journalists who took up their cause, deinstitutionalization was not entertained as a viable solution to the problem. Yet during the heyday of the deinstitutionalization movement between 1955 and 1982, as the result of release, transfer and more rigorous involuntary commitment criteria, the number of patients in state asylums decreased from 559,000 to 120,000 (Salinsky & Loftus, 2007, p. 6).

Sources of Deinstitutionalization

The systematic decline in the patient census would seem to suggest a policy-driven response to the awful conditions of state asylums. It was, instead, the result of an assortment of initiatives, laws, developments and reactions occurring over several decades that, at best, were only loosely connected to each other, and that only coincidentally brought about what later came to be known as deinstitutionalization. Although the path to reducing the state asylum patient census was long and meandering, there are significant markers along the way.

Federal Initiatives

In 1949 the Council of State Governments met to discuss the custody and care of the chronically mentally ill. Data collected via surveys before the meeting showed not only the extent of overcrowding in state asylums across the country, but also expressed the considered opinion of survey respondents that a significant number of institutionalized patients would better benefit from community care (Council of State Governments, 1950). The council's call for psychiatric research aimed at finding the causes of madness and determining the least restrictive treatment approaches was echoed several years later by state governors in their annual meeting. Their recommendation that community-based psychiatric programs not only could staunch the steady flow of the mad into state asylums, but could also siphon mad patients from the state asylums and back into the community received considerable publicity that kept both the crisis and the solution of what later would be called deinstitutionalization in public and political awareness.

Although the horrifying exposés by Maisel and Deutsch, among others, had prompted the American Psychiatric Association to urge its members to become vigorous advocates for increased funding of state asylums, by the late 1950s the professional organization was recommending they be shut down completely and their patients be transferred to the psychiatric wards of general hospitals, community-based day treatment programs, veterans hospitals, private mental hospitals and nursing homes (Solomon, 1958). That recommendation was repeated by the federally funded Joint Commission on Mental Illness and Health whose eclectic membership included not only psychiatrists, but also neurologists, whose historic opposition to state hospitals was well known, and representatives from lay organizations, including the American Legion. After a five year study of state asylums, the commission concluded that the number of chronically mentally ill returned to the community could more than double if federal funds were made available to create a network of community-based treatment programs (Ewalt, 1979).

The commission's conclusions were supported by President John F. Kennedy, who appointed a government interdepartmental task force to develop strategies for implementing them. Early in 1963, the president submitted the task force's proposal to Congress, and in a press conference statement reminded both elected officials and the public at large about the urgent need for reform:

> I have sent to Congress today a series of proposals to help fight mental illness....
> [O]ur chief aim is to get people out of State custodial institutions and back into
> their communities and homes, without hardship or danger.... If we launch a broad,
> new mental health program now, it will be possible within a decade or two to
> reduce the number of patients now under custodial care by 50 percent or more....
> We, as a nation, have neglected too long the mentally ill.... It affects all of us and
> it affects us as a country. I am hopeful that beginning today this country will
> move with a great national effort in this field so vital to the welfare of our citi-
> zens [Woolley & Peters, 2008].

In late 1963 Congress passed the proposals in the form of the Community Mental Health Centers Act. Under its aegis, federal matching-formula funds were provided for the development of community mental health centers that would provide short-term inpatient care for acutely mad persons, outpatient counseling services, partial hospitalization programs, twenty-four hour emergency services, and community education and consultation programs. With what was confidently believed to be a strong community-based service net soon in place, the rate of deinstitutionalization accelerated (Morrissey, 1989).

Two other federal programs accelerated that rate. Medicaid, enacted in 1965, picked up much of the tab for nursing home care. Since states paid no more than one-half of Medicaid costs, there was a strong financial incentive to transfer the aged mad from state asylums to nursing and personal care homes. In just a few years, in fact, this shift in the locus of institutional custodial care nearly doubled the number of mad residents in nursing homes across the country (Scull, 1984, p. 149). Enacted in 1972, Supplemental Security Income (SSI) guaranteed welfare payments to those released from state asylums into the community. Unlike Medicaid, however, SSI was entirely federally funded, thus increasing the financial incentive for deinstitutionalization. Because many of those ex-patients could neither return to their families nor care for themselves, and because SSI required no aftercare, this federal initiative also, ironically, was a disincentive to the development of community-based housing. Thus a significant number of the deinstitutionalized mad found themselves homeless, or living in welfare hotels and board-and-care homes of varying quality that had sprung up to accommodate them or, sometimes, in jails and prisons (Scull, 1984).

Pharmaceutical Justification

The development of powerful psychotropic medications, especially chlorpromazine, both hurried along the process of deinstitutionalization and justified it. Touted as a miracle drug, chlorpromazine was introduced in the United States in 1954 and aggressively marketed under the trade name Thorazine by the pharmaceutical company Smith-Kline and French, which had purchased the rights from the Laboratoires Rhône-Poulenc in France. Although it was promoted as a treatment for the disorganized thinking and behavior of the severely mad, Thorazine was not immediately appealing to most state asylum psychiatrists, who not only were resistant to drug therapies, but were also unimpressed with the results of the published French drug trials.

To increase the marketability of the drug, Smith-Kline and French put together a Thorazine task force to market the drug and sponsored two American studies. In the first study, Thorazine was administered over several months to 142 noninstitutionalized psychiatric patients and was found to "reduce severe anxiety, diminish phobias and obsessions, reverse or modify a paranoid psychosis, quiet mania or extremely agitated patients, and change the hostile, agitated, senile patient into a quiet, easily managed patient" (Winkelman, 1954, p. 18). In the second study, Thorazine was administered to thirty institutionalized patients diagnosed with schizophrenia. The results were not just favorable, but given the intractability of this severe type of madness, they were nothing short of astonishing. Patients who had been institutionalized for years and whose madness had never been ameliorated by any therapeutic interventions not only became symptom-free but also were able to rationally and insightfully discuss their madness with psychiatrists (Kinross-Wright, 1955).

Armed with these findings, the Thorazine task force redoubled its marketing efforts, promoting the drug to psychiatrists as well as in the news media. The promise that Thorazine held for transforming madness into rationality was treated with such enthusiasm that one participant in a promotional conference sponsored by Smith-Kline and French commented that its "atmosphere approached that of a revivalist meeting" (Bowes, 1956, p. 530). A short eight months after introducing the drug to the American market, and in the absence of any scientific investigations into its long-term effect, Smith-Kline and French boasted that Thorazine was being administered to more than two million institutionalized and noninstitutionalized mental patients (Swazey, 1974).

While it would be an exaggeration, though an oft-repeated one, that Thorazine and other psychotropic drugs like it were solely, or even largely, responsible for emptying state asylums, they certainly justified the deinstitutionalization trend, as well as the community care of those who otherwise would have been institutionalized (Gronfein, 1985). The apparent success of the psychotropic drugs in managing severe madness also had a more subtle consequence: it reinforced a medical model of madness. Psychotropic drugs became the therapeutic intervention of choice, both inside state asylums and in the community-based programs that originally were envisioned as providing a broad range of therapeutic, supportive and rehabilitative services.

Left and Right Ideology

Given the increasing commitment to a medical model of madness, it is ironic that an entirely antithetical model was gaining ground and that it, too, was used to justify deinstitutionalization. A provocative body of European and American scholarly literature, often labeled as "anti-psychiatry," started to emerge on the scene in the early 1960s. Thoroughly resonant with the political tumult, intellectual iconoclasm and concern for civil rights of that decade, the literature variously declares that madness is nothing more than a label, a metaphor for problems of living in an unfair and unjust world, or a perfectly rational adjustment to an irrational society. Psychiatry, to the anti-psychiatrists, is a tool of oppression; psychiatric therapeutics are state-sanctioned methods of torture; state asylums are bastions for social control; the medical model of madness is scientifically worthless and socially harmful (Breggin, 1970; Cooper, 1967, 1978; Foucault, 1965; Goffman, 1961; Laing, 1960, 1967; Scheff, 1966; Szasz, 1970, 1974). The anti-psychiatry canon included the following:

- In the past men created witches: now they creat mental patients [Szasz, 1970, p. xx].
- Madness is the destructuring of the alienated structures of an existence and the restructuring of a less alienated way of being. The less alienated way of being is the more responsible way of being [Cooper, 1978, p. 5].
- Since in the majority of cases of mental illness the underlying illness is unproved, symptomatic behavior has to be discussed in terms that do not involve the assumption of illness [Scheff, 1966, p. 36].
- There is no such "condition" as "schizophrenia," but the label is a social fact and the social fact a political event [Laing, 1967, p. 100].
- Strictly speaking, disease or illness can affect only the body; hence, there can be no mental illness. If there is no mental illness, there can be no hospitalization, treatment, or cure for it [Szasz, 1974, p. 267].

Although particularly appealing to New Left academics, scholars and civil rights activists, the anti-psychiatry movement also attracted support from the opposite end of the political spectrum. While not exactly arguing for an alternative view of madness, far Right groups, such as the John Birch Society, nonetheless endorsed the anti-psychiatry movement's critical stance towards psychiatry, arguing that the specialty is part of a broader communist conspiracy promulgated by Jews. Although the Left and the Right could not be further apart ideologically, both viewed psychiatry as a conspiratorial effort to subvert the rights and the well-being of the masses in order to advance the interests of the few—although, of course, for the Left the "few" were capitalists, for the Right communists. Both also rejected any idea that psychiatry could be reformed, calling instead for its elimination as a specialty (Dain, 1994).

This wide spectrum of political support for anti-psychiatry meant that grassroots groups could easily find justification for involvement in the movement. Individuals who defied the stigma of madness by either publicly identifying themselves as mad or denying they were, joined with ex-patients of asylums to form advocacy groups, such as the Insane Liberation Front, the Mental Patients Liberation Front, and the Network Against Psychiatric Assault. Newsletters, such as the *Madness Network News*, that circulated among them further personalized the politics of anti-psychiatry by publishing personal accounts, poetry and journalistic reports, all from the points of view of those labeled mad. These grassroots groups made slow but steady incursions into public and political life during the 1960s and 1970s. Their members became involved in public fora, legislative hearings, and special commissions on mental health related issues. Believing that the proposed community mental health centers could become self-help collectives and drop-in centers run by ex-patients and even the patients themselves, they became outspoken proponents of deinstitutionalization (Dain, 1994).

The appeal of the anti-psychiatry movement also was reflected in a growing genre of popular literature. While autobiographical and fictional accounts of madness and institutionalization have been around as long as asylums, this version of the genre was more psychologized and highly politicized. It acted as a site for the disputes of the anti-psychiatry movement by raising questions about the meaning of madness, the nature of reality, the differences between diagnostic label and personal identity, the production of psychiatric knowledge, the nature and necessity of therapeutic intervention and of institutional control (Benzinger, 1969; Dawson, 1961; Kesey, 1962; Stefan, 1965; Plath, 1963). Also broaching those questions were popular films, such as *The Snake Pit* (1948), *Fear Strikes Out* (1957), *David and Lisa* (1962), and the disturbing documentary *The Titicut Follies* (1967) filmed at Bridgewater State Hospital in Massachusetts and initially banned from public screening by that state's supreme court.

In its cumulative impact, the anti-psychiatry movement influenced professional, political and public discourse about madness and its treatment and control. It did not specifically endorse deinstitutionalization, nor did it single-handedly cause it; but anti-psychiatry certainly legitimated deinstitutionalization as a social policy.

Appraising Deinstitutionalization

In his 1963 address, President Kennedy had set a measurable target of a 50 percent reduction in the state asylum population by 1983; by that date, that target had been well surpassed. The state asylum population had decreased nearly 80 percent.

So the question must be asked: Was deinstitutionalization a good thing? The answer depends, in part, on how the neologism "deinstitutionalization" is defined in the first place. As a *policy*, most, but certainly not all, agree that it was. Situated within a larger civil rights initiative, the policy was predicated upon the principle that even the most chronically mad of patients have fundamental human rights that are ignored and violated in the state asylum system. The policy of deinstitutionalization — in that it released mad patients from a system that was "bankrupt beyond remedy" (Robitscher, 1973, p. 146) into community settings where their rights became a kind of social capital on which patients could trade to live dignified and productive lives — was progressive and humane (Cameron, 1978; Clarke, 1979; Grob, 1987). It also was scientifically enlightened. In that the policy broke with the past, it represented a significant shift in both the understanding of madness and its treatment (Rochefort, 1984).

There are those who take issue with this view of the policy of deinstitutionalization, arguing that it was predicated on a naïve idealism, rather than on pragmatic social science inquiries. Rather than considering whether institutionalized mad patients would even benefit from community care, let alone what kind of community care would benefit them, the policy was based on the untested assumption that community care always is better than institutional care (Lerman, 1985; Mechanic, 1989; Reich, 1973). Other dissenters are more critical. They argue that the idealism of the policy masks a more cynical intent — to shift custodial care of the mad from the state to the community in order to relieve states of the onerous financial burden of caring for the mad, even while ensuring that a profitable "trade in lunacy" (Parry-Jones, 1972) will be carried out by a wide range of differently qualified mental health workers and by the owners and managers of nursing homes, group homes, welfare hotels, and board-and-care homes (Rose, 1979; Scull, 1984).

If deinstitutionalization is defined as a *practice* most, but certainly not all, agree that it was, in the end, not a good thing. By 1983, the target date President Kennedy had set for a 50 percent reduction in the state asylum patient population, the political winds had shifted in the direction of reducing government programs. More than 700 community mental health centers already had been funded, but they represented less than half of the centers needed to accommodate the return of state asylum patients to the community (Dowell & Carlo, 1989; Foley & Sharfstein, 1983); and federal funds for meeting that need had been severely reduced. In addition, the accelerated reviews of people on the federal disability rolls conducted during the administration of President Ronald Reagan left hundreds of thousands of former state asylum patients without income until Congress was able to revise the rules, thus restoring the benefit.

As they were decanted into the community, former state asylum patients often ended up living in facilities in hostile communities poorly prepared for their release; in badly managed and rundown welfare hotels or board-and-care homes; on the streets and; sometimes in jails and prisons (Isaac & Armat, 1990; Lamb, 1984; Mechanic & Rochefort, 1990; Rubin, 2007; Wyatt & DeRenzo, 1986). Critics of the practice of deinstitutionalization find the sentiment of then Democratic senator Daniel Moynihan of New York particularly prescient. He wrote the following in a 1989 letter to the *New York Times*: "What if, on the occasion of the bill signing in 1963, someone had said to President Kennedy: 'Wait. Before you sign the bill you should know that we are not going to build anything like the number of community centers we will need.... The hospitals will empty out, but there will be no place for the patients to be cared for in their communities. A quarter-century hence the streets ... will be filled with homeless, deranged people'? Would he not have put down his pen?" (Moynihan, 1989, p. A16).

Even the most ardent of defenders of the practice of deinstitutionalization acknowledge that it has not lived up to expectations. They contend, however, that the practice has stimulated the development of successful community programs that provide not only shelter for former patients of state asylums, but also training in life and job skills; improvements in assessing the service needs of the chronically mad and in adjusting state policy to redress those needs; and necessary changes to close the service gaps in Medicaid and Supplemental Security Income. The defenders also argue that while some deinstitutionalized patients indeed have been released into substandard community care and have been exploited by ruthless entrepreneurs in the "lunacy trade," most have not (Clarke, 1979; Lamb, 1991; Mossman, 1997; Okin, 1985).

Aftermath

The deinstitutionalization movement, the concomitant establishment of more rigorous involuntary commitment criteria, and occasional state budget cuts combined to reduce the state asylum patient census from 559,000 in 1955 to less than 39,000 in 2006. As a consequence, many state asylums across the country were shut down. They were left abandoned, razed to the ground or, in a few instances and as the result of successful activism by historic preservationists, restored to their original glory and transformed into business offices, condominiums, and upscale shops and restaurants.

What of the newly mad? Some do find their way into surviving state asylums, but in these days the largest number of available beds for their care has shifted across service providers. The acutely and chronically mad now are more likely to be cared for in private psychiatric hospitals, veterans' hospitals, psychiatric units in general hospitals, residential treatment centers, and in nonspecialized medical/surgical wards in general hospitals (Salinsky & Loftus, 2007) than they are in the once handsome buildings whose moral architecture Thomas Kirkbride had envisioned as providing refuge and succor.

5

Asylum Patients

Though this is madness, yet there is method in't. —Hamlet

ALTHOUGH THEIR HISTORY WOULD seem to prove otherwise, asylums always have been idealized as places where "the mad would settle as the cat to her corner, giving up their visions and mad ways" (Holmes, 2001, p. 71). Of course, how the mad really "settle" in to asylum life is more fickle and certainly less cozy than either the historic idealization or the poetic metaphor would ever allow.

Moral Career of a Mental Patient

From the founding of the first asylums in the United States through the present day, a growing collection of asylum memoirs has developed into its own fascinating genre. Part exposé, part captivity tale, part political manifesto, part redemption narrative, the genre gives voice to those who in so many ways would otherwise have been "politically and socially erased" (Thomson, 2000, p. 348). The experiences of these authors vary widely, even *wildly* if only because of their differing personal circumstances, historical contexts, geographical locations and institutional altercations, but those experiences can be distilled into a common element—a "moral career," i.e., a sense of self and of identity that is slowly and steadily shaped as much as by the experiences of institutionalization itself as by any real or imputed madness (Goffman, 1961).

125

Going In

A moral career begins with entry into an asylum. But an explanation of how that precarious first step is taken, whether voluntarily or involuntarily, and why, often serves as the prelude to a published asylum memoir.

Voluntary Admission

Some asylum memoirists launch their moral careers as mental patients by voluntarily admitting themselves into asylums. Although many do so with a certain confidence that they would be the better for it, this decision is rarely ever easily made. It often is the result of a reluctant acknowledgment that behavior, thoughts or emotions (or all three) are no longer within the bounds of prevailing cultural norms, cannot be brought into line, and cannot be concealed from others.

The reasons for concealment, or at the very least attempts at concealment, vary. For Lisa Wiley (1955), who had been hectored by voices since she was a child, the fear of embarrassing her mother, who already had been deeply humiliated by her husband's institutionalization years before, was reason enough to hide her madness until she could do so no longer. When the voices demanded she renounce God and her strict religious upbringing, she voluntarily admitted herself to an asylum, incurring the very reaction of her mother that she had feared most:

> The interview with the psychiatrist was very disappointing, for I knew more than he did—so I thought. It was very brief. I told him what I had done and about the voices that I thought I heard at the first of the summer and that there was no hope for me. I told him I had been dead for a good many weeks. He didn't take me very seriously for he was used to people telling him all kinds of things like that.... When I went home I didn't tell mother about the interview, for she would not have permitted me to go to such a place. However, a few days letter a letter came from this hospital saying that the doctors felt I needed a period of hospitalization to get over my nervous condition, and Mother would have to go through some red tape to get me in. Mother was very cross at me. She said, "See what you've done." It disgraced her terribly [p. 49].

Tracy Thompson's (1995) motivation for concealing her madness was both personal and professional. She had just landed a position as a journalist for the prestigious *Washington Post* newspaper. But "the Beast," as she referred to the depression she had experienced for years, overwhelmed her with a force "like a psychic freight train of roaring despair" (p. 4), leaving her filled with self-doubt, anxious, withdrawn and suicidal. She voluntarily admitted herself into a hospital psychiatry ward, no longer willing, or able, to conceal her madness from herself or others:

For years, in fact, I had devoted considerable energy and enterprise to the act of appearing normal. My zeal in imitating health grew in direct proportion to my shame at knowing there was something wrong with me, even though I lacked a clear idea of what that was. This way of living had worked, in the short term. I had fooled a lot of people for a long time; I had even, at times, fooled myself. But the costs had been steep: years of tumbling in and out of depressive episodes, years of unhealthy dependence on the approval of others, of ravenous emotional neediness which had threatened to consume every man I had tried to get close to, and which had doomed me to long periods of loneliness and isolation. So the real culprit, then, was me [p. 178].

The struggle to maintain some self-integrity, even while conceding that the self is the "real culprit," is evident in Elyn Saks' (2007) memoir, *The Center Cannot Hold*. Now an esteemed professor of law, Saks has battled madness all of her life and has had several periods of institutionalization. She recollects the one time, while a student at Oxford University, that she voluntarily admitted herself, and did it in her own time and on her own terms in order to preserve what little dignity she had left:

That night was terrible. I lay awake in a pool of sweat, unable to sleep, a mantra running through my head: I am a piece of shit and I deserve to die. I am a piece of shit and I deserve to die. I am a piece of shit and I deserve to die. Time stopped. By the middle of the night, I was convinced day would never come again. The thoughts of death were all around me; I realized then that they had begun during the summer before, like a small trickle in a creek where I had gone wading. Since then, the water had been steadily rising. Now it was deep and fast and slowly threatening to cover my head. The next morning, haggard and beaten, I managed to call the hospital and reach Dr. Smythe. "I'm so glad you called," she said. "Please, come in as soon as you can." That lonely night had served its purpose. No one had locked me up against my will. I entered the hospital voluntarily. If I were going to be a mental patient, at least it would be by my choice and no one else's [pp. 61–62].

To Jim Curran, the difference between being admitted, as opposed to committed, to an asylum was just as crucial for self-dignity as it was for Saks. Curran had "sat and watched with a kind of helpless horror" (Kraugh, 1937, p. 33) as his business and then his personal life collapsed around him during the Great Depression. When he confides in his physician that he fears he is having a nervous breakdown, the physician replies that there is no such thing—that, in fact, what he is suffering from is "emotional depression," and "the encouraging angle of that is that depressive patients practically always get well (p. 115). Heartened by that prognosis, Curran admitted himself into the St. Charles State Hospital: "I had come of my own volition. Now there's a technicality. It meant that I was rated as 'admitted,' not 'committed.' It meant that I did not lose my citizenship" (p. 116).

For the voluntary patient who, in some ways, has capitulated to madness, entrance into the asylum sometimes brings relief, as it did for Curran, who found it a welcome respite from the stresses and strains of daily life: "In the Hospital they gave us a place to rest; they gave us every help to build us up physically; they planned our lives for us so that we would not be forced to make plans for ourselves while our minds were befuddled; and they relieved us of the necessity for adjusting ourselves in a world that could not understand us while our illness was upon us" (pp. 152–153). It did also for Susanna Kaysen (1993), who, as a depressed and suicidal 18-year-old, admitted herself into the "parallel universe" (p. 5) of McLean Hospital in Belmont, Massachusetts, for what she believed would be a short rest. Over what became the many months of her stay in McLean, one of the oldest asylums in the nation, she began to reluctantly acknowledge the safe haven it provided her:

> For many of us, the hospital was as much a refuge as it was a prison. Although we were cut off from the world and all the trouble we enjoyed stirring up out there, we were also cut off from the demands and expectations that had driven us crazy. What could be expected of us now that we were stowed away in a loony bin?... In a strange way we were free. We'd reached the end of the line. We had nothing more to lose. Our privacy, our liberty, our dignity: All of this was gone and we were stripped down to the bare bones of our selves. Naked, we needed protection, and the hospital protected us. Of course, the hospital had stripped us naked in the first place—but that just underscored its obligation to shelter us [p. 94].

The madness certainly does not disappear upon voluntary admission, but the security, perhaps even the invisibility, that comes with isolation from the demands of the larger world, coupled with the promise of a cure, often brings the kind of "salvation" that Pulitzer Prize winning novelist William Styron describes in his "memoir of madness," *Darkness Visible* (1990):

> [T]he hospital was my salvation, and it is something of a paradox that in this austere place with its locked and wired doors and desolate green hallways—ambulances screeching night and day ten floors below—I found the repose, the assuagement of the tempest in my brain.... This is partly because of sequestration, of safety, of being removed to a world in which the urge to pick up a knife and plunge it into one's own breast disappears in the newfound knowledge, quickly apparent even to the depressive's fuzzy brain, that the knife with which he is attempting to cut his dreadful Swiss steak is bendable plastic. But the hospital also offers the mild, oddly gratifying trauma of sudden stabilization—a transfer out of the too familiar surroundings of home, where all is anxiety and discord, into an orderly and benign detention where one's only duty is to try to get well. For me the real healers were seclusion and time [pp. 68–69].

Nevertheless, for others voluntary admission is a surrender to madness and a humiliating blow to self-dignity. This was the case for Russell Hampton (1975). As a 29-year-old doctoral candidate, he had reason to be proud of his considerable educational achievement; but he could no longer cope with the waves of panic and despair that made studying, eating and sleeping impossible. He voluntarily admitted himself into an asylum:

> Entering a compound for mental patients is a most frightening experience. It doesn't matter whether it's a private hospital, a public one, or a ward of a general hospital. The implication is inescapable: "I am unable to care for myself. Without help I cannot survive." Precisely the status of an infant. For some persons this may not constitute a particular insult to the self; for me it was unforgettable and almost intolerable. Still, it had come to that.... I was helpless. A deeper wound to the self-integrity I could not imagine [pp. 15–16].

Tracy Thompson (1995) had the same experience. She had only just signed the admission paperwork when she demanded that she be allowed to leave. It was not just the experience of entering an asylum that changed her mind—although that was frightening enough—but the fear that in doing so, even voluntarily, she had irreparably altered the way others would perceive and understand her:

> At that moment, the horror of mental illness became physical. It meant *this:* an existence in ugly space, the mind fettered by drab walls and wire mesh, life reduced to childish makework and getting by. The room I stood in was a vivid expression of the psychic isolation which had dogged my life, which I had fled from and waged war against with long hours at the office, the never satisfied craving for tokens of achievement and acceptance, a frenetic social life. Now, despite all my efforts, I was about to be locked up with a bunch of drug addicts and schizophrenics, the pathetic flotsam of life, people whose hands shook and who pissed on themselves and who made valentines to lovers they would never have. Was this what people saw when they looked at me? Was this what they would see from now on? [pp. 153–154].

Involuntary Commitment

The circumstances and methods by which persons may be deprived of their liberty and involuntarily committed to asylums have been subjects of considerable disagreement and debate since the very founding of asylums. In 1885, for example, a survey of procedures found that in some states persons could be involuntarily committed upon court order but without a medical certificate; in others, with a medical certificate but without a court order; in others still, only as a result of a judicial hearing before a judge; and in the remaining few, only as a result of a jury trial (Wines, 1885). A century later, involuntary commitment procedures had been formalized and somewhat standardized across the country, and as a result of advocacy, activism and civil suits, more procedural protections have been built in to guard the substantive rights of those who are subject to the proceedings (Miller, 1987).

What has not changed from one century to the next, however, is the role of the "circuit of agents and agencies" (Goffman, 1961) that make involuntary commitment possible. Variously comprising family and friends, physicians and mental health professionals, police officers and judges, courts and sometimes general hospitals and even jails, the agents and agencies confer with each other and leave their subjects as distant third parties to their own fate. The bitterness and sense of betrayal that are the inevitable consequence of the activities of this circuit are persistent themes in asylum memoirs.

Take Elizabeth Packard as an example. In 1860 her husband, a prominent Calvinist minister, committed her to the Illinois State Hospital for the Insane because he believed that her public disagreement with him on theological matters was evidence of madness. He was under no burden to prove his charge; under state law, a married woman could be held indefinitely in an asylum solely on the authority of her husband and with the agreement of the asylum superintendent. Packard (1866) describes her first confrontation with the circuit of agents who brought her against her will to the asylum where she would spend the next three years:

> I was kidnapped in the following manner—Early on the morning of the 18th of June, 1860, as I arose from my bed, preparing to take my morning bath, I saw my husband approaching my door with two physicians, both members of his church and of our Bible-class—and a stranger gentleman, Sheriff Burgess. Fearing exposure, I hastily locked my door, and proceeded with the greatest dispatch to dress myself. But before I had hardly commenced, my husband forced an entrance into my room through the window with an axe! And I, for shelter and protection against an exposure in a state of almost entire nudity, sprang into bed, just in time to receive my unexpected guests. The trio approached my bed, and each doctor felt my pulse, and without asking a single question both pronounced me insane. This was the only medical examination I had. This was the only trial of *any kind* that I was allowed to have, to prove the charge of insanity brought against me by my husband. I had no chance of *self defense* whatever [p. 43].

Packard was released from the state asylum as incurably mad; upon her return home, she was imprisoned in a boarded up room by her husband. She managed to toss a letter out of a window to a friend, who brought it to the attention of a local judge. He issued a writ of habeas corpus and scheduled a trial a trial to determine if Packard indeed was mad. The trial began on January 12, 1864, and after six days of testimony, including Packard's impassioned defense of her religious beliefs that had so antagonized her husband, the jury took just seven minutes to reach its verdict. Packard was declared sane.

The verdict prompted Packard to begin publishing parts of the journal she had secretly kept while in the asylum. In doing so, she exposed the mortifying experiences of being institutionalized: the curtailment of freedom, the communal living under constant watch and criticism, the powerlessness in the face of an echelon of sometimes indifferent, sometimes abusive ward attendants, staff and physicians, all of which made it difficult, if not impossible to maintain self-integrity, let alone the sanity Packard avers she had never lost in the first place. She also vigorously lobbied for changes in the law. As a result of her efforts, the state of Illinois passed the "Bill for the Protection of Personal Liberty" that required a trial by jury before any person could be involuntarily committed to a state asylum; and a number of states adopted what came to be known as "Packard Laws" that limited the power of asylum superintendents to admit and detain patients, especially women who had no legal standing independent of their husbands (Sapinsley, 1991).

19th Century Protofeminist Asylum Memoirs

Agnew, A. (1886). *From under a cloud or, personal reminiscences of insanity.*

Brinckle, A.P. (1887). "Life among the Insane."

Davis, P. (1885). *Two years and three months in the New York Lunatic Asylum at Utica.*

Lathrop, C.C. (1890). *A secret institution.*

Lunt, A. (1871). *Behind bars.*

Metcalf, A. (1876). *Lunatic asylums: and how I became an inmate of one.*

Russell, A.B. (1898). *A plea for the insane by friends of the living dead.*

Smith, L. (1879). *Behind the scene; or, life in an insane asylum.*

Stone, E. (1842). *A sketch of the life of Elizabeth T. Stone, and of her persecution.*

Trautman, R., & Trautman, B. (1892). *Wisconsin's shame. Insane asylums or the American Bastile!*

Packard's memoir of her asylum years can be read as a protofeminist manifesto. She rails not only against the inequality of women in general and their inferior status in marriage in particular, but also against the patriarchal arrangements of the asylum and the authoritarianism of its male superintendent. When, as an example, she asked Andrew McFarland, the superintendent of the Illinois State Hospital for the Insane, for "liberty to support myself, as other wives do who cannot live with their husbands," his reply spoke volumes about the status of women in 19th century society: "The only right course for you is to return to your husband, and do as a true woman should do; to be to him a true and loving wife, as you promised to be by your marriage vow, unto death, and until you do consent to do so, there is no prospect of getting out of this place!" (Packard, 1866, p. 134).

"No prospect of getting out of this place" looms as a threat, regardless of gender, age, or historical context to those who are involuntarily committed, thus intensifying their sense of betrayal by the circuit of agents and agencies. Frances Farmer (1972) vividly describes how a quarrel with her mother resulted in her involuntary commitment when her mother called asylum officials to take her away:

I began to scream and tried to run, but they grabbed me.... I screamed every filthy word I knew at my mother, and then, in consuming fear, I was reduced to begging her to help me. "Oh God, Mama, don't do this. Don't do this to me." She turned away, and as the men pulled me to my feet, I began to kick. They each grabbed a leg, jerked off my shoes and clamped heavy leather manacles around my ankles, trussing me up like a pig on the slaughter line. A thick roll of gauze, stuffed in my mouth, silenced me.... And so it was, on May 22, 1945, at 3:25 in the afternoon, I was delivered bound and gagged to the state asylum like a dog gone mad [p. 32].

Farmer never believed herself mad, so her incredulity at being involuntarily committed was only compounded by her fear that she would never be able to prove herself sane. As a devotee of the anti-psychiatry movement, Mark Vonnegut (1975) had little reason to believe that there is even anything called "schizophrenia," let alone that he had it. But when his attempts to reframe his madness in spiritual terms—"the Sanskrit word for crazy means touched by the gods" (p. 60)—left him raving and delusional, his famous father, author Kurt Vonnegut, and a friend—Mark's "allies"—drove him to an asylum and involuntarily committed him: "Why are they taking me to a hospital? Why is everything whizzing by faster and faster? Why am I holding my breath? Why do I feel so strange? Whatever is wrong is very strange. This will doubtless be a very strange hospital.... When [my allies] left me, when three guys dressed in white started walking me down that long hall, half holding me up, half holding me down, I understood. I had gone too far" (p. 112).

Like Vonnegut, who eventually recovered and became a pediatrician, Margaret Aikens McGarr (1953) did not consider herself mad, although she had no particular ideological reason for rejecting the label. Her sense of betrayal, therefore, is not just a consequence of having been involuntarily committed to Manteno State Hospital in Illinois, but also of having to face the fact that family and friends had not understood her in the way that she had understood herself:

I had been torn from my home, my loved ones—and borne away to an "institution." The worst that could happen to me, it seemed then, had happened.... Yes, there I was—there I stood, looking sheepishly about me. I was shorn of the dignity of clothing—*my* clothing, which was being snatched from me and hastily tabulated on a record sheet by the white-clad attendants of this "Psychopathic Hospital" where I had been taken by people I had every reason to trust. People who, supposedly, meant only the best for me; wanted me cured of what was troubling me so that I could be speedily returned to them and normal society in a perfectly normal, natural state—mentally. But I could not believe then that I was not right. I was as sane as any of them; perhaps a little high-strung; my nerves a bit frayed, due to overwork and too much to think about. But certainly far, far from being mentally unbalanced. It had all come so suddenly—this taking me away, bringing me here. What did it all mean? As I stood there I had strange, uneasy feelings that I was being betrayed—especially when the person who brought me here had suddenly left me. I felt so alone—entirely deserted [p. 2].

Mindy Lewis (2002) was just shy of 16 years old when her mother dragged her to the Department of Child and Welfare Services, and then to the family court, begging the sympathetic judge to do something about her truancy, marijuana smoking and incorrigibility. The judge ordered she be involuntarily committed to a New York psychiatric facility. Lewis' feeling of having been betrayed quickly transformed into anger when the charges against her were reiterated by her parents at the intake conference: "The intake conference was almost more than I could bear, everyone talking about me as if I weren't there. My stepfather showed up and spouted his bullshit. And my mother—so charming, so innocent, with her heels and make-up. What a hypocrite! She tried kissing me good-bye, but I walked away" (p. 5).

Whether they walk away, are carried away or are dragged away, the involuntarily committed often have been handed off from agent to agent, agency to agency, each with a distinct agenda and each, by words and actions, expediting their transition from the civilian to the mental patient role, from free life to asylum life. For Seymour Krim (1961), author and elder statesperson of the Beat Generation literary movement, once that transition had taken place, he was not only officially labeled mad, but also was perceived as always having been mad. Involuntarily committed to a "private laughing academy" in New York after "the thousand unacknowledged human (not literary) pressures in my being exploded" (p. 114), all of the considerable successes in his civilian life were ignored, and he was retrospectively reconstructed as a kind of congenital madman, far "beyond reasoning with, [to be] treated like a child; not brutally, but efficiently, firmly and patronizingly. In the eyes of this enclosed world I had relinquished my rights as an adult human being" (p. 114).

A Digression on the Circuit of Agents

Some asylum memoirists have more than enough reason to feel betrayed by family and friends. They were tricked, manipulated, or lied to and about. Never visited or communicated with, their involuntary commitment was tantamount to abandonment. For those who returned home, whether released as incurable, as was the custom in the 19th century, or as stabilized or even cured, family and social relations often had been irreparably altered for the worse.

But the rather recent emergence of another subgenre of asylum literature, this one best described as creative nonfiction by kin and kith, reveals that families and friends often worry incessantly about the well-being of those who have been institutionalized and agonize over the role they played as agents in that process. The origin of this subgenre can be traced to the 19th century, not so much in the published memoirs or voluminous family histories that were so popular in that era, since the stigma of madness would have rendered such revelations unseemly, as in the often misspelled and grammatically incorrect notes scribbled on the back of postcards and sent to asylum superintendents for responses, such as these sent to Henry Hurd, superintendent of the Eastern Michigan Asylum in Pontiac (Bogdan Collection, 2008; used with permission):

AUGUST 1880

Dear Sir,

Please is my wife any better since you last wrote me. Please ask her if she would like to see me or her sisters. Please give me her answers in her own words.
    yours truly in haste

DECEMBER 1880

Dear Dr.

We are thinking of sending Mrs. L a Christmas box with little remembrances from each of us. Do you approve of it?
Is there any danger of her getting too much excited over it.
An early reply will oblige yours truly

JULY 1881

Dr Hurd,

I have this day sent a letter containing picture to Mrs. L. As I was her most intimate girl friend please let me know how she receives it and if she recognizes the face. I take much interest in her and sincerely hope you can benefit and help her.
    Respectfully,

JULY 25, 1881

Mr. H.M. Hurd we received your letter of July 13th with pleasure we were glad to hear that our Daughter had so improved in health of body and mind we would be pleased to hear from you again we are quite ancious to have her come home as soon as it will be safe and best for her we have just got through our wheat harvest
    We remain yours with respect

JULY 31, 1882

Dear Sir,

Your letter of July 6th received in due time. I am very much greeved all the time to hear that my dear Husband does not gain in the least and to see that he can not write me one line, does he say anything about me or his little Daughter, does he refur to his delusions very often and does he get angry when he talks about them, do you think he will ever get any better by staying whare he is and do you think it would be posable for me to live with him if I should have him brought home please answer this week and oblige
    yours very truly

These days, the same worries and concerns can be read in popular creative non-fiction, a subgenre of asylum literature in which the tools of fiction are used to tell a detailed, richly characterized, dramatic and often suspenseful story of the author's interactions with, and on behalf of, a mad family member or friend. The pseudonymous Sarah Lorenz (1963), for example, describes the frustrating years she and her husband spent trying to help their son, whose madness created chaos in every part of their, and his, lives. Their worries did not cease when they finally and reluctantly institutionalized him. They watched while one type of therapeutic procedure after another failed to bring him any relief, endured the blame that staff placed on them for causing his madness, and nearly depleted their savings in paying for his care.

With two young children to care for after he committed his wife to an asylum, Alton Brea (1968) was left to wonder about all of the signs of her madness he had missed during their years together. In retrospect, he saw many, and was humiliated by the thought that others had seen what he had not. In the context of the asylum, her madness was unmistakable to him, and his regular visits left him so emotionally exhausted that he could no longer care for their children. After months of institutionalization his wife was released as cured, and they worked to restore their marriage and their family life. Even though Brea ends his memoir with a detailed, although admittedly amateurish, psychological analysis of his wife that locates the cause of her madness in both her genetics and her upbringing by her authoritarian and emotionally distant parents, he still questions his decision to commit her, illogically wondering if he could have made the madness, which he himself diagnosed as originating in both nature and nurture, somehow disappear by being a better husband.

The theme of what could have been, or what should have been, runs deeply through this subgenre of asylum literature. With his brother having spent most of his adult life in one asylum or another, Jay Neugeboren (2003) wonders what went wrong, and what it would take to restore the easy sociability and quick wit he remembered his brother having when they were children. Since the steady parade of mental health professionals who interacted with his brother inside and outside of the asylums either had wildly contradictory answers to his questions or none at all, he is left to imagine what it must be like to be his brother, and what must be done to protect his best interests. Like many memoirists, Neugeboren finds himself in a quandary when he advocates for his brother: "[I]f I complained too much, or confronted [his] health care workers with their inadequacies, or sent off the long letters I often composed in my head (to *The New York Times* to hospital and state officials, to doctors, etc.), I feared they would only take out their resentment of me on [my brother]—that they would (as had happened before) simply talk with me less, care for [him] less, and/or ship him off to a ward where he would receive even less attention (and more drugs) than he was now receiving" (pp. 12–13). After years of worry, and of advocacy that was sometimes successful but more often not, Neugeboren once again had to commit his brother to yet another asylum. For the first time in his memory, "there are no tears in my eyes. Nor do I find myself cursing the hospital, or [my brother's] therapists, or life, or the universe. I feel, simply, very sad, and enormously tired" (p. 299).

Jonathan Aurthur (2002) also writes about the exhaustion of taking care of his son Charley who, at the age of twenty-three, committed suicide after numerous periods of institutionalization and numerous diagnoses. The first time a psychiatrist recommended he commit his son, Aurthur was as appalled as he was resistant, his mind quickly conjuring up images of "Nazi nurses and electroshock and lobotomies" (p. 4). But months later, and after dealing with one crisis after another, the "feeling of burn-out and exhaustion, the desperate wish to have somebody else, *anybody* else, responsible" (p. 239) consumed him, and he signed the papers that committed his son to what would be the first in a series of asylums that, from time to time, would take over his care.

Michael Greenberg (2008) was reluctant to do the same for his adolescent daughter, whose madness sometimes left him feeling that he was "in the presence of a rare force of nature, such as a blizzard or flood; destructive, but in its own way astounding too" (p. 4). He stares at the X where he is to sign his name on the consent form and realizes that to do so is not only to turn his daughter into a mental patient, but also to subject her to an asylum regime that would, by both necessity and intention, blunt her astonishing uniqueness. He signs the form, goes to the asylum every day and stays, even when he is not allowed for some reason to see her; wracked with guilt, he considers revoking his consent. "Then what?" he muses. "We have no isolation room [at home], no training, no sedatives or meds.... The blunt weight of the fact stops me cold; we need this place" (p. 46).

Adaptation Alignments

Since their founding, asylums have evolved from "total institutions" (Goffman, 1961) which segregate their inpatients from larger society and formally administer all aspects of their lives, to more open institutions that allow some freedom of activity both inside and outside of the asylums' grounds. Regardless of type, however, asylum life requires adaptation. And while inpatients may be very innovative, trying out different coping and adjustment behaviors throughout their moral careers, several types of adaptation alignments appear regularly in asylum memoirs.

Role Distancing

Whether voluntarily admitted or involuntarily committed, new inpatients often do not want to be seen or known as mad, or at least *as* mad as the other institutionalized patients. Thus, they may engage in role-distancing by vigorously denying they are mad, withdrawing, avoiding interactions as much as possible, or even offering fabricated accounts of who they are and why they have been institutionalized.

For Elizabeth Packard and other 19th century women who saw themselves as victims of duplicitous husbands and asylum superintendents, role-distancing is evident not only in their strenuous assertions, given at every opportunity, that they are not mad, but in their advocacy of their fellow patients whom they believed were indeed mad. Keeping a wide and somewhat condescending distance between self and others, Packard (1866) explains her mission while she was institutionalized in the Illinois State Hospital for the Insane: "[B]y the omnipotent power of God's grace, I was inspired with moral courage sufficient to espouse the cause of the oppressed and the defenceless, even at the risk of becoming one of their number by doing so.... And like Queen Esther, I felt willing to cast my lot with these despised captives, if necessary, to be their deliver" (p. 87).

Like Packard, Lydia Smith (1879) had been involuntarily committed by her husband, who had abducted her from their home and brought her to a private asylum in New York; she later was transferred to the Kalamazoo Asylum in Michigan, where she remained for four years. Smith knew she was ill; she frequently was too exhausted to care for her children, and too nervous to be a good wife to her husband. But she never thought she was mad. Her asylum memoir, therefore, is a study in role-distancing as she continually perambulates the line she believes distinguishes self from others, and sanity from madness. In the preface to her asylum memoir, she writes:

> It is the author's design to call attention to this subject for the benefit of the really insane who are not capable of self-defence, and who have none of the privileges granted to a free and enlightened people, but are cruelly and inhumanely treated under the ordinary asylum usage. It is the author's design also to call attention to another class who are more favorably situated, if possible, than the really insane. It is those who are not insane, and who are kept confined in an asylum either from a false belief in regard to their condition, on the part of their friends, or from a desire on their part to keep them thus confined [p. ii].

Journalist Norah Vincent (2008), in contrast, knew she was mad. Depressed, suicidal, she admitted herself into a locked psychiatric ward of a general hospital. Despite the torpor of her emotional state, she realized the "loony bin" was fertile ground for her as a writer, so over the ensuing year she admitted herself into three different asylums, not as a pseudopatient, but as a writer desperate to regain her emotional stability. In her asylum memoir, Vincent walks a much more precarious line than Smith had more than a century before—a line not just between sanity and madness, self and other, but between observer and participant:

> I thought I was in a foreign country, and so, like every frisky tourist whose intrusiveness is pure entitlement, I was curious about the customs—and possessive, too. I wanted these people to myself, to make them mine in word and sentence. These were living dolls, characters ready made for me, shuffling by in all their google-eyed magnitude and efflorescent distress. I liked them that way, and I watched. I did not accept then that I was one of them, and that the foreign country, the theater, the rabbit hole, was not out there but in my head [pp. 4–5].

Role-distancing also takes place in more subtle interactional ways. When a new patient is introduced to the other patients in the asylum ward or wing, an opportunity arises to etch out some role distance by comparing self to others. For instance, when Jack Kerkhoff (1952), a successful reporter and editor, admitted himself to Traverse City State Hospital in Michigan after attempting suicide, he was introduced to the others in his wing by a patient who confided he was being pursued by mobsters and was only using the asylum as a temporary safe house. The patient then points out each of the men on the ward: the religious maniac, the stroke victim who would be better off dead, the glutton who craved attention as much as he craved food, and the piano player who is "as crazy as a loon" (p. 14). The introductions give Kerkhoff pause: he knows he is mad and that without help he could not fight the urges to take his own life, but he is relieved that he is not *as* mad as his fellow patients. "I'm beginning to feel better already," he tells his companion. "When I look at some of the other patients, I realize that I am not so badly off" (p. 18).

To maintain that same perception, Daphne Scholinski (1997) had to hide one of her diagnoses from the other adolescents on her ward in the asylum. Upon admission she rather liked the idea that she was given multiple diagnoses. "I knew this was a major deal; it was like being a Disciple or a Latin King," she writes, "it was your identity in the hospital" (p. 15). But she was none too pleased that one of those diagnoses was Gender Identity Disorder. So when she and the other adolescents on the ward would sneak to the nurses' station and look up their diagnoses in the *Diagnostic and Statistical Manual of Mental Disorders*, putting them on a crude continuum of "freakiness," she never revealed that particular diagnosis, telling everyone instead that she had a Conduct Disorder, thereby staking a claim for being the least "freaky" of the inpatients on the ward.

Role-distancing, however, also can be breached. For Tracy Thompson (1995), whose introductions to the other patients in the hospital psychiatry ward only assured her she was not mad and did not belong there after all, an encounter with a new patient traversed the distance she maintained between herself and the other patients. This new patient, rail-thin, red-haired and pale-complexioned, had to be tackled to the floor by several attendants after she smashed the telephone into the wall and then attempted to hurl herself through a glass door. This was Thompson's first encounter with "someone who fit the classic description of crazy, the image of *Jane Eyre's* madwoman in the attic" (p. 165), but it was not her florid madness that was so disconcerting to Thompson, rather, it was that she could no longer maintain her role distance: "I was her peer in the eyes of the world. No matter how different I felt myself to be from her, the outside world classified us both, for the moment, as mentally ill. By coming here, [she] had confronted me with this fact. Now I shared her taint, as unmistakable as the smell of poverty, as obvious as the itch of lice" (p. 165).

Intransigence

Whether a total institution or an open one, in every asylum there are rules to be followed, restrictions on freedom to be abided by, staff in authority to be obeyed. For some inpatients, adaptation to the regime of asylum life takes the form of obstinacy, if not rebellion. Their intransigent acts may be done individually or collectively with other inpatients, and can be unruly or not; but they involve such things as working the system to gain resources, job assignments, free time and space; creating or trading in a shadow economy that exchanges items such as cigarettes and food for other material things, privileges or protection; surreptitiously finding ways to have social interactions with outsiders; palming medications; and even attempting escape which, in the lingo of the asylum, is rather romantically referred to as "elopement."

Kate Millett (1990), once damned with faint praise in a *Time* magazine cover story as the "Mao Tse-Tung of Women's Liberation," refuses at first to adjust to the asylum to which she was involuntarily committed by her sister. She spits her medication into the pocket of her blouse when no one is looking. There it was, "safe. Evidence—that I did not even throw it away, only saved it to explain, demonstrate, prove that I was given no choice" (p. 205). She wanders off the grounds, not so much as an attempt to escape as an attempt to recover some of the independence she had lost by being institutionalized.

But like many asylum memoirists, Millett also comes to realize that the mortifying consequences of such intransigent acts far outweigh the fleeting sense of triumph they create. Her ploy with the medication ends when a nurse grabs her, pries open her mouth, and responds to her strident defense of her civil liberties by forcing her to swallow not only the pill she was hiding under her tongue, but also the pills she had been secreting in her pocket. Her meander off the grounds of the asylum is brought to an end by two nurses who trundle her into a car and bring her back to her ward. And like many asylum memoirists, Millett appreciates the quandary such acts of rebellion put inpatients in: in the short term, they may be affirmations of a pre-asylum self; but in the peculiar logic of the asylum, they eventually will be seen as nothing more than confirmations of madness:

> And I am found out. The final laugh. Witch and pretender. A Joan, a heretic. And they have me now. I am in their dungeon and their jail. From this room—if you refuse the skylight and stand your ground, wanting out, wanting the trees outside and the roads—from this room you will go to another. To solitary, then cell after cell, farther and deeper.... This is their punishment, their lesson. Every night I will be tortured thus. And if I resist they will tie me down to inoculate me with this horror, this eight hours of hellfire. Exhausted into the gray light of morning [pp. 221–222].

Mindy Lewis (2002) also learns quickly that intransigence has consequences. While in the asylum she smoked and had sex with other patients, hid razor blades in anticipation of a suicide attempt, saved and traded her medication. Her defiance was quickly interpreted by staff as a deterioration of her mental state and, in a combination of therapeutics and punishment, she was given a sodium amytal injection to calm her and then was confined in the "quiet room" with its spartan furnishings and padded walls.

While rebellion and resistance carry risks, another form of intransigence, no less defiant, rarely does—unless detected. Lydia Smith (1879) was determined to chronicle all of the abuses she and other patients experienced in the Kalamazoo Asylum in Michigan, and to initiate wide-sweeping reforms once she "eloped"—her plan to escape made necessary by her certainty that she would never be released. And so she obeyed the asylum's rules, acted the tightly scripted role of the mad inpatient, and was passively, if not pleasantly, defiant in doing so. Her description of her interaction with a physician reveals the intransigence of this strategy: "I spoke so pleasantly and candidly, and looked so indifferent, as though I thought nothing of the past, so that, with all his skill and penetration, he could not detect the true state of my feelings" (p. 86). She elaborates on this ingratiating strategy:

> I was a prisoner, without the means of defending myself; I possessed no weapons but my hands and my tongue. I knew those two members were useful, but I must be very careful how I use them. I must be discreet, must be wise, not appearing to be so; must feel my way along carefully, and, more than all, must stoop to do things distasteful to me. I must act a part. I must flatter [the physicians'] vanity. I must seem not to remember the past, or only as an insane freak, and think it all a

delusion. I would be cheerful, and even gay, and tell them how much their treatment was helping me, and praise their skill. Every opportunity that presented itself to me I would take advantage of in one way or another, just as the circumstances called for. But above all, I must flatter them [p. 87].

Colonization

After an often unsettled period of adjustment most new inpatients finally tend to settle down into the predictable, if not humdrum, daily routine of asylum life. For some, the routine is a welcome respite from having to cope with a social world they could no longer handle and sometimes could no longer even comprehend.

That was the case for Clifford Beers (1908). A Yale graduate who had just embarked on a career in the insurance business, he finally had been overcome by the lingering fears that he, like his brother before him, was going mad. As a result, he attempted suicide. After a stay in a general hospital and a private sanitarium, he was committed to a private asylum where he "became accustomed to the rather agreeable routine" (p. 49). His comparative content, he writes, "had not been brought about by any decided improvement in health. It was due directly and entirely to an environment more nearly in tune with my ill-tuned mind" (p. 50). For Beers, however, the harmony between mental state and institutional environment turned dissonant; after a peaceful period of settling down, he became violent and was transferred to a state asylum where he remained more than a year before being released as cured.

Jane Doe (1966) settled down quickly. Out of work, out of friends, and out of money, the award-winning scriptwriter and radio broadcaster, who had dropped her first name "Mary" for the ghoulish charm of being known as "Jane Doe," was committed to Estrelita State Hospital in California for "grandiose thinking with paranoid content and delusional systems" (p. 20). Although she refused to label her wildly irresponsible and dangerous attempts to cope with her fast-paced career and maintain her extravagant lifestyle as madness, she quite quickly settled down in Ward 8. For her, the "problems of earning a living were eliminated," and with a roof over her head and three square meals a day, she finally could relax (p. 43).

For others, though, settling down is tantamount to giving in. Actor Frances Farmer (1972), involuntarily committed to Western Washington State Hospital for the Insane for the first of two times in 1944, the dull routine, the terrifying hydrotherapy treatments, and the abuses of asylum life broke what she believed was her free spirit but what others had seen as her most florid symptoms of madness. "I was unnaturally calm at the end of three weeks," she recollects, "for I had been systematically deenergized. All personality was washed away and all that was left was a water-logged robot. I had been tamed" (p. 173).

There is a danger in being tamed, however. Becoming colonized co-opts the sense of self, and can deprive the inpatient of ingenuity and autonomy, both of which are necessary for the successful completion of the therapeutic regime, and for release. That was what Jim Curran realized after he had settled down. He was depressed and suicidal when he admitted himself into an asylum, but he settled down quickly: "I became what is known as 'hospitalized.'... To be hospitalized indicates that a patient is improved, and is becoming well adjusted—i.e., to hospital life" (Krauch, 1937, p. 196). His biographer then goes on to explain that "he becomes so well adjusted that he no longer wishes to leave—at least, not for the present. He keeps putting the idea off to some future day, when perhaps—perhaps he will do something about it. If it isn't too much trouble. But what he really wants to do is to remain within the warmth and safety and security of the hospital. And while he is in this mood, he is not ready or fit to live anywhere else either" (pp. 196–197).

Russell Hampton (1975) had the same experience, as he writes in his asylum memoir: "Now I have a new set of problems to cope with. At this point I was struggling with the hospitalization syndrome. My initiative and what little drive I had left were consumed in becoming a product of the ward routine. The mechanics of bathing, dressing, eating, reporting to the various activities, and ostensibly participating in the group and individual therapy sessions became ends in themselves. To cope with the regime was now my goal" (p. 56).

Conversion

Although asylums always have offered diverse activities, from therapeutic, to social, to recreational, all are carried out under the watchful eye of staff, in the company of like-situated persons, and often on the grounds of the asylum itself. Asylum life does not, and in fact cannot, resemble "real life." Some inpatients adapt to this alien environment by conversion, i.e., by surrendering whatever remains of a personal sense of self and taking on the psychiatric identity of mad persons. More bluntly stated, they become exactly what the asylum expects them to be.

But asylum memoirists often ruminate more on the *process* of conversion—the submission to the demands and expectations of the asylum, and the gradual giving up of a personal sense of self and identity—than on the outcome. Adeline Lunt (1871), as an example, describes how she and other inpatients are "hewn down to the similitude of sticks and stones" by the tedium of asylum routine, "a passive state of being [with] all impulses or natural emotions ... made prostrate to the law of obedience" (p. 225). Margaret Starr (1904), involuntarily committed in a jury trial on the testimony of two physicians who had never even interviewed her, concludes that the "idea, the knowledge, that you are being treated as insane while in a lunatic asylum with only lunatics as associates is unparalleled for cruelty; for it dooms you to be a *nonentity!*" (p. 109).

As a champion of women's right to self-determination, Kate Millett (1990) found herself defeated by asylum life. She muses how the institutional arrangements of the "loony-bin," as she refers to it, co-opted her sense of self and of identity: "Odd how the shape of an institution, its intentions and definition, affects its inmates.... The very purpose of the bin and what all understand by its meaning predicate madness. To remain sane in the bin is to defy its definition" (p. 218). Decades later, Norah Vincent (2008) agrees:

> You adopt the mindset of the place. You become docile, subservient, frightened, dull, unthinking, susceptible to the mysterious self-fulfilling power of the rule. You loathe the tone of your own voice as you mewl and cower to the dingbat shoving you your meds or taking away your pen. You are demeaned by the routine as you regulate your life by mealtimes, loitering in the hall at eight, twelve, and six. You change as you acquiesce rudeness, becoming less, becoming small, a picker, a stealer, a scratching stray licking the hand that defeats it [pp. 41–42].

But the tightly ordered regime of the asylum, its unassailable hierarchy, and its panoptic gaze sometimes are cited by memoirists for helping them finally confront their madness and do what they can to deal with it. That was true for Jane Hillyer (1926). Involuntarily committed after months of battling what she calls "the thing," she finally came to acknowledge her madness when a physician one day does nothing more than call her by name:

> [M]y own name had a magical effect. I had one of those curious experiences in which one sees oneself. I saw what she saw. A human being had turned into a beast; its hair was in a mat over its eyes, its face twisted and marred by rage and pain, the upper part of the body was incased in stiff canvas from which a wrecked negligee hung in limp, faded folds. "Is this Jane Hillyer?" she repeated. I made a swift turn and threw myself face downward upon my bed, Yes, this *thing* was "me," the *thing* that had brought me to my feet in the middle of the night months before with its sinister prophecy had indeed ceased to haunt, and had become incarnate; it had made its spring and landed full and square. "Yes," I answered. "Yes, *this* is 'me'" [p. 83].

While Hillyer had to assimilate madness into her sense of self and of identity before she finally could deal with it, Russell Hampton (1975) had to hold it at abeyance when the routines and contingencies of asylum life finally stripped away all pretences and left him with the realization that he indeed was mad. He came to see "it," as he refers to his madness, as his adversary:

I came to regard the pathology I was experiencing as really not a part of me....
And a struggle began between "it" and "me" for dominance of the person I had
come to know as RH. This tactical change in strategy (not consciously deliberate,
I can assure you) enabled me to use one facet of my character to advantage—
stubbornness. This kind of attitudinal shift then made my personality liability of
stubbornness into an asset. I now felt that I would hold out longer than "it"
could.... As I've said, there was not a sudden burst of psychological insight, no
glorious peak of experience, no sudden cataclysmic freedom. One day I just had
several moments of calmness, of freedom from anxiety and despair.... There were
a few more moments when I dared hope that I would live normally again [pp.
57–58].

Asylum memoirists, then, suggest that as an adaptation alignment, conversion can bring about surrender or struggle. In either case, the inpatients'
senses of self and of identity have been slowly and steadily shaped not just
by their madness, whether real or imputed, but also by the contingencies and
the hazards of asylum life.

A Digression on Pseudopatients

Interestingly, the keenest observations on the moral career of mental
patients are made by pseudopatients, i.e., people feigning madness. They are
in a unique position to appraise the effects of asylum life on their otherwise
stable sense of self and of identity.

In 1887 at the suggestion of the editor of *World*, a New York City newspaper, Nellie Bly, the non de plume of aspiring 23-year-old journalist Ellen
Jane Cochran, admitted herself to New York City's Blackwell's Island in
order to file a "plain and unvarnished" (Bly, 1887, p. 1) narrative on the treatment of mad patients in this notorious asylum. Pretending to be mad by babbling irrationally and wandering around her boardinghouse room all night,
Bly was taken into custody by the police, brought before a sympathetic judge,
examined by a physician who was convinced she was under the influence of
belladonna, the deadly nightshade plant that in small doses acts as a narcotic,
and then taken to Bellevue Hospital, the "third station" (p. 24) on her way
to the asylum. There she was examined by another physician who took her
adamant denial that she was a "woman of the town," a polite euphemism for
prostitute, as evidence of her being "positively demented ... a hopeless case"
of hysteria (p. 29). And from there, finally, she was taken to Blackwell's Island
Asylum where she would spend ten days until friends secured her release.

Bly's recollection of the awful conditions, mistreatment by ward attendants, horrible food, and the pitiable mad patients, some of whom she was
convinced were as sane as she was, was detailed in the series "Ten Days in
a Madhouse" published in *World* and in a book by the same title. Bly was

immediately transformed into the country's most famous "girl stunt reporter" (Lutes, 2002). But it is her resistance to being transformed from a civilian to a mental patient that forms the subtext of her reportage. Throughout her ten days at the asylum, Bly refused to compromise her sense of self as a sane, rational, intelligent person; in fact, it can be argued, she was never *more* sane, rational and intelligent than she was over those ten days (Kroeger, 1994). She spoke out against the abuses she witnessed, lobbied for warmer blankets, advocated on behalf of the silent or silenced mad patients on her ward, and negotiated with ward attendants and physicians. Yet, in the eyes of all who interacted with her, she *was* a mental patient, and ipso facto mad:

> I always made a point of telling the doctors I was sane and asking to be released, but the more I endeavored to assure them of my sanity the more they doubted it.
> "What are you doctors here for?" I asked one, whose name I cannot recall.
> "To take care of the patients and test their sanity," he replied.
> "Very well," I said. "There are sixteen doctors on this island, and excepting two, I have never seen them pay any attention to the patients. How can a doctor judge a woman's sanity by merely bidding her good morning and refusing to hear her pleas for release? Even the sick ones know it is useless to say anything, for the answer will be that it is their imagination."
> "Try every test on me," I have urged others, "and tell me am I sane or insane? Try my pulse, my heart, my eyes; ask me to stretch out my arm, to work my fingers, as [the doctor] did at Bellevue, and then tell me if I am sane." They would not heed me, for they thought I raved [p. 72].

In 1973, Stanford University psychology and law professor David Rosenhan set out to answer the question of whether the salient characteristics that lead to a diagnosis of madness reside in the mental patient or in the context of the asylum. He gathered four men and three women, none of whom had a history of mental illness, to join him as subjects in an intriguing and controversial experiment. Over the ensuing months, the eight pseudopatients were admitted into a dozen different asylums in five different states on the East and West coasts, on the basis of a single symptom: they reported hearing an unfamiliar voice that said "hollow," "thud," and "empty." With the exception of altering identifying demographic information, the pseudopatients truthfully answered all intake questions about their current lives and their childhoods. Seven of them were diagnosed as schizophrenic, one as manic-depressive (bipolar), and each was immediately admitted. Their lengths of institutionalization ranged from seven to fifty-two days, with an average length of nineteen days.

Once admitted, the pseudopatients ceased simulating any symptoms of madness and behaved as they always had. Curiously, their bluff was called by a scattering of other mental patients who recognized they were sane, but

never by the staffs of the asylums to which they were admitted. And Rosenhan suggests a reason why: the pseudopatients had *become* their diagnoses
and, as a consequence of this newly constructed self, everything they did
and said was interpreted through that frame. And so were their early lives.
Rosenhan offers the example of one of the pseudopatients who had had a
close relationship with his mother but a distant one with his father during
childhood; during adolescence and throughout his adulthood, on the other
hand, he grew close to his father, but sought some distance from his mother.
His present relationship with his spouse was warm and close, and except for
an occasional spat, free of discord. He enjoyed a good relationship with his
children and rarely spanked them for misbehavior. Retrospectively reconstructed, however, in light of his diagnosis of schizophrenia, this is how his
history appears in his discharge notes:

> This white 39-year-old male ... manifests a long history of considerable ambiva-
> lence in close relationships, which begins in early childhood. A warm relation-
> ship with his mother cools during his adolescence. A distant relationship with his
> father is described as becoming very intense. Affective stability is absent. His
> attempts to control emotionality with his wife and children are punctuated by
> angry outbursts and, in the case of the children, spankings. And while he says
> that he has several good friends, one senses considerable ambivalence embedded
> in those relationships also [p. 253].

Rosenhan's pseudopatient study prompted sharp criticism from the psychiatric profession for its deceitful methods and inherent biases (Spitzer, 1975,
1976), but its description of how the transformation from civilian to mental
patient is not just a change in role, but also a fundamental change in the way
self and identity are perceived and treated by others has much in common
with accounts in many asylum autobiographies. Unlike many of those autobiographies, though, Rosenhan refuses to accuse asylum staff of being malicious or ignorant in their expediting of that transformation; rather, he
attributes their readiness to label as mad everything the pseudopatients did,
from writing in journals to lining up in the hall for dinner, as a consequence
of the demands and expectations of the asylum environment in which they
worked. "In a more benign environment, one less attached to global diagnosis," he writes, "their behaviors and judgments might have been more benign
and efficient" (p. 258).

As the controversy over the article waned, Harry Lando (1976) reveals
he was the 9th pseudopatient in the Rosenhan study. Diagnosed as schizophrenic, he was admitted to the psychiatric ward of a large public hospital,
where he remained for 19 days. Lando's experiences in the ward were "over-
whelmingly positive" (p. 51) and, he claims, because they contradicted Rosenhan's findings, they were not included in the published study. Lando suggests

that future research should focus less on why staff failed to detect simulated madness, and more on the one experience he did share with the other pseudopatients: "how staff actively misinterpret behaviors that would be viewed as normal within a different context" (p. 52).

As a parenthetical note, psychologist and author Lauren Slater (2004) tried to replicate the Rosenhan study by going to nine hospital emergency rooms with the single complaint that she was hearing a voice saying "thud." Although never committed, she was diagnosed with psychotic depression "almost every visit," and was prescribed a total of 25 anti-psychotics and 60 antidepressants. "It becomes fairly clear to me that medication drives the decisions, and not the other way around," she concludes. "Rosenhan's point that diagnosis does not reside in the person seems to stand" (p. 86). In the face of criticism about her method and conclusions, however, as well as skepticism about the veracity of her account, Slater contends her experiment was not a scientific study and should not be critiqued as one (Slater, 2004, 2005; Lilienfeld, Spitzer, & Miller, 2005; Spitzer, Lilienfeld, & Miller, 2005).

Getting Out

As much as asylums may be needed by both the mad and the family and friends who care about them, most inpatients eventually are released. Those who voluntarily admitted themselves may request release and, unless there are compelling reasons to believe they lack the capacity to make this decision, they will be discharged.

Voluntary admission usually is prompted by an acknowledgment, albeit often a painfully reluctant one, that behavior, thoughts or emotions are out of line and out of control. In the refuge that the asylum then becomes, the restoration of balance, self-management and restraint is what some asylum memoirists, such as William Styron (1990), point to as reason for requesting release: "I began to get well, gradually but steadily. I was amazed to discover that the fantasies of self-destruction all but disappeared within a few days after I checked in, and this again is testimony to the pacifying effect that the hospital can create, its immediate value as a sanctuary where peace can return to the mind" (p. 70).

For others, though, it is less a sense of restoration, let alone cure, that motivates a request for release than a sense of improvement, however incremental. In her asylum memoir, Norah Vincent (2008) discusses how she self-consciously altered her interactions with staff to make her release possible by steering her answers to their questions "progressively toward the lighter side of disaster, going from 'I'm not as bad as I was,' to 'Getting better, I think,' to the unequivocal, 'I'm ready to go now, please'" (p. 90). The physicians signed her release the morning of the tenth day of her voluntary institutionalization, and for the next six hours, tasting freedom, she waited for the paperwork to wend its way through the asylum bureaucracy; "but [I was] anxiety ridden at the prospect of it [freedom] being somehow revoked, or worse, eroded by my paperwork's slow, careless passage through the clogged procedural channels of the hospital bureaucracy" (p. 92).

Once released Vincent ran for blocks, fearing she might be chased by asylum physicians who had changed their minds. When no one came for her, she slowed to a walk, feeling "glorious to be out of breath, to have a wallet and shoelaces, and a meandering gait, and my own sweet, whimsical will again" (p. 94). For other asylum memoirists, however, the realization that their moral career as mental patients, albeit voluntary ones, does not end with their release, weighs more heavily. Elyn Saks (2007) insisted on release from the asylum she had voluntarily admitted herself to, ignoring the staff's caution that she might not be ready to resume her university studies. Telling anyone who asked that she had been on vacation, and keeping her follow-up psychiatric appointments secret, she lived in fear that every lapse in concentration, every stray thought, every behavioral faux pas meant that her hold on mental health was more tenuous than she could ever imagine.

For Susanna Kaysen (1993), the fear took a different form—the stigma, or the "general taint" (p. 124), as she refers to it, of having been institutionalized followed her in unexpected ways. McLean Hospital's address is as well known in Massachusetts as the White House's address is to the nation, so listing 115 Mill Street as her last address on job applications, an apartment lease and a driver's license application form signaled to everyone that she was a recent mental patient. She knew that fact altered the way they thought about her, making them wonder if she "could think straight [and] not say crazy things" when they occurred to her (p. 124). So she stopped giving herself away, and in doing so developed the same combination of fascination and revulsion for the mad as that with which others treated her.

> Insane people: I had a good nose for them and I didn't want to have anything to do with them.... I can't come up with reassuring answers to the terrible questions they raise. Don't ask me those questions! Don't ask me what life means or how we know reality or why we have to suffer so much. Don't talk about how nothing feels real, how everything is coated with gelatin and shining like oil in the sun. I don't want to hear about the tiger in the corner or the Angel of Death or the phone calls from John the Baptist. He might give me a call too. But I'm not going to pick up the phone. If I who was previously revolting am now this far from my crazy self, how much further are you who were never revolting, and how much deeper your revulsion? [p.125].

Management of a Spoiled Identity

Upon release, and quite regardless of whether they had been unjustly institutionalized, voluntarily admitted, or involuntarily committed, former mental patients are left with the general taint of madness that adheres to their moral careers. The management of this "spoiled identity" (Goffman, 1963, p. 3) requires a certain finesse and is likely to be a long, even a lifetime, endeavor if only because of the "stickiness" of psychodiagnostic labels (Rosenhan, 1973, p. 253).

Any number of asylum memoirs begin and end with going in and adapting to asylum life, however brief that period of time may have been, and little if any mention is made by the authors of getting out, or of adjusting to the "real world" once they have. But that is not always the case. Take Clarissa Caldwell Lathrop (1890) as an example. Having secured her release from the New York State Asylum at Utica with the help of an asylum reformer who filed a writ of habeas corpus on her behalf, Lathrop found it necessary to hide her history as an inpatient in order to secure employment and find her place in a new community. By "wear[ing] a smile and work[ing] away with feverish avidity" (p. 324) she keeps questions about her recent past at bay and reveals nothing about herself except that which she chooses.

This process of "passing" (Goffman, 1963, p. 58), or concealing the stigmatized attribute, in this case madness, is always an anxious endeavor, if only because of the fear of being found out. Jane Hillyer (1926) describes the first dinner party she attended after being discharged from the asylum. Reasoning that if she "fired only interrogations" (p. 150) at the partygoers she could fend off their questions to her, she managed to get through the evening. In college after her discharge, Mindy Lewis (2002) refuses to talk about her past. Although finding it quite easy to make friends, she remains wary and keeps them at arm's length. "I feel like I am sitting on a large egg, which, if exposed to too much warmth, will crack open," she writes, "and the loathsome secret of my difference will come busting messily out, frightening people" (p. 192). Elyn Saks (2007) managed to get through several years of her academic career by only selectively disclosing to close friends. But she struggled with what she knew to be the stigma of madness when she thought about forming new friendships: "The gaps in your life—how do you explain them? You can always make up stories, but beginning a friendship with a lie about your life doesn't feel very good. Or you can say nothing about how you spent the last few years, which strikes people as odd. Or you can choose to tell them about your illness, and find out the hard way that most people aren't ready to hear about it" (p. 288).

Passing often is not a fixed strategy for managing a spoiled identity; but it is used in relation to some people and some circumstances when, as Saks' rumination indicates, the perceived costs of revealing that identity outweigh the perceived benefits. Other asylum memoirists use a compromise strategy that straddles the line between concealment and disclosure. Tracy Thompson (1995), as an example, feared that she simply did not have the energy to pass when she returned to work as a newspaper journalist, so when pressed for details about where she had been over the previous month, she straightforwardly replied that she had been hospitalized for depression, and said not one more thing about it. This strategy of "covering," of naming the stigmatizing attribute by putting it on the table, as it were, makes it easier for both the person and others to "keep the stigma from looming large" (Goffman, 1963, p. 125) and to carry on with their interaction.

Acknowledging madness figures into another management strategy: developing relationships with both sympathetic supporters and other like-stigmatized persons. By joining self-help groups or regional and national organizations having to do with mental illness, ex-asylum patients not only can find refuge from the stereotypes, fear and negative appraisals that often greet them upon their return to the social world but also support and direction in advocatory activities that will redress them. Clifford Beers (1908) ended up taking a leadership role in creating a formal network of support, and in doing so spearheaded one of the most vigorous psychiatric reform movements in history. Discharged from the asylum in 1903, he founded the National Committee for Mental Hygiene and attracted not only other ex-asylum patients as members but also prominent psychiatrists and psychologists who together brought about major changes in legislation and funding for mental health services (Dain, 1980).

There is a hazard, though, that this management strategy requires living in a "half world" (Goffman, 1963, p. 24) by allowing little distance between the former condition of madness and the latter condition of stabilized, in remission, or cured, or the former role of inpatient and the latter role of citizen. Mindy Lewis (2002) recognized that. She joined the Mental Patient Liberation Project in New York City, a nascent grassroots political action group comprised of people like her who had been asylum inpatients. "United by a shared moral indignation" (p. 209) the group became her family, albeit a "dysfunctional" one (p. 210); but she quickly found herself absorbed by and with the problems and the politics of madness and asylums. Putting the past behind her became increasingly more difficult.

Often groups and organizations such as this produce "exemplary moral tales" (Goffman, 1968, p. 37) of persons who overcame their madness or who succeeded despite, or perhaps even *because*, of it. But these tales can be used by individuals to manage their spoiled identities as well. Certain she was cured of her madness during her asylum stay, that in fact she had been "reborn" (p. 95), Margaret Aikens McGarr (1953) situates her identity in the context of just such an exemplary moral tale, and in doing so, preempts any attempts to further stigmatize her: "It is said that people who have had a 'psycho' or 'psychio' experience (I suppose 'mentals' are all such), have a great awareness, a keenness of mind that causes them to so manage their affairs that they often become very wealthy and even make their friends rich at times through their suggestions. And again—others become humanitarians, giving of themselves for the good of others. I am of that latter class" (p. 215).

For some asylum memoirists, however, exemplary moral tales hide the remnants of a spoiled identity. After three years in three different asylums Daphne Scholinski (1997) was discharged a few days after her insurance finally ran out, and went on to earn an undergraduate and a graduate degree in art. Invited to speak about her asylum experiences to the United Nations Fourth World Conference on Women, later interviewed on a number of prime time television shows, and invited to lecture at colleges and universities across the country, her public identity is that of a self-proclaimed psychiatric survivor. But her private identity is not:

> The hospitals are in the past, but that's not where they live in my mind. Three or four times a week I have night terrors. Even now, after all these years, I'm running, being chased, or hiding. I hold my breath. I hold it as long as I can. It's like I'm trying to hold it all in.... Then my breath pushes out of me, really hard; it comes out in ragged whimpers. My hands start to move, I claw at my face.... I try to think of nothing. I practice the trick of going numb, the trick I perfected in the hospital, the trick that has bound me to the past. I pretend I don't care.... I think I'm finding peace, but I'm not [pp. 199–200].

As Scholinski points out, the stigma of madness and of the mental patient role adheres to identity. The disavowal of either one or both is a strategy of resistance taken by a few asylum memoirists in their recollections of how they managed their spoiled identities. For the 19th century women, such as Elizabeth Packard (1866) and Lydia Smith (1879), whose accounts of unjust institutionalization make up the subgenre of protofeminist asylum memoirs, the legal vindication of their sanity provided a powerful tool to resist the stigma's stickiness: after all, if they were never mad, then they were prisoners of the asylums, never mental patients. But the very reforms these, and other, women engendered in their subsequent advocatory campaigns made it increasingly unlikely that such egregious miscarriages of justice would continue to send otherwise sane people to asylums in the first place. So how do more contemporary memoirists resist the stigma of madness?

Some redefine it. While Russell Hampton (1975) acknowledges that the anxiety attacks and waves of depression that brought him into the asylum in the first place, and that dogged him after his discharge, are indeed "emotional devils" (p. 15), he finally concludes that their origin was in his body, not his mind. By relocating the problem from the psyche to the soma—in his case in hypoglycemia, i.e., an abnormally low level of blood sugar—he puts up some resistance to the stigma of madness.

Kate Millett (1990) takes this strategy a long step further. For years after her discharge from the asylum, she was self-consciously absorbed in and by her psychiatric diagnosis, taking large daily doses of lithium and dutifully attending therapy sessions where she "recites the formula" by confessing that without psychiatric help she is irascible, antagonistic and frustrating, i.e., incurably and forever mad (p. 263). After an invited presentation to the National Association for Rights, Protection and Advocacy, in which she railed against the psychiatric profession and the asylum system, she decides to stop taking lithium and experiences not a recurrence of florid madness as she had been warned of, but a patience, serenity and tolerance that causes her to redefine not just her own madness, but in a bold act of resistance, madness in general:

> We do not lose our minds, even "mad" we are neither insane nor sick. Reason gives way to fantasy—both are mental activities, both productive. The mind goes on working, speaking a different language, making its own perceptions, designs, symmetrical or asymmetrical; it works. We have only to lose our fear of its workings. I do not speak of Alzheimer's disease or any other condition where the mind's function itself appears to be hampered. I mean plain old "insanity." And I say it doesn't exist [p. 315].

Silent and Silenced Voices

Asylum memoirs are written by people with a certain amount of social capital: they are literate, have the resources to bring their manuscripts to the attention of publishers and their final products to the reading public and, whether ever "really" mad or not, possess the lucidity to set out narratives about meaning, reality and identity. For every asylum memoir ever published there are many more, finished or not, on yellowing pages in boxes on closet shelves or on dusty floppy disks in desk drawers.

Back-Warders

Some asylum memoirs remain unwritten for no other reason than they cannot be written. The chronic mad patients who have occupied the back wards of asylums across the country and throughout history are silent on all of the points about the meanings of madness, the moral careers as mental patients, and the stickiness of psychodiagnostic labels that preoccupy the published asylum memoirists. Not only do these back-warders have no voice, they rarely ever have anyone to speak for them, so they contribute neither autobiography nor biography to the genre of asylum literature.

Sometimes, though, they are described. When first established in the United States, asylums borrowed the European tradition of allowing the interested public to stroll around the grounds and some of the buildings and take a gander at the mad patients. The Reverend Manasseh Cutler, for example, describes his 1787 visit to the Pennsylvania Hospital: "We next took a view of the *Maniacs*. Their cells are in the lower story, which is partly underground. Their cells are about ten feet square, made as strong as a prison.... Here are both men and women.... Some of them have beds, most of them clean straw. Some of them were extremely fierce and raving, nearly or quite naked" (Cutler & Cutler, 1880, p. 280).

Cutler was just one of so many visitors to the Pennsylvania Hospital that managers erected a fence to "prevent the Disturbance which is given to the Lunatics confin'd in the Cells by the great Numbers of people who frequently resort and converse with them" (cited in Deutsch, 1937, p. 64). The managers also decided to charge 12.5 pence in an effort at discouragement. Paradoxically, the charge only increased the interest and by the early 1800s the newly established West Wing of the hospital had become a "convenient lounge for idlers" and "fashionable ladies" alike, who now paid 25 pence to take their pleasure from mad patients. "The morbid curiosity displayed by a majority of the visitors to the Hospital is astonishing, and their pertinacity in attempting, and fertility in pretexts and expedients, to gain admission to the 'mad people' is not less so," lamented the clerk-librarian in a report to the hospital managers. "Even females who have tears to bestow on tales of imaginary distress, are importunate to see a raving madman, and do not hesitate to wound the diseased mind by the gaze of idle curiosity, by impertinent questions, and thoughtless remarks" (cited in Morton & Woodbury, 1973, p. 156).

Thomas Kirkbride (1880) decried the public exhibition of mad patients as "an outrage upon common humanity and common decency," and insisted in his detailed plan for asylum construction and management that it "ought not be tolerated anywhere or under any circumstances" (p. 238). Yet even he was not opposed to interactions between the public and mad patients in asylum-sponsored activities where the strictest rules of décorum applied to patients and visitors alike, and where the interactions facilitated moral treatment. Whether it was a 4th of July celebration on the asylum grounds ("Fourth of July," 1843) or a guest lecture replete with a "magic lantern" show (Haller

& Larsen, 2005) or a lunatics' ball where mad dancing partners watched their feet "going sadly astray" ("Lunatics' Ball," 1874, p. 15), chronically mad patients always were observed, compassionately or not, sometimes interacted with, but rarely ever talked to.

Kirkbride, like so many asylum superintendents who would follow over the decades, also was not opposed to back ward visits by philanthropists, politicians and journalists, hoping, perhaps, that their visits would increase both public confidence in the mission of asylums and, of course, funding. The noted British author Charles Dickens (1842), for example, was invited to visit the State Hospital for the Insane in Boston, where he filed this report of his congenial encounter with an intractably mad patient:

> Leaning her head against the chimneypiece, with a great assumption of dignity and refinement of manner, sat an elderly female.... Her head in particular was so strewn with scraps of gauze and cotton and bits of paper, and had so many queer odds and ends stuck all about it, that it looked like a bird's nest. She was radiant with imaginary jewels; wore a rich pair of undoubted gold spectacles; and gracefully dropped upon her lap, as we approached, a very old greasy newspaper, in which I dare say she had been reading an account of her own presentation at some Foreign Court.
>
> I have been thus particular in describing her, because she will serve to exemplify the physician's manner of acquiring and retaining the confidence of his patients. "This," he said aloud, taking me by the hand, and advancing to the fantastic figure with great politeness: "This lady is the hostess of the mansion, Sir. It belongs to her. Nobody else has anything whatever to do with it. It is a large establishment, as you see, and requires a great number of attendants. She lives, you observe, in the very first style. She is kind enough to receive my visits, and to permit my wife and family to live here.... She is exceedingly courteous, you perceive," on this hint she bowed condescendingly, "and will permit me to have the pleasure of introducing you...."
>
> We exchanged the most dignified salutations with profound gravity and respect, and so went on. The rest of the madwomen seemed to understand the joke perfectly (not only in this case, but in all the others, except their own), and be highly amused by it. The nature of their several kinds of insanity was made known to me in the same way, and we left each of them in high good humour [pp. 54–55].

A few asylum memoirists also include descriptions of some of the intractably mad patients they themselves encountered in the back wards of asylums, and cobble together something akin to biographies out of the snatches of conversations and the rumors that ran rampant through the wards. Yet even these patients remain as unfamiliar, indeed as unknowable, as the backwarders whose photographs were published in the post–World War II asylum exposés of Alfred Maizel (1946) and Albert Deutsch (1948).

A statistical snapshot of the 333 long-stay patients—those who had been institutionalized at least three years as of April 1, 1999, in Massachusetts asylums—sheds a little light on who might be left in state asylums across the country, and sheds even more light on why they remain (Fisher et al., 2001). For the majority of them, as Table 2 indicates, it is not madness alone that confines them to asylums that had been all but emptied by the deinstitutionalization movement; rather, it is their complicating behavioral and medical problems that prevent their transfer to nursing homes, halfway houses or residential treatment centers, let alone their discharge into the community. While many of these 333 long-stay patients had been institutionalized for many more than the three year criterion set for this statistical snapshot—some, for many decades—the data reveal nothing about their moral careers as mental patients. These back-warders, like the others who remain in state asylums across the country, are unlikely to ever author asylum memoirs.

Racial Minorities

If black patients had penned asylum memoirs, much could be learned about how racism acts as both a contingency and a certainty in this institutional context. In this genre of literature, however, there are no black authors.

Historically, race has been a deciding factor in how, and even *if*, blacks were treated in the nation's asylums. In the pre–Civil War years in the North, blacks either were segregated within asylums or denied admittance entirely, quite regardless of whether they were slaves or free. The prevailing mores of the community in which the asylum was located seems to have determined the policy. In eastern states that had a higher proportion of blacks, the common practice was to segregate those admitted. Worcester Asylum in Massachusetts, for example, admitted several blacks soon after it opened in 1833 and segregated them in a brick shop on the grounds. In midwestern states that had comparatively lower proportions of blacks, such as Indiana and Ohio, the prevailing practice was to deny them admittance, although in some states mad blacks were routinely sent to jails and almshouses that accepted all dependent blacks, but kept them segregated from white inmates (Grob, 1994).

Just like the chronically mad confined in the back wards of asylums, mad black patients on occasion are talked about, even if they are rarely ever talked to. This somewhat japing newspaper report by a visitor to the Philadelphia Almshouse in 1832 offers a glimpse into the madness of a couple of black inmates:

> The next place of visitation was the part devoted to lunatics. In the yard of the building were many whose sad estate had called for the use of chains and the straight jacket. One black man laughed at the awkwardness of his situation, but professed himself happy, excepting a single want—*viz. a chew of tobacco....*

Table 2: Selected Demographic and Diagnostic Characteristics of 333 Long-Stay Psychiatric Patients in Massachusetts State Asylums*

CHARACTERISTIC	N (%)
Sex	
Male	228 (69%)
Female	102 (31%)
Race	
Caucasian	285 (88%)
African American	16 (5%)
Hispanic	10 (3%)
Other	14 (4%)
Educational Attainment	
< High School	125 (51%)
High School	116 (38%)
> High School	66 (22%)
Primary Diagnosis	
(data reflect multiple diagnoses some patients)	
Schizophrenia	255 (76%)
Mood Disorder	34 (10%)
Psychiatric disorder	23 (7%)
due to medical condition	
Borderline intellectual	26 (8%)
functioning/retardation	
Personality Disorder	58 (18%)
Lifetime Problem Behaviors	
(data reflect multiple behaviors some patients)	
Unable to care for self	272 (83%)
Dangerous	244 (74%)
Suicidal	134 (41%)
Self-Injuring	142 (43%)
Sexually Assaultive	59 (18%)
Substance Abuse	245 (75%)
Fire-setting	64 (19%)
Property Destruction	154 (47%)
Refused Medications	172 (52%)
Medical Problems	
(data reflect multiple problems some patients)	
Obesity	102 (31%)
Respiratory Disease	29 (24%)

Hypertension	57 (17%)
Gastrointestinal Disorder	57 (17%)
Heart/Circulatory Disease	56 (17%)
Diabetes	46 (14%)
Thyroid Disease	41 (12%)
Seizure Disorder	39 (12%)
Tardive Dyskinesia	38 (12%)
Stroke/Organic Brain Disorder	23 (7%)
Urogenital Disorder	21 (6%)
Visual Impairment/Blind	20 (6%)
Speech Disorder	19 (6%)
Hearing Impairment/Deaf	10 (3%)
Hepatitis	11 (3%)
Cancer	9 (3%)
Infectious Diseases	5 (2%)
Huntington's Disease	2 (1%)
Parkinson's Disease	2 (1%)
Other Medical Disorders	126 (38%)

(Adapted from Fisher et al., 1999, pp. 1053–1054)

Individuals for whom data were missng for a given variable were excluded from calculations of percentages.

There was one colored man, whose sober, mournful look, and timid, distressful step, excited our special notice. He had been, some months before, brought into that place in a state of insanity. He had conceived the idea that he was Michael the archangel, and he had, for two months, trod with a step, and spoken with an authority, which he thought belonged to the archangelic character. But in an evil hour for him and his supremacy, there was brought in another colored lunatic. The imaginary Michael confronted him, and, stretching forth his hand in an authoritative manner, and assuming a tone of high command, he said, "See that you do me obedience in this place, and give me proper service. I am Michael the archangel."

The newly arrived lunatic looked with a smile of complacent benevolence upon his assuming brother, and, lifting his hand with a slight motion, he replied, "I know thee Michael, and I know thy high office; but I am He that formed the archangel and all the universe, and I shall destroy it."

The abashed Michael shrunk with awe from his superior; his hand, elevated in command, dropped listless at his side; his authoritative mien disappeared; the commanding elevation of the head was gone; the firm step was no more seen. He shrank away from observation as one stripped of all authority, and has ever since looked even "less than archangel fallen" ["A Visit to the Philadelphia Alms House," 1832, p. 128].

In the southern states where, on the eve of the Civil War, free and enslaved blacks comprised more than one-third of the population, the mad among them could not be easily ignored. Asylum policies, however, were far from consistent in dealing with them. Some southern asylums simply refused to admit blacks. Others admitted them into the patient population, while still others segregated them in facilities that were not just separate but unequal.

The Public Hospital for the Insane and the Disordered of the Mind in Williamsburg, Virginia, later renamed the Eastern Lunatic Asylum, is an interesting case study of the antebellum institutional response to blacks suffering from madness. Established in 1773, it was the first public asylum in the country devoted solely to the mad, and it admitted free blacks from the very start, housing them in the same facilities with whites and subjecting them to the same asylum routines. Free blacks, most of them itinerant laborers, constituted approximately 7 percent of its patient population (Savitt, 1978).

Under the 1841 to 1862 superintendency of John Minson Galt II, the asylum expanded from a single building to seven, and its patient population from 30 to 300. Among those patients were mad slaves, admitted under the orders of Galt himself for the first time in 1846, at a cost of $1.50 per week charged to their owners. Although black women patients, regardless of whether free or enslaved, were strictly segregated in an outbuilding, no such efforts were made with the men, who were fewer in number. In Galt's (1848) words, "No particular strictness is observed in isolating the white from the coloured patients; nor under the arrangement adopted in this respect, is there the slightest difference in management originating from the presence of the two races in the same asylum" (p. 27).

There may have been a difference in treatment, however. Reasoning in a manner consistent with the racial prejudices of the times, Galt theorized that free blacks, unused to control, would be less amenable to the kind of moral treatment he advocated, and therefore more likely in need of mechanical restraint in straightjackets or chains. It remains matters of conjecture as to whether the asylum's black patients indeed were restrained more often than white patients, as well as to whether black patients were offered the same quite progressive moral treatment regime that included outplacement, bibliotherapy and even talk therapy, as were white patients, and to the same effects. And with no published memoirs by black patients of the Eastern Lunatic Asylum, the influences of both race and racism on their moral careers as mental patients must remain a matter of conjecture as well.

As a parenthetical note, Galt died in 1862 just after the Union army seized Williamsburg. His death is attributed to an overdose, whether accidental or not, of opium, a drug he prescribed with some enthusiasm for his patients. Upon his death, Gillet Watson was appointed superintendent, but as the Union army began evacuating the city, he sent this urgent telegram on August 20, 1862, to President Abraham Lincoln:

Sir—

I am senator of the Wheeling Government & under Gov. Pierepoint appointment am Supt of the Eastern Lunatic Asylum. Williamsburg is now being evacuated by the Union forces. Under these circumstances the safety of my life requires that I shall leave in a very few hours—When I leave all the officers and servants will leave so that the Unfortunate inmates will be left locked up without any one to minister unto them. I have made known this condition of things to Genl Dix and Genl McClellan and they have done nothing! I now communicate it to you which is the last effort I can make [Basler, 1953, p. 387].

Despite President Lincoln's urging that he "remain as long as you safely can, and provide as well as you can for the poor inmates of the Institution" (Basler, 1957, p. 387), Watson and all but one of the attendants fled the asylum, leaving nearly 300 patients locked in the buildings. The remaining attendant, Sommersett Moore, handed over the keys to Union officers and saved the lives of patients, black and white, who surely would have died of privation over the weeks to come.

At the end of the Civil War, and in the face of persistent warnings that madness would be the price of freedom for emancipated blacks, seven asylums were established for the "colored insane." Like all asylums during these years, they quickly became overcrowded, understaffed and underfunded, but when compared to white or segregated asylums, these historic black asylums had their share of unique problems that surely would have acted as contingencies on the moral careers of their patients. Most were located in isolated rural areas, making it difficult for family members and friends to visit; most were staffed largely, if not exclusively, by white physicians and attendants, transforming them into microcosms of the racial tensions of larger society. Historic black asylums are listed in Jackson (n.d.): Central State (1870–1965): Petersburg, VA; Eastern North Carolina (1880–1965): Goldsboro, NC; Mt. Vernon (1902–2969): Mt. Vernon, AL; Crownsville (1911–1962): Crownsville, MD; State Park (1914–1966): Columbia, SC; Lakin (1926–1954): Point Pleasant, WV; Taft (1933–1955): Taft, OK. Those in the Deep South hired out their patients to neighboring white farmers to work the land and pick cotton and, under a tacitly accepted peonage system, sent them to work as servants in the homes of both white community members and asylum superintendents and staff.

There were other unique factors, too, in these historic Black asylums before they were integrated, or for other reasons closed completely, that very well could have affected the moral careers of their patients. Crownsville State Hospital, as an example, integrated its staff in the late 1940s and developed a strong partnership with the surrounding Black community that provided volunteers to visit with the patients and supervise activities, as well as employment opportunities and social support for discharged patients. Lakin State

Hospital for the Colored Insane, as another example, was staffed by blacks from its start, and not only required that all attendants have a high school diploma and all aides a certificate of completion of a nine-month training course, but also that all staff live in rooms adjacent to the wards. Staff, therefore, did not just work with patients, but recreated and socialized with them on a daily basis (Jackson, no date).

In the wake of Emancipation, southern states codified the subordinate position of blacks in society. The so-called Jim Crow laws mandated the segregation of blacks in public spaces such as schools, on public transportation, as well as in public accommodations and facilities, and barred black males from exercising the right to vote. To escape the public humiliation, the race riots and mob violence, thousands of southern blacks fled to Kansas and Oklahoma in the "Kansas Exodus" of the 1880s, and tens of thousands more to eastern and midwestern cities during the "Great Migration" of 1916–1919 (Gregory, 2007). Some of that great number fled to Washington, D.C., where most lived in dire poverty and where a steadily increasing number of them found themselves committed to St. Elizabeth's Hospital, founded by Dorothea Dix in the mid–1800s to provide care for the enlistees and veterans of the armed forces, as well as for the residents of the District of Columbia. Once there, these "strangers within our gates" (Evarts, 1916, p. 287) were segregated in deteriorating wards, and encountered racial stereotyping and prejudices from the predominantly white staff that were trained to think that madness was evidence of the failure to adjust to a changing social environment. And how was that failure racialized? In the words of one prominent member of staff:

> With this in mind, we can understand why insanity should be on the increase in the colored race, for of it is being demanded an adjustment much harder to make ... than any other race has yet been called upon to attempt.... During its years of savagery, the race has learned no lessons in emotional control, and what they attained during their few generations of slavery left them unstable. For this reason we find deterioration in the emotional sphere most often an early and persistent manifestation [of severe madness] [Evarts, 1914, pp. 394 & 396].

Staff were content to take note of deference, dependence and congenial unpaid labor as evidence of some improvement in the "emotional sphere" of black patients, or, in other words, in the behaviors expected of blacks in a still racially stratified society. Beyond that, little effort was made to improve their condition and some time-honored treatments, such as hydrotherapy for agitated patients, were withheld, resulting in a higher rate of seclusion and mechanical restraint for distressed black patients (Gambino, 2008).

Once again, the contingencies of racially segregated living conditions in the asylum, racialized theories of madness, racial stereotyping and prejudices on the moral careers of black patients at St. Elizabeth's are not described in asylum memoirs. But there are hints, penned by staff, in patient records:

- The nurse reported to me today that the patient [Harriet Cross] has talked very freely to the other patients, evidently more freely than on examination, telling them that she was sent here on a mission from God [cited in Gambino, 2008, p. 401].
- When asked the date, Jacob Jeffries replied, "Every date is the same around here." When asked how much money he was worth, he replied, "I am not worth a cent while I am in here" [cited in Gambino, 2008, p. 398].
- Abraham Tibbs said, "The onliest time I got good sense is when I'm working for nothing [in the asylum], but when I ask for pay like you would, then I am out of mind and insane" [cited in Gambino, 2008, p. 400].
- Leonard Perry resents being questioned and is inclined to dispute the examiner's right to ask him anything [cited in Gambino, 2008, p. 401].
- [The patient] believes that white people are very much opposed to the colored people and would oppress them in every way possible. That is just his way of thinking owing to his mental condition, I suppose [cited in Gambino, 2008, p. 402].

The conflation between race, mental condition and the asylum environment persists unrelieved by the 1964 Civil Rights Act that ended racial segregation in public facilities. At the time of this writing, black mental patients are four times more likely to be diagnosed as schizophrenic (Barnes, 2004; Minsky et al., 2003), have significantly longer asylum stays (Bolden & Wicks, 2005), and are less likely to be treated according to prevailing evidence-based treatment protocols than white mental patients (Wang, Demler, & Kessler, 2001). They are unlikely to ever interact with professionals of their own race while institutionalized since less than 2 percent of all psychiatrists, 2 percent of all psychologists and 4 percent of all social workers self-identify as Black and only a small proportion of these professionals work in asylums (Ellis, 2009). Once discharged, Blacks are substantially more likely to be institutionalized again over the ensuing twelve months than are whites (U.S. Surgeon General, 2001). Yet, in the absence of published asylum memoirs, the effects of all of these factors and more on their moral careers as mental patients are not known.

The same may be said of Native Americans. After the scandal-ridden Hiawatha Asylum for Insane Indians was shut down in 1931, and with it the local chamber of commerce's publicity campaign that invited the public to "Come See the Crazy Indians!" Native Americans often were segregated either in St. Elizabeth's Hospital, for those belonging to federally recognized tribes, or in state asylums for those who did not. Segregation was a matter not just of race, but of presumed dangerousness. The equation of madness with inherent savagery persisted in psychiatric thinking for generations, and often provided the justification for cruel or indifferent treatment of institutionalized Native Americans (Cooley, 2001). To this day, and just like blacks, Native Americans have longer asylum stays than white patients and higher rates of readmission upon release (U.S. Surgeon General, 2001). All of these things—racial segregation, racialized theories of madness, and racial stereotyping and prejudices—would act as contingencies on the moral careers of Native American mental patients. Once again, however, the absence of published asylum memoirs leave the workings and the effects of those contingencies to the imagination.

Immigrants

The United States always has been a nation of immigrants. People from all over the world come to this country, sometimes with little more than the clothes on their backs, settle in its major cities and small towns, find jobs, raise families, and eventually assimilate to some degree or another. Along the way they encounter the inevitable challenges, the ignorant stereotypes and, sometimes, the virulent nativism of those who for whatever reasons are threatened by their presence. Some distinguish themselves as leaders, others as little more than social problems, and still others find their ways into their adopted country's asylums.

During the 1820s, for example, approximately 54,000 Irish immigrated to the United States; most of them were middle class, from the Protestant northern counties and assimilated quite easily. Two decades later, at the height of the Great Famine, another 780,000 came to this country, but the majority of these Irish immigrants were poor, from the Catholic southern counties, and were unwelcome. And while they transformed the cultural, political, economic and religious landscapes of cities such as Boston, Massachusetts, they also overran state institutions, including asylums. Irish immigrants constituted 41 percent of the patients at the Boston Lunatic Hospital in 1846; a mere five years later, that figure had doubled (Torrey, 2001).

The lives of that second wave of Irish immigrants were hard; the poverty and cultural dislocation they experienced were theorized to contribute to what appeared to be their high rate of madness. But those social facts offered only a partial explanation for the disproportionate number of Irish in state asylums. In his 1855 report on "insanity and idiocy" in the state of Massachusetts, Edward Jarvis wrote the following:

> There is good reason for supposing that the habits and condition and character of the Irish poor in this country operate more unfavorably upon their mental health, hence producing a larger number of the insane in ratio of their numbers than is found among the native poor. Being in a strange land and among strange men and

things, meeting with customs and surrounded by circumstances widely different from all their previous experience, ignorant of the precise state of affairs here, and wanting education and flexibility by which they could adapt themselves to their new and unwonted position, they necessarily form many impracticable purposes, and endeavor to accomplish them by unfitting means. Of course disappointment frequently follows their plans. Their lives are filled with doubt, and harrowing anxiety troubles them, and they are involved in frequent mental, and probably physical suffering. The Irish laborers have less sensibility and fewer wants to be gratified than the Americans and yet they more commonly fail to supply them. They have also a greater irritability.... Unquestionably, much of their insanity is due to their intemperance, to which the Irish seem to be peculiarly prone, and much to that exaltation which comes from increased prosperity [pp. 61–62].

Jarvis suggests that an admixture of circumstance and character made Irish immigrants particularly prone to madness, but other of his colleagues had much harsher assessments. The superintendent of Blackwell's Island concluded that a "low order of intelligence" and "imperfectly developed brains" accounted for the disproportionate number of Irish immigrants institutionalized in that New York City asylum (Parsons, 1857, p. 79). The eminent psychiatrist Isaac Ray explained that the low curability rate of Irish immigrant asylum patients was due to the fact that they were a "very ignorant, uncultivated people" who were incapable of developing the requisite insight that would assure their discharge (Ray, 1863, p. 33).

The Irish certainly were not the only immigrant group singled out for such opprobrium. From the late 19th century through the early 20th century, more than 18 million immigrants came to the United States (Dowbiggen, 1997). Soon, the number of foreign-born mad patients either equaled or eclipsed the number of native-born in virtually every public asylum in the country. Worried that therapeutic regimes would be unsuccessful in treating mad patients for whom the English language and the norms and rules of American culture were unfamiliar, and that hereditary patterns not only would assure that madness would spread through subsequent generations but that it would also taint the germ plasms of otherwise mentally healthy native-born white Americans, some asylum superintendents and psychiatrists played a significant role in advocating such legal remedies as immigration restriction. In 1884, for example, the American Medico-Psychological Association unanimously supported a resolution urging Congress to increase its efforts to deny "defective classes" of immigrants entry into the country; in 1903, as another example, the organization lobbied for a congressional bill that would allow the deportation of any immigrant who was institutionalized in an asylum or had been adjudicated as criminally insane within three years of his of her arrival in the country (Blumer, 1903).

The American Medico-Psychological Association took pride in "mak[ing] ourselves felt in these great public issues which are now pressing upon the country" (Bancroft, 1908, p. 14). In many ways, this public activism fundamentally changed the speciality of psychiatry by extending psychiatric control into everyday life, as well as into the social problems of a rapidly changing nation. Psychiatrists believed they could play a crucial role in bettering society by encouraging mental hygiene, bringing alcoholics, drug abusers, gamblers, prostitutes, criminals and other ne'er-do-wells under psychiatric control, as well as by treating the mad (Grob, 1994). Although this new agenda effectively shifted attention from the asylum to society—from the chronically mad to the socially, and arguably morally, dysfunctional and consequently freed many psychiatrists from the burden of having to ply their trade only in a total institution context—the specialty found common ground, albeit *shifting* common ground, on the issue of eugenics.

Eugenics, literally translated as "good in birth" or "well born," was both a scientific ideology and a vigorous social movement based on the research on the evolution of human differences conducted in the 1880s by the English scientist Francis Galton. Using data from biographical dictionaries and alumni records at Oxford and Cambridge universities, he concluded that talent and genius were inherited; thus, for the betterment of society and the improvement of the human race, it was imperative that gifted and intelligent people have more children.

Eugenics ideology spread quickly to the United States, where a generous philanthropic gift from Mary Harriman, widow of the railroad baron E.H. Harriman, established the Eugenics Record Office (ERO) in Cold Spring Harbor, New York. Reflecting the Galton tradition of positive eugenics, the ERO trained field workers to collect pedigrees of families with unique characteristics and talents, held "Fitter Family" and "Better Baby" contests at state and county fairs, disseminated reams of self-help and informational literature, and produced documentary films to be screened at schools and churches. At the same time, the ERO reacted to the unsettling changes in American society by developing an increasing interest in what can be termed "negative eugenics." It created batteries of intelligence, literacy and other tests to identify the "unfit," a pliable term used to label criminals, alcoholics and drug abusers, chronic paupers and ne'er-do-wells, the "feebleminded," i.e., those with a mental age of eight to twelve years who could pass for normal, and the mad—in other words, the very types of people who were the subjects of the widening net of psychiatric control—and to discourage their reproduction by involuntarily sterilizing them.

After the United States Supreme Court upheld involuntary sterilization in *Buck v. Bell* (1927), a case involving Carrie Buck, an allegedly feebleminded young woman institutionalized in Virginia, thirty states went on to pass involuntary sterilization laws (Table 3). Although the court in *Skinner v. Oklahoma* (1942) later unanimously struck down those state laws that allowed the involuntary sterilization of convicted criminals, concluding that they violated the Equal Protection Clause of the 14th Amendment, it never did so for other types of allegedly "unfit" people. Thus, the practice of involuntary sterilization continued in some states until the 1970s, by which time more than 63,000 institutionalized and imprisoned people across the country had undergone this "surgical solution" (Reilly, 1991).

In recent years, the governors of six states—California, Indiana, North Carolina, Oregon, South Carolina and Virginia—have offered official apologies to those who had undergone involuntary sterilization. They also have offered symbolic gestures of contrition. In Virginia, a highway marker was erected to the memory of Carrie Buck, whose test case helped establish the model eugenics law that was replicated in one state after another; in Oregon, December 10 was declared a "Human Rights Day"; and in North Carolina, health care and educational benefits were extended to any of the surviving 7600 residents who had been involuntarily sterilized under state law that was not repealed until 1974 (Stern, 2005a).

State asylums were particularly convenient places not only for the study of family histories of madness, but also for the practice of negative eugenics. One former mental patient, Marion Marle Woodson (1932), who under the pseudonym "Inmate, Ward 8" published a memoir of his years as a patient in the Eastern State Hospital in Vinita, Oklahoma, describes the impact of the state's passage of the new sterilization law on his fellow patients:

> The patients on the receiving ward are in seething unrest. The two thousand men and women in the institution are in a foment. I suspect that this is true in every asylum in the state.... The spectre of sex sterilization has been thrust over us. The legislature has passed and the governor has signed a measure permitting the desexualization under certain circumstances, of any male or female inmate who is not too aged to procreate. And the patients are frightened, wrought up, angry and muttering. They know little about the law, therefore they are the more frightened.... They gather in knots and discuss the fate which may be hanging over them.
>
> But they do not do it where the attendants can hear. They are afraid to do that.... And so the fears, the loneliness, and the near hopelessness of the Locked-ins have an added terror [p. 112].

The "added terror" certainly loomed for all asylum patients; by 1940, more than 18,000 of them had been involuntarily sterilized (Table 4). At Norwalk State Hospital in Norwalk, California, for example, it loomed large for foreign-born patients. Mexicans constituted 7.8 percent of the new admissions between 1921 and 1930, yet they were involuntarily sterilized at rates

Table 3: State Criteria for Eugenical Sterilization

STATE	INSANE	FEEBLE-MINDED	IDIOTS	IMBECILES	EPILEPTICS	HABITUAL CRIMINALS	SEXUAL PERVERTS	MORAL DEGENERATES	MENTAL DEFECTIVES	SYPHILITICS	OTHER
Alabama		X									
Arizona	X										
California	X	X	X			X			X		
Delaware	X	X			X				X		
Idaho	X	X			X	X		X			
Indiana	X	X			X						
Iowa	X	X				X		X			X
Kansas	X	X				X					
Maine		X									
Michigan	X								X		
Minnesota	X	X									
Mississippi	X	X	X		X						
Montana	X	X			X						
Nebraska	X	X									
New Hampshire		X									X
North Carolina									X		
North Dakota	X	X				X	X	X	X		
Oklahoma	X	X	X	X	X	X					
Oregon	X	X				X	X	X	X		
South Carolina	X	X	X	X	X						
South Dakota		X									
Utah	X	X	X	X	X	X					
Vermont	X	X	X	X							
Virginia	X	X	X	X	X						
Washington	X	X				X	X	X	X		
West Virginia	X	X	X	X	X						
Wisconsin	X	X				X	X				

(Adapted from the Harry Laughlin Papers and used with permission of Truman State University) of 11 percent for females and 13 percent for males (Stern, 2005b, p. 111). While there are no comparable national data, the sheer number of immigrant patients in asylums across the nation assured that the "added terror" of involuntary sterilization acted as a contingency on their moral careers as mental patients. In the absence of published asylum memoirs by immigrants, however, how this acted as a contingency, and to what effect, is a matter for speculation.

The "added terror" of involuntary sterilization may be over, but immigrants still constitute a significant proportion of state asylum patients. Some have been institutionalized for the psychological consequences of war, famine, torture or ethnic cleansings in their native countries; others for the psychological consequences of poverty, unemployment or homelessness in their adopted one (Appleby, Luchins, & Freels, 2006). Their moral careers as mental patients, however, remain unexamined.

Children

While there are a number of published memoirists who reflect on spending part, or even much, of their adolescence confined in asylums (e.g., Kaysen, 1993; Lewis, 2002; Schiller & Bennett, 1994; Scholinski, 1997), the same cannot be said of those who spent part, or even much, of their *childhoods* in asylums. Although most state asylums from their inception admitted them, the early history of the institutionalization of mad children has yet to be written.

The more recent history, though, can be cobbled together. Concerned that child patients were getting neither the attention nor the treatment they needed, a number of state asylums created separate children's units. Allentown State Hospital in Pennsylvania opened its Children's Institute, the first of its kind, in 1930 and several state asylums quickly followed its lead (Klopp, 1932). In 1945, the American Psychiatric Association created a set of standards for the treatment of children, and recommended the establishment of separate children's units in all state asylums. In the post–World War II years, with the changing nature of the family and the increasing case-finding functions of public education, public welfare, the juvenile court, and the newly established community child guidance centers, those specialized asylum units filled quickly.

The moral careers of children as mental patients most often began with probate court commitment hearings after petitions had been filed, usually by their parents but just as likely by the social service or juvenile justice systems, alleging mental illness and the need for treatment. Most of these children had been grappling with their spoiled identities for some time before

Table 4: Number of Sterilizations Performed in State Asylums Through 1940

State	Males	Females	Total
Alabama	0	0	0
Arizona	10	10	20
California	5,329	4,310	9,639
Connecticut	19	337	356
Delaware	206	71	277
Georgia	6	68	74
Idaho	2	10	12
Indiana	213	177	390
Iowa	83	91	174
Kansas	1,035	724	1,759
Maine	0	10	10
Michigan	71	234	305
Minnesota	113	266	379
Mississippi	135	320	455
Montana	16	20	36
Nebraska	53	90	143
New Hampshire	24	166	190
New York	0	41	41
North Carolina	90	150	240
North Dakota	123	174	297
Oklahoma	70	232	302
Oregon	287	321	608
South Carolina	0	0	0
South Dakota	0	0	0
Utah	44	43	87
Vermont	1	12	13
Virginia	936	1,365	2,301
Washington	141	245	386
West Virginia	0	18	18
Wisconsin	0	0	0
Total	9,007	9,505	18,512

(Adapted from the Harry Laughlin Papers and used by permission of Truman State University)

they were committed to state asylums. They had been counseled by school counselors, private therapists, juvenile probation officers, or child guidance social workers; some had spent time in foster care, detention centers, private residential treatment programs, or specialized programs or camps (Leon, Uziel-Miller, Lyons, & Tracy, 1999; Scharer & Jones, 2004). But what remains not well known is how they experienced the unfolding of their moral careers as mental patients in these specialized state asylum units that were designed to provide "a living situation that was stable, safe, and predictable, with reasonable limits and expectations, and an opportunity to develop the necessary skills, within their ability, to experience social and academic success" (Decker, 2008, pp. 283–284), but were asylums, nonetheless. Although their experiences sometimes are narrated by others (Roth & Roth, 1984; Szajnberg & Weiner, 1989, 1996), not much is heard from the children themselves or, for that matter, the adolescents or adults who as children had been institutionalized.

In regard to children, a curious thing occurred contemporaneously with the deinstitutionalization movement: the number of private, for-profit asylums increased dramatically, and the number of children admitted to them did as well. From 1980 through 1986, for example, when the last of the adult state asylum patients were being decanted into the community, the number of children admitted to private psychiatric asylums and residential care programs increased by four times and the total days of care provided increased by more than three times, which "made minors an especially expensive (or lucrative) patient population" (Mayes, Bagwell, & Erkulwater, 2009, p. 85). Yet researchers find that nearly one-half of these children were being admitted inappropriately, "served inadequately, and had the length of their stay in the hospital controlled by the coverage limits of their insurance policy rather than by actual need" (Friedman & Kutash, 1992, p. 130).

When insurers began balking at the costs in the early 1990s and turned to managed behavioral health-care organizations to contain them, the average length of asylum stay for children dropped significantly and cheaper psychotropic drugs took the place of expensive face-to-face therapeutic interventions (Mayes, Bagwell, & Erkulwater, 2009). Many of the bespoke private asylums closed their doors, and it has became increasingly difficult to find beds for those children who are in need of them, as a recent *Boston Globe* investigation reveals (Goldberg, 2008):

> Parents and advocates report that in recent weeks across the state, at least a dozen children and teens in crisis—threatening violence to themselves or others—have waited three, five, even seven days in hospital emergency rooms or medical wards for psychiatric beds. In some cases, they've been sent home to be monitored in hopes the danger would pass or a bed would open.

By all accounts, the state has made significant progress toward solving the problem of "stuck kids"—children with mental illness deemed well enough to leave hospital psychiatric units but stuck in them for lack of treatment programs outside. But while it has gotten easier for children to leave the state's mental health facilities, which should make more beds available, it appears to have gotten harder, in some cases, to get in [p. 1].

All of these economic, political, professional and ideological factors, and more, act as contingencies on the moral careers of mental patients, even if they are children and know nothing of contingencies and, perhaps, even less of moral careers. But how their sense of self and of identity is slowly and steadily shaped by the experiences of institutionalization, and with what short and long term effects, how they manage the lifelong stickiness of the psychiatric labels used to diagnose and classify them, is awaiting narration by the children themselves.

6

Asylum Therapeutics

Canst thou not minister to a mind diseased; pluck from the memory a rooted sorrow; raze out the written troubles of the brain?—Macbeth

BETWEEN THEIR ENTRIES INTO ASYLUMS and their exits from them, if indeed they do ever exit, asylum patients experience therapeutic regimes to steady their moods, control their erratic behaviors, order their chaotic thoughts, silence the voices in their heads, and occupy their long days. From a historical perspective, the sheer range of asylum therapeutics is nothing short of astonishing. From the early humoural therapies of bleeding, purging and vomiting; to tranquilizing chairs, gyrators, confining cribs, wet blankets and straightjackets; to the inductions of fevers and seizures and the removal of teeth, appendixes, ovaries and sections of colons; to lobotomies, psychotropic drugs, and group and occupational therapies asylum patients have been whirled, doused, restrained, cut, fevered, shocked, doped and talked to in efforts to restore their sanity.

This wide range of asylum therapeutics invites two mutually exclusive interpretations. The first construes the range as illustrative of the steady progression of benevolence over malevolence, science over ignorance, and therefore perhaps not so much of a "range" after all, but "a long road upward" (Deutsch, 1937, p. 495) from unenlightened to enlightened therapeutic interventions. The second, in contrast, construes the range as little more than a hodgepodge of fads and fancies in search of science (Whitaker, 2002).

For advocates of each of these extreme positions there is no middle ground and, given the vituperative tone of the debate, rapprochement is unlikely. The editors of the journal *History of Psychiatry*, for example, declared that "this controversy is now closed" (1995, p. 241), meaning that two warring opponents would no longer find the journal an arena for carrying on their hullabaloo (Mersky, 1994; Scull, 1995), but suggesting instead by that somewhat obtuse declaration that all argument about asylum therapeutics has been resolved and is now over.

It would be as unwise to toll the end of the controversy as it would be to ignore it altogether. But there is a middle ground between the two extremes that opens a door for analysis, and that is to treat asylum therapeutics as inextricably intertwined with not only the social forces of the particular historical moment, but also with the extant body of scientific knowledge, as scrawny as it may have been (Braslow, 1997). If scientific knowledge itself is socially and historically contingent, then it, too, will change over time, thus helping to explain why asylum therapeutics come, often with great fanfare, and go, often without it, as well as why some of their most prominent promoters and practitioners have been judged so harshly by history.

Therapeutics are the "translation of abstract knowledge into socially acceptable recipes for intervention and practical action" (Scull, 1994, p. 2). The phrase "socially acceptable" in some ways complicates any examination of asylum therapeutics. It suggests that the meaning of therapeutics must be found not only in the larger social and scientific contexts, but also within the more intimate context of the asylum as an institution, and the even more intimate context of the physician-patient interaction (Braslow, 1997; Rosenberg, 1992). If society, science, institution and interaction share a system of beliefs about the relationship between the mind and the body, and between madness and sanity, and if the therapeutic practices are perceived to be manifestations of those beliefs and expected to be effective, they very well may be.

That said, they often are not. Thus that phrase "socially acceptable" also opens the door for an examination of what happens when there is no convergence between society, science, institution, interaction and therapeutics. Virtually every asylum therapeutic has been surrounded by controversy, not just in retrospect, but at the times they were being promoted and practiced. Some of the controversies arose from disputes between psychiatric practitioners. Some of those were personal and petty, others were substantive disagreements about scientific knowledge, professional practices, efficacy and ethics; only a few were made public and fewer still would have been known by the asylum patients upon whom the therapeutics were being practiced. Others arose from spates of bad publicity, and some from the organized resistance of former and present asylum patients. Just as the controversy over asylum therapeutics is far from closed, the controversy *about* any given asylum therapeutic remains open for examination.

Mechanical Restraint Controversy

Mechanical restraints—chains, manacles, jacket waistcoats, leather wristlets, hand straps—may never have been mistaken for therapeutics in the early asylums in the United States; but they were considered both acceptable and necessary for the management and control of mad patients whose lack of reason, as prevailing beliefs averred, reduced them to "wild beasts." The importation of moral treatment from England into the country in the early 1800s was both the cause and the effect of a shift in beliefs about madness as well as about the treatment of the mad. Its emphasis on ordered routines, gentle persuasion, and unruffled firmness called into question the use of mechanical restraints, the skills of physicians who preferred them, and the deeply held belief that the peculiar character of Americans, with their rugged individualism, faith in freedom, and daring spirits, rendered them difficult to control if and when they became mad. The controversy over the use of mechanical restraints in asylums, then, not only pitted American physicians against English physicians—who "considered the non-restraint system as one of their greatest contributions to medical progress" (Tomes, 1988, pp. 190–191)—but also American physicians against each other as they debated the necessity and the efficacy of mechanical restraints, and American physicians against themselves as they struggled with the daily task of dealing with the mad.

The Iron Fist in the Velvet Glove:
Mechanical Restraint in the Age of Moral Treatment

The career of Benjamin Rush, who served on the Pennsylvania Hospital medical staff from 1783 until his death in 1813, embodies much of that controversy. The "Father of American Psychiatry" and one of the signatories of the Declaration of Independence, he believed that madness could be diagnosed, classified, treated and cured. A remarkable therapeutic innovator, he purged, blistered, vomited and bled his patients; administered herbal concoctions and drugs; and twirled them in a purpose-built gyrator until their noses bled. Yet at the same time, Rush also embraced the humanitarian principles of moral treatment, even though his methods are as unique as the American version of madness he was treating:

> [T]he first object of a physician, when he enters the cell, or chamber, of his deranged patient, should be, to catch his eye, and look him out of countenance. The dread of the eye was early imposed upon every beast of the field. The tyger, the mad bull, and enraged dog, all fly from it: now a man deprived of his reason

partakes so much of the nature of those animals, that he is for the most part easily terrified, or composed, by the eye of a man who possess his reason....

A second means of securing the obedience of a deranged patient to a physician should be by his VOICE.... In governing mad people it should be harsh, gentle, or plaintive, according the circumstances....

The COUNTENANCE of a physician should assist his eye and voice in governing his deranged patients. It should be accommodated to the state of the patient's mind and conduct. There is something like contagion in the different aspects of the human face, and madmen feel it is common with other people....

The CONDUCT of a physician to his patients should be uniformly dignified, if he wishes to require their obedience and respect. He should never descend to levity in conversing with them. He should hear with silence their rude or witty answers to his questions, and upon no account ever laugh at them, or with them.

ACTS of justice, and a strict regard to truth, tend to secure the respect and obedience of deranged patients to their physician. Every thing necessary for their comfort should be provided for them, and every promise made to them should be faithfully and punctually performed....

A physician should treat deranged patients with respect, and with all the ceremonies which are due to their former rank and habits of living. Carpets upon the floors of their rooms or cells, curtains to their beds, taste in the preparation and manner of serving their meals, will all serve to prevent distress and irritation, from a supposed change in their condition of life....

And lastly. A physician acquires the obedience and affections of his deranged patients by ACTS OF KINDNESS [Rush, 1812, pp. 175–180].

Rush's version of moral treatment may have emphasized more firmness than kindness, and expected more obedience than insight in return, but it was a response to the changing zeitgeist about the nature and treatment of madness. Although committed to its humanitarian principles, Rush refused to surrender mechanical restraints, particularly that of the specially designed tranquilizing chair. About that chair, for which he is probably best remembered, he wrote in an 1810 letter to his son: "I have lately contrived a chair and introduced it to our Hospital to assist in curing madness. It binds and confines every part of the body [and] lessens the impetus of the blood toward the brain.... Its effects have been truly delightful to me. It acts as a sedative to the tongue and temper as well as to the blood vessels. In 24, 12, 6, and in some cases in 4 hours, the most refractory patients have been composed. I have called it a *Tranquilizer*" (Butterfield, 1951, p. 1052).

For Rush, any dissonance about using the tranquilizing chair in the age of moral treatment was resolved by asserting that it was a far more humane type of mechanical restraint than the straightjacket, and that it was only one of a variety of "coercive" treatments that by regretful necessity simply had to be part of the arsenal of every physician treating the mad:

If all the means that have been mentioned should prove ineffectual to establish a government over deranged patients, recourse should be had to certain modes of coercion....

1. Confinement by means of a strait waistcoat, or of a chair which I have called a tranquilizer.... The tranquilizer has several advantages over the strait waistcoat or mad shirt. It opposes the impetus of the blood towards the brain, it lessens muscular action every where, it reduces the force and frequency of the pulse, it favours the application of cold water and ice to the head, and warm water to the feet, both of which I shall say presently are excellent remedies in this disease; it enables the physician to feel the pulse and to blood without any trouble, or alter-ing the erect position of the patient's body; and, lastly, it relieves him, by means of a close stool, half filled with water, over which he constantly sits, from the fac-tor and filth of his alvine evacuations.

2. Privation of their customary pleasant food.

3. Pouring cold water under the coat sleeve, so that it may descend into the arm pits, and down the trunk of the body.

4. The shower bath, continued for fifteen or twenty minuets. If these modes of punishment should fail of their intended effects, it will be proper to resort to the fear of death [Rush, 1812, pp. 181–182].

In their 1844 meeting, the Association of Medical Superintendents of American Institutions for the Insane (AMSAII) were not asked to endorse the tranquilizing chair as a particular method of mechanical restraint, nor the "fear of death" that was the last resort of Rush, but it did resolve that any "attempt to abandon entirely the use of all means of personal restraint is not sanctioned by the true interests of the insane" (Curwen, 1875, p. 7). Arguing that mechanical restraint is itself a "moral instrument," the members agreed with one of its own who urged pride in the belief that "we have an American practice in the use of restraint, which is at once benevolent, enlightened, and practicable" (Shrady, 1859, p. 61).

Pride, however, was something that Thomas Kirkbride, with whom moral treatment is more intimately associated, refused to enjoy. Kirkbride was conflicted over the necessity of using mechanical restraints, confessing to members of the AMSAII that he "never saw [mechanical restraints] in use without a feeling of mortification, nor without asking [myself] if it was really necessary" (Nichols, 1855, p. 92). Yet under his medical superintendency at the Pennsylvania Hospital for the Insane, straightjackets, canvas suits and bed straps were used in the treatment of mad patients, but only sparingly, and only for the most intractably violent patients who were demonstrable threats to themselves or to others.

While Kirkbride may not have shared his colleagues' enthusiasm about mechanical restraints, the continued use of them made those who use them targets of criticism and ridicule by their British colleagues with whom they always had had a close and supportive relationship. The broadside by one of those colleagues, J. Mortimer Granville, a prominent asylum reformer and head of the Lancet Commission that had investigated the conditions of British asylums, was keenly felt by both American asylum physicians and the AMSAII:

The social treatment of the insane may be broadly, but not inaccurately, divided
into three periods or stages of development: the barbaric, in which the lunatic
was simply regarded as a wild and dangerous animal from which society needed
protection, and that might be kept in chains, tamed, or destroyed, as convenience
should dictate; the "humane," in which some compassion began to be felt for the
victim of what was believed to be a supernatural visitation; and the remedial, in
which madness has come to be recognized as a malady, and measures have been
directed to its cure.... It is surprising, but unhappily it is notorious, that in the
United States the treatment of lunatics can hardly be said to have made progress
even in the stage of development which we have reluctantly described as the
humane.... The governors, and especially the medical superintendents of asylums
in the States, will, doubtless, indignantly repudiate the charge of being behind the
age, more particularly when it is understood that the imputation involves, as it
most assuredly does, a very serious reflection on their professional acumen and
social sagacity.... Nothing has been more conclusively proved by the experience
of an extended practice than that the treatment of insanity with restraints is neither rational nor scientific.... If the medical superintendents of American asylums
resort to the old system, they do so in the face of patent facts, and their practice
has no claim to be classed as medical, hardly can it be called humane.... It is
scarcely believable, but we are almost forced to the conclusion, that our friends
across the Atlantic have not yet mastered the fundamental principles of the remedial system. They adhere to the old terrorism tempered by petty tyranny [Gran-
ville, 1875, pp. 705, 706, 707].

The outraged and humiliated American asylum physicians were somewhat
feebly defended by another British physician, John C. Bucknill, who had spent
several months in the United States visiting asylums. But in a book detailing
his experiences, published just a year later, Bucknill, too, excoriated them
for their continued use of mechanical restraints:

With regard to the constantly repeated proposition of American superintendents,
that they maintain and defend the use, but not the abuse, of mechanical restraints,
I have only to remark that the use of such restraint must always be an abuse
whenever and wherever it may be avoided or substituted by a more skillful mode
of treatment, inflicting less suffering upon the patients.... Our American brethren
tell us, indeed, that there is some wonderful peculiarity in the American character
which distinguishes it from that of the parent race in the old country in prefer-
ring the restraint of instrumental bonds to that of moral influence.... It can, however, scarcely be doubted by those who know even a little of America and the
"inherent quality" attributed to the "universal Yankee" of peculiar resistance to
moral influences and rebellion against kindly and sympathising treatment is an
unjust and unfounded libel upon him.... The essence of the non-restraint system
is to lead the lunatic by such remains of mental power and coherence as the
physician can lay hold upon, and where there has been least mind there will be
the slightest means of moral guidance; but to make the men of the United States
an exception because they, more than others, have learned how to rule themselves, is a blundering censure upon their culture and their virtues.... Verily, we
believe that this spread-eagle apology for the bonds of freemen is the most feeble,
futile, and fallacious which could be possibly imagined [Bucknill, 1876, pp. 84,
85, 86].

Bucknill's condemnation of mechanical restraints hardened the resolve of the older generation of asylum superintendents and physicians to continue the practice, but it embarrassed the new generation that was poised to take over the leadership not just of the AMSAII but also of the emerging specialty of psychiatry. For them, promoting non-restraint in the asylums in which they worked was "the mark of a new, more scientific approach to psychiatry" (Tomes, 1988, p. 214).

Mechanical Restraints in the Age of Scientific Psychiatry

By the late 1880s, the "great restraint controversy" was no longer great, and not even much of a controversy anymore. Its fading away had as much to do with the concomitant fading away of moral treatment as it did with anything else. The use of mechanical restraints, after all, was a crucial therapeutic decision "only so long as moral influences were conceived as important factors in the cure of insanity" (Tomes, 1988, p. 217). With moral treatment gone; asylums filled beyond capacity with a staggering array of mad patients; and an emerging psychiatric interest in somatic therapeutics, the arguments for and against mechanical restraints were now being couched in utilitarian, rather than moral, terms. The questions now were about which patients needed restraint and why, under what conditions and whose orders, and for how long.

In *Youngberg v. Romeo* (1982) the United States Supreme Court ruled that asylum patients have a constitutionally protected right to reasonably safe conditions of confinement, freedom from unreasonable bodily restraints, and minimally adequate training. The only standard for determining whether these patient rights have been protected is whether professional judgment in ordering restraint or seclusion in fact had been exercised. In the court's opinion, that judgment must be considered presumptively valid. The decision, however, left the utilitarian questions unanswered.

The debate over the answers to these questions might have been vigorous behind closed asylum doors, but a consensus emerged in the contemporary psychiatric literature about the efficacy of mechanical restraints. A review of articles published between 1972 and 1994 finds that restraints work in that they reduce patient agitation and prevent patient injury; and the vast majority of asylums would find it impossible to operate efficiently without their use (Fisher, 1994, p. 1590).

The literature also recognized that nonclinical factors such as cultural biases, staff role perception, lack of staff training, and administrative attitudes influence the use of restraints as much as, if not more, than clinical factors. It also found that the use of mechanical restraints "can have substantial deleterious physical and (more often) psychological effects" on mental patients (Fisher, 1994, p. 1590), a finding most certainly influenced by the testimony of former patients who as members of the National Association of Psychiatric Survivors were taking on the utilitarian daily practices of asylums. In a series of roundtable discussions about alternatives to involuntary treatment sponsored by the National Institutes of Mental Health in the early 1990s, for example, these psychiatric survivors described the experience of being restrained as something akin to rape or physical abuse, as aversive and far from therapeutic, as a human rights rather than a utilitarian problem (Blanc & Parrish, 1990). As one psychiatric survivor argues:

> I was taken to this prison called a hospital, in handcuffs and leg shackles.... You wonder how these things begin. These things helpers call "treatment." ... You wonder how a system so sophisticated, so technologically advanced, can treat people with such cruelty. Of course, it is not the system at all.... It is *people* who lock the people into seclusion rooms, and it is people who affix the leather cuffs or the chains or the gauze strips. It is people who do this and do not have the courage to confront the unimaginable. It is people who believe they must do what they must do and that what they must do is the expedient thing. It is people who justify torture. "We're only trying to help. We don't know what else to do," they say, with their refrigerated voices [Unzicker, 1995, p. 15].

The human rights perspective on restraints was revived by the *Hartford* (CT) *Courant* in a series of investigative reports on restraint deaths that had occurred across the country between 1988 and 1998 (Weiss, 1998). Finding that most of these deaths go unreported, the investigation was able to uncover 142 restraint deaths cited in public records, 85 of which had occurred in psychiatric wards of general hospitals and in public and private psychiatric asylums; the remainder occurred in group homes and special schools for the developmentally delayed and nursing homes for the elderly. Arguing that the deaths reveal that restraints are still used as much, if not more, for "for discipline, for punishment, for the convenience of the staff" (Weiss, 1998, p. A-1) than for patient protection, the newspaper called for better staff training, stronger oversight, uniform standards, and the creation of a national database for storing and sharing restraint-related information.

The national response to the investigative report was immediate. The Health Care Finance Administration, the federal agency that administers Medicare and Medicaid, released a set of interim guidelines under the title "Patients' Rights Condition of Participation," regulations that limit the use of both restraints and seclusion in public and private hospitals and asylums that receive Medicare and Medicaid funding. Its standards specify that restraint and seclusion must never be used for coercion, discipline, staff convenience or staff retaliation; be limited to emergency situations and used only after less restrictive alternatives have failed; be authorized by a physician or independent licensed practitioner who also must evaluate the patient in question within one hour of the intervention; never be written as a standing order; and be time limited with a maximum time of four hours for adults, two hours for adolescents and children between the ages of nine and seventeen years, and one hour for children under nine years of age, with continual monitoring during the time period (Health Care Finance Administration, 1999).

A year later, an inspector general's investigation found inconsistent implementation of the federal guidelines across the country, and between public and private asylums. For example, 21 percent of the states allow "any trained," "authorized," or "qualified" person to restrain or seclude patients in public asylums, as do 27 percent of the states in private asylums; 43 percent of the states limit the period of restraint to the age-dependent one to four hour block in public asylums, but only 9 percent do the same in private asylums; 85 percent of the states meet the federal requirement of continual patient assessment during restraint or seclusion in public asylums, and 48 percent do so for private asylums. The report recommended that the Health Care Finance Administration "work aggressively with states ... to quickly raise psychiatric hospital compliance ... [and that] particular attention should be given to policies for private psychiatric hospitals" (Brown, 2000, p. 18).

A more aggressive reaction came in the form of the proposed Patient Freedom from Restraint Act of 1999 (H.R. 1313), a bill that mandated restraints be used only as a "last resort" and that every instance of use be logged along with its rationale and a plan for avoiding its use in the future and filed with the state's protection and advocacy agency. Substantial penalties, including civil fines and loss of federal funds, would be levied against any violations. The bill, however, never became law.

The restraint controversy faded after these federal initiatives were put into place, but it is easily reinvigorated each time individual cases of inappropriate or deadly restraint of asylum patients are made public. The stereotype of the mad as wild beasts in need of mastery indeed may have faded, too, over the centuries since mad patients were chained to the walls of the basement of the Pennsylvania Hospital; but it is patients who fit that old stereotype who most recently revived the restraint controversy. These "outliers," as they are referred to, are unpredictably violent to self and others and unresponsive to standard therapeutic interventions. Loopholes in federal and state laws allow asylums to seclude and restrain patients, often for months and even years at a time. One instance is recounted in the case of César Chumil (McElway, 2009). Chumil, a native of Guatemala, spent nearly 30 years in the Western State Hospital in Virginia. A violent schizophrenic who had repeatedly assaulted staff members, he spent most of those years in either an 8-point stationary restraint or a 4-point ambulatory restraint. His last few years at the hospital were spent in a specially designed "containment suite" that isolated him completely from other patients, which the State Human Rights Commission ruled was an inappropriate form of seclusion, carried out "more for the convenience of staff than for his well-being." Chumil finally was transferred to a less restrictive environment in a facility closer to his family, but died three weeks later of colon cancer. "His last days," according to his attorney, "showed the failure of a system that had lost sight of the patient." For asylum officials, the practice is necessary for the safety of the patient and the staff; for advocates, the practice is a human rights violation and is indicative of an asylum system that lacks both patience and creativity in caring for the intractably mad (Potter, 2009).

Somatic Therapeutics Controversy

The relationship between the mind and the body has been no less of a preoccupation of philosophers as it has been of asylum physicians. After all, whether the mind and body are monistically seen as one, or dualistically interpreted as separate but to some debatable extent interactive has a great deal to do with which asylum therapeutics will be favored.

American alienists and psychiatrists inherited a dualistic understanding from their European mentors. They equated the mind with consciousness; and because consciousness is always rational, they theorized that madness must emanate from the body or from some unstable connection between the mind and the body somewhere in the brain. So romanticized, madness was transformed into a legitimate subject of medical inquiry, control and treatment (Porter, 2002).

But exactly *where* in the body, or more specifically in the brain, madness originated was a matter of considerable debate. The humoural doctrine, dating back to the 4th century B.C., enjoyed a rather longer allure to American asylum physicians than it did to their European counterparts, an allure that lasted long past the doctrine's scientific credibility. Fundamental to the doctrine were the four "vital spirits" of blood, phlegm, black bile and choler, or yellow bile, that circulated through the body and whose balance was thought to be essential for both physical and mental health. The restoration of that balance through purging, vomiting, sweating, blistering, leeching, cupping and especially bleeding, was one of the favored asylum therapeutics well into the 19th century.

Benjamin Rush, Pennsylvania Hospital's therapeutic innovator, was a particularly vocal proponent not just of bleeding, but of "copious" bleeding that took 20 to 40 ounces from a mad patient in a single instance. In his rather idiosyncratic approach to therapeutics that combined humoural medicine with a manipulative version of moral treatment, Rush describes how he dealt with one of his patients—a young man filled with remorse for having killed his friend in a duel—who had demanded a pistol so that he could end his own life. Rush refused, explaining that the pistol shot would only disturb the other patients and spray his cell with blood; but he offered to "take away his life in a more easy and delicate way, by bleeding him to death, from a vein in his arm, and retaining his blood in a large bowl." Mutual expectations now in place, the young man agreed, and Rush ordered the asylum apothecary to take 20 ounces of blood from his arm. Upon doing so, the young man fainted, and was much calmer upon waking. When Rush visited him the next day, he found him "still unhappy; not from despair and hatred of life, but from a dread of death; for he now complained only, that several persons in the hospital had conspired to kill him. By the continuance of depleting remedies, this error was removed, and he was soon afterwards discharged from the hospital" (Rush, 1812, pp. 129–130).

Rush's influence on asylum therapeutics was considerable, and continued long after his death. But by 1854, the enthusiastic use of bleeding as cure-all for all types of madness had waned; indeed, it might be argued, it had vanished almost completely. It was in that year that Pliny Earle, by then a visiting physician and lecturer, published a meticulously researched treatise on the practice of bleeding that opens with the query "To bleed or not to bleed: that's the question" (Earle, 1854, p. 9). The answer, culled from the annual reports of American asylum superintendents, was resounding: bleeding, especially the "copious" type of bleeding advocated by Rush, not only produced few lasting therapeutic, let alone curative, effects, but in the long-term actually risked exacerbating the patients' madness, even while it depleted their overall physical health.

Earle's treatise tolled the demise of bleeding as an asylum therapeutic, although less "copious" versions of it in the form of leeching and cupping continued for another few years. It also tolled the demise of the humoural doctrine that had so influenced early asylum therapeutics. Asylum physicians, however, were keen to move on. Their growing experience with institutionalized mad patients, coupled with their unsteady professional standing, made a more scientific understanding of madness and its treatment both appealing and necessary. They turned their attention away from the fluids of the body to its solids, i.e., its nerves, fibers and organs, most particularly the brain. In doing so, however, they split along an ideological and thus also a therapeutic faultline. Some American asylum physicians persisted in dualistic thinking, maintaining that mind and brain, just like mind and body, are related if not separate entities, and that either, or both through their interactions, can become disordered or diseased, thus producing madness. Therefore, either or both would be the necessary target of therapeutic interventions. William White, superintendent of St. Elizabeth's Hospital, made that point clear in a letter to a colleague:

> As you may know, for a number of years, I have been writing and talking about the necessity for considering the organism as a whole and proceeding on the hypothesis that no adequate understanding of mental disease will ever be had except that it proceeds upon this basic assumption: that there is no way of understanding the psyche and its various manifestations either in health or disease,— no way of appreciating its placement in a general biological scheme of things, except as we study its evolution from this standpoint, and when we do this we must necessarily come to a realization that the history of the psyche is as old as the history of the body.... Recognizing the inextricable interrelations of somatic and psychic phenomena as expressions of the living organism as a whole, it is manifestly as illogical and as dangerous for future progress to approach the problems of that organism exclusively from either the somatic or the psychic side [cited in Grob, 1985, p. 113].

Other asylum physicians, however, turned away from mind-body dualism, embracing instead a monistic view of mind and body as inseparable and, more specifically, of the mind as nothing more than a function of the brain. Henry Cotton, superintendent of Trenton State Hospital in New Jersey, set out this position in a *New York Times* editorial addressed to lay readers whose own notions of the mind-body relationship very well may have been changing along with their understanding of the social world and their life circumstances. After describing how he eliminated all forms of mechanical restraint in the asylum, Cotton continued:

> Elimination of restraint is at best of negative character, it does not solve the real problem offered by insanity, it sheds no light on causation, and contributed nothing to a genuinely effective curative and preventive system. Recognition of this impasse was what finally led to new methods of treatment for which the hospital at Trenton has become known—methods based upon the idea that every mental difficulty has a physical basis—and, consequently, that anything which has a damaging effect upon brain tissue is certain to be attended by abnormalities of the mind.... That thousands of minds have been restored through frank recognition of the physical basis of insanity ... should be a matter of real encouragement to the lay public as well as to the medical profession [Cotton, 1932, p. 10].

This new biological model of madness that Cotton and others promoted spawned therapeutic "revolutions," often spearheaded by larger-than-life psychiatric entrepreneurs that were as dramatic as they were short-lived. Those revolutions, in turn, raised lingering questions about the ties of these therapeutics to science and to the scientific method, their efficacy and ethics, as well as doubts about their promoters' character and their specialty's credibility in what was becoming a crowded and competitive medical marketplace.

"Every Mental Difficulty Has a Physical Basis"

As early as the 4th century B.C., Hippocrates claimed to have cured a case of arthritis by pulling the patient's rotting tooth; Benjamin Rush also cured a patient of crippling arthritis of the hip by extracting his abscessed tooth. These two healers, centuries apart in time and worlds apart in geography, both theorized that focal infections of the teeth can cause systemic disease (Francke, 1973).

This germ theory of disease reached its height of popularity when, in a series of unrelated laboratory studies conducted during the late 1800s, the bacteria responsible for such diseases as typhoid fever, diphtheria, malaria, cholera, tetanus and syphilis were isolated. The infectious disease of syphilis, of course, was well known to asylum physicians; patients suffering from neurosyphilis, the tertiary stage of syphilis, accounted for a significant proportion of the asylum population.

Perhaps it was the experience with tertiary stage syphilitic patients, and the promise offered by the isolation of the bacterium responsible for it, that first led Henry Cotton to theorize that other types of madness might have a similar etiology. In 1907 Cotton had been appointed the medical superintendent of Trenton State Hospital in New Jersey, the first state asylum built as the result of the advocatory efforts of reformer Dorothea Dix. He was appalled at what greeted him: deplorable conditions, a demoralized and sometimes brutal staff, hopeless and helpless mad patients. Determined to reform the asylum, he improved its physical facilities, hired and trained new staff, and demanded they spend more time with patients and keep detailed notes of their interactions. To Cotton, these reforms were immediately necessary, but also strategic; they paved the way for his most pressing reform—the transformation of the already archaic asylum into a modern hospital where the mad would be cured by the best that medicine had to offer (Scull, 2005).

Cotton, like so many of his psychiatric peers, was certain that madness was a disease of the body, not of the mind, and that as a disease it had a single cause that could be remedied with a single cure (Noll, 2006). Influenced not only by the popular germ theory of disease, but also by a growing body of medical literature that focused on infected teeth as the cause not just of systemic diseases such as arthritis, but of madness as well, he became convinced that bacterial infection "spread pathological changes to the blood stream (toxemia) and the brain, thus providing the key to the puzzle of intractable mental disorder" (Ramchandani, 2007, p. 290). Confirm the source of the infection, he reasoned, remove it, and madness would be cured.

To that end, Cotton extracted the rotting teeth of 50 patients, all chronic back-warders, but with disappointing results. Reasoning then that the mad patients also had swallowed the saliva that was infected by tooth decay, he later removed the tonsils of 25 of them, with outstanding results: 24 who had undergone the full treatment of exodontia and tonsillectomy were discharged as recovered (Scull, 2005). Buoyed by this success, Cotton "started literally to 'clean up' [the] patients of all foci of chronic sepsis" (Cotton, 1923, p. 437), removing not only their teeth and tonsils, but parts of their stomachs and small intestines, their appendixes, gallbladders, uteri, thyroid glands and, especially, their colons in the asylum's new surgical suites.

Why the colon? Certainly there was a lingering influence of humoural theory in targeting this part of the digestive system. But there was also a growing body of medical literature that was implicating infections of the colon, especially the proximal segment known as the right colon where ingested materials are absorbed, as the cause of dementia praecox, now known as schizophrenia. It was there that ingested materials could ferment, or the movement of fecal material out of the body could be slowed or even stopped, thus increasing the risk of infection. If indeed madness was the result of this infection, the cure was obvious: remove the infected portion of the colon.

It is important to appreciate that in the early 20th century, focal sepsis and its surgical cure were well within the bounds of both medical knowledge and acceptable medical practice (Porter, 1997). The controversy that eventually engulfed this surgical cure for madness had less to do with the changing contours of medical knowledge than with its zealous use and the exaggerated claims of a few psychiatric entrepreneurs.

Bayard Taylor Holmes, a surgeon and bacteriologist, was one of those psychiatric entrepreneurs. His own meticulous laboratory research conducted over a decade had led him to the conclusion that focal sepsis of the colon was the cause of dementia praecox. Although his research finding required careful follow-up and replication before it could be considered valid, Holmes was eager to act on it. In a Chicago, Illinois, hospital in 1916, he performed an appendicostomy—a surgical opening of the tip of the diverticulum of the right colon to irrigate the bowel—on a 28-year-old former medical student who had been suffering from dementia praecox for a decade. Post-surgery, he irrigated the patient's colon with a mixture of water and magnesium sulfate. The patient, who was Holmes' own son, died four days later. Perhaps this unfortunate death should have sent Holmes back into the laboratory to reexamine his findings; instead, he hurried into the surgery suite, where he quickly operated on two more dementia praecox patients. Buoyed by the fact that both were "apparently improved" (Holmes, 1916, p. 702), Holmes then prematurely claimed in a published medical journal article that he had found both the cause and the cure of dementia praecox.

Such hyperbolic claims almost always invite close scrutiny, but Holmes dismissed a colleague's refusal to "pervert my laboratory findings to fit some preconceived theory" as nothing more than professional jealousy (cited in Noll, 2006, p. 306) and continued performing appendicostomies and colonic irrigations on dementia praecox patients. Before his death in 1924, Holmes and several surgeons instructed by him had performed a total of 22 appendicostomies, but with decidedly mixed results. Although still certain he had unlocked the impenetrable mystery of dementia praecox, Holmes was ignored by his medical colleagues. Why? No doubt the answer lies in the fact that he was overshadowed by Henry Cotton.

Between 1918 and 1925, Cotton and his medical team performed 300 partial or full colectomies on asylum patients diagnosed with dementia praecox; 25 percent of the patients recovered, but 33 percent died, most of them from peritonitis (Scull, 2005, p. 259). Despite these low cure rates and disturbingly high mortality rates, Cotton sought every opportunity to make his colleagues, state politicians, and the general public aware of his revolutionary surgical cure for madness. He published articles in prestigious medical journals, delivered papers in professional meetings, and gave talks to medical school students and community groups, urging parents to consider colectomies for their children as a prophylactic to head off future behavioral and mental problems, as he himself had done for his own two sons (Scull, 2005). Cotton credited himself with having single-handedly broken through the therapeutic nihilism of his profession and instilling hope for the cure of intractable madness. The prospect of witnessing what had been thought impossible—back-warders finally leaving the asylum, sans teeth, an organ or two, and a segment of the colon, of course—seemed to many reason enough not to question this surgical therapeutic.

Curiously, it was not the disturbing mortality statistics, or any scientific refutation of focal sepsis theory or, for that matter, questions about the ethics of performing surgeries on patients often too mad to appreciate what was happening to them, let alone to give consent, that brought about the end of surgical therapeutics at Trenton State Hospital. Rather, it was Cotton's pandering to the politicians and the larger public, trying to sell them on a surgical solution to madness and to raise money for the transformation of the asylum into a modern hospital, that provoked his peers to urge an investigation into his surgical practices and outcome data. The specially constituted Bright Investigating Committee, a legislative committee looking into waste and fraud in state government, did just that in 1925 in a series of hearings that were voraciously reported on by the press that always had favorably covered Cotton and his work. It took testimony from "a parade of disgruntled employees, malicious ex-patients, and their families, testifying in damning detail about brutality, forced and botched surgery, debility and death" (Scull, 2005, p. 176). Although vigorously defended by a few of his peers, the hearings took a toll on Cotton. Becoming increasingly erratic and disorientated, he no longer attended the Committee hearings, and was quietly removed from his duties as the medical superintendent of Trenton State Hospital. Interestingly, the psychiatrist whose whole career was predicated upon the belief that madness was a disease of the body attributed his own breakdown to heart and kidney ailments that were exacerbated by the stress of the investigation, as the *New York Times* reported: "It was said today that [Cotton] was suffering from a nervous disorder as well as an acute ailment. Dr. Cotton took to his bed late Wednesday afternoon on his return to his home ... from the State House, where he had attended a session of the Bright investigating committee, which is examining into conditions at the hospital following charges that patients were ill-treated there.... It is said that the strain of these investigations has aggravated Dr. Cotton's condition" ("Dr. Cotton," 1925, p. 4).

While secreted away, recovering from his breakdown, Cotton missed the testimony of Phyllis Greenacre to the Bright Investigating Committee. The young psychiatrist had spent months reviewing patient files at Trenton State Hospital at the request of Cotton's mentor, Adolf Meyer, then an esteemed professor of psychiatry at Johns Hopkins University. Looking at records of patient outcomes, Greenacre realized that Cotton's claims of successfully curing dementia praecox through surgical procedures were wildly exaggerated. What particularly drew her attention was a group of patients who had undergone the most aggressive surgical interventions; of those 62 patients, 17 had died immediately of postoperative shock or peritonitis, and several more had lingered for months before dying, and therefore were never calculated as surgical mortality statistics. Only five had recovered completely; an additional three were improved but still symptomatic; and the remainder were unimproved, leading Greenacre to conclude that "the lowest recovery rate and the highest death rate occurs among the functional cases who have been thoroughly treated.... [T]he least treatment was found in the recovered cases and the most thorough treatment in the unimproved and dead groups" (cited in Scull, 2005, p. 200).

Greenacre also hunted down ex-patients and interviewed them extensively. She became convinced that many who had been discharged as cured or as improved were, in fact, neither. All of these observations and data analysis were put into a report that was all but ignored by the Bright Investigating Committee, so distracted it apparently was by a barrage of obfuscating data, learned opinions, and ad hominem attacks by Cotton's peers who were called to his defense, as well as by Cotton himself. What had begun with such vigor ended with a whimper: the Bright Investigating Committee dismantled its grandstand and assured its critics that it no longer had an interest in the therapeutics practiced by Cotton at the Trenton State Hospital.

The ruling gave Cotton carte blanche to continue his surgical procedures on mad patients, lecture across the country and Europe, and continue to build a lucrative private practice from the most wealthy patients seeking admittance into the Trenton State Hospital. Yet he could not escape controversy. A Swiss psychiatrist was appalled at what he observed upon his extended visit: hundreds of mad patients without teeth, aggressive surgical interventions upon the scantiest laboratory findings of focal infection, slipshod recordkeeping and inflated recovery rates. Another investigation, this one at the behest of the hospital's board and conducted by the director of the New Jersey Department of Institutions and Agencies, examined the records of 645 patients who had undergone colectomies or pericolic membranotomies and compared those to the records of 407 patients who had not undergone these surgeries. His findings were unsettling (Table 5).

Despite Cotton's persistent claims of surgical success in curing madness, the data showed otherwise. In addition, the mortality rate of patients who underwent the most invasive of the surgeries, the colectomy, remained startlingly high. This study, just like the one Greenacre had conducted years before, seemed to reveal the futility of trying to cure madness through surgical techniques.

From his new position as director of research at Trenton State Hospital, Cotton reacted with defiance and became more determined than ever to convert his peers, politicians and the public to his cause. Eager to return to his post as medical superintendent, from which he had been quietly removed

Table 5: "End Results" of 645 Major Operative Cases and 407 Non-Operative Cases

	Colectomies (N = 309)	Pericolic Membranotomies (N = 336)	Nonsurgical (N = 407)
Died	44.7%	13.7%	18.0%
In Asylum	32.7%	55.4%	30.2%
Released/Recovered	7.6%	12.5%	26.5%
Released/Improved	7.4%	13.4%	16.7%
Released/Unknown	6.1%	5.0%	8.6%

(cited in and adapted from Scull, 2005, p. 265)

after the Bright Investigating Committee hearings, he argued before the hospital board that it must have been undetected infections that accounted for the high surgical mortality rate, therefore, if *all* of the teeth, not just the obviously infected ones, were extracted from *all* surgical candidates, the mortality rate would significantly decrease.

Cotton died soon after launching this campaign to increase the number of surgeries that had been virtually halted in the face of scandals, internecine battles, and disconfirming findings at Trenton State Hospital. He was eulogized in the *Trenton Evening Times* as a "great pioneer whose humanitarian influence was, and will continue to be, of such monumental proportions" ("Death Notice," 1933, p. 6).

While Cotton might be retrospectively written off as nothing more than a "maniacal Trenton psychiatrist" (Shorter, 1997, p. 112), the fact remains that what he believed and what he practiced were inextricably linked to the social context and the state of medical knowledge in the early 20th century. While he had his detractors and critics, they were either unable or unwilling to challenge that link. Part of the strength of that link was due to the favorable publicity he garnered. The national press, for example, lauded his work, and in doing so stirred up public optimism that what heretofore had been impossible—the cure of dementia praecox—now was within easy reach. So enticing was this hope that not only did the families and friends of the Trenton State Hospital patients agree to, or at least not disagree with, the surgeries performed, but wealthy people across the country also brought their loved ones to Cotton for a surgical cure (Scull, 2005). The air of despair that had always surrounded madness seemed finally to be lifting. A *Trenton Evening Times* article mocked those who would suggest otherwise:

> Dr. Henry A. Cotton ... can hardly ask for a better endorsement of his new methods of treating insane patients than is contained in the statement that within the past two years the discharge rate from the institution has overtaken the admission rate.... Jealous rivals may ridicule what they call the "tooth-pulling" treatment practiced by Dr. Cotton but results count, and when one can show that his methods have measurably increased the number of cures and made a noticeable decrease in the hospital population, which for years has shown a steady increase, he can afford to laugh at his critics and feel encouraged that he is pursuing his experiments in the right direction ["Treating the Insane," 1921, p. 6].

The Bright Investigating Committee aside, politicians also lauded Cotton not for the science of focal sepsis theory, but for fiscal savings to the state that the resulting surgical therapeutics offered. Across the nation, the number of state asylum patients had increased 36 percent, from 187,791 to 255,245 between 1910 and 1923 alone (Torrey & Miller, 2001, p. 288), far outpacing the increase in the general population, thus leaving the distinct impression that madness was epidemic. State asylums quickly became over-crowded, understaffed, and although also underfunded, extremely expensive for states to maintain. Thus the prospect of checking the increase in mad-ness, emptying asylums, and surgically transforming those who had been debilitated by madness into useful and productive citizens was particularly appealing to the fiscal bottom line.

Many of his peers also lauded Cotton's surgical therapeutics, as evi-denced not only by their passionate defense of them during the Bright Inves-tigating Committee hearings, but also by their equally passionate desire to transform their own aging asylums into modern hospitals for the cure of mad-ness. In Missouri, for example, dental surgeons volunteered their expertise and equipment to perform exodontias on 724 patients in the state asylum; citing "sufficient improvement" in a "number" of them, they hoped to con-vince the state to fund a state-of-the-art dental surgical suite in the aging asylum ("Dental Surgery," 1920, p. 7). Cotton's surgical therapeutics also had the imprimatur of the prestigious Mayo Clinic and of the British Medical Association. In fact, in Great Britain, where his theory of focal sepsis remained popular well into the 1940s, exodontia and colectomies were routinely per-formed on asylum patients, as were sphenoidotomies. The latter, which involved the surgical opening of the sphenoid sinus, was touted as a cure for criminal insanity (Fairley, 1991).

Although a significant body of medical knowledge on the etiologic rela-tionship between focal sepsis and dementia praecox had developed over the years Cotton was performing surgeries on mad patients, a much smaller body of carefully designed and experimentally controlled studies found no evi-dence that the surgical removal of focal sepsis, by itself, brought about recov-ery (Kopeloff & Cheney, 1922; Kopeloff & Kirby, 1923). These findings, and Cotton's subsequent dismissal of them, were the topics of contentious debate when presented at the annual meeting of the American Psychiatric Associ-ation in 1922; yet calls for a thorough investigation of his work, and fainter calls for abandoning it altogether, were shouted down (Scull, 2005).

In the tactful language of the profession and of the era, the wisdom of Cotton's approach—if not its science and ethics—was less acrimoniously debated in exchanges of letters between some of the most prominent physi-cians of the time. William White, superintendent of St. Elizabeth's Hospital, for example, disclosed in a 1919 letter to the superintendent of the Georgia State Sanitarium that Cotton's focus on infected teeth "is a most unfortunate one" since "anything that impairs the general health of the individual may be a factor in causing a mental break" (cited in Grob, 1985, p. 109). In 1922, the associate editor of *Southern Medicine and Surgery*, prompted by a man-uscript submitted by Cotton, wrote to a colleague that Cotton was "infected with red ants"; not only was he depriving his patients of their teeth and colons, but he was "injudicious in his attitude and unsound in his reasoning" (cited in Grob, 1985, p. 110). The editor urged his colleague to send data about how the treatment of asylum patients has been contravened by inadequate state funding, rather than by ignorant physicians, so that he could counter Cotton's argument that only physicians schooled in the theory of focal sepsis and trained in advanced surgical therapeutics would be successful in treating the mad. Even Adolf Meyer, mentor and ardent defender of Cotton, was more circumspect in a 1927 letter to a Norwegian colleague, saying that his own assessment of Cotton's claims did not give him "the impression [that] his own figures could be anywhere near correct," that his claimed success in treating madness might be "due to the atmosphere of action and helpfulness which pervade the place, and that the diagnosis and estimation of the condition in the discharged cases is strongly colored by a policy rather than a painstaking scrutiny of the cases." Finding it "deplorable" that there had not been more control over Cotton's surgical therapeutics, Meyer emphatically concluded that "such an experiment will hardly ever be possible again" (cited in Grob, 1985, p. 115).

The focal sepsis theory of madness lingered for some time after Cotton's death in 1933, but even at Trenton State Hospital, the enthusiasm for performing the most invasive and riskiest of the surgical therapeutics, the colectomy, waned considerably. Teeth were still being pulled and tonsils were still being removed in state asylums across the country, but different ideas about the relationship between the mind and the body led to different surgical therapeutics and, despite Meyer's pronouncement that that they would never be possible again, different experiments on mad patients.

Gynecological surgeries are a case in point. While Cotton did perform oophorectomies (the removal of one or both ovaries), salpingectomies (the removal of the fallopian tubes), and enucleations of the cervix, reasoning that these organs, too, were susceptible to focal sepsis and thus causal of madness, gynecological surgeries were being done with much more enthusiasm by other physicians at other asylums.

The notion that women's madness was intimately related to their sexual organs can be traced to Hippocrates, who, in the 4th century B.C., theorized that the wombs of women who were not fulfilling their biological destiny of procreation meandered about their bodies causing all manner of mental distress that he termed hysteria, literally translated as "wandering womb." While it is true that not all women asylum patients were diagnosed with hysteria, in fact in the United States not all that many were, the disproportionate number of women patients vis-à-vis men kept this theory of madness very much in play.

But just exactly how asylum physicians reasoned through the relationship between women's bodies and their minds varied and was the source of considerable contention. Some rejected the idea altogether, and not all of them were the women physicians who were allowed to work in asylums for the first time in the late 1800s with the expectation that their "inherent constitution" would cause them to "exhibit more sympathy in the care of their afflicted sisters than might be expected from the so-called sterner sex" ("Relation of Diseases," 1887, p. 765). After comparing the results of the gynecological examinations of mad women patients in the Willard Asylum in upstate New York with those of mentally healthy women of the same social class, Alice May Farnham found comparably high incidences of sexual organ disease in both groups, leading her to conclude that if it were "really so powerful an agent in the production of insanity it would be a matter for wonder that, with the alarming prevalence of such disorders, so few women exhibit profound nervous disturbances" (Farnham, 1887, p. 544). In his role as surgeon at the Manhattan State Hospital on Ward's Island in New York City, Leroy Broun routinely performed gynecological surgery, but only with the goal of improving the physical, as opposed to the mental, conditions of the patients. And while he acknowledged that the mental recovery of patients sometimes was hastened by the physical relief surgery provided, he saw no reason to remove the otherwise healthy reproductive organs of mad women in order to alter their mental state, as some of his colleagues across the country were doing. "It is contrary to all surgical experience," he said in a paper delivered to his colleagues, "to expect that the removal of the normal ovaries and tubes in a woman during her active sexual life can result other than disastrously to the nervous system even in women having no mental alienation— how much more so with those who have a weakened nervous potentiality ... or in those already insane" (Broun, 1906, p. 411).

Other asylum physicians engaged in the kind of specificity logic exemplified by Hippocrates, i.e., a line of reasoning that argued for a causal link between women's sexual organs and madness (Zetka, 2008); and in this case, not all of them were practitioners of the emerging specialty of gynecology. Richard Bucke, medical superintendent of the Asylum for the Insane in Ontario, Canada, is a case in point. Stating that the uterus and the mammary glands render all women more emotional and irrational than men, he went on to argue that it therefore was only logical to conclude that diseases of the uterus and mammary glands were the causes of madness in those women who were institutionalized. Gynecological surgery, then, was their only hope for a cure. He held out the results of 161 of those surgeries as proof of his hypothesis: 62 of the women recovered completely, 43 improved mentally, 52 improved only physically, and 4 died (cited in Mitchinson, 1982,

p. 471). When asked to speak on these findings to his American colleagues, however, Bucke was confronted by W.P. Manton, the first gynecologist hired to work in an American asylum, in this case the Eastern Michigan Insane Asylum. Manton insisted that he had "never yet, either in asylum practice or in private practice, seen a case of insanity, other than puerperal, that could be attributed to pelvic disorder alone. And I am also ready to state," he went on before an audience of his colleagues, "that I have never yet seen a mental cure of insanity through purely surgical procedures" (Bucke, p. 103).

The spirited debate that followed captured the conflicting opinions within the specialties of psychiatry and gynecology, and between them, and were as much about the status of each as well as about the proprietary control of mad women as they were about etiologic theories and asylum therapeutics (Theriot, 1993; Zetka, 2008). In fact, so heated had that debate become among American asylum physicians that even George Rohé, medical superintendent of the Second Hospital for the Insane in Cantonville, Maryland, retreated from specificity logic in the face of sustained and vocal criticisms of the gynecological surgeries he performed. Although he stood by his finding that 14 of the 34 mad women he operated on were "physically and mentally cured" by the surgeries, and that an additional 5 had improved, he reluctantly acknowledged the possibility that the etiologic relationship between diseased sexual organs and women's madness might not be as specific as he originally had imagined:

> If it is true that pelvic disease is prevalent among insane women (an assertion easily confirmed or refuted by further observation) the question arises, Has the pelvic disease any etiologic relation to the mental disturbance? Upon this point, much more extended clinical observation is desirable. I incline to the belief that there is such an etiologic relation. But my experience is as yet too limited to establish that opinion as an axiom. The personal equation which governs every observer's work has not yet been determined. Others, with the same material might arrive at a different conclusion. But no one has a right to deny the accuracy of my observations, or the validity of my inferences, unless upon a similar basis of personal experience. I refuse to recognize the authority of any critic "up a tree." He must come down from his perch and meet facts with facts. Arguments based upon prejudice will not answer [Rohé, 1895, p. 625].

Because contemporary feminist scholars argue convincingly that the history of women's madness is the history of the changing nature of the role and status of women vis-à-vis men in a historically patriarchal society (Cayleff, 1988; Micale, 1995; Showalter, 1998), no arguments about gynecological surgical therapeutics seem unprejudiced. For those asylum physicians who rejected the specificity logic of Rohé but who remained committed to surgical intervention as a therapeutic, the alternative radical logic (Zetka, 2008) was equally biased. It reasoned that body does not unilaterally affect mind, but that the mind-body relationship, particularly in women, who were thought to be by nature emotionally labile, is more complex than it is for men. Therefore, not only can sexual organs reflexively affect the mind, and the mind reflexively affect the sexual organs, producing such things as menstrual disorders and infertility, but the mind can also take the raw materials of the historically situated everyday conflicts of women—the balance between the roles of wife and mother, the drive for independence, the rejection of gender role stereotypes, the expressions of sexual desire, as examples—and psychosomatically transform them into bodily symptoms. Clara Barrus, in her study of 100 women patients in the Middletown State Hospital in New York, for whom she found a high rate of sexual organ disease and disorder, advocated this position:

> The causes of insanity in women may be, nay, they probably are, as varied, and many of them identical with, the causes of insanity in men; for we have to always remember that both before and after one is a wife and mother (and consequently subjected to the forms of puerperal and lactational insanity), one is a human being, and the elements that enter into the causation of mental aberration in women will develop along the line of the experiences and inheritances that come to her as a human being, *with the addition* of those which come to her as a human being of the female sex. Therefore, domestic troubles, reverses of fortune, worry and overwork, and excesses both in drink and in sexual matters, are among the causes of insanity in both men and women, together with the predisposing causes of bad heredity, of consanguinity of parents, of epilepsy, etc. Besides these, women have the additional physical and mental strain resulting from the physiological crises which come to them as women—the establishment of puberty, the regularly recurring monthly period through their menstrual life (when uninterrupted by diseased conditions or by pregnancy); pregnancy itself, and the attendant perils of partuition; the puerperal state, and lactation; then having undergone all of these, the grand climacteric.... One is led to ask why the generative organs should play a more important part in women than in men in the causation of disease. Gynaecologists explain it by saying that the ganglionic system of nerves in women is more developed than in men.... The intimate relation between the sympathetic and the cerebro-spinal nervous systems, their reciprocal action on each other, explains why we witness so many reflex functional disturbances from local lesions. At the same time we know that the gravest lesions of the reproductive organs do not cause mental disturbance in some women, while the slightest local trouble affects others profoundly, and out of all proportion to the extent of the lesions found. For an explanation of this fact we must consider the instability, in individual cases, of the central nervous system, and its susceptibility to disturbing influences.... [I]n the face of the fact that the majority of insane women present varying degrees of local lesions, one conclusion, at least, may be reached. We should examine each case as soon as possible to find out whether or not there is any abnormality, and finding it, remove it as far as possible; by doing so we shall have lessened the degree of nerve irritation, and shall have at least removed some of the "stumbling blocks" in the way of the patient's recovery [Barrus, 1895, pp. 477, 478, 484].

While this complex mind-body relationship set out by Barrus certainly did not preclude the need for gynecological surgery, as she pointed out, it did make choosing surgical candidates from the large population of women asylum patients a more arduous task. If only women whose madness was specifically caused by their sexual organs were operated upon, as opposed to those whose madness was caused by some complexly reflexive interaction between mind, body and life circumstances, then the cure rate surely would increase.

It was this logic that legitimated gynecological surgery as an asylum therapeutic, as opposed to a relief from physical suffering, well into the 1950s when asylums across the country ceased performing the last of these gynecological surgeries—clitoridectomy—on women patients whose excessive sexual desire led to a diagnosis of nymphomania. Interestingly, it was neither findings of psychiatric nor of medical research that halted the practice. Rather, it was the changing times and women's relation to them. As sexual attitudes liberalized, sexual expressions were normalized by large scale studies of the sexual feelings and behaviors of ordinary people; further, as sexual desires made the stuff of popular culture, the diagnosis of nymphomania and its classification as a sexual deviation that required institutional treatment and control all but disappeared (Groneman, 2001).

"A Therapeutic Noble Deed"

As early as the 1860s European physicians were describing a kind of "premature dementia" that struck young people, leaving them incoherent and confused. These early studies were largely observational in nature and concentrated more on describing the presenting symptoms of delusions, hallucinations, and disordered thinking than on hypothesizing a cause. It was Emil Kraepelin, the German psychiatrist who is posthumously remembered as the "father of modern psychiatry," who labeled this debilitating form of madness "dementia praecox" and hypothesized that it almost certainly was the result of heredity factors and chemical disturbances in the brain. The Swiss psychiatrist Eugen Bleuler suggested in 1908 that the diagnosis be renamed "schizophrenia," which he found more descriptive of the "splitting of the mind" that was the hallmark of this form of madness. But Bleuler, too, was certain its cause was biological, arising from some kind of toxicity that is separate from any of the more psychological influences. Once the diagnosis had been established, the number of asylum admissions for schizophrenia increased rapidly; and asylum physicians, left to hypothesize about its elusive cause, launched a series of experimental and often short-lived therapeutic assaults on it.

One of those therapeutic experiments was conducted by Robert Carroll at Highland Hospital in Asheville, North Carolina. Although the asylum boasted a range of therapeutics from hydrotherapy, diet and exercise, and electroconvulsive shocks, to psychotherapy, it was Carroll's experiments with the injection of horse blood into the cerebrospinal fluid of his schizophrenic patients that the asylum's glossy promotional brochure failed to mention (Highland Hospital, 1943).

Carroll was struck by observations reported in the medical literature that schizophrenic patients sometimes improved during the leucocytosis stage of infectious processes. It is during that stage that the body increases its production of white blood cells to fight off the infection. By replacing 25 cc's of cerebrospinal fluid with an equal amount of horse serum, Carroll was able to produce aseptic meningitis in schizophrenic patients. The resulting fevers and inflammation of the brain, he reasoned, would not only stimulate the body's immune system to attack the meningitis, but to repair what he suspected was the damaged choroid plexuses of the brain, the areas where cerebrospinal fluid is produced and where many medical researchers had been looking for some time in an effort to solve the mystery of schizophrenia. Once repaired, Carroll hypothesized, these sections of the brain could resume their function of maintaining the extracellular environment needed for optimal brain function. Carroll treated five cases at Highland Hospital with this experimental therapeutic and reported "temporary or permanent improvement" in each (Carroll, 1923).

Although skeptical of his theory, asylum physicians at the Philadelphia Hospital for Mental Disease used the horse serum therapeutic on a total of 49 patients, with interesting results: 6 schizophrenic patients went into remission, 28 showed continuing improvement, 14 showed either temporary improvement or none at all, and one died of a preexisting condition. Since the evaluative terms of "remission" and "improvement" are not defined, a sample of the case studies offer some glimpse into how the efficacy of this treatment was assessed, as well as into the experience of being an institutionalized schizophrenic (Carroll, Barr, Berry, & Matzke, 1925):

Case 38—R.K., white male, age 29 ... A case of paranoid dementia praecox of several months' duration. Symptoms: Restive, negative, seclusive, at times assaultive in reaction to tormenting hallucinations. Given five treatments. Is much brighter, talks and laughs quite normally, cheerful and helps willingly with hard work. Had formerly been regarded as a dangerous patient. His parents regard him as cured. Final result, remission [p. 697].

Case 26—C.N., female (colored), age 37 ... A case of hebephrenic dementia praecox. Symptoms, silly, foolish, untidy, evasive, hallucinated and at times excited and violent. Given five treatments, has had no attacks of excitement since last treatment (two months ago). Is quiet, tidy and works on ward, still foolish and reacts to hallucinations. Final result, better institutional adjustment [pp. 694–695].

Case 42—H.Y., white male, age 34 ... A case of paranoid dementia praecox of several year's duration.... Symptoms: seclusive, paranoid, hallucinated and very fearful. Given four treatments. For a time appeared much better; talked coherently about his former ideas and hallucinations, laughing about them, but suddenly relapsed and became violent and homicidal in his actions. Final result, nil [p. 697].

Case 40—F.H., white male, age 22 ... A case of catatonic dementia praecox of several weeks' (?) duration. Symptoms: Mute, restive, and negative. Filthy in habits and very destructive. A "runaway." Given five treatments without a particle of improvement; in fact, grew worse. Final result, nil [p. 697].

Interestingly, Carroll never wrote a case study of one of his most famous patients, Zelda Fitzgerald, in whom the horse serum injection produced a moment or two of encouraging lucidity after three days of recurring high fevers, vomiting and debilitating headaches. Diagnosed as schizophrenic, the writer, artist, dancer and wife of novelist F. Scott Fitzgerald was admitted into the Highland Hospital in 1936 and was reluctantly discharged four years later with a note from Carroll that absolved her famous husband of any blame should she relapse. Carroll wrote:

> Mrs. F's history shows a definite cyclic tendency and we look forward with apprehension to her inability to meet emotional situations, to face infections, or to indulge in alcohol, tobacco or drugs without a rapid return to her maniacal irresponsibility. Let it be known that Mrs. F. is capable of being absolutely irresponsible and intensely suicidal. Her present condition, however, is one of gentleness, reasonable capacity for cooperation and yet with definitely reduced judgment maturity [cited in Cline, 2002, p. 376].

Indeed, Fitzgerald did relapse and was readmitted to Highland Hospital several times over the ensuing years. She died there, along with eight other patients, in a fire in 1948. By that time Carroll had retired and his aseptic meningitis cure for madness, if not exactly discredited, was relegated to the margins of asylum therapeutics by long-term follow-up studies of patients and detailed single case studies that showed its effects were short-lived at best (Barr & Berry, 1926; Rudolf, 1931; Viner, 1933). However, interest in the role of the choroid plexus in schizophrenia continues to this day. Research studies often find anomalies in these brain structures in schizophrenic subjects (Carlson, Weingart, Guarnieri, & Fisher, 1997; Rudin, 1980; Sandyk, 1990).

Carroll was just one in a line of psychiatric entrepreneurs who were experimenting with fever induction to cure madness. Inspired both by Louis Pasteur's finding that high temperatures could kill bacteria—a finding that led to the pasteurization of food—and the success of the Austrian physician Julius Wagner von Jauregg in slowing or killing the spirochete that caused syphilis by inducing fevers in tertiary stage syphilitic patients, they began experimenting with a variety of febrile agents. In asylums across the country, tertiary stage neurosyphilitic patients were inoculated via intravenous injection with tertian malaria, a rarely fatal type of malaria caused by the protozoan *Plasmodium vivax*. After an incubation period of about a week, the patients would experience chills and nausea, followed by raging fever of more than 106 degrees Fahrenheit that lasted several hours. Over the next several days, fevers would alternate with chills until the patients were administered quinine sulfate to terminate the malarial infection, but not before a few milliliters of their blood were extracted to be used to infect the next batch of syphilitic patients. By the 1920s published case studies showed that more than half of all treated patients either went into full remission or showed at least some improvement, and the popular press had proclaimed the procedure a "therapeutic noble deed" (cited in Brown, 2000, p. 380). Subsequent studies, few of which were empirical in nature, generally repeated these findings (Braslow, 1997).

Malarial fever therapy effectively transformed the asylum physician-patient relationship. The prevailing attitude of both had probably reflected the larger social attitude, i.e., syphilis is the consequence of moral failure. Prior to malarial fever therapy, asylum physicians had little to offer their patients except the arsenical compound Salvarsan, coupled with a good dose of moral condemnation; after it, they began engaging their patients in a therapeutic dialogue, listening to them and soliciting their ideas and their cooperation for a course of treatment. In the absence of empirical studies that proved its efficacy, "it is possible that shared belief and the altered relationship brought about by changes in perception created malaria fever's apparent biological success" (Braslow, 1997, p. 93).

Syphilitic patients comprised as much as 20 percent of the asylum population, so the prospect of slowing or arresting the progression of the infection was encouraging, and stimulated more psychiatric entrepreneurship over the pre-penicillin decades. Harry C. Solomon, of the Boston Psychopathic Hospital, in an effort to avoid some of the drawbacks of malarial fever therapy, reported some positive results from injecting *Spirochaeta morsus-muris*, better known as rat-bite fever, into syphilitic patients, producing skin rashes, violent shaking and relapsing fevers. *Time* magazine reported with some enthusiasm the attempt to replicate those results on a sample of Illinois asylum patients with tertiary syphilis. Of the 72 patients, 14 showed some mental improvement, 30 showed some physical improvement, and 10 died, although only two of those deaths were attributed to the treatment ("Rat Bite," 1929).

Malarial fever therapy had its critics, though. While it was apparently successful in treating those patients whose madness was the result of the tertiary stage of neurosyphilis, it did little, if anything, for those whose madness had nothing to do with an infectious spirochetal bacterium. It was also expensive and tricky to dispense, requiring the careful matching of blood type between donor and recipient, and the laboratory confirmation that it was tertian malaria and not some other type that was being administered. Despite these caveats, malarial fever therapy was used on tertiary stage neurosyphilitic patients well onto the 1950s.

Despite the lack of evidence of their efficacy, fever therapies of all kinds also were administered to patients whose madness was not the result of syphilis, or for that matter any other organic cause. Mad patients not only were inoculated with malaria and rat-bite fever, but also were wedged between condenser plates and bombarded with short-waves, confined in infrared or carbon filament diathermy cabinets, wrapped in electric blankets, or submerged in hot water, all in attempts to raise their body temperature and produce something akin to the what Wagner von Jauregg, who was awarded the Nobel Prize in 1927, had done with some success for his neurosyphilitic patients.

The idea that fever can cure madness is as old as medicine itself. As early as the 4th century B.C. Hippocrates noted that malarial fever could have a calming effect on epileptics; later, Galen described a case of melancholy cured by malarial fever. Physicians over the centuries described such things as hysterical fits remedied by cholera fever, and even the remediating effects of typhoid fever on patients in overcrowded and unsanitary asylums that were particularly prone to typhoid epidemics. Interestingly, for just as long, physicians have noted that fevers can cause madness as well (Whitrow, 1990). This historic interest in fever cures effectively ended in the 1950s, however, with the discovery that penicillin cures syphilis. With the consequent decline in the number of tertiary stage syphilitics admitted to asylums, fever cures as a therapeutic for any type of madness effectively were rendered obsolete. However, interest in it still arises occasionally, one instance being described in Curran et al. (2007): Parents and clinicians often report that behaviors of autistic children improve during episodes of fever. The responses of 30 parents to the Aberrant Behavior Checklist were collected during and after their autistic children's episodes of fever. Data were compared to responses from parents whose autistic children were fever-free during similar time intervals. Fewer aberrant behaviors, i.e., irritability, hyperactivity, stereotypy and inappropriate speech were recorded for the febrile autistic children. All improvements, however, were transient.

"As Dramatic as Medieval Magic"

When Princeton mathematician John Forbes Nash, Jr., was admitted to Trenton State Hospital in 1961, its vainglorious medical superintendent Henry

Cotton had been dead for decades and his surgical therapeutics for focal sepsis were largely forgotten. Nash, inventor of a theory of rational behavior that later would earn him a Nobel Prize and was the subject of a best-selling biography, *A Beautiful Mind* (Nasar, 1998), and an Academy Award–winning film by the same title, underwent a somatic therapeutic that once was hailed as "dramatic as medieval magic" because of the hope it brought to "hundreds of thousands of persons otherwise condemned to a life of constant nightmare" (Ratcliff, 1938, p. 38).

Insulin shock therapy had come to the United States in the 1930s and had quickly eclipsed surgical therapeutics for madness in popularity. While "shock" was a familiar medical concept, it was not introduced into psychiatry until 1926 when French psychiatrist Constance Pascal theorized that dementia praecox (schizophrenia) was the result of "mental anaphylactic reactions" and could be cured by shocking the brain and the autonomic nervous system into equilibrium with any one of a number of different agents, including colloidal gold, milk and turpentine (Barbier, Serra, Loas, & Breathnach, 1999). When insulin, a pancreatic hormone that regulates blood sugar or glucose, was discovered, it, too became an agent for producing the kind of non-convulsive shock to the brain that Pascal considered therapeutic. A deficit of insulin, of course, produces hyperglycemia, better known as diabetes; but an excess, which was of much more interest to asylum physicians, shocks the brain by depriving it of glucose, and can lead to coma and sometimes even death.

While European asylum physicians were somewhat quietly experimenting with injecting their mad patients with insulin, it was a young neurologist, Manfred Sakel, working in a German asylum, who assumed the entrepreneurial role of promoting insulin shock therapy as a cure for madness. He had been injecting heroin addicts with insulin to ease them through the withdrawal stage; one of those addicts, a schizophrenic, slipped into a coma that Sakel, apparently startled by the reaction, quickly reversed with an injection of glucose. To Sakel's surprise, the patient's schizophrenic symptoms improved. On the basis of this single observation, Sakel was convinced he had discovered the cure for schizophrenia.

Although Sakel engaged in a great deal of post hoc theorizing to explain why the induction of an insulin coma should have a remitting effect on schizophrenic symptoms, he and his protégés never agreed on a coherent rationale (Braslow, 1997; Vallenstein, 1986). Nevertheless, schizophrenic patients flooded his private sanatorium in Vienna, Austria. His claim that he was able to bring 50 of the first 58 recent onset schizophrenics he treated to full or partial remission was widely reported, even if it was never replicated in European medical circles or, for that matter, in American medical circles. He also treated others, including Vaslav Nijinsky (1890–1950), whose experience is recounted in *The Diary of Vaslav Nijinsky* (Acocella, 1999; Porter, 1989): One of the most gifted dancers in history, Nijinsky was treated with insulin coma therapy by Sakel while institutionalized in a private Swiss asylum. The creator/choreographer of such ballets as *The Rite of Spring*, *Prelude a l'Apres-midi d'un Faune*, and *Jeux* considered his madness as nothing more than genius: Sakel, however, thought otherwise. Nijinsky was diagnosed with schizophrenia, and for a brief time his grandiose symptoms were relieved by insulin coma therapy. Nijinsky's four volume diary, hastily written in 1919, provides a disturbing glimpse into his descent into madness.

Sakel not only had been visited by American psychiatrists eager to learn this new therapeutic, but he also had come to the United States to personally supervise sessions of insulin coma therapy. On one of those visits, he lectured to more than a thousand of his American colleagues; the following day the *New York Times* lauded insulin coma therapy as "one of the great milestones in the treatment of mental ills" ("Dementia Praecox," 1937, p. 11). In 1938 Sakel emigrated to the United States. Eschewing offers of professorships, he opened a private practice and took a position as an attending physician and researcher at Harlem Valley State Hospital in New York. Soon after his arrival, a medical journalist described how "the living dead" were being restored to sanity by what was known in Europe as "Sakel's Technique":

> In the special wards reserved at the [Harlem Valley] hospital ... for the newly-discovered insulin shock treatment I saw some 15 patients stretched in death-like coma on their beds. At 7 o'clock that morning each had received a huge dose, by hypodermic injection, of insulin.... For nearly five hours after that they lay unconscious, oblivious alike to their actual surroundings and, presumably, to the unreal world of their disordered minds.... At noon I saw the patients awakened. The sweet, life-saving insulin-counteracting solution of sugar and water was poured into the stomach through a rubber hose inserted in the nostril. The waking process was horrible to watch.... The patients retched and choked. They uttered terrifying, animal-like sounds. Some vomited the vital sugar.... There was not time to wipe up the vomitus, or to change soiled bedding. Attendants moved swiftly, tightening restraint sheets to keep the awakening patients from throwing themselves out of bed as they thrashed about. Arms, rigid as boards, were thrust into the air, fingers spread stiffly apart. Inhuman grimaces distorted the unconscious faces.... The scene I witnessed at Harlem Valley Hospital is being repeated daily in many public and private hospitals through the United States and foreign countries. Patiently, heroically, physicians and nurses and attendants are performing over and over again the deft, life-saving ministrations I watched [Stafford, 1938, pp. 334–335].

The journalist went on to report the results of the insulin coma therapy at Harlem Valley Hospital, the first asylum in the United States to institute this therapeutic: of the 52 patients treated at the time of the report, 6 had completely recovered, 15 were "much improved," 22 were "improved," and 9 were "unimproved." Sakel apparently was content with a cure rate much lower than he had achieved in Europe, reasoning that most of the patients in his first American sample were chronic, rather than recent, onset schizophrenics, and therefore were more resistant to treatment.

Like the somatic therapeutics that went before it—surgeries and fever inductions, the ones that were contemporaneous with it—metrazol and electroconvulsive therapy, and the one that would soon follow—prefrontal lobotomy, insulin coma therapy was unpleasant for mad patients and carried considerable risk. While Sakel never could explain how insulin coma therapy worked, he certainly insisted on how the "Sakel method" of administering it should be performed (Doroshow, 2006). Patients were to be slowly built up over weeks or even months to tolerate increasing doses of insulin until they finally lapsed into comas. This "coma dose" would continue until asylum physicians concluded they had derived the greatest possible benefit from the depletion of glucose in their brains, a period of time generally measured in hours. The comas then were terminated with either an injection of an intravenous glucose solution or the administration of a sugar solution via a nasogastric tube. This therapeutic was thought most effective when it was repeated perhaps as many as 50 or 60 times over the ensuing months.

The dramatic effects of insulin coma therapy on the patients was thoroughly described by the journalist who had shadowed Sakel soon after his arrival at Harlem Valley Hospital. Although the therapeutic tended to alter memory, a few first person narratives written by patients can be found in the literature. One of these patients was William Moore, a World War II veteran who, after earning a college degree in social studies, was committed to Binghampton State Hospital in New York, diagnosed with schizophrenia. During his many months there, he penned his autobiography and later raised the money for its publication. A few years after his discharge, Moore, a pacifist, atheist and civil disobedient, strapped a sign to his chest proclaiming "Equal Rights to All!" and hiked the Sand Mountain area between Tennessee and Alabama on his way to the office of the governor of Mississippi. He was shot to death by a local who took offense. Moore's death prompted a wave of "civil rights hikers" to follow suit during the turbulent 1960s ("The South," 1963), and in 2008 the city of Binghampton erected a monument in his honor. While he is best remembered as a civil rights activist, he might also be remembered as a former mental patient who never rejected his diagnosis, but who remained unconvinced that the 55 insulin coma therapy treatments he was subjected to had anything to do with his remission:

> *Treatment 1:* D-day and H-hour came. This morning between 7:00 and 7:30, a group of us were taken to a side room and given our injection of insulin. I had

previously asked other patients how they like this treatment. Answers varied from, "Not bad. You just die every morning," and "Sometimes it is hell," to "It isn't bad at all. You just lie down and go to sleep." I didn't really feel any strong emotion about the idea of treatment. It couldn't be avoided, so I was resigned....

Treatment 2: The head nurse-attendant asked to read my notes. He asked about the remark, "People may destroy my mind, but they cannot pervert it!" "You don't think they are trying to pervert it, do you?" he asked. My answer, summed up, came to something like this: "To the extent that they are trying to make me conform to another's 'normal,' and not to my own 'normal,' it is perversion...."

Treatment 16: Everyone should take insulin treatment. Then they will know beforehand what all my life I have wondered about—how it feels to die, what it is like to pass from this life into the next. For the coma one goes into during treatment is just what happens when the insulin eats up the sugar in the blood or something; it is dying of starvation, kind of, the only real difference being that we are brought back to life, we are returned to the world we left....

Treatment 40: "If I should die before I wake, I pray the Lord my soul to take." I died. The Lord took my soul. Then, at the end of the treatment, He gave it back to me....

Treatment 47: When I came to, I asked the new doctor ... "How many treatments do I have to take?" "As many as you think you need." "How many is that?" "Don't pin me down."

Treatment 55: Two sheet straps were fastened across my body. Someone was sitting on my legs. Someone was behind me, looking down in my face. A person was on each shoulder, holding it down. At least eight people were around the bed. I couldn't move a muscle. There was something nightmarish about the whole thing. Yet, when the one injecting the glucose asked how I was, I could only reply, "All right" [Moore, 1955, pp. 244–248].

While insulin coma therapy may mimic the experience of dying, its actual mortality rate was approximately 2 percent, with most patients dying from complications such as heart failure, aspiration pneumonia, cerebral hemorrhage and hypoglycemic encephalopathy (Kolb, 1941). With its relatively low mortality rate, the question remained as to its efficacy. Sakel himself had never been particularly precise in assessing his own results, and used evaluative terms such as "cured" and "improved" without bothering to operationally define them. When pressed, he was content to appeal to the therapeutic optimism insulin coma therapy had inflated: "For even if the hypoglycemic treatment of psychoses accomplishes only a part of what it promises," he wrote, "it nevertheless has a value beyond its therapeutic claims, for it should now enable us to work backwards from it to the nature and cause of schizophrenia itself" (cited in Valenstein, 1986, p. 38).

The question of efficacy, however, was more rigorously addressed in a study of 1,039 schizophrenic patients treated with insulin coma therapy in New York asylums in 1938. Efficacy would best be addressed by comparing that experimental group to a control group of mad patients, matched for diagnosis, age, gender, race and socioeconomic class, who were not treated with insulin coma therapy. This study, however, used an unmatched comparison group comprised of patients who had been admitted to the same asylums between 1935 and 1936, when insulin coma therapy was not yet available. The added rigor of the study called into question Sakel's hyperbolic claims, yet still buoyed therapeutic optimism: overall, 65 percent of the schizophrenic patients treated with insulin coma therapy showed some degree of improvement, compared to only 22 percent of the untreated comparison group (Malzberg, 1938). The study's results, especially in the absence of any other new therapeutics for schizophrenia, stimulated intense interest. By 1941, according to a U.S. Public Health survey, 72 percent of the country's 305 reporting public and private asylums were using insulin coma therapy, not only for schizophrenia, but also for other types of madness (Kolb, 1941).

A caveat in that first large-scale study, however, predicted the eventual decline in the popularity of insulin shock therapy. "Do remissions and improvements last?" the author had queried. "Only with the passage of time can the question be fully answered" (Malzberg, 1938, p. 552). Indeed, the passage of time, measured by long-term follow-up studies conducted in the United States and Europe, consistently showed that the improvement observed in schizophrenic patients was, for most of them, short-lived (Bourne, 1953; Malzberg, 1939). At four years post-treatment, in fact, only 17 percent of them had maintained improvement, a percentage comparable to that for untreated controls (Rivers & Bond, 1941).

By 1961, when Princeton mathematician John Forbes Nash, Jr., was institutionalized in Trenton State Hospital, insulin coma therapy was on the wane. In many asylums the special units where the therapeutic was administered were being used for other treatment regimes, and the highly skilled nurses and attendants, the crème-de-la-crème of the asylum staff, were reassigned. Insulin shock therapy, in its day, had enjoyed a great deal of cachet. Not only were the facilities in which it was administered modern and well-equipped, and the staff efficient and highly trained, but the patients were also given a great deal of highly personal care which, in the end, may have significantly contributed to the therapeutic's initial success (Doroshow, 2006). Nash himself was declared "in remission" after a course of treatment, and was discharged. Although he had nothing good to say about insulin shock therapy, referring to it as "torture" and sometimes using the words "Insulin Institute" as his return address, he did have an "interlude of enforced rationality," as he termed it, upon his discharge from Trenton State Hospital (Nasar, 1998, p. 294). Two years later, however, he was involuntarily committed to a private asylum; two years after his discharge from that asylum, he was involuntarily committed once again. From that point on, as Nash wrote in his Nobel Prize autobiography:

I became a person of delusionally influenced thinking but of relatively moderate behavior and thus tended to avoid hospitalization and the direct attention of psychiatrists.... So at the present time I seem to be thinking rationally again in the style that is characteristic of scientists. However this is not entirely a matter of joy as if someone returned from physical disability to good physical health. One aspect of this is that rationality of thought imposes a limit on a person's concept of his relation to the cosmos. For example, a non–Zoroastrian could think of Zarathustra as simply a madman who led millions of naïve followers to adopt a cult of ritual fire worship. But without his "madness" Zarathustra would necessarily have been only another of the millions or billions of human individuals who have lived and then been forgotten ["Autobiography," n.d.].

Nash never experienced metrazol shock therapy. Created by László von Meduna, a Hungarian physician, it competed with insulin shock therapy for a time as a feat of "medieval magic." Meduna had examined the brains of deceased epileptic patients and compared them with those of schizophrenic patients. Convinced that there were subtle nerve cell differences between the two groups, a bit of received wisdom that had been circulating through the medical field for some time but that had never been proved, he concluded that epilepsy and schizophrenia were mutually antagonistic (Valenstein, 1986). Perhaps, he reasoned, it was the convulsions that kept epileptics from developing schizophrenia; therefore, if convulsions were induced in schizophrenics, their madness might be cured.

To that end, in 1934 he injected 11 schizophrenic patients with camphor, an oil found in the wood of the camphor laurel and used for centuries as a tonic in Asian medicine. This first trial produced convulsions in less than half of the patients, yet two of them improved enough to be discharged, and a third improved enough to participate in the asylum's occupational therapy program (Gazdag, Bitter, Ungvari, Baran & Fink, 2009). Hoping to produce a higher rate of convulsions, Meduna then tried metrazol, a synthetic preparation also known as cardiazol, that in small doses acts as a circulatory and respiratory stimulant. His first trial with the drug produced remarkable results: a patient suffering from catatonia, a type of schizophrenia, who had been immobile for four years and unable to attend to his own bodily functions, got out of bed, dressed himself and showed an interest in his surroundings after five metrazol-induced convulsions (Valenstein, 1986). After treating several more patients Meduna published his findings: 10 of the 26 patients "recovered," 3 showed "good results," and 13 showed "no improvement."

Metrazol shock therapy quickly became the therapeutic of choice in Europe, largely as a consequence of Meduna's entrepreneurial activities. It did not take long for word of its success in treating schizophrenia to reach American asylum physicians. By 1940 almost every public and private asylum in the country was using metrazol, not just for the treatment of schizophrenia, but for mood disorders, especially depression, for which it was thought to be particularly efficacious. It terminated severe depressive reactions in 90 percent of cases (Bennett, 1938).

What was the experience of metrazol shock therapy for patients? Thirty-seven patients who had received metrazol shock therapy at Rockland State Hospital in Orangeburg, New York, were interviewed about the experience (Starks, 1938). Although few could recall their initial sensory impressions upon being injected with the drug, those who could described smelling ether, hearing a buzzing in the ears, and feeling a stiffening of the muscles and a whirling sensation in the head. With a few exceptions, most of the patients found the course of metrazol shock therapy unpleasant. "They're very painful," one patient explained. "You get like blown up and you go unconscious, like something boils up" (p. 701). And a significant number of them feared they would die as the result of the treatments. "Sometimes I thought they'd rock you to sleep for good. You think everything dies in you. Everything fades away," another patient explained. "I felt every time I took that as if I was going to die" (p. 701). Despite the fact that 6 of the 37 interviewed patients saw no therapeutic value in the treatments, experiencing them instead as punishments, the remaining patients evaluated the physical results of metrazol shock therapy in quite favorable terms, saying they experienced more energy and alertness. The emotional results also were quite positively evaluated. One patient described feeling less discouraged and pessimistic. "I don't worry now," she explained. "I feel calm because I make the best of everything now" (p. 704). Another, who had been institutionalized for more than two years, said he had better control of his thoughts. "Impressions become more clear and distinct," he clarified. "One seems to observe things and judge. Before, impressions were not voluntary. Now, all the difference in the world. The impressions are fresher, not the same old things, and they are voluntary" (p. 705).

This early and rare look into the subjective experience of a therapeutic regime would seem to indicate that the positive results of metrazol shock therapy outweighed the negative, at least from the subjective point of view of the patients. There was reason, however, to be skeptical of the findings. Metrazol shock therapy produced retrograde amnesia, so few patients had many accurate memories of their treatment. What they may not have remembered was the latency period between the injection and the convulsion; during that several minutes, most patients became frightened, anxious and often difficult to manage (Braslow, 1997).

Asylum physicians had reason to become increasingly concerned about the use of metrazol shock therapy. Unlike insulin shock therapy, in which sugar or glucose served as a fast-acting antidote to the convulsions, there was no antidote for metrazol. Asylum physicians, therefore, had little if any control over the convulsions that often were so violent that they raised the patients' risk of experiencing bone fractures, dislocations, and shattered teeth. In Bellevue Psychiatric Hospital in New York City, for example, the incidence of fractures for schizophrenic children who were given metrazol shock therapy was so alarmingly high that asylum physicians were encouraged to administer beta-erythroidin hydrochloride to diminish the strength of muscular contractions (Cottington, 1941), a practice that became widely prescribed for adult patients as well (Rosen, Cameron, & Ziegler, 1941). The drawbacks are illustrated by Bennett (1972, p. 131): "Just before [a] patient received her last metrazol convulsive shock treatment she pleaded with me beseechingly as I was about to give the intravenous injection, saying, 'Doctor, is there no cure for this treatment?' Once a visiting doctor watching us give the metrazol treatment asked if we ever had any incontinence with treatment. I replied, 'Sometimes, in the doctor.'"

But the larger concern for asylum physicians was the nagging question of efficacy. Like insulin shock therapy, metrazol shock therapy seemed to produce improvements only in the short run; and despite Meduna's insistence that it was a cure for schizophrenia, its most lasting positive effects were for patients diagnosed with depression. While that may have been considered an achievement in and of itself, a new type of shock therapy—electroconvulsive—was proving itself easier to administer and with better long-term effects than either metrazol or insulin. Meduna himself had lost interest in metrazol, turning his attention, instead, to carbon dioxide therapy, in which neurotic patients in multiple sessions were made to inhale the chemical compound. The resulting "cerebral stimulation," Meduna believed, would relieve them of their anxiety, phobias and inhibitions (Meduna, 1950). Without Meduna's continuing entrepreneurship, and with high risks and low results, metrazol shock therapy all but disappeared from American asylums during the 1950s. The Food and Drug Administration revoked its approval of the drug in 1982.

Electroconvulsive Shock Therapy

Despite the failure of both insulin and metrazol to bridge the gap between the promotional rhetoric that had transformed them into asylum therapeutics well before their efficacy had been proven, and the reality of their high risks and low long-term rewards for mad patients, psychiatric interest in shock as a therapeutic remained high. By 1941, nearly every public and private asylum in the United States was using ECT—electroconvulsive shock therapy—tried out for the first time in the country just a year earlier at the Parkway Sanitarium in Chicago, Illinois (Pulver, 1961). Hailed as "the penicillin of psychiatry" (Shorter & Healy, 2007, p. 3), ECT nonetheless has been the most stigmatized and vilified of the shock therapies—the grist for bad press, the stuff of urban legend and grade-B movies, and the target of political activism and identity politics.

Electroconvulsive shock therapy originated in Italy, the result of research on the hippocampus of the brain conducted by Ugo Cerletti. The hippocampus, or "Horn of Ammon," already known to play a role in learning and memory, also was suspected of playing a role in epilepsy. To test that hypothesis Cerletti electrically induced convulsions in dogs and then examined their brain tissues. Upon hearing Meduna's claim that metrazol-induced convulsions cured schizophrenia, Cerletti considered the possibility that electrically induced convulsions would do the same, and with less distress for the patients. Cerletti was just as aware as the public at large that massive jolts of electricity are fatal; news coverage of accidental electrocutions and of state-sanctioned ones in the form of the electric chair left no doubt of that fact. So to determine the voltage for inducing convulsions rather than death, Cerletti and his young assistant, Lucio Bini, visited a Rome slaughterhouse. There they learned that there was a wide margin between a convulsive jolt of electricity (120 volts) and a fatal one (400 volts), and that to cause death, a one to two-and-half minute continuous charge of electricity was required. Assured by that margin of safety, Cerletti and Bini made their intentions known to try electroconvulsive shock treatment on schizophrenics (Shorter & Healy, 2007).

They were given that opportunity in 1938 when the police admitted a man, found wandering through the train station in a confused state, to the Clinic for Nervous and Mental Diseases that Cerletti headed in Rome. Diagnosed as schizophrenic, the patient known as "S.E." was strapped to a table, with electrodes fixed to his temples with rubber bands and given 80 volts of electricity for a quarter of a second. His body trembled slightly, but he did not lose consciousness. Ten minutes later the second dose of 80 volts, this time for a half-second, was administered, with the same results. Overhearing Cerletti and Bini's heated discussion about whether they should continue, "S.E." cried out, "Not another one! It's deadly!" (cited in Impasto, 1960, p. 1113). A third dose of 80 volts for three-quarters of a second was administered nonetheless, but that, too, failed to produce a convulsion. A week later they tried again, this time with a 92-volt charge for a half-second. "S.E." convulsed for more than a minute, then stopped breathing for nearly a minute and a half. Bini describes what followed: "Thereupon we observed with the most intensely gratifying sensation the characteristic gradual awakening of the patient 'by steps.' He rose to a sitting position and looked at us, calm and smiling, as though to inquire what we wanted of him. We asked: 'What happened to you?' He answered: 'I don't know. Maybe I was asleep.' Thus occurred the first electrically produced convulsion in man, which I at once named electroshock" (cited in Valenstein, 1986, p. 51).

After several more treatments over the next month, "S.E." was very much improved; he was coherent in his speech, aware of his surroundings, and was no longer bothered by persecutory delusions. He was presented to the Royal Academy of Medicine in Rome by Cerletti and Bini and, for the purpose of demonstration, was given yet another jolt of electricity in front of the flabbergasted audience. While accolades poured down on Cerletti and Bini for finding the cure for schizophrenia, "S.E." was released from the clinic and returned home. Two years later he was committed to another asylum in Milan, once again diagnosed with schizophrenia (Shorter & Healy, 2007).

The enthusiastic reaction to electroconvulsive shock therapy by professional peers, the press and the public would seem to suggest that electrical shocks had never before been considered a treatment for madness. Indeed, the use of *non-convulsive* electrotherapy can be dated to the 1st century A.D. when the malaise and headaches of the Roman emperor Claudius were treated by the application of a torpedo fish—better known as an electric ray—on his forehead. Electroichthyotherapy was used over many subsequent centuries for the treatment of alcoholism, demon possession, epilepsy and "carnal passions," in which case the gall of an electric eel was placed on the genitals (Delbourgo, 2006).

In colonial America, the harnessing of electricity for psychiatric purposes not only was consistent with the Enlightenment emphasis on science, but also on its rejection of the dualistic philosophy that saw mind and body as separate entities (Delbourgo, 2006). Perhaps no other colonial figure better embodies Enlightenment thinking than Benjamin Franklin, whose experiments with electricity are the stuff of legend. But what may be less familiar is Franklin's belief that melancholia, mania and hysteria, the prevailing diagnostic categories of that age, could be effectively treated by electricity. He himself had on two occasions accidentally received a massive jolt of electricity from Leyden jars. The jars, made of glass, filled with water or lead shot, and covered with conducting metal foil, were capable of storing a charge from an electrostatic generator and releasing it on demand. While the jolts did not harm him, although he did experience amnesia for each of the accidents, the incident did prove that large shocks to the cranium were survivable and, in fact, might be therapeutic (Beaudreau & Finger, 2006).

To test that hypothesis, Franklin administered shocks to "C.B.," a twenty-four-year-old who had suffered for ten years with hysterical seizures so violent that she could not be restrained by several strong people and that had left her on the verge of madness. "C.B." was most likely the sister of Cadwallader Evans, a Scottish educated physician whom Franklin was mentoring. The year was 1752, and "C.B.'s" recollection of the remedy, penned in a letter to Evans, almost certainly is one of the first personal narratives of the treatment of madness published in the United States:

> At length my spirits were quite broke and subdued with so many years affliction, and indeed I was almost grown desperate, being left without hope or relief. About this time there was great talk of the wonderful power of electricity; and as a person reduced to the last extremity, is glad to catch at any thing; I happened to think it might be useful to me. Altho' I cou'd have no encouragement from any experiment in the case, I resolv'd to try, let the event be what it might; for death was more desirable than life, on the terms I enjoy'd it. Accordingly I went to Philadelphia, the beginning of September 1752, and apply'd to B. Franklin, who I thought understood it best of any person here. I received four shocks morning and evening; they were what they call 200 strokes of the wheel, which fills an eight gallon bottle, and indeed they were very severe. On receiving the first shock, I received the fit very strong, but the second effectually carried it off; and thus it was every time I went through the operation; yet the symptoms gradually decreased, till at length they intirely left me. I staid in town two weeks, and when I went home, B. Franklin was so good as to supply me with a globe and bottle, to electrify myself every day for three months. The fits were soon carried off, but the cramp continued somewhat longer, though it was scarcely troublesome, and very seldom returned. I now enjoy such a state of health as I would have given all the world for, this time two years [Evans, 1754, p. 85].

Although Franklin, who was not a medical doctor, was cautious about the use of electrical shocks to treat hysteria, reasoning that "C.B.'s" anticipation of a cure may have done more to relieve her symptoms than the shocks could ever have done, he did encourage his European colleagues who already were experimenting with the electrical treatment of a variety of medical maladies to try administering shocks to the institutionalized mad who were suffering from melancholy (Beaudreau & Finger, 2006). Indeed, in some European asylums, cranial shocks were administered to melancholic patients, with mixed results; but the slow growth of American asylums in the late 18th century and early 19th century diminished interest in its use.

A rather unexpected convert to Franklin's hypothesis that electrical charges to the cranium could remedy madness was an itinerant physician named T. Gale, who practiced medicine in various locales throughout upstate New York. In 1802 Gale published a massive treatise on electrotherapy in medicine, and provided detailed case studies of three melancholic patients he had successfully treated with the administration of electric shocks. One, a despondent young man who had slit his own throat in an abortive suicide attempt, was turned into a "new man" after several electric shock administrations and remained well three years later (Gale, 1802, p. 127). Another, a violent older man who became delusional after being cheated out of money, was so resistant to the treatment that Gale required the assistance of twenty men to restrain him. The man was restored to sanity after several jolts of electricity over the course of two days (p. 130). But it was Gale's interaction with his third melancholic patient, a young woman who had become terrified at the sight of her husband after the birth of their child, that provides the most insight into the role of the physician in persuading and cajoling a patient to submit to what must have been a terrifying treatment:

> I observed all the decorum...; used all the address in my power to ingratiate myself into the number of her friends, which consisted then of her mother only; this I knew was previously necessary, as I could have no opportunity of administering to her in that situation. Her husband came to the house—I observed her terror—I laid hold of this opportunity to gain upon her feeling; I would not suffer him to come nigh her, pretendedly so: It had the intended effect. To be brief, it was not long before I was able to persuade her to take a little wine; after this, under the appearance of entertainment, we got her to the machine, when I passed some very light shocks in all the before mentioned directions. We regaled her with all the lively appearances in our power. The next day she could be induced to smile; this gave me great encouragement. I alternated light shocks, with wine, diluted brandy, &c. and as her mind began to be caught with lively appearances, we endeavored to furnish all the variety that was possible. The consequence soon was, all that gloominess of mind was dispelled, and she gradually assumed the appearance of cheerfulness; her digestion was promoted, and she began to take nutricious food freely. To be short, in four or five weeks she was able to unite with her husband again in keeping house [pp. 126–127].

Throughout the 19th century non-convulsive electroshock treatments, such as those described by Franklin and Gale, were used within the contexts of medical practices and private sanitariums and health farms, rather than in asylums. The apogee of its use was during the post–Civil War years when the hustle and bustle of the rapidly modernizing society raised concerns about a veritable epidemic of neurasthenia, or nervous exhaustion. Described as a "chronic, functional disease of the nervous system" (Beard, 1880, p. 115), neurasthenia was thought to be especially amenable to electroshock treatments that toned up the nerves, revitalized the nervous energy and repaired the nerve tissues of "brain-workers," i.e., the emerging professional class. To that end, physicians used electrical belts and vibrators, low frequency generators, static machines, and a variety of other innovative devices to treat their well-heeled patients and ready them for their important role of rebuilding American society after the ravages of the Civil War (Kneeland & Warren, 2002). Public and even private asylums, however, were not filled with these kinds of patients. Rather, the asylums were teeming with lower and middle class men and women whose madness did not so much exhaust as disorientate, baffle and delude them. They were packed with patients who had little prospect of ever being discharged, let alone being remade into productive citizens. Electroshock as a therapeutic, then, had little appeal to, or function within, asylum settings.

But the same cannot be said of electro*convulsive* shock treatment. Cerletti and Bini's therapeutic innovation spread widely across Europe. In its wake, papers touting it as a remedy for both schizophrenia and depression were delivered at major medical conferences and published in leading psychiatric journals; and new machines were designed to deliver higher currents of electricity. In many ways, the outbreak of World War II in Europe facilitated the rapid spread and acceptance of electroconvulsive shock therapy. Pharmacies had been emptied of drugs in order to assist the war effort, and the insulin for insulin shock therapy, at the time the preferred treatment for schizophrenic patients, was almost impossible to secure (Shorter & Healy, 2007).

World War II also brought electroconvulsive shock therapy to the United States. A number of psychiatrists, such as Lothar Kalinowsky, who had trained with Cerletti and Bini, were forced to flee the rising tide of fascism and take refuge in the United States. Although other American psychiatrists already had experimented with electroconvulsive shock therapy, it was Kalinowsky's use of it at the New York State Psychiatric Institute that captured the attention of the press:

> Although [it is emphasized] that hope for any "miracle cure" must not be pinned on the new method, as the experiments have been in progress only a few months and findings are inconclusive, it was reported that "considerable success" had resulted in treatment of certain types of insanity.... Adherents of the electric-shock method contend that metrazol sometimes is an uncertain treatment, and that the process of injection of the chemical into the veins has disagreeable features that sometimes instill fear in the patient. The electric treatment, they say, at least is not unpleasant, so the patient may be more inclined to cooperate with the physician in future treatments ["Insanity Treated," 1940, p. 17].

Within a short time, asylum psychiatrists from all over the United States were coming to New York to train with Kalinowsky. Their enthusiastic reaction to electroconvulsive shock therapy is illustrated by survey results: 129 of the 305 asylums polled in 1941 reported using electroconvulsive shock therapy (Kolb, 1941); just six years later, an unpublished survey found that 9 out of every 10 public and private asylums were using the therapeutic (Shorter & Healy, 2007).

Part of the reason for the popularity of electroconvulsive shock therapy was its relatively low cost and its ease of administration. But the largest part of the reason had to do with its effectiveness and its efficacy. Asylum physicians and staff observed its success in relieving the symptoms of madness, particularly those of major depression, and early studies showed that when compared to untreated patients, those patients who had undergone electro-

convulsive shock therapy showed much more rapid and sustained improvement (Alexander, 1953; Tillotson & Sulzbach, 1945). There were risks, however. Before the drug curare was introduced to block neuromuscular
connections and eliminate the violent convulsions, the rate of fractures upon
administration of electroconvulsive shock treatment was 9 out of every 1,000
cases, a rate, by the way, that was less than one-quarter of that for metrazol
shock treatment (Valenstein, 1986). After the introduction of curare in the
late 1940s, and later succinylcholine, the rate was negligible. And whether
with curare or not, electroconvulsive shock treatment produced amnesia,
although the question remained unanswered as to whether it was the result
of a psychological reaction to the therapeutic or a physiological change in the
brain (Janis, 1948).

In some ways, asylum physicians considered amnesia therapeutically
advantageous in that patients, especially those who were depressed, were no
longer able to ruminate on past failures and disappointments. For patients,
however, memory loss often was much more problematic; it was a frightening shadow that eclipsed personal identity and a sense of generational continuity and that always darkened to some degree the sense of optimism when
symptoms remediated. A 24-year-old patient who had been institutionalized
after an attack of mania caused him to leave university in his senior year
before taking his final exams described his experience of memory loss in an
essay he wrote for a psychology class upon returning to university in 1946:

> I woke up sometime later feeling completely refreshed, not tired or logy, or
> drugged with sleep, just ready for a big day.... I began looking around. I was in a
> large cream colored room with fifteen or twenty beds neatly made, and covered
> with white counterpanes. It looked like a hospital, but why should I be in a hospi-
> tal? I shut my eyes and tried to think. But nothing came.
> "What is the date?" I asked myself.
> "I haven't any idea."
> "What day of the week is it?"
> "Don't be silly."
> "What month is it?"
> "I don't know."
> "What year is it?"
> That shouldn't be hard. But I wasn't sure. It was later than 1941. I tried to out-
> smart myself by asking how old I was and then figuring one year. But I didn't
> know how old I was [Alper, 1948, p. 206].

Responding to patients' concerns about memory loss, asylum physicians
experimented with ways to reduce it. They decreased the dosage of electricity, tried passing a direct rather than an alternating current through the brain,
and placed the electrodes on top of the skull rather than on either side of the
head in order to spare the non-motor parts of the brain responsible for memory and sensation from the direct current of electricity. Each of these strate-

gies was successful to some extent in preserving memory (Shorter & Healy, 2007).

So with its high efficacy rate, the use of drugs to reduce the drama of brutal convulsions and the fractures they often produced, and the use of measures to reduce memory loss, how did electroconvulsive shock therapy become so stigmatized? One contributing factor certainly had to do with the unanswered questions about how it worked. Cerletti had hypothesized that the shock of the convulsion caused the brain to release a vitalizing substance that he labeled "acro-amines"; his attempts to isolate that substance, however, were unsuccessful. By 1950, American physicians and researchers had constructed fifty separate theories on how electroconvulsive shock treatment worked (Gordon, 1948); and although each theory had ardent proponents and just as ardent detractors, the prevailing consensus was that the curative mechanism of electroconvulsive shock therapy "still is to a large extent obscure" (Alexander, 1953, p. 60).

That obscurity invited speculation and representation. Undoubtedly the most unsettling and contentious of the many theories about how electroconvulsive shock therapy worked was that it permanently damaged the brain. This theory is in many ways more interesting for its political implications than its scientific ones. It was seized upon by the burgeoning anti-psychiatry movement during the 1960s and 1970s and became the lynch-pin of its critique of psychiatry as a tool of oppression and social control. The movement raised disturbing questions about the extent to which institutionalized patients were able to give informed consent for the treatment, were allowed to withdraw consent once given or, for that matter, were even asked to give consent in the first place (Culver, Ferrell, & Green, 1980). It asserted that certain classes of institutionalized patients—women, racial minorities, gays and lesbians, the poor and the young—whose roles in society were rapidly, and to many, disconcertingly, changing, were at the greatest risk for having their minds and their brains altered by electroconvulsive shock therapy (Fine, 1974; Szasz, 1973). It presented case after case of institutionalized patients who were administered electroconvulsive shock therapy with no adjunctive treatment whatsoever; who lay strapped to beds in wards or even hallways, fearfully awaiting their turns with what variously was known as the "buzz box," the "shock factory," the "power cocktail" and the "stun shop," some of them under the guise of treatment, others for punishment for misbehavior (Petit, 1974).

Representatives and self-proclaimed "survivors" of the anti-psychiatry movement did a great deal to tarnish the appeal of electroconvulsive shock therapy. They circulated horror stories and political treatises through their various newsletters, held public demonstrations outside asylums, testified before legislative bodies, and published a "shock doc roster" that named physicians who administered or authorized the controversial therapeutic and their institutional affiliations (Frank, 1978). As a result of the movement's efforts, states as far-flung as Utah, Alabama, Massachusetts and California restricted or regulated its use ("Regulation," 1976).

Obscurity about the source of the curative power of electroconvulsive shock treatment also invited representation. The 1949 film *The Snake Pit* was the public's first glimpse not only into overcrowded public asylums, but also of what was being touted as the miracle cure that would empty them. The protagonist, a recently married young woman, is confused, delusional and under the sway of hectoring disembodied voices. Although a short course of electroconvulsive shock treatments finally remediates her symptoms long enough for her treating psychiatrist to uncover the trauma that caused them, the graphic representation of the treatment raised the question as to whether the cure was worse than the madness. Over subsequent years, the cinematic representations of electroconvulsive shock therapy returned to that question. But it was the quintessential anti-psychiatry film, *One Flew Over the Cuckoo's Nest* (1975), based on the Ken Kesey (1962) novel by the same name, that swayed public opinion the most. The film depicts a fiercely nonconformist protagonist who feigns madness to avoid a jail sentence and is sent to a state asylum where he engages in a constant battle of wills with the staff. After rousing his fellow patients to revolt, he is subdued and sent to the "shock shop" for punishment. A mouthguard is stuck between his teeth and electrodes are placed on his temples. Fully conscious when the jolts are delivered, he convulses horribly and later returns to the ward in a zombie-like state that, in the end, is more feigned than real.

The effect of this film on public attitudes about electroconvulsive shock treatment, let alone about madness and asylums, was considerable; in post-screening surveys, the majority of audience members considered it barbaric and punitive and would refuse to allow an institutionalized family member or friend to undergo it (O'Shea & McGennis, 1983). Interestingly, the attitudes of medical students changed in a negative direction as well. After viewing the electroconvulsive shock therapy scene in *One Flew Over the Cuckoo's Nest*, as well as scenes in three additional films, 33 percent of the surveyed medical students, who had little accurate information about the therapeutic in the first place, decreased their support for it; and 25 percent of them indicated that they would dissuade a family member or friend from undergoing it (Walter, McDonald, Rey, & Rosen, 2002).

Fictional and autobiographical accounts of electroconvulsive shock therapy worked in a fashion similar to films in shifting pubic attitudes in a negative direction (Hilton, 2007). Sylvia Plath's *The Bell Jar* (1972), a semi-autobiographical account of madness, is a particularly compelling example. Plath had received a course of electroconvulsive shock treatments in the 1950s and committed suicide a few years later. Posthumously published in the United States, her book provides a harrowing account of the treatment: "Then something bent down, and took hold of me, and shook me like the end of the world. Whee-ee-ee-ee-ee, it shrilled, through an air crackling with blue light, and with each flash a great jolt drubbed me till I thought my bones would break and the sap fly out of me like a split plant. I wondered what terrible thing it was that I had done" (p. 118). This apparent risk of suicide after the treatment, already suggested by the 1961 suicide of writer Ernest Hemingway, who had shot himself in the head a few days after going through a second course of electroconvulsive shock treatments for depression, further darkened the public attitude about the treatment. "It was a brilliant cure," he had told his biographer just a short time before his suicide, "but they lost the patient" (Hotchner, 1967, p. 308).

If a case is needed to illustrate the hardening of attitudes about electroconvulsive shock therapy there are few better than that of Thomas Eagleton. The 42-year-old Missouri senator, nominated as the running mate of Democratic candidate Senator George McGovern in the 1972 presidential election, publicly revealed that he had been hospitalized on three separate occasions for "nervous exhaustion and fatigue" and had undergone two courses of electroconvulsive shock treatments (Lydons, 1972, p. 1). McGovern stated firmly that it was his intention to keep Eagleton on the ticket; less than a month later, and under pressure from all corners, he asked for, and received, Eagleton's resignation (Kneeland, 1972). The Eagleton case is complex less for its politics than for its psychology. It exposed social fears about madness and reified its stigma; it showed distrust not only in those who have been labeled mad, but in those whose profession it is to treat them (Reston, 1972); and it revealed qualms about electroconvulsive shock as a therapeutic. While the American Psychiatric Association weighed into the Eagleton case by submitting a carefully worded public statement about the nature and extent of depression, it said nothing that redressed the qualms. It neither vigorously defended nor attacked electroconvulsive shock. After carefully explaining how the treatment is administered, and that it has a high success rate in the remediation of depression, that statement went on to say that not all psychiatrists favored its use and some considered it "a drastic and barbaric procedure" (Rensberger, 1972, p. 11).

The split in psychiatric opinion about electroconvulsive shock treatment was yet another factor that contributed to its decline in popularity. The split occurred most obviously along specialty lines, with psychiatrists more favorable towards its use than psychanalysts who were trained in the Freudian method of talk therapy. But it also occurred along more practical lines that pitted private practice psychiatrists, who could discretely administer the therapeutic to carefully chosen patients in their offices or clinics, against asylum psychiatrists who sometimes used it as a "one-size-fits-all" therapeutic, against a smaller group of asylum psychiatrists who experimented with what came to be known as "regressive" electroconvulsive shock therapy that involved a daily blitz of treatments often over several days in succession.

One early practitioner of this controversial innovation was Lauretta Bender. Between 1942 and 1947, Bender administered 20 to 40 shocks each day to 98 children hospitalized for schizophrenia in the children's ward of the psychiatric division of Bellevue Hospital in New York City. The children ranged in age from 4 to 11 years old. According to Bender (1947):

> There was very little anxiety in relation to the treatment [although] some children showed preoccupation with the meaning of the shock experience. Girls clearly related it to sexual intercourse and fantasy. Boys concerned themselves with aggressive implications as with the possibility that it was punishment or that they might not recover consciousness. Children in or near puberty showed the most marked anxiety. Some of the youngest mute children were negativistic and resistive sometimes to the point of panic. However, most of the children would lend themselves passively and actively to the treatment both physically and psychologically [p. 167].

The results of regressive electroconvulsive shock treatment on young schizophrenic children? None, as far as remediating the symptoms of schizophrenia, such as disturbances in thought and language, social withdrawal and emotional lability. Half of the children returned home, and half remained institutionalized. However, Bender concludes, "[I]t is the opinion of all observers in the hospital, the school rooms, of the parents and other guardians that the children were always somewhat improved by the treatment inasmuch as they were less disturbed, less excitable, less withdrawn, and less anxious. They were better controlled, seemed better integrated and more mature and were better able to meet social situations in a realistic fashion. They were more composed, happier, and were better able to accept teaching or psychotherapy in groups or individually" (p. 168).

A follow-up study, however, called into question both the effects and the efficacy of regressive electroconvulsive shock therapy with schizophrenic children, not to mention the very diagnosis of childhood schizophrenia. Seven years later, 30 children who had been treated in Bender's program were residing in the children's ward in Rockland State Hospital in New York. They and two additional children were the subjects of a follow-up study that found that for the nine children for whom the diagnosis of schizophrenia was "definite," the regressive electroconvulsive shock therapy produced "much improvement" for four of them; "improvement" for two; and "no improvement" for three.

The three who remained unimproved were, in fact, in a "regressed, deteriorated condition" when readmitted (Clardy & Rumpf, 1954, p. 617). For the 20 children for whom the original diagnosis of schizophrenia was called into question, most improved immediately after the regressive electroconvulsive shock treatments, but relapsed into considerably worsened states quite soon after (p. 617). For the three remaining children now diagnosed as psychopathic, the treatment had significantly worsened their conditions, although other types of adjunctive therapies had improved two of them over subsequent years.

Phrases such as "no improvement," or "regressed, deteriorated condition" are not operationally defined, but the experiences of the children with regressive electroconvulsive shock therapy are described in brief case studies:

- 10-year-old boy with IQ of 122, who had been reared in "a disorganized, strife-torn home where he witnessed and was subjected to much physical violence," spoke of an intense desire to kill the doctor who treated him with ECT. He also was hostile to mom for committing him. Before admission to Rockland, he assaulted mom and then attempted to jump out of apartment window [p. 621].

- 11-year-old boy with IQ of 130 who at 7 "had been exposed to sexual experiences by an irresponsible, alcoholic father," described his reaction to ECT a year after treatment: "When I heard the word 'shock' I thought they would put me in something like an electric chair. I was scared to death of them! I thought maybe I'd die, but after I woke up I wasn't so scared any more. But I felt like a bunch of rocks were going around in my head; I mean I had a headache! I was just as tense as I was before, and I was mixed up about things as before. I don't think they did me any good, because when I came here I was just as bad as ever. I couldn't do any school work so good any more" [p. 621].

- 9-year-old girl with IQ of 107 who had felt severely rejected at home, and who at 7 had played truant and engaged in sexual practices with older boys, expressed "considerable resentment" for ECT five years before. "They are only for crazy people, and I hope I'm not crazy. I had awful headaches and then I went to sleep. Only when I woke up I didn't feel like I slept at all. I think I'd have gotten better without them" [p. 621].

The follow-up study finds that the effects of regressive electroconvulsive shock treatment "were temporary and resulted in no sustained improvement in the patterning of behavior. Relapses occurred in all cases, necessitating continued hospitalization" (p. 620), and any improvement seen in the children over subsequent months and years was due largely to "transference or attachment, giving the child contact with suitable parental substitutes" (p. 622). It concludes with a warning that highlights the schism between practitioners of standard electroconvulsive shock therapy and those advocating it in its regressive form:

It appears to the writers that one should be fearful of giving electric shock therapy to very young children—those four or five years old—for we have no good understanding of what pathology may take place in the child's brain or the later effect of shock treatment on the personality that is only in the developmental stage. It seems that one would be justified in giving this treatment when the child has remained in a chronic state, or is deteriorating, and when all other measures have failed. Important consideration must also be given to the psychological influence of shock experience on the long-range emotional and social maturation of youngsters treated in their formative years. Perhaps some clues have been given by the children's personal reactions and their interpretations as reported here [pp. 622–623].

One of those children was Ted Chabasinski. Sent at the age of six to the children's ward of the psychiatric division of Bellevue Hospital by a social worker who was overseeing his foster home placement, he was diagnosed as schizophrenic and given a daily course of regressive electroconvulsive shock treatments. Chabasinski, now an attorney who is active in the psychiatric survivors' movement, recollects his experience:

I wanted to die but I really didn't know what death was. I knew that it was something terrible. Maybe I'll be so tired after the next shock treatment I won't get up, I won't ever get up, and I'll be dead. But I always got up. Something in me beyond my wishes made me put myself together again. I memorized my name, I taught myself to say my name. Teddy, Teddy, I'm Teddy.... I'm here, I'm here, in this room, in this hospital. And my mommy's gone.... I would cry and realize how dizzy I was. The world was spinning around and coming back to it hurt too much. I want to go down, I want to go where the shock treatment is sending me, I want to stop fighting and die ... and something made me live, and to go on living. I had to remember never to let anyone near me again ["Personal Stories," n.d.].

The practice of administering electroconvulsive shocks to children, let alone doing so in a regressive protocol, deeply divided the psychiatric profession. In order to negotiate the controversy, it was recommended that the regressive protocol be used only for the most severely decompensated schizophrenic asylum patients for whom other somatic therapeutics, such as insulin and metrazol shock, had been unsuccessful. In a controlled research study, 30 chronic schizophrenic patients institutionalized at the Veterans Administration hospital in Chillicothe, Ohio, were administered three electroconvulsive shock treatments daily over the course of five days. These were profoundly disturbed patients, some of whom could not attend to their bodily functions and all of whom were withdrawn and actively hallucinating. The immediate effect of the course of treatment illustrates why the word "regressive" is so descriptive: they became childlike, relying on others to spoon-feed them and taking delight in playing children's games. When compared to a group of untreated controls, those administered regressive electroconvulsive shock therapy eventually showed significant changes in what might be called "ward behavior." Still too ill to be discharged, they nonetheless became more social, more attentive to their bodily functions and less assaultive, and these changes persisted a year post-treatment (Garrett & Mockbee, 1952). Subsequent studies confirm these findings (Brussel & Schneider, 1951; Exner & Murillo, 1977; Glueck, Reiss, & Bernard, 1957; Murillo & Exner, 1973).

Despite the hope this protocol held for chronic back-warders—not for a cure, but for an amelioration of some symptoms—regressive electroconvulsive shock therapy was never widely used, considered by many to be "too drastic" even for otherwise hopeless patients (Rothschild, VanGordon, & Varjabedian, 1951, p. 150) and even "unconscionable" in its ethical implications (Frankel, 1973, p. 5). With the introduction of powerful psychotropic medications in the mid–1950s, it all but disappeared from the armamentarium of asylum therapeutics.

In the face of scientific controversy, internal schisms, unfavorable cultural representations and the anti-psychiatry movement, and in the context of rapidly liberalizing social and political attitudes and a growing emphasis on civil rights, the use of electroconvulsive shock therapy in public asylums declined considerably from the 1960s and well into the 1990s. In private asylums, however, its use continued unabated, with interesting consequences: the typical electroconvulsive shock therapy patient was no longer the poor, disenfranchised patient of a public facility, about whom ideological arguments about social control were most convincing, but the white, middle class, voluntary patient whose insurance covered the treatment (Thompson, Weiner, & Myers, 1994).

In 1996 a spread of several pages in the *Washington Post* announced "Shock Therapy: It's Back" (Boodman, 1996). In fact, electroconvulsive shock therapy had never left, although the relative silence about it for 30 or more years may have left the impression that it had. The article rehashes much of the controversy surrounding the therapeutic—how it works and why, the persistent questions about memory loss, the transparency of the financial ties between psychiatrists who use the therapeutic and companies that manufacture the devices for administering it, the nagging issue of informed consent—but generally overlooks the behind-the-scenes strategies of some psychiatric entrepreneurs to save the controversial therapeutic from the fate of the previous shock therapies, insulin and metrazol.

The American Psychiatric Association, stung by public criticism of electroconvulsive shock therapy and by the schism within its own membership, had formed a task force to evaluate the therapeutic. Its report, published in 1978, gave the imprimatur of the organization to the controversial procedure by stating that it was an appropriate therapeutic for the treatment of suicidal depression, and drug-resistant mania and catatonia, but interestingly, given its original use, not for chronic schizophrenia. The association lays out the conditions for obtaining informed consent, conducting pre- and post-assessments of patients, planning both adjunctive pharmacological and psychological therapies as well as maintenance courses of electroconvulsive shock therapy (American Psychiatric Association, 1978).

Once its report was published, the American Psychiatric Association initiated a public relations campaign that created a generally favorable, albeit quite brief, media interest in the therapeutic (Andre, 2009; Hirshbein & Sarvananda, 2008). But more important, the report stimulated a vigorous effort to scientize electroconvulsive shock treatment. Led by Max Fink and Harold Sackeim, arguably its most vocal proponents, the scientizing movement organized conferences, sought grants to fund research, formed the International Psychiatric Association for the Advancement of Electrotherapy, and founded a new journal, *Convulsive Therapy*, which later was retitled the *Journal of ECT: Dedicated to the Science of Electroconvulsive Therapy and Related Treatments*. This scientizing movement had one overarching goal: to place the controversial therapeutic "in a framework of a history of progression in science and medicine ... extol[ling] its place among modern psychiatric treatments" (Hirshbein & Sarvananda, 2008, p. 11).

The electroconvulsive shock therapy of the 1980s and forward, of course, barely resembles that of previous decades. With anesthetics and muscle relaxers, unilaterally placed electrodes and ultra-brief pulses of electricity, gone are the brutal convulsive thrashings, the strong attendants holding down legs and arms, the dislocations, shattered teeth and fractured bones. Many contemporary first-person narratives, as a matter of fact, now extol its virtues (Berhman, 2002; Dukakis, 2006). But it was the ideological agenda of Fink, Sackeim and others that went the greatest distance not just in scientizing but also in destigmatizing the controversial therapeutic. Endorsements of it flowed in not just from the American Psychiatric Association, but the American Medical Association, the United States Surgeon General, and the World Psychiatric Association (Shorter & Healey, 2007). Electroconvulsive shock therapy had finally made what appeared to be a somewhat respectable comeback, much to the outrage of its detractors, who continue to vociferously assail its science, efficacy, ethics and respect for human rights (Andre, 2009).

Research on the therapeutic continues, but the many controversies that have shadowed it since its inception remain unresolved by it. A sample of recent research findings highlights one of those controversies—the administration of electroconvulsive shock therapy to what might be considered the most vulnerable types of patients, i.e., the young, the old, racial minorities, the developmentally delayed and pregnant women:

- Autism is increasingly being diagnosed in children. There is speculation that certain types of autism may be early expressions of catatonia, for which electroconvulsive shock therapy is effective. What may be the greatest deterrent to the use of electroconvulsive shock therapy for autistic children is the widespread negative reaction to the therapeutic in the public as well as among medical professionals. This reaction must be overcome before clinical trials can begin (Dhossche & Stanfill, 2005).

- Although electroconvulsive shock therapy increasingly is being administered to the elderly, little research on its effects and efficacy has been published. A review of the literature finds nine studies, all with small sample sizes, no control or comparison groups, and using only short-term follow-up assessments. More research is urgently needed (Tielkes, Comijs, Verwijk, & Stek, 2008).

- In a retrospective pilot study, black patients receiving electroconvulsive shock therapy were compared to white patients who were matched for age and gender. Black patients had higher seizure thresholds and were more likely to require additional shocks than white patients. Further research is needed to examine the relationship between race and seizure threshold (Dawkins, Ekstrom, Hill, Isaacs, & Golden, 2000).

- Research on administering electroconvulsive shock treatment to developmentally delayed patients who also have a psychiatric disorder was reviewed. Forty-four patients were found in the literature; for 84 percent of them electroconvulsive shock therapy was effective, but almost half of them relapsed. Controlled studies are needed to establish the efficacy and safety of electroconvulsive shock therapy for developmentally delayed patients (vanWaarde, Stolker & van der Mast, 2001).

- A review of the literature on the administration of electroconvulsive shock therapy to pregnant women finds a total of 339 reported cases. In those studies reporting efficacy data, complete or partial remission of psychiatric symptoms is noted in 78 percent of the cases. Fetal or neonatal complications, including two deaths, are reported in 22 percent of the cases, although not all of these complications were directly attributable to the therapeutic. Although it appears that electroconvulsive shock therapy is effective for the treatment of depression during pregnancy, more controlled and long-term studies are needed (Anderson & Retle, 2009).

Lobotomy

Case 1: "63 year old lady who complained of nervousness, insomnia, depression of spirits, anxiety and apprehension.... The patient was a master at bitching and really led her husband a dog's life.... She was a typical insecure, rigid, emotional, claustrophobic individual throughout her mature existence" (Freeman & Watts, 1950, p. xviii). Her scalp was cleaned and daubed with gentian violet. Three incisions were made into the violet markings and an auger was used to make holes in her skull over the left and the right frontal lobes of her brain. A blunt knife-like instrument with a retractable wire loop was inserted four centimeters down into the exposed surface of her brain. The wire loop was rotated full circle to cut a round core of neural fibers, withdrawn one centimeter to cut another core, and another centimeter to cut a third core. The instrument was withdrawn and then reinserted at a different angle and three additional cores of neural fiber were removed in a surgical procedure that took approximately one hour (El-Hai, 2005).

Four hours after the surgery the patient stated she felt much better; later that evening she was alert, cheerful and hungry. On the following day she answered questions correctly, first in simple monosyllables and then with more detail:

Q: Are you content to stay here?
A: Yes.
Q: Do you have any of your old fears?
A: No.
Q: What were you afraid of?
A: I don't know. I seem to forget.
Q: Do you remember being upset when you came here?
A: Yes, I was quite upset, wasn't I?
Q: What was it all about?
A: I don't know. I seem to have forgotten. It doesn't seem important now
[Freeman & Watts, 1950, p. xix].

Upon returning home she was somewhat shrewish and demanding of her husband and friends, and not at all self-conscious. "I can go to the theatre now and not think whether my shoes pinch or what the back of my hair looks like," she said, "but [I] can really concentrate on the show and enjoy it" (Freeman & Watts, 1950, p. xx). Five years after the surgery she had a convulsion and broke her wrist, and then became steadily more indolent and even abusive. Alice Hood Hammatt died of pneumonia in 1941, just two weeks after the fifth anniversary of her surgery. She was the first person in the United States to undergo a prefrontal lobotomy. Over the next several decades, as many as 50,000 more patients would undergo this "great and desperate" cure for madness (Valenstein, 1986).

Hammatt was not an asylum patient at the time of her surgery. Indeed, her physicians, neurologist Walter Freeman and neurosurgeon James Watts, initially reasoned that the surgery would be of no benefit to the "chronic deteriorated patients" who inhabited the back wards of asylums across the country and who already were the subjects of insulin and metrazol shock therapies. Rather, they proposed that lobotomies be considered for "a small group of specially selected cases in which conservative methods of treatment have not yielded satisfactory results" (Freeman & Watts, 1937, p. 30). Patients in out-patient psychiatric settings who were dealing with the kind of agitated depression Hammatt was experiencing or with chronic anxiety or chronic obsessions seemed to them to be the most amenable to the surgery. All of that, however, would soon change.

The surgery was not the brainchild of Freeman and Watts. Although the frontal lobes of the brain had been of considerable interest to researchers for some time and had been surgically excised in experiments on chimpanzees conducted by John Fulton of Yale University, the first lobotomy performed on a human subject was done by Egas Moniz, a Portuguese neurosurgeon. Consistent with the prevailing scientific reasoning of the time, Moniz considered the frontal lobes of the brain to be the seats of psychic activity. Madness, he therefore postulated, must be the result of the thoughts, ideas and emotions stored in their nerve fibers becoming "fixed." If these pathologically fixed nerve fibers could be surgically destroyed, then madness could be cured (Pressman, 1998).

To that end, his first "leucotomy," as he labeled the surgery, was conducted in 1935 on a middle-aged woman who had been institutionalized for more than three years for depression, anxiety and paranoid delusions. Holes were drilled in her skull and alcohol was injected into her frontal lobes to destroy the nerve fibers. A few hours post-surgery she was responsive to simple questions; two months after the surgery, an attending psychiatrist noted that she was calm although still somewhat depressed, and had no paranoid delusions. Moniz declared her cured and immediately proceeded to perform leucotomies on seven more institutionalized mad patients, with decidedly mixed results. On the eighth patient, Moniz tried a different approach. Rather than destroying the nerve fibers with alcohol, he severed them with a leucotome, a knife-like instrument with a retractable wire loop that could core the nerve fibers from the frontal lobes, a surgical innovation that be believed would increase the likelihood of a cure. After 20 leucotomies, and on the basis of only brief post-surgery observations, Moniz declared that seven patients had been cured, seven had improved, and six were unimproved; none, however, had improved sufficiently enough to be released from the asylum, and several had to have a second leucotomy in an attempt to relieve their persisting symptoms of madness (Valenstein, 1986). It was Moniz's monograph on these first 20 patients that had drawn the attention of Walter Freeman, then a professor of neurology at George Washington University who also had a thriving private practice with his neurosurgeon colleague, James Watts.

The story of how Freeman, and to a much lesser extent Watts, came to eclipse Moniz in both fame and notoriety is the story of the growing controversy over the surgical procedure they were calling a lobotomy. After Hammatt's apparently successful surgery, the physicians quickly lobotomized five more psychiatric outpatients, with mixed immediate results: two were able to return to work, two others relapsed within a couple of months, and the remaining patient, a 47-year-old woman who had lost a great deal of blood when a couple of blood vessels accidentally were severed during the lobotomy, now suffered seizures and incontinence and remained anxious and forgetful (El-Hai, 2005). Freeman and Watts, however, were cautiously confident in the prefrontal lobotomy, confident enough, in fact, not only to present a paper on their first six patients to the Southern Medical Association, but also to have contacted the press for advance publicity. While colleagues attending that meeting were far from unanimous in their support of the surgery, the press coverage was favorable. *Time* magazine for example, quoted one attendee who declared the prefrontal lobotomy a "noted example of therapeutic courage" and generally dismissed those who challenged the procedure on scientific or ethical grounds as "lesser experts" ("Southern Doctors," 1936, p. 67).

The meeting was more heated than the press described, and Freeman was more restrained than he ever would be in the future. But some glimpse of the rather flippant style that would come to characterize both his speaking and writing was offered by Freeman at that meeting when he informed his audience that while the prefrontal lobotomy held promise for a select group of patients, the fact remained that "every patient probably loses something by this operation, some spontaneity, some sparkle, some flavor of the personality, if it may be so described" (Freeman & Watts, 1937, p. 30).

What is this "sparkle" that lobotomy patients lose? Passing reference is made in all of Freeman and Watt's presentations, published papers and interviews to a certain slipshod sociability of patients post-lobotomy, to a lassitude and a distraction. It was not until the publication of their massive textbook in 1942 and its second edition in 1950 that the consequences of the loss of "sparkle" are described (Freeman & Watts, 1950, pp 139–181):

- Disorientation to time, place and self.
- Inertia that may produce "wax dummies" who have to be tickled and prodded into activity.

- Euphoria.
- Restlessness that may have to be remediated by electroconvulsive shock treatments.
- Food cravings and sloppy eating habits.
- Affective incontinence, i.e., a tendency to react with unrestrained joy, sorrow or anger to rather trivial events.
- Childishness, usually manifested as stubbornness.
- Loss of dignity, shame, reserve and self-consciousness.
- Incontinence and sloppy bathroom habits.
- Reduction of creative talent.
- Reliance on concrete rather than abstract or strategic thinking.

By the time Freeman and Watts had published the first edition of their definitive text on lobotomies they already had rejected Moniz's proposition that madness was the result of thoughts, ideas and emotions stored in the nerve fibers of the frontal lobes becoming "fixed," and suggested, instead, another metaphorical explanation: madness is the result of "perverted activity" in the frontal lobes, which have to be "partially inactivated" to reduce "the sting" of madness (Freeman & Watts, 1942, p. 294). By that time, they had found it necessary to lobotomize some of their patients a second time in order to achieve satisfactory results. By that time, they had lobotomized their first child, a nine-year-old whose tantrums were unrelieved by the surgery; and they had botched the lobotomy of Rosemary Kennedy, the eldest daughter of Joseph and Rose Kennedy and sister of the future president of the United States. Both the child and Kennedy had to be institutionalized. By that time, their medical colleagues were complaining among themselves more about the ethics of courting publicity than the ethics of the surgery, while the press lauded Freeman, Watts and the surgery over and over again in uncritical and often hyperbolic articles. By that time, the first patient narrative, titled "Psychosurgery Cured Me," had been published in a popular magazine. The author was Harry Dannecker, a toolmaker from Indiana who upon losing his job had become nervous, irritable, tense and suicidal. His wife, a librarian, brought home newspaper clippings that trumpeted the success of lobotomy in cases like his. So, with her encouragement, he contacted Freeman, who assured him that a lobotomy had six-in-ten odds of curing him. A week after the surgery Dannecker was discharged, and, by his accounts, was not just his former self, but an entirely new, and better, person:

> Back home again, I began taking a new interest in life. I worked on the lawn, painted and repaired the house and did most of the housework.... I acquired new

pleasure in visiting with friends.... I was able to plan and think logically.... Other things returned, too. Slowly, but they returned. My sense of humor, for example. I found myself cracking jokes with friends and injecting an occasional witty remark in conversation. I could even joke about the operation and join in kidding myself about a person getting along better with less brain [Dannecker, 1942, pp. 11–12].

Dannecker joined Freeman and Watts at medical conferences to give a personal, first-hand account of the restorative effects of the lobotomy, and reached out to others with "afflictions" to "give them heart and courage" to have the surgery (p. 12). Sadly, Dannecker relapsed several years after the publication of his story; he had a second lobotomy that resulted in profound inertia and confusion and never recovered.

By that time, Freeman and Watts had abandoned their initial conviction that lobotomies should be performed only on a small group of specially selected cases of depressed and anxious outpatients, and were scouring the nation's overcrowded asylums for candidates for the surgery among the chronically mad. It is perhaps some measure of the controversy surrounding lobotomies that asylums were at first reluctant to provide surgical patients, despite the significant economic incentive for doing so. One asylum superintendent had done the math. He had 180 candidates for lobotomies; at $250 per surgery the total cost would be $45,000. He estimated that 18 of the patients would die, half of the remaining would be improved enough to be more easily, and less expensively, cared for in the asylum; and the remaining half would improve enough to be discharged. Thus the asylum would be relieved of the care of 99 patients, with a total savings over a ten year period of $351,000 ("Neurosurgical Treatment," 1941). Despite the appeal of this argument, it is estimated that between 1940 and 1945, fewer than 1,000 lobotomies were performed on asylum patients by Freeman, Watts and the scores of physicians they had trained (El-Hai, 2005).

What transformed the lobotomy from a surgery of last resort for agitated and depressed outpatients to a surgery of first choice for the psychotic and institutionalized mad? Certainly the economic argument was a strong incentive. Asylums were horribly overcrowded, retention rates were high, staffing rates were abysmally low. Already hothouses for therapeutic innovations, from surgeries to insulin and metrazol shock, asylums were well primed for yet another. Just as certainly, the change in attitude was influenced by "clinical drift" (Pressman, 1998, p. 43), i.e., the experimental lobotomies that Freeman and Watts' protégés were performing on patients who did not match the original protocol. At Pennsylvania Hospital, for example, asylum physicians lobotomized 22 institutionalized psychotic patients and reported the majority had improved enough to discharge them from the asylum

(Strecker, Palmer, & Grant, 1942). Freeman and Watts's perception of the benefits of lobotomies seemed to grow "in direct proportion to the expansion of the diagnostic categories considered appropriate for the procedure" (Pressman, 1998, p. 144). Soon they were arguing that the institutionalized mad should not be left to languish in asylums when the lobotomy held out some hope, if not for their full recovery, then at least for their improvement.

All of that said, it had to be a different kind of lobotomy if it were to be used in asylums. The original prefrontal approach required a surgical suite, a neurosurgeon, and a large staff, equally skilled in nursing and "mothering" (Ewald, Freeman, & Watts, 1947, p. 211), to tend to patients throughout what was almost always a long and very difficult recovery period, none of which most asylums had. And while asylum physicians were noting a high rate of relapse among the lobotomized chronic mad, it had to be the kind of lobotomy that could be effectively used as an "intermediate treatment" for those asylum patients who were not responding to other therapies but were not yet "sufficiently intractable" to justify the extensive brain damage that would be caused by the standard prefrontal lobotomy (Freeman, 1949, p. 9). Such a lobotomy, of course, could also be performed on outpatients, as a kind of prophylactic against worsening madness.

This different kind of lobotomy was the transorbital lobotomy. Pioneered by an Italian psychiatrist, Amarro Fiamberti, the transorbital method accessed the frontal lobes of the brain through the bony eye socket. Impressed by the method, but not yet willing to inform his partner, Watts, of it, Freeman began to practice it on cadavers, using an ice pick from his home to crack through the bone and then moving it back and forth, rather like a windshield wiper, to sever the nerve fibers. Confident that he had mastered the technique, he was ready to try it on a patient.

Sally "Ellen" Ionesco was a 29-year-old patient in Freeman's private practice. For some time she had been in the throes of rapid mood swings, alternating between periods of depression that left her bedridden and periods of mania that made her violent. In 1946, Freeman anesthetized her with three short bursts of electroconvulsive shock, pinched her upper eyelid between his thumb and forefinger, easing it well away from the eyeball, and inserted the ice pick into the conjictival sac. He bent down on one knee while aligning the ice pick parallel to the bony ridge of her nose and then pulled its handle as far laterally as the rim of the eye socket allowed in order to sever the nerve fibers at the base of the frontal lobe. Returning the instrument half way to its initial position, he then pushed it into the frontal lobe to a depth of seven centimeters from the margin of the upper eyelid. "Then comes the ticklish part," he explains. "Arteries are within reach" (Freeman & Watts, 1950, p. 55). He moved the ice pick 15 to 20 degrees medially and 30 degrees laterally, returned it to the mid-position, and withdrew it with a twisting motion, all the while exerting pressure on the eyelid to prevent hemorrhaging. While in subsequent transorbital lobotomies the procedure would be immediately repeated through the other eye socket, he asked Ionesco to return several weeks later for that part of the procedure (El-Hai, 2005).

Left with swollen black eyes, Ionesco returned home for a long recovery that required fulltime care. Her mood swings disappeared, and after some time she was able to work as a nurse, and later as a nanny. Freeman declared her surgery a success, but like so many lobotomy patients, whether prefrontal or transorbital, her good health was impermanent, although not short-lived. As she aged, her mental state declined; she hallucinated and had delusions of persecution (El-Hai, 2005). Although at age 88 she could no longer remember what Freeman's office looked like or, for that matter, what Freeman himself looked like, she remembered him as "a great man" ("My Lobotomy," 2005).

Freeman performed several more transorbital lobotomies in rapid succession in his office, all with similar results as the Ionesco surgery, with the exception of the fourth patient, who hemorrhaged when he sliced a blood vessel. The patient recovered in the hospital but soon began having epileptic seizures. Freeman's notes indicate that the patient never really recovered and had to be cared for by his family (Valenstein, 1986). After nine successive surgeries, Freeman finally asked his colleague Watts to join him, asking him to hold the ice pick while he took a photograph. Watts's adamant refusal effectively ended their partnership. In the second edition of their text, Watts explains why:

> It is Freeman's opinion that transorbital lobotomy is a minor operation.... If he is correct in his view [it] should take precedence over more time consuming psychiatric techniques. On the other hand, if [it] is a major operation, as I believe it is, it should be performed only rarely in mental cases that are not disabled. In both mental and physical disease, surgical intervention should be reserved for cases in which conservative therapy has been tried and failed or in cases where such treatment is known to be ineffective. It is my opinion that any procedure involving cutting of brain tissue is a major surgical operation, no matter how quickly or atraumatically one enters the intracranial cavity. Therefore, it follows logically, that only those who have been schooled in neurosurgical techniques and can handle complications which may arise should perform the operation [Freeman & Watts, 1950, pp. 59–60].

Freeman was left on his own to promote the new procedure and to find candidates for it. To that end, he began visiting state asylums. Arriving first at the state hospital in Yankton, South Dakota, in 1946, he was invited to perform transorbital lobotomies on a dozen chronic schizophrenics, patients who a decade before he would have thought inappropriate for the surgery. The following year he revisited Yankton and then went on to perform 13 transorbital lobotomies on schizophrenic patients in Western State Hospital in Steilacoom, Washington, where the success of the surgeries was trumpeted by the press. But it was in 1948 that Freeman started in earnest his nearly decade-long "head-hunting trip" (El-Hai, 2005, p. 243), crisscrossing the country to find patients in state asylums, and picking up a few "alcoholics, criminals, frustrated businessmen [and] unhappy housewives," all eager for a cure of what ailed them, along the way ("Medicine," 1947, p. 45).

Not content with the assembly-line lobotomies he was performing at large state asylums on patients selected for him by asylum physicians, Freeman proposed a "mass lobotomy" project that would bring the benefits of the surgery to smaller and more isolated asylums. In 1952 he convinced the West Virginia Board of Control to fund what he was calling the "West Virginia Lobotomy Project." Over a twelve day period, he lobotomized 228 patients from four small asylums in the nation's poorest state. Julius McLeod, then an 18-year-old attendant at Lakin State Hospital, the state's segregated asylum for blacks, remembers how the lobotomies were performed and his reaction to them: "[Freeman] took a surgical looking nail and a surgical looking hammer, and he drove the nail between the bridge of the nose and the eyes, one on each side. He pushed in one or two times, up through the frontal lobe, crossed it a couple of times, moved it back and forth.... After all this time, I still can't put into words what I felt other than anger and disgust. These people were human, not cattle" (Wells, 2009).

Helen Culmer arrived as a nurse at Lakin State Hospital just as the West Virginia Lobotomy Project began, and assisted Freeman in performing lobotomies. She recalls the press of people, not just physicians and nurses, but also laypeople from the town, who came to watch the procedure:

> [Freeman] came, and I held the patient's head and he did the lobotomy. He had an instrument—to me it looked like a nail, a great big nail. It had a sharp point, and he inserted this in the corner of the individual's eye and banged it with a mallet, I guess it was. And then he pulled from one side and pulled to other side. It wasn't easy.... It wasn't easy to watch ... and I know that we lost one patient because they couldn't stop the bleeding and I can't remember if any others died.... It wasn't—it wasn't what I thought it might be. To me it was cruel. But that was my opinion. Remember, I've seen all kinds of things in my line of work, so if I stopped and dwelled on each little thing, I'd be hurting ["Oral Histories," 2005].

Freeman published the results of the West Virginia Lobotomy Project in the prestigious *Journal of the American Medical Association* (Freeman, Davis, East, Tait, Johnson, & Rogers, 1954). He reported that four of the 228 patients died as the result of their lobotomies, and of the remaining 224 patients, 85 (38 percent) were released from the asylums over the postsurgery year. One of the criticisms levied at Freeman and other physicians who were performing lobotomies was that their claims to success were suspect in the absence of comparison or control groups. In this project, he actually had a comparison group comprising patients whose relatives had refused permission for the surgery. Of that group, comprising 202 patients, two had died within a year of the project and only 5 (2.5 percent) had been discharged. The difference in the discharge rate for the two groups gives face validity to Freeman's claims that "the lobotomy gets them home."

The report, replete with before and after photographs of patients, which provide another kind of "face validity" in that the "distorted expressions of fear, hate and torment give way to relaxed and sometimes smiling friendliness" (p. 941), does not further analyze the differences between the lobotomized and the comparison patients; but it gives interesting glimpses into the loss of "sparkle" that results from the transorbital lobotomy, just as it did from the more invasive prefrontal. When lobotomized patients are discharged, he explains, they will go through a couple of weeks of "relaxed friendliness, indolence, some confusion, and forgetfulness," but this "rather easy period" would be followed by a more protracted "echo" period of "irritability, defiance and perhaps resurgence of complaints" (p. 941). Indeed, visits to the homes of the 85 patients who had been discharged revealed that their adjustment varied greatly. Although Freeman offers no data on these visits, he states that some were working or attending school, some were keeping house "in a more or less effective fashion," some were in "less satisfactory condition" and had to be closely supervised by family members (p. 942).

The report is significant for other data which are not elaborated upon, but that exacerbate the controversies over the transorbital lobotomy. The 85 patients who returned home after their lobotomies were not the only discharged patients; an additional 50 had returned home but had proven themselves too difficult for relatives to handle and had to be readmitted to the asylums (p. 941). In addition, 47 (21 percent) of the lobotomized patients had shown no improvement whatsoever, and 17 patients had to have a second lobotomy the following year because they either had shown insufficient improvement or had relapsed.

The cost of the West Virginia Lobotomy Project was $2,300. In this poverty-stricken state, the per diem cost of housing a mad patient was $2.04. Freeman calculated a $48,000 savings to the state in the year following the project, thus showing the financial bottom line for "getting them home." The project was re-funded. The next year Freeman and his associates lobotomized an additional 285 West Virginia patients, 115 more the following year, and 159 more the next year, claiming an overall success rate, as measured by discharge alone, of 38 percent, for a grand total of 787 patients (p. 942).

A 38 percent discharge rate for patients, most of whom had been diagnosed with schizophrenia, was, in fact, remarkable—no other therapeutic could assure that—but the questions lingered as to the quality of life for the discharged patients, and as to how they fared in the longer term. To address the latter concern, Freeman (1962) conducted a brief statistical follow-up as patients reached their fifth through eighth years post-lobotomy. Of the 703 still alive, 309 (44 percent) were now living outside of the asylums. As to the quality of their lives, Freeman quite cleverly concluded that "the losses in intelligence, memory and other measureable abilities are due to the [pre-existing] psychosis, not to lobotomy" (p. 1134).

By the time he died in 1972, Freeman personally had performed nearly 3500 lobotomies. He had trained dozens of physicians to perform the relatively simple, but revolting, procedure, and they had gone on to train dozens more. It is estimated that by the time of Freeman's death, 50,000 lobotomies, both prefrontal and transorbital, had been performed in the United States (Pressman, 1998). The bulk of those lobotomies had been carried out on state asylum patients, but during the heyday of lobotomies they were performed across "the institutional geography of American psychiatry, which included private asylums, general hospitals, university medical centers, psychiatric research institutes, and veterans hospitals" (Pressman, 1998, p. 147). Patients included the chronically mad who were languishing away in the back wards of state asylums; those in the throes of acute episodes of madness; the depressed, fearful and anxious who could function, but not well, outside of the asylum. They included more women than men, veterans of World War II, whites and racial minorities, straights and gays, Catholics, Protestants and Jews, the poor and the rich and those in between, urban and rural dwellers, the educated and the illiterate.

Those lobotomized also included children. In the second edition of their massive text, Freeman and Watts (1950) offer brief case studies of several children they lobotomized, two of whom died as the result of the surgery. One of the surviving children was Case 262. "Linda" was six years old, destructive, rebellious, solitary, silent, and overly concerned with cleanliness. Although at two separate hospital visits she had been diagnosed with encephalitis, Freeman labeled her schizophrenic and he and Watts performed a prefrontal lobotomy. After a brief period of improvement, she relapsed, and a second prefrontal lobotomy was performed. Her recovery was slow, but she began talking more and was less destructive with her dolls and toys, although she continued to tear her clothes and run wildly around the house (p. 441). Several years later, "Linda" still talked very little and had made no progress in "helping around the home" (p. 442), although photographs taken of her during her recovery seemed, in Freeman's eyes, to show that her "spirits" had been lifted (p. 444). Acknowledging that "children are difficult to influence" (p. 515) and that at best, a lobotomy could be expected to "smash their fantasy life beyond repair" (p. 536), Freeman and Watts had less interest in lobotomizing children than some of their protégés did (Andy, 1966), that is, until Freeman developed the transorbital procedure. At the Langley Porter Clinic in San Francisco, California, Freeman performed transorbital lobotomies on seven adolescents whose anxiety had been unrelieved by psychotherapy. Bringing three of them to a talk he gave at the clinic, he was met with a hostile audience. One of those adolescents was Howard Dully, who recalls the altercation between the famous lobotomist and his audience:

> It was a big auditorium, and it was full. The seats were raised, angling away from the stage, almost like an operating theater, so that everyone was looking down on us. There were a lot of people there. We sat on chairs onstage with Freeman off to the side, standing behind a podium with his notes. He talked a little bit about what he had done to us. He asked each of us a few questions. He recorded that I answered "in quite a low voice, and didn't have very much to say." Neither did Richard [another adolescent lobotomy patient]. Maybe he got freaked out by all the people, or the lights. He wasn't able to answer the questions Freeman asked him. Freeman got frustrated, and pushed him to try harder. Richard said, "I'm doing the best I can." Freeman pushed him to try again. Someone in the audience shouted something. Freeman explained that we had all had our surgeries quite recently, and besides, we were only children. Someone asked him how old I was — remember, I was a big kid. When Freeman said I had just turned twelve, the doctors were shocked. Only twelve? It was outrageous. The doctors started shouting and yelling. Freeman shouted back. Soon the whole place seemed out of control [Dully, 2007, p. 102].

Perhaps having anticipated some dissent, Freeman had brought hundreds of Christmas cards from grateful lobotomy patients and their family members to the Langley Porter talk. Throwing them on the table, he shouted at the audience, "How many Christmas cards do you get from *your* patients?" (cited in Valenstein, 1986, p. 274). He was booed off the stage, and the meeting was quickly adjourned.

The year was 1961 and in many ways it was as much of a turning point in attitudes about the lobotomy as it was of Freeman's career as a lobotomist. Press coverage of lobotomies, which generally had been as favorable as they were plentiful, had decreased significantly and what was published had a decidedly more critical tone (Diefenbach, Difenbach, Baumeister, & West, 1999). Novels such as *All the King's Men* (Warren, 1946) and *The Naked Lunch* (Burroughs, 1959) further tarnished the surgical procedure, as did the play *Suddenly, Last Summer* (Williams, 1958), later made into a popular film. The public also was getting a glimpse at the role of lobotomy-like procedures in a future technologically totalitarian society in novels such as *The Invisible Man* (Ellison, 1952) and *Limbo* (Wolfe, 1952) and in films such as *A Clockwork Orange*. Freeman's career as a lobotomist was fairing as badly in the eye of the medical profession as the procedure was in the public's eye. His medical privileges were revoked at one hospital after he defied policy and administered an "emergency" electroconvulsive shock treatment to a woman who had been brought to the hospital by the police, and at a second hospital after he severed a blood vessel while performing a prefrontal lobotomy on a patient he had lobotomized twice before. She died as a result of the surgery. Although hers was the last lobotomy he ever performed, Freeman remained enthusiastic until the day he died about the surgery's ability to "bring them home." His enthusiasm, however, was long past being shared by his colleagues, the public or the media. What had happened to turn the tide of opinion from lauding the lobotomy as "an example of therapeutic courage" ("Southern Doctors," 1936, p. 67) to judging it "the most uniquely infamous" (El-Hai, 2005, p. 1) therapeutic in American history?

Certainly the changing times had much to do with this sea change in attitude. In the early years Freeman had been unabashedly brazen in defending not only the surgery as a therapeutic, but also its unsettling results as efficacious. "We want a little indifference, a little laziness," he told a journalist, "a little joy of living that patients have sought in vain for so long." It bothered him not one iota that a patient could be turned into a "careless happy drone" by a lobotomy, explaining that it is "better than [going] through life in an agony of hate and fear of persecution" (Kaempffert, 1941, p. 74). No matter how hard pressed by skeptical colleagues, Freeman never provided anything more than a metaphoric description of lobotomy outcomes: some patients were no more than "wax dummies," others were like "good solid cake but no icing." Whatever the outcome, it was always cast as preferable to the pre-lobotomy psychiatric condition. "We are quite happy about these folks," he and Watts (1950) wrote about the 25 percent of their prefrontal lobotomy patients who had regressed to the level of what they referred to as "domestic invalids and household pets.... [A]lthough the families may have their trials and tribulations because of indolence and lack of cooperation, nevertheless when it comes right down to the question of such domestic invalidism as against the type of raving maniac that was operated on, the results could hardly be called anything but good" (p. 198).

The use of the word "good," and other words such as "improved," "adjusted" and "better" that Freeman relied upon over and over in his many published follow-up studies of lobotomized patients is equally problematic. Since the terms are never operationally defined, almost always conflated with institutional discharge, and the evaluation is never made in relation to a control group of patients who had never been lobotomized, the meanings of the words are elusive; and the apparent success rate of lobotomies cannot be assailed.

The same opaqueness can be found in the published reports of other practitioners of both the prefrontal and the transorbital lobotomies, most of whom were more responsive to criticisms about the lack of scientific rigor in lobotomy studies than Freeman ever was. Henry Worthing (1949) and his colleagues at Pilgrim State Hospital in Brentwood, New York, where as many as 2,000 lobotomies were performed between 1946 and 1959, also fall back onto what they readily admit are "subjective" evaluations of the first 350 patients lobotomized there. They discuss "betterment" in symptoms (p. 623), "improved appearance and subjective state" of the patients (p. 624), "behavior improvement" (p. 625) and "personality loss" (p. 653) without defining the terms. Their study ends, as so many of Freeman's do, with a few selected case studies that as the years went on would raise the question of whether any lobotomy patient is ever "better off" for the surgery:

[*Case No. 4:*] This woman, born in 1898, was admitted to Brooklyn State Hospital, where she was diagnosed as dementia praecox, catatonic type. She was transferred to Pilgrim State Hospital in 1936. Since 1940, she was assaultive and noisy; she wet and soiled and was a feeding problem. Prefrontal lobotomy was done on June 10, 1947. She is now obese, quiet, smiling, friendly, does a small amount of work. There is massive regression and chronic hallucinations, but she is clean [p. 647].

[*Case No. 38:*] Born in 1923, this man was admitted to Pilgrim State Hospital on February 18, 1942. The diagnosis was dementia praecox, catatonic. There was no reaction to adequate therapy; he was subsequently regressive, disturbed, and hallucinated. Lobotomy was performed on January 16, 1948, followed by a gradual improvement in behavior. The patient was released on convalescent care.... At home, he was somewhat childish but in the main well behaved. He is idle, requires some slight supervision and is dependent.... His parents are grateful, since they had never been able to adjust to the idea of leaving him in the hospital, and yet could not manage him at home before the lobotomy [p. 649].

[*Case No. 49:*] This man, born in 1922, had had a previous attack at Pilgrim State Hospital when he was treated by one of the authors. He was readmitted June 22, 1945, after which there was failure with both insulin and electric shock. Lobotomy was done on February 19, 1948, after the patient had been in a withdrawn state, actively hallucinating for more than a year. There was striking improvement. The patient described his previous hallucinations with insight — as happens after insulin. Released on convalescent care April 18, 1948, he was discharged one year later. He was well-adjusted, working, without apparent residual defect; but he began drinking and is said to have indulged in marijuana. There was a full relapse and he was re-certified [as insane] [pp. 649–650].

[*Case No. 231:*] Aged 57, this man was diagnosed with dementia praecox, paranoid, onset more than ten years ago. There were delusions of persecution, economic incapacity, withdrawal from family, letters to authorities. He was admitted to Pilgrim State Hospital in 1947. In the hospital, he was furiously resistive, actively hallucinated, resentful, grandiose, unapproachable.... Lobotomy was done on February 8, 1949.... The patient admitted that he had been "imagining things." He became friendly and approachable. On close examination, residual psychotic content was noted.... The man was released June 4, 1949. On first report, he was comfortable, but economically dependent. He was well-behaved. "No loss of intelligence in conversation' was observed, but 'no will to work" [p. 654].

By the time Freeman had paraded three lobotomized adolescents before an audience of medical professionals in 1961, the loss of "sparkle" he had so flippantly referred to when he began his lobotomy mission decades before was no longer perceived as a "good" outcome, and certainly not as a "preferable" one. Indeed, the best results of the lobotomy — inertia, inattentiveness, lack of initiative, blunted affect, docility — were leading to the conclusion "that the treatment was worse than the disease" (Mashour, Walker, & Martuza, 2005, p. 412).

For the anti-psychiatry movement that was burgeoning during that era, the loss of "sparkle" would become not so much a clinical as a civil rights issue. Most members of this movement were themselves "psychiatric survivors" of insulin, metrazol and electroconvulsive shock treatments. The best outcomes of lobotomies pretty well assured that there were few, if any, survivors of the surgery among them, but the movement found plenty of reason to take on the cause. The 1960s, after all, was a tumultuous decade: violent crime rates were increasing, war protests were disrupting university campuses, racial conflicts were burning cities, and all kinds of people who had been pushed to the margins of society — the poor, women, racial minorities, gays and lesbians — were pushing towards the center. A high-tech lobotomy was being proposed as a cure for the nation's ills.

Five days of race riots in Detroit, Michigan, in 1967 resulted in $32 million in property damage and left scores of people dead and thousands arrested. It was arguably the most violent urban revolt of the 20th century and a portent of racial conflicts yet to come (Grimshaw, 1969). While politicians, pundits and the public were grappling with the origins and consequences of the riot, a letter published in the *Journal of the American Medical Association* by three Harvard University neuroscientists proposed both a cause and a cure. Arguing that social and economic stresses alone could not adequately explain why only some black residents rioted, or why only some of those who did were assaultive, they reasoned that the most violent of the rioters were brain-damaged. They concluded by asking for "intensive research and clinical studies of individuals committing violence" in order to "pinpoint, diagnose and treat ... people with low violence thresholds before they contribute to further tragedies" (Mark, Sweet, & Ervin, 1967, p. 895).

Although the letter's authors never specifically mentioned surgical corrections of the alleged brain damage or, for that matter, the lobotomy, the impression they left of the need for a medicalized program of behavior modification had frightening social and political ramifications. When the authors received $600,000 in grants from the National Institutes of Mental Health and the Law Enforcement Assistance Administration to pursue this line of inquiry, concerns redoubled. The publication of their book, *Violence and the Brain* (Mark & Ervin, 1970), details their experiences in treating uncontrollably violent patients with a stereotaxic procedure that uses a three-dimensional coordinate system to locate the precise area of the brain causing the violence so that brain tissue can be removed, brain lesions can be created, or electrodes can be implanted. The authors consider the surgery a viable procedure not only for the urban rioters who had first piqued their interest, but also for protesting students, and even rogue police officers and corrupt public officials. While far from the blind technique of damaging the frontal lobes of the brain with an ice pick, this procedure was considered by the antipsychiatry movement as nothing more than a high-tech lobotomy with much higher social and political stakes than the ice-pick surgery ever had (Breggin, 1972).

The story of this type of surgical procedure is a complicated, albeit quite short, one. Because the procedure was aimed at the modification of violence, rather than madness, the full story is best left to others (Breggin, 2007; Chavkins, 1980). But to the extent that the controversy over what was now being called psychosurgery also influenced the vilification of the lobotomy, it is significant. When the *Washington Post* reported that three inmates with histories of uncontrollable violence had parts of the amygdalas in their brains destroyed by stereotaxic surgery in an experimental program in behavior modification at Vacaville Prison in California (Aarons, 1972), the reaction was swift. Lambasted as the "return of the lobotomy" (Breggin & Greenberg, 1972), the experiment conjured images of government-funded mind control programs that targeted the poor racial minorities who were disproportionately represented in the prison population. Psychosurgery, the lobotomy included, now became a civil rights issue, and "it was not long before [it] was being debated in the popular press, in congressional hearings, in symposiums at scientific and professional meetings, in conferences on science, medicine, and ethics, and in legal circles" (Valenstein, 1986, p. 287).

The legal implications of psychosurgery were highlighted in the high profile case of *Kaimowitz v. Department of Mental Health* (1973). In this case, Louis Smith, who was suspected of having raped and murdered a student nurse, had been held in a state asylum in Michigan for 18 years under the state's criminal sexual psychopath law. In an experimental program funded by the state legislature, Smith had consented to undergo psychosurgery to test the efficacy of the procedure against hormone treatments to reduce violence. A suit was brought to prevent the surgery; the court ruled that as a matter of law, involuntarily confined patients cannot give legally adequate consent to experimental psychosurgery because the three basic elements of informed consent—competency, knowledge, and voluntariness—cannot be reliably assessed in relationship to such an invasive and irreversible procedure.

The Kaimowitz decision became a major talking point in hearings that led to the creation of the National Commission for the Protection of Human Subjects of Biomedical and Behavior Research, established in 1974. But the commission also responded specifically to the lobotomy. After taking testimony and reviewing the literature, it refused to endorse either the prefrontal or the transorbital lobotomy, but it did conclude that more modern psychosurgical procedures, such as the stereotaxic procedure, might be of therapeutic value for carefully selected patients (Culliton, 1976).

By the time the National Commission issued its

A Primer on the Politics of Psychosurgery

*1944: Porteus and Kepner (1944) predict that post–World War II social strains will necessitate an increase in lobotomies to deal with the distress they cause and to quell unrest.

*1952: The Central Intelligence Agency commissioned an investigation into the use of the lobotomy to "neutralize" Communists (El-Hai, 2005).

*1956: An investigative journalist claims that the 21 American soldiers who refused repatriation after the Korean War had been lobotomized by the Chinese (Lamb, 1956).

*1968: Secret experimental psychosurgery performed in California on violent prisoners (Valenstein, 1986).

*1969: In *Physical Control of the Mind,* Delgado recommends a $1 billion government initiative to control the human brain with the ultimate goal of creating a "psycho-civilized society."

*1970: In *Violence and the Brain,* Mark and Ervin recommend stereotaxic psychosurgery for controlling violent behavior.

*1973: The president of the Hastings Institute, William Gaylin, reassures a senate subcommittee on health care that psychosurgery would not be the method of choice for any totalitarian regime bent on taking over the United States ("Protection," 1977).

---

report, the lobotomy as Freeman and Watts knew and practiced it had all but disappeared. Fewer than 350 of the surgeries were performed each year during the decade of the 1970s, even fewer over subsequent decades. From today's perspective the surgery is "uniquely infamous" and Freeman is one of "the most scorned" physicians in recent history (El-Hai, 2005, p. 1). But it is the fall from grace of both the procedure and its most passionate promoter and practitioner that is of the most sociological interest. That was a fall through decades of changing ideas about the relationship between the mind and the body, between madness and sanity, between physician and patient; it was a fall through evolving notions of civil and human rights, and it was a fall through different perspectives on how much "spontaneity, sparkle and flavor" (Freeman & Watts, 1937, p. 30) a person, even a *mad* person, can lose and still be a person.

As for Egas Moniz, who performed the first lobotomy on a human, he was awarded the Nobel Prize in Medicine in 1949 for his innovative surgery. Since the mid–1990s there has been a small-scale, but certainly persistent, campaign to persuade the Nobel Foundation to rescind Moniz's prize. Spearheaded by relatives and friends of American lobotomy patients, the letter-writing campaign finally elicited a response from the Nobel Foundation: it acknowledged Moniz's prize is controversial and heavily criticized; while it said nothing about the demand to rescind it, it did stand behind an essay posted on its website by a prominent psychiatrist that concludes, "I see no reason for indignation at what was done in the 1940s as at that time there were no other alternatives" (Jansson, 1998; "Psychosurgery," n.d.).

Psychotherapeutics Controversy

Although the mind-body relationship has preoccupied ancient philosophers and asylum physicians alike, it was not until the antebellum era that "the psychological" acquired cultural prominence (Pfister, 1997). Its emphasis on subjectivity, i.e., on the impressions, emotions, thoughts and opinions that are associated much more with the mind than with the body or even the brain, generated a host of new psychotherapeutic professsions, from clinical psychology and psychiatric social work, to recreational and occupational therapies, that became part of the armamentarium of asylum medicine.

It was not that early asylum physicians had no appreciation of psychotherapeutics. Even the "Father of Psychiatry," Benjamin Rush, whose passion for bloodletting and the tranquilizing chair are legendary, had a complex theory of the mind, its "derangement" and its treatment. Believing the mind to be immaterial, Rush nonetheless described its "faculties": the passive, i.e., intellectual faculties of memory, understanding, conscience and a sense of deity; and the active, i.e., voluntary faculties of will, imagination, and passions (emotions). Any of these can become "deranged" and cause madness (Carlson, Wollock, & Noel, 1981). Take the passions as an example. Rush proposed two classes of them: those that defend a person from a real or supposed evil, and those that impel the person towards a real or supposed good. Of the first class, grief, fear and anger are the passions most vulnerable to derangement; in the second, love. A derangement in the passion of love, by way of another example, may take the form of what Rush referred to as the "morbid excess" of hopeless or unrequited love (Rush, 1812, p. 312), which causes hysteria, hypochondriasis, fever, dyspepsia and madness. For Rush, the most efficacious remedy was psychotherapeutic. Although he did recommend bleeding and blistering, as he did for virtually every type of madness, he aimed the rest of the therapeutics at the mind rather than the body or brain. To that end, he recommended that asylum physicians treat love-stricken patients by encouraging them to find new lovers; directing them to dwell on the imperfections and bad qualities of the unresponsive persons they desire; advising them to avoid the company of these persons and to engage in constant activities so as to forget them entirely; extinguishing any sparks of hope that their love will ever be requited; and by inciting more powerful passions, such as ambition.

Rush's theory of the mind and of its passions pays homage to early Greek philosophers who often talked of the passions in medical terms, variously conceiving them as the sources of madness, the symptoms of madness, or the states of mind that must be rectified for madness to be cured (Jackson, 1990). These philosophies certainly influenced moral treatment as well. The treatment of mad patients at the Pennsylvania Hospital for the Insane under the superintendency of Thomas Kirkbride, the figure most closely associated with moral treatment in the 19th century, provides an illustration. Although Kirkbride theorized that madness was a "functional disease of the brain," he indicted the passions or emotions as one of its primary causes. Grief, anxiety, fear, worry, desire, guilt, he argued, could adversely affect the brain; but if talked about, the madness could be cured. Thus a significant part of moral treatment was accessing the minds of mad patients, overcoming whatever resistance they had to talking about their emotions and expressing their otherwise unexpressed thoughts, encouraging introspection, and persuading them to feel and to think differently (Tomes, 1994).

For the lovesick, the guilt-stricken, and the fearful, this was not often a protracted or particularly painful process. But the delusional posed a challenge. Their feelings and thoughts had become fixed in their minds, in Kirkbride's thinking, and were not easily unfixed by gentle probing and moral suasion. Kirkbride noted early in his career that delusional patients clung to their delusions even more tenaciously when confronted, so if he could not distract them with the activities of moral treatment—the walks, lectures, magic lantern shows and recreational activities on the beautiful grounds—then he counseled them to distract themselves. "Say little about them," he counseled one young patient whose "unnatural feelings" about his father had made him mad, "introduce the subject rarely if ever" (quoted in Tomes, 1994, p. 218).

Kirkbride died in 1883. His death not only tolled the end of moral treatment but trumpeted the emergence of the somatic therapeutics that focused on treating the body and the brain rather than the mind. But this biological psychiatry revolution was far from hegemonic. Competing with it, even while it was struggling to find its own place in asylum therapeutics, was psychoanalysis. Both a theory of the mind and a set of techniques for treating it, psychoanalysis became hugely popular in the newly introspective and self-focused antebellum era in the United States.

Psychoanalysis was the brainchild of Sigmund Freud, the Viennese neurologist whose early research on the gonads of eels and the nervous systems of crayfish led to research on brain injuries and diseases in human patients, and finally and most significantly, to the study and the treatment of the mind. At that time, the late 1800s, matters of the mind belonged more to philosophy than to medicine; but Freud set out to change that. Over the years he developed a complex theory of the mind that was both structural and dynamic in nature, and a set of techniques for accessing and treating the troubled mind that emphasized the one thing the competing somatic therapeutics had little interest in—talk.

Freud came to the United States for the first and only time in 1909 to deliver a series of invited lectures at Clark University in Worcester, Massachusetts. Although he arrived with eagerness, he left disappointed. The Americans he encountered on his brief sojourn struck him as neurotic, prudish, materialistic and immature; the country, as a whole, struck him as iconoclastic and much too individualistic to ever succeed as a democracy. Dismissing the country as a "gigantic mistake" and as a "bad experiment conducted by Providence," Freud's antipathy to the United States and its citizens not only never diminished, but also fueled his critique of western civilization that preoccupied him for the decade or so before his death in 1939 (Kaye, 1993).

Americans, however, *loved* Freud. His theory of the mind filled up the "empty self" which was being depleted by the breakdown of community, tradition and moral authority in modernizing society, and healed the loss of generational continuity being created by the rapid expansion of urban, industrial mass society. It infiltrated the vocabulary, words and phrases such as "the unconscious," "id," "ego," "phallic symbol" and "Oedipal Complex" increasingly were used by Americans to represent and understand themselves and others. Its considerable influence also could be seen in art, literature, poetry, music, film and theatre (Roth, 1998).

Although Freud had his devotees in the United States before his visit in 1909, he gathered considerably more after that visit. Local psychoanalytic societies were established as meeting places for the exchange of ideas between psychiatrists interested in Freudian theory and practice. These enthusiasts, however, were more than aware from the start that psychoanalysis as a practice had little, if any, role as an asylum therapeutic. The protracted one-on-one sessions between analysts and analysands, the years of commitment required, made it unsuitable in state asylums that already were filling up with patients who were as demographically as they were diagnostically diverse. And, of course, psychoanalysis as a practice was wholly unsuited for the treatment of the most intractable of the mad, the psychotics. Freud said so himself in a 1928 letter to a colleague: "I do not like these patients.... I am annoyed with them.... I feel them to be so far distant from me and from everything human ... [a] curious sort of intolerance, which surely makes me unfit to be a psychiatrist" (cited in Lynn, 1993, p. 64). Therefore, much of the discussion in these local meetings, and later in the American Psychoanalytic Association, which was formed in 1911, centered on the practice of psychoanalysis in private asylums and clinics, and in outpatient offices, i.e., in settings where patients were more likely to be well-heeled, literate, articulate and not laboring under the burden of delusions and hallucinations.

Psychoanalysis, however, did influence asylum therapeutics in two important ways. First, an increasing number of analysts were becoming psychiatrists, and an increasing number of psychiatrists were being trained in psychoanalysis. The first increase was due to a new standard promulgated by the American Psychoanalytic Association that required training candidates to have completed at least one year of psychiatric residency; the second, to the incursion of psychoanalysis into university and hospital training programs not just in psychiatry, but in clinical psychology and psychiatric social work (Shorter, 1997). Therefore, by mid-century the majority of staff who were psychotherapeutically working directly with asylum patients were well-versed in psychoanalytic theory, even if the contingencies of their work made its practice nearly impossible.

A visit from Frieda Fromm-Reichmann, to Worcester State Hospital in Massachusetts, where the staff had enthusiastically embraced psychoanalytic theory, provides an illustration. Fromm-Reichmann, who later would be immortalized as "Dr. Fried" in both the novel *I Never Promised You a Rose Garden* (Green, 1964) and the film by the same title, was one of only a few analysts who had an interest in treating psychotic patients with psychoanalysis. And she had some success. The Worcester staff read of her techniques, including sitting on a floor day after day in the company of an unspeaking psychotic patient who finally acknowledged her presence by offering her a urine-soaked cigarette. When Fromm-Reichmann was told by a Worcester psychiatric resident that he was trying that same technique with one of his psychotic patients, she responded in her heavy German accent: "I'm so sorry, but zat was a mistake I made long ago. Ve all make mistakes, you see. Ze problem is that sooner or later ve get tired of sitting in the 'quiet room' smoking urine soaked cigarettes. Ve must accept our limitations like ve accept those of our patients. I now think that ve should not promise a patient something that ve are not willing to deliver forever. Otherwise ve vill be tested until ve fail and so fulfill their paranoid predictions" (Calloway, 2007, p. 81).

The second way psychoanalysis influenced asylum therapeutics was that it provided an ongoing critique of the efforts of asylum psychiatry to scientize itself by developing increasingly complex diagnostic categories and treating madness as a disease. The critique was predicated upon the premise, a la Freud, that if everyone is "only approximately normal" then madness is not an exception to the norm but an expression of it. Therefore, it is not a disease, should not be endlessly categorized and subcategorized, and cannot be cured. In fact, the attempts to cure it by the somatic therapeutics and later by the psychopharmaceuticals were particularly derided by psychoanalysts who believed that symptoms should be read, not eradicated, so that their psychogenic causes will be revealed. Making those causes, such as adverse childhood experiences, rather than their symptoms the object of therapeutic intervention, they argued, is the only way to restore the patients' well-being.

In the end, this ongoing critique did little to change asylum therapeutics or the practice of them, if only because of the insurmountable obstacles posed by the asylum itself. Reading symptoms rather than eradicating them was antithetical to the management function of the asylum; treating symptoms rather than eradicating them required time which most asylum physicians did not have, and cooperative, i.e., articulate, introspective and intelligent patients, which many asylum patients were not. But the critique, in a curious way, did affect *who* was left to practice asylum therapeutics. Half of all psychiatrists whose practice was asylum-based in 1941 had gone over to psychoanalytically-informed private practice by 1962 (Shorter, 1997, p. 181), leaving behind those who had a strong commitment to somatic and later to psychopharmacological therapeutics to work in asylums. By the late 1970s, in some state asylums, more than 90 percent of psychiatrists were foreign-born; problems in communication and with cultural competence also encouraged the turn away from face-to-face counseling and towards somatic and psychopharmacological therapeutics (Haveliwa-la, 1979).

The cachet of Freudian psychoanalysis as a practice has declined precipitously over recent years; expensive and time-consuming, it can no longer meet the quick-fix needs of most Americans in a late-modern society. Freudian psychoanalytic theory, too, has come under increasing attack for being unscientific, untestable, racist, classist, homophobic and sexist (Hale, 1995). Nor has it held up well in those asylums where it is practiced. When the effects of psychoanalysis alone, psychoanalysis with drugs, drugs alone, electroconvulsive shock therapy alone, and milieu therapy alone were compared, schizophrenic patients improved the most with drugs alone followed by electroconvulsive shock treatment alone, than they did with any other therapeutic (May, 1968). When the parameters were expanded to include psychotherapy in general, i.e., the mélange of theories and practices that were influenced by Freudian psychoanalysis, schizophrenic patients still showed considerably more improvement with drugs alone than they did with psychotherapy alone (Grinspoon, Ewalt, & Shader, 1972).

Psychopharmacology Controversy

In 1954 the drug chlorpromazine changed asylum therapeutics. Its trade name, Thorazine, is an homage to Thor, the Norse god of thunder. The drug calmed patients, reduced their delusions and hallucinations, and rendered them more amenable to adjunctive therapies. And it did all of that not only for patients whose madness was acute and of short duration, but also for those chronically mad whose presence in the back wards of asylums across the country was a continuing reminder of the failure of modern psychiatric therapeutics and those who practiced them. The Pulitzer Prize winning poet Robert Lowell, whose attacks of what is now known as bipolar disorder led to his repeated hospitalizations, said this about Thorazine: "I could hardly swallow my breakfast because I so dreaded the weighted bending down that would be necessary for making my bed. And the rational exigencies of bed making were more upsetting than the physical.... My head ached.... I felt my languor lift, then descend again" (Hamilton, 1982, p. 218).

While Thorazine alone hardly emptied asylums, it did contribute to the steadily declining patient census during what has become known as the deinstitutionalization movement that began in the 1960s. Marketed as the "chemical lobotomy," the round orange pill—despite its powerful effects, it soon became evident—could "get them home" faster, cheaper, and more expediently than the ice pick.

Thorazine might have raced into the asylum armamentarium with all of the thunder befitting its trade name, but remedies of various kinds had been administered to mad patients from the very start of the asylum movement with the establishment in 1751 of the Pennsylvania Hospital. The "kitchen physics" of the pre-asylum era — the herbs and plants used by the apprentice doctors, empirics, ministers, root workers and medicine men for the folk treatment of madness — became the *materia medica* of the asylum. Indeed, the board of managers of the Pennsylvania Hospital enthusiastically received a proposal by the founders to establish a physics garden on the hospital grounds that would provide physicians easy access to the ingredients for their remedies. (The garden, however, was not created until two centuries later when the Philadelphia Committee of the Garden Club of America and the Friends of Pennsylvania Hospital planted it as a bicentennial project in 1976.)

An easily accessible physics garden might have provided asylum physicians with remedies to ameliorate the symptoms of madness, but it did little for remedying a more pressing problem. The very purpose of the asylum — to congregate large numbers of mad patients in a secure place — begged for remedies for their management and control. As the practice of using mechanical restraints such as chains, manacles, jacket waistcoats, leather wristlets and hand straps became increasingly controversial, and as asylums became more crowded, asylum physicians became more interested in compounded drugs for achieving the same effects. In the early years of the asylum movement, opium was much relied upon as a tranquilizer and sedative. The "Plant of Joy" had been in use in folk medicine for millennia, and asylum physicians found it "most effectual and salutary," especially for calming paroxysms of mania and wild delusion (Woodward, 1850, p. 1). But opium also had deleterious side effects, most notably nausea and constipation, the latter of which often required a reliance on the anachronistic humoural treatment of purging with salts, cremor tartars, senna, calomel or jalap in order to relieve the distress.

The asylum law reformer Elizabeth Packard (1868) wrote about the deleterious effects of opium treatment that asylum physicians were slow to appreciate. She describes a fellow asylum patient, a "little, beautiful fawn-like creature" (p. 203) whose long course of opium treatment for her nervous condition eventually drove her to suicide:

> Her nerves were unstrung, and lost their natural tone by the influence of opium, that most deadly foe of nature.... The opium was expected to operate as a quietus to her then excited nervous system; but instead of this, it only increased her nervous irritability. The amount was then increased, and this course persisted in, until her system became drunk, as it were, by its influence. The effect produced was like that of excessive drinking, when it causes delerium tremens. Thus she became a victim to that absurd practice of the medical profession, which depends upon poisons instead of nature to cure disease [p. 204].

Indeed, the "poisonous" properties of opium finally were recognized by asylum physicians. Concerns, too, developed over time about "morphinomania," that is the accumulation of opium in the body; those concerns would grow into warnings about the perils of addiction that, ironically, would bring many opium addicts into asylums as patients (Carlson & Simpsom, 1963).

Mercury, a powerful toxin, also was administered, primarily for cases of mania. E.H. Smith, a physician at the New York Hospital, recounts the successful treatment of a 17-year-old Irish immigrant who "suddenly was taken insane" on a walk over a country field in 1796 (Smith, 1797). Upon being admitted to the asylum, she was so violent that she tore off the strait-waistcoat used to restrain her, not once, but three times. She sang loudly, assumed bizarre postures, and failed to recognize her mother and brothers when they visited. Refusing to open her arms to expose a vein, she was bled with six ounces of blood taken from her temples and forehead, but to no effect. Theorizing that if a powerful action could be excited in the "absorbent system," i.e., the lymphatic system, then vital energy would be diverted from the muscles "and awaken the torpid power of the brain, stomach and bowels" (p. 183), Smith administered three drachms of mercurial ointment.

> [S]he grew calm and rational; took food.... She also had her cloaths put on, and was removed to a clean bed, in the nurse's room. The mercurial friction was discontinued. This interval of reason was only for a few hours. She became as violent as ever; broke every frangible article in the nurse's apartment; and again tore off her cloaths. She was reconducted to her cell.... The mercurial frictions were renewed. They excited a gentle salivation, and brought back her reason.... [S]he mended gradually till the 7th of September, when she was well enough to return to her family [p. 183].

The phrase "mad as a hatter" is often associated with Lewis Carroll's classic children's book, *Alice in Wonderland* (1865), but it was coined decades before to describe a type of madness peculiar to milliners in the hat-making industry. A mercury solution was used to turn fur into felt, and in poorly vented working conditions, milliners breathed in the toxic fumes. The symptoms associated with the accumulation of mercury in the body were loss of coordination, trembling ("hatters shakes"), slurred speech, memory loss, depression, irritability and anxiety—the Mad Hatter Syndrome.

Camphor also was used in the early years of asylums, as was digitalis, or foxglove, the former to stimulate the nervous system, the latter to slow the heart rate. It is worth noting that as asylum physicians accumulated experience in dealing with the mad and began to make finer diagnostic distinctions between them, they became more circumspect about their treatment. Benjamin Rush is a case in point. In his magnum opus he reflected on 30 years experience of treating the mad at the Pennsylvania Hospital. He urged asylum physicians to abandon the practice of giving large doses of opium to manic patients in order to sedate them, and to consider giving them small doses to prevent sleep, thus "gradually wast[ing] their excitability" (Rush, 1812, p. 200). He strongly recommended against the use of both camphor and digitalis in cases of mania, since neither, in his considerable experience, did much to calm frenetic behaviors and thoughts.

Rush's tenure at the Pennsylvania Hospital ended with his death in 1813, several decades before folk medicine remedies would start gradually giving away to psychopharmaceuticals, i.e., specially compounded drugs for the treatment of madness. The fact that some, maybe even many, early asylum patients indeed were helped, if not cured, by opium, camphor and digitalis, among other folk remedies, and, it should be added, by the humoural treatments of bleeding, purging, vomiting and blistering, gives some support to the contention that if society, science, the physician and the patient share a system of beliefs about the relationship between the body and mind, and between madness and sanity, and if therapeutic practices are perceived to be manifestations of those beliefs, they are expected to be effective and they often are. While it is true that early asylum superintendents had a tendency in their annual reports to inflate their success in treating the mad, and that prominent physicians such as Rush may have shared that proclivity, the fact remains that the reports and reminiscences are replete with cases of patients who got well enough to go home from the asylum and never returned.

Psychopharmacology

By the mid–1800s several strands of controversy began to intertwine: increasingly overcrowded asylums perpetuated the use of mechanical restraints despite the considerable argument about their use, engendered fears that madness was epidemic, and increased skepticism about the skills of asylum physicians and, more generally, about the claim for status in the medical profession by the new specialty of psychiatry.

First Wave

In a small but significant way the introduction of sedatives addressed, even if it did not completely redress, these controversies. These early sedatives had the potential of diminishing or even eliminating the use of mechanical restraints. Although none, with the exception of potassium bromide, was ever touted as a cure for madness, all could significantly alter the milieu of the asylum, from loud and chaotic to quiet and orderly, thus also changing the practice of asylum psychiatry. The fact that the early sedatives were created in research laboratories strengthened the link between medical research and psychiatric practice, thus increasing the scientific bona fides of the latter (Warner, 1986).

One of the first of those synthesized sedatives was morphine, a derivative of the newly maligned opium. Administered orally when first introduced and then later subcutaneously via the newly invented hypodermic needle, it was ideal for both the quick management of aggressive and agitated patients and the general sedation of melancholic and delusional patients. By the mid–1800s morphine was the most widely used drug in asylums, its praises sung by one of the most prominent asylum superintendents of his generation, Samuel Woodward, of the Worcester Asylum in Massachusetts: "The manner in which morphine has been used in this and other hospitals in this country, continuing until the symptoms have subsided, then omitting it and seeing them return, then again and again removed by the renewal of this medicine, affords unequivocal evidence of its power to subdue maniacal excitements, relieve the delusions of the insane, and restore the brain and nervous system to a sound and healthy state" (Woodward, 1850, p. 62). Such was the cachet of morphine that even Thomas Kirkbride, the champion of moral treatment, used it extensively. At any given time, anywhere from 75 percent to 88 percent of the mad patients at his Pennsylvania Hospital for the Insane had been sedated with morphine (Tomes, 1984, p. 195).

The discovery that potassium bromide can decrease the frequency of what were known as hysterical seizures, i.e., seizures with a psychological as opposed to an organic origin, paved the way for the use of various bromide compounds in asylums. Used to relieve stress and anxiety by sedation, the bromides were, like morphine, administered with no expectation that they would do little more than provide temporary respite. i.e., until a Scottish physician practicing in Shanghai, China, came upon something he named "bromide sleep."

Neil Macleod administered 2.5 ounces of sodium bromide to a morphine-addicted woman, producing a "bromide sleep" of several days from which she could not be roused. When the administration of sodium bromide ceased, she gradually awakened and reported no craving for morphine. Macleod then hypothesized that the bromide sleep for a five to nine day period would produce the same cessation of craving for alcoholics and also would terminate an acute attack of mania. He replicated the treatment in eight more patients and achieved the desired results in all but one case. In that case, the patient died of pneumonia (Macleod, 1900).

While asylums had their share of morphine addicted and alcoholic patients, Macleod's conclusion that a sedative could cure, as opposed to temporarily relieve, acute mania by resting the nervous system was appealing. His reports had been republished in American psychiatric and medical publications, most notably *Merck Archives*, which not only endorsed bromide sleep only for the cure of acute mania, but suggested that it may "prove a powerful and effective means of dealing with *all* maladies of the nervous system" ("Bromide Sleep," 1900, p. 111). Since it was nervous maladies of all kinds that were filling asylums and stoking the fear that madness was epidemic, American asylum physicians were intrigued by the remedy, and eager to try it. Their experiments, however, were decidedly mixed in their outcomes. Archibald Church, a professor at the Chicago Medical College, used it with great success on a morphine addict who, upon awakening, not only lost his desire for the drug but also had a renewed feeling of "strength [and] buoyancy" (Church, 1900, p. 293). Church's second patient, however, died during the course of the treatment, most likely from the cumulative effects of the bromide.

Church's subsequent conclusion that bromide sleep is effective, yet more risky than Macleod had acknowledged, put somewhat of a damper on its use in the United States. Some asylum physicians continued the treatment, much more for morphine addiction and alcoholism than for the spectrum of nervous disorders, and did so with some reported success; but most considered the risk of overdose too high. It would be a few more decades before barbiturates would reintroduce the idea of sleep therapy, or "prolonged narcosis," as it came to be termed.

Perhaps the best known of the early sedatives, and the one that had the longest span of use as an asylum therapeutic, was chloral hydrate. Developed in the mid–1800s as a new type of chloroform that could be taken orally, its hypnotic effects proved useful for temporarily sedating asylum patients. Because it also had such widespread medical uses — from a topical antiseptic for boils to stopping asthma attacks — it may have been the single drug that finally tolled the end of the practice of humoural medicine in the United States (Warner, 1985).

Chloral hydrate's popularity was a product of its relatively low cost and the ease of administration of the tasteless, odorless and colorless drug. It was not pushed into asylum use by pharmaceutical companies, as chlorpromazine (Thorazine) much later would be, but was vigorously promoted by academic pharmacology and psychiatry. As a sedative, it quickly eclipsed opium, the bromides, and other remedies in popularity both in outpatient and inpatient medical and psychiatric practice. But in specific regard to asylum patients, the need for a drug like chloral hydrate for sedation far outstripped the growing concerns about its effects. Numerous studies began reporting adverse side effects, contrary reactions, and the potential for abuse and addiction, as well as the kind of psychotic reactions that brought patients into asylums in the first place; yet its appeal to asylum physicians never really waned (Snelders, Kaplan, & Peters, 2006).

Even its public vilification did little to dampen their enthusiasm. Chloral hydrate always has been deeply steeped in urban lore and in popular culture. It was the stuff of the infamous knockout drops of the Mickey Finn cocktail whose consumers, it was rumored, would finally awake days later to find themselves shanghaied to China or, perhaps, enslaved in a white slavery prostitution ring. It was the sad demise of many a literary heroine, including Lily Bart in Edith Wharton's *House of Mirth* (1905), and the reason for the evil machinations of literary psychiatrists such as Dr. Seward in Bram Stoker's *Dracula* (1897). It was rumored to have caused the untimely death of the world renowned actress Sarah Bernhardt (Snelders, Kaplan, & Pieters, 2006), was later implicated in the suicide of Marilyn Monroe and the death of Anna Nicole Smith, and was the source of the debilitating addiction of Mary Todd Lincoln, the widow of the 16th president of the United States (Baker, 1987).

These and other sedatives comprised the first wave of psychopharmaceuticals. And, for the most part, they did exactly as they promised to do. Ironically, though, they replicated in chemical form the very mechanical restraints they promised to eliminate. In the face of growing controversy over the "chemical restraint" of asylum patients, these drugs, too, eventually were abandoned. With the exception of chloral hydrate, these early sedatives were dismissed as nontherapeutic. The quest for drugs that actually could cure, rather than temporarily relieve, madness was redoubled (Braslow, 1997).

Second Wave

The second wave of psychopharmaceuticals began at the turn of the 20th century with the synthesis of barbital and later of phenobarbital, but these powerful hypnotics and sedatives still initially were for the purpose of calming, not curing. With none of potassium bromide's side effects, such as a nasty taste, and with a therapeutic dosage well below a toxic dosage, thus decreasing substantially the likelihood of overdose, the barbiturates were aggressively marketed by pharmaceutical companies. In 1939, for example, one hundred tons of barbiturates were sold in the United States. While not all of this massive quantity found its way into asylums, the fact remains that asylum physicians enthusiastically administered it to mad patients (Cozanitis, 2004).

Many mad patients enthusiastically received it, eager for its sedative effect. Jane Hillyer (1926), for example, describes her desire, indeed, her *craving* for Veronal, the first of the more than 2,000 synthesized barbiturates, to relieve her of the stresses of coping with asylum life and with her own madness:

The sun was just beginning to sink behind the trees.... It would be hours before it was time to sleep—for Veronal. I continued my imperious demands. "Maybe they will break their old rules; maybe I can have it earlier if I make a fuss"; they did, a little. Yet long before the nurse stood before me with a glass of clear water and that magic white tablet—it always seemed the one cool, white thing in the world—long before then, I heard my own voice, cracked and strange mingling with the unearthly cries of other patients [p. 8].

The barbiturates not only calmed and soothed mad patients, but if continuously administered they also, like the bromides, produced protracted sleep. In the years between the use of the bromides to produce prolonged narcosis in both addicted and manic patients and the advent of barbiturates, a hypothesis was put forward that schizophrenic patients would benefit from this therapeutic as well. A Swiss psychiatrist, Jakob Klaesi, reasoned that the hallucinations and delusions that are the hallmark symptoms of schizophrenia may be expressions of an overactive nervous system. Therefore, if prolonged narcosis could reduce the activity of the nervous system these symptoms would diminish, if not disappear, thus rendering the patient more amenable to adjunctive psychotherapy (Palmer & Paine, 1932). Klaesi injected a total of 26 schizophrenic patients with a barbiturate mixture to keep them in a state of prolonged narcosis for 10 days, making sure that on each day there was enough of a dosage reduction that they could be roused to eat and use the toilet. Eight of the patients improved well enough to either be discharged or transferred to another, less closely supervised, asylum ward; but three of the patients died. Although Klaesi argued their deaths were due to preexisting medical conditions and not the therapeutic, the fact remained that in all subsequent uses of the barbiturates to produce prolonged narcosis, the mortality rate hovered between 3 and 5 percent. Other complications were noted as well: barbital rash, cardiovascular collapse, bronchopneumonia, acute renal insufficiency with anuria, respiratory depression, dehydration fever, toxic confusional states, occasional brief delirious episodes, and withdrawal type convulsions at the termination of treatment (Arieti, 1959). Gowran (1944) describes its use: Prolonged narcosis also was used to return battle-fatigued soldiers to the front lines. A barbiturate is administered intravenously and while the soldier is in a half dreaming, half-awake state, the psychiatrist questions him about his troubles and fears. The soldier, relaxed completely, talks on, losing all the anxieties he has kept bottled up inside. Dazed and happy as a result of the narcosis, he will have no memory of combat. For the next three days he will have rehabilitation and then return to the front lines. So successful is the narcosis treatment that 75 percent of all afflicted soldiers return to the front lines within ten days.

Prolonged narcosis, deep or continuous sleep therapy as it later was termed, required not only repeated injections of the barbiturate agent but also, given its risks of complications, close monitoring throughout the several day period of narcosis. Not only did nurses and attendants have to rouse the patient to eat and use the toilet, but they also had to sit at the bedside for the entire duration of the treatment to record verbatim every word the patient mumbled, as well as to describe in written detail the emergence of the patient from the sleep. Each of these was thought to reveal something about the nature of the madness the patient was experiencing and therefore would inform the adjunctive psychotherapy that would follow (Palmer & Paine, 1932).

Despite its complications, relatively high mortality rate, and high nursing cost, prolonged narcosis was used in many asylums across the United States, although it never quite achieved the popularity it enjoyed in Europe (Windholz & Witherspoon, 1993). Its use as a therapeutic, however, began to diminish in the 1930s with the introduction of insulin and metrazol shock therapies, and later of electroconvulsive therapy. It all but disappeared as an asylum therapeutic by the 1960s.

In retrospect, prolonged narcosis is remembered more for the scandals in which it was implicated than for any efficacy it had as a therapeutic for the treatment of madness. In Great Britain, for example, the Ward 5 "sleep room" of William Sargant at St. Thomas' Hospital in London was the subject of considerable controversy. A standard bearer for the somatic therapeutics and an expert on brainwashing, Sargant administered repeated electroconvulsive shocks to his patients whom he had put into prolonged narcosis by large doses of barbiturates. His goal was not to ready them for psychotherapy, which he disdained, but to "re-pattern" their thinking. One of his patients, now a physician herself, was interviewed in a recent BBC Radio 4 documentary titled *Revealing the Mind Bender General* (Maw, 2008). She had been admitted to St. Thomas' in 1970 for postpartum depression and was sent to Ward 5, where she was put into a prolonged narcosis and received as many as 25 electroconvulsive shock treatments. Although she has little memory of her time in Ward 5, she recalls clearly that her consent for the treatment had never been sought, nor was it ever given. Virtually all of her prehospitalization memories were eradicated by the treatment; in her words, she was little more than a "walking zombie" for three months after her discharge.

Similar treatments were being conducted at McGill University's Allan Memorial Institute in Montreal, Canada, by Ewen Cameron, who had served as president of the American Psychiatric Association in the early 1950s, and later of the World Psychiatric Association. While his colleague Sargant was interested in re-patterning, Cameron was focused on "*de*-patterning," i.e., breaking up preexisting memories, thoughts and patterns of behavior in order to create a "clean slate," free of madness. To that end, he isolated patients in specially built boxes in a converted horse stable on the hospital grounds, with goggles on their eyes and cardboard tubes on their arms to prevent them from touching themselves. After sensory deprivation was complete, he induced prolonged narcosis that lasted from 15 to 30 days, with as many as three electroconvulsive shocks administrations daily. Hypothesizing that patients in prolonged narcosis were particularly suggestible, he played a continuous loop of tape over the many days the patients were asleep, with the goal of replacing their own memories with the propagandist messages on the tape. This process of "psychic driving," as he referred to it (Cameron, 1956), was of great interest to the Central Intelligence Agency, which, it later was revealed, generously funded these de-patterning experiments on unwitting mad patients. In 1988 the Central Intelligence Agency settled a class action suit by nine former patients for $750,000. In 1994, seventy-seven of the former patients whose de-patterning had reduced them to a childlike state were awarded $100,000 each by the Canadian government; but 250 additional claimants have been denied compensation (Moore, 2007).

Prolonged narcosis also was deeply implicated in the Chelmsford Private Hospital scandal in Sydney, Australia, where between 1963 and 1985, Harry Bailey put hundreds of mad patients into barbiturate-induced deep sleeps for two to three weeks, and gave them daily electroconvulsive shocks. Because the barbiturate dosage he administered was so high, the patients could not be roused; thus they had to be fed through nasogastric tubes and were left to urinate and defecate in their own beds. Although Bailey claimed an 85 percent success rate in the treatment of a range of disorders, from schizophrenia, depression, drug addiction, and alcoholism to anorexia, 87 of his patients died as a result of the prolonged narcosis therapeutic, and several hundred were left psychologically or physically disabled. Although there were a number of coronial inquiries into Bailey's administration of prolonged narcosis, it was not until three years after his suicide that the Chelmsford Royal Commission began an inquiry into his practice. In 1990, it filed a twelve-volume report, replete with the sordid details of Bailey's flamboyant personal as well as professional life. As a result of the report, prolonged narcosis, or deep sleep therapy as it was called in Australia, was banned (Kaplan, 2009).

By the 1960s prolonged narcosis, whether induced by barbiturates or other drugs, had all but disappeared in asylums in the United States. As a therapeutic it always had competed to some extent with the shock therapies of insulin, metrazol and electroconvulsive shock treatment; and although hailed, just as they had been, as the cure for schizophrenia, prolonged narcosis always produced decidedly mixed outcomes, and did so in the face of high risks for complications and death. And, like the shock therapies, it seemed to defy any attempts to explain how it worked when it actually did work (Valenstein, 1986).

The second wave of psychopharmaceuticals also brought two drugs that essentially changed the diagnostic distribution of asylum patients. In the early decades of the 20th century asylums contained a large proportion of patients suffering from dementia caused by pellagra. Because its cause was at first unknown, pellagra was thought to be a communicable disease and those who were diagnosed with it often were shunned in their communities as well as isolated in asylums once they were admitted. A series of observational studies, however, convinced some asylum physicians that pellagra was the result of a dietary overreliance on corn, which from an epidemiological perspective explained why a disproportionate number of patients diagnosed with it could be found in southern asylums. And it also explained why pellagra outbreaks occurred *in* asylums among patients who had been admitted for other types of madness. At the Mount Vernon Hospital for the Colored Insane in Mount Vernon, Alabama, for example, 88 black patients came down with pellagra in 1906, and more than half of them eventually died from it. Because the staff who attended them were not affected, the prevailing idea that pellagra was an infectiously communicable disease could be dismissed. Since it was diet that differentiated the stricken patients from the staff, with the patients being fed a monotonous corn-based diet and the staff having a choice of more nutritious foods, it was theorized that corn lacked a basic nutrient for the maintenance of good health. That nutrient, niacin, or vitamin B3, was isolated several years later. With public education programs, crop diversification initiatives and the fortification of processed food such as flour with niacin, pellagra was eradicated by the mid–20th century, thus assuring no new asylum admissions for pellagra-induced dementia (Rajakumar, 2000). For those patients already institutionalized, the administration of niacin, then known as nicotinic acid, often reversed their dementia and restored their physical health enough to ensure their discharge (Fouts, Helmer, Lepkovsky, & Jukes, 1937).

The "miracle drug," penicillin, also changed the diagnostic distribution of asylum patients. An antibiotic, penicillin eradicated the spirochetal bacterium *Treponema pallidum* that causes syphilis. In the early part of the 20th century, asylums across the country were filled with patients diagnosed with neurosyphilis, also known as general paresis or as general paralysis of the insane, the tertiary stage of the disease. Demented, delusional, moody and difficult to deal with, the stigma of their disease also meant that many of those patients had been rejected by their families and friends, and they were isolated and often treated with disdain in the asylums. While a host of treatments ranging from injections of mercury and arsenic to fever inductions were available—and were to some extent effective in checking the progression of the disease, although not without complications or risk of death—it was not until penicillin was proven effective in the mid–1940s that anyone could speak with confidence about a cure (Timberlake, 1955; Weickhardt, 1948). As a result of early stage diagnosis with new instruments such as the Wasserman and the Lange Colloidal Gold tests, and of the administration of penicillin to institutionalized neurosyphilitics, syphilitic patients all but disappeared from asylums by the early 1960s.

Third Wave

The third wave of psychopharmaceuticals crested in the mid–20th century with the introduction of mood stabilizers such as lithium carbonate, antidepressants such as imipramine (Tofranil), and anxiolytics such as meprobamate (Miltown and Equanil) for the treatment of anxiety (Ban, 2001). The drugs had a significant impact on asylum life. By variously controlling the aggression and overactivity of some patients, and the distress and despondence of others, the necessity of using the more controversial therapeutics—electroconvulsive shock treatment, prolonged narcosis, mechanical restraints and seclusion—declined. The pharmaceutical management of patients opened the way for adjunctive therapies, such as psychotherapy, occupational and recreational therapies—all of which since the long-ago days of moral treatment had played somewhat minor roles in asylum life—to achieve prominence in what was now optimistically being envisioned as a program of rehabilitation. These third wave drugs also altered the daily interactions between asylum patients and staff. They reduced aggressive altercations and self-harm, as well as the destruction of asylum property (Ferguson, 1957).

The history of asylum therapeutics is, in so many ways, a history of the search for optimism. It is rife with certainty that some therapeutics will turn the diabolical docile, that others are milestones in the treatment of madness. The same may be said of the third wave psychopharmaceuticals. As the deinstitutionalization movement developed mid–20th century on and rates of discharge increased, the optimism that these drugs finally would "bring them home" was considerable, as demonstrated by the following:

> Today, the most exciting news in medicine is this: for the first time in history, we're beginning to gain on mental illness.... Five years ago, almost no one would have thought it possible. Yet today, in dozens of mental hospitals, it's a routine miracle, made possible by the great advances and discoveries in the treatment of the mentally ill with new drugs. Spurred on by the increasing understanding of the brain as a physical organ which can be treated by chemical and pharmaceutical means, a world-wide hunt is on for new medicines, new cures, new knowledge about brain disorders.... Our progress against the brain disorders has

amounted to a major breakthrough. And we have seen only the beginning [Beck, 1958, p. G16].

The mood stabilizers, antidepressants and anxiolytics also were aggressively marketed for both psychiatric and general medicine outpatient administration. In 1957, for example, 36 million prescriptions were written for Miltown, an anxiolytic "Happy Pill" that promised to reduce the anxieties and tensions of fast-paced, consumer-orientated life. That number, by the way, amounts to one prescription per second throughout that year. Urged on by glossy advertisements, the popular press, and even the antics of America's first television star, Milton Berle, who variously dubbed himself "Uncle Miltown" and "Miltown Berle," people flooded their physicians' offices with requests for the drug. Unable to keep up with demand, pharmacies hung signs in their windows declaring "Out of Miltown," and "More Miltown Tomorrow." Pharmaceutical companies also raced to produce competitive anxiolytics. Librium soon appeared on the scene, followed by the wildly popular Valium and, more recently, Prozac, the most prescribed and profitable psychopharmaceutical in history (Metzl, 2003). But it was the neuroleptics, such as chlorpromazine (Thorazine), that were the reason for the most optimism. As a major tranquilizer Thorazine reduced the delusions and hallucinations of the chronically mad, made them more amenable to adjunctive therapies and, in combination with the political, economic and ideological forces that gave rise to the deinstitutionalization movement, contributed to the emptying of asylums across the country.

Thorazine is not without its own complications and risks. In the short term, it causes drowsiness, thirst, blurry vision, weight gain, tremors and stiffness of the muscles of the extremities, causing what has come to be known as the "Thorazine Shuffle." Its long-term use can cause tardive dyskinesia, an irreversible neurological disorder characterized by uncontrollable movements of various parts of the body, especially the lips, mouth, tongue and fingers. Thorazine blocks dopamine receptors; because dopamine is implicated in the creation of delusions and hallucinations, it diminishes those hallmark symptoms of psychosis. But dopamine also courses through the neuronal circuits of the brain that have to do with attention and pleasure; thus it also puts patients into a mental fog, deadens their feelings, limits their spontaneity, and dampens their sense of joy. In that way alone Thorazine lives up to its marketing slogan as "the chemical lobotomy."

Mindy Lewis (2002), who as an adolescent was involuntarily committed to a state asylum, recollects her first encounters with the "Thorazine zombies" who would be her fellow patients for many months:

> Half the patients are on high doses of Thorazine. It's easy to tell who. Their faces are bloated, their skin an unnatural pink. That's because Thorazine makes you

hypersensitive to light. It dries you out, sucking out all of your life force, replacing it with a chemical stupor.... There are other side effects. Trembling hands. Itching skin. Tongues that won't work, just get in the way—dry, swollen slabs of muscle flopping uselessly in parched mouths that all the water in the world can't quench. If you get dehydrated, your bowels refuse to work and your skin erupts. You're in trouble when you can't bring yourself to get up and go to the water fountain. The Thorazine zombies sit motionless for hours. That's what they are— the living dead [p. 20].

Despite the fact that it was never intended as a cure for psychosis, Thorazine often was touted as one. In 1955, the year after it was introduced in the United States, the venerable *New York Times* reported on it eleven times, repeatedly using or, at the very least suggesting, the word "cure," while never mentioning the short- and long-term side effects that even the lay public was seeing in the former asylum patients who had been discharged into the community (Whitaker, 2002). Lauded as a "wonder drug" and a "miracle pill" by the press, the fact remains that Thorazine was, and is, an "imperfect therapeutic"; it reduces relapse in the short, medium and, to a lesser extent, long term, but does so with adverse effects that not only are unpleasant, even intolerable, for users (Adams, Awad, Rathbone, & Thornley, 2007), but that also forever publicly brands them as former asylum patients. And it does not work at all for as many as 30 percent of all schizophrenic patients.

That is one of the reasons another neuroleptic, clozapine (Clozaril), was greeted with such enthusiasm. It did not produce humiliating side effects, it improved tardive dyskinesia, and it produced improvement for a significant number of "treatment-resistant" schizophrenics. Clozaril, however, almost never even found its way into asylum therapeutics. In its European clinical trials, it caused agranulocytosis, the failure of the bone marrow to produce enough white blood cells to fight off infections, and an alarming number of study subjects died as a result. In the late 1980s, however, the U.S. Food and Drug Administration licensed it for use in treatment-resistant schizophrenia, although in practice it could be administered to anyone.

In what can only be called a characteristic fashion, the media promoted Clozaril as the drug that "awakens" chronic schizophrenics from their madness. In a cover story on schizophrenia, *Time* magazine reported that with the drug, asylum physicians "finally have reason to be optimistic" (Wallis & Wilworth, 1992, p. 57). The optimism of patients was evident in the story, as well. In a late-modern twist on the "lunatics' ball," the centuries old tradition of encouraging asylum patients to dance with invited community members, nearly 200 present and former patients of Case Western Reserve's affiliated hospitals in Cleveland, Ohio, attended a dinner dance covered by the magazine. None would have been able to attend without Clozaril. They represented the 10 percent of schizophrenic patients who experience a dramatic reawakening with the drug. The effect, enthused one of those patients, is like being reborn.

Rebirth, though, came with a substantial price tag. Having anticipated a relatively small number of treatment-resistant schizophrenic patients, and having insisted on its own representatives conducting the blood tests needed to detect agranulocytosis, the Sandoz Pharmaceutical Company set the price for an annual per patient supply of Clozaril at $9,000, more than ninety times the annual per patient cost of Thorazine. The cost caused an outcry. During a symposium on the drug sponsored by the American Psychiatric Association, protestors stormed the room, demanding the drug be made available at a lower cost. Some insurance companies refused to pay for it, as did government subsidized treatment programs (Healey, 2002). Sandoz finally backed down, but only a little. It agreed to sell the drug without company blood testing, thus reducing the annual per patient cost to $4,160, still far beyond the reach of so many schizophrenic patients. As the *Time* cover story reported, the prohibitive cost was the single greatest factor in the discrepant use of the drug across the country. The state of Minnesota, for example, had 4,300 eligible treatment-resistant schizophrenic patients in its state asylums, and administered the drug to 1,000 of them. California, on the other hand, had nearly 60,000 eligible patients and had administered the drug to just 1,300. In the country's veterans hospitals, only 300 of their more than 9,000 eligible patients had received the drug.

Other drugs followed, most notably risperidone (Risperdal), olanzapine (Zyprexa), aripiprazole (Abilify), and quetiapine (Seroquel). Unlike Clozaril, they do not cause agranulocytosis; like Clozaril, they generally do not cause tardive dyskinesia, the "Achilles heel" of the antipsychotic drugs (Healy, 2002, p. 249).

It may have been, in fact, that Achilles heel of tardive dyskinesia that had first made Thorazine a lightning rod for the anti-psychiatry and the mental patients' liberation movements in the 1960s; but it is the mind-body relationship or, more specifically, the mind-*brain* relationship, that is the foundation for more recent attacks on *all* of the neuroleptics used to treat schizophrenia (Torrey & Miller, 2001; Whitaker, 2005). The complex and controversial biological argument goes like this:

- Since the introduction of Thorazine in 1955, and the development of other neuroleptics, there has been a significant increase in severe mental illness in the United States;

- This increase can be measured by the number of "patient care episodes" calculated by the U.S. Department of Health and Human Services to estimate the number of people treated each year for mental illness in psychiatric hospitals, residential treatment facilities and ambulatory care facilities. In 1955 there were 1.028 episodes per 100,000 of the population; in 2000 there were 3.806 such episodes, a nearly four-fold increase;

- The increase also can be measured by the number of recipients of Social Security Disability Insurance (SSDI) or Supplemental Security Income (SSI), both typically given to the disabled mentally ill. In 1955, the rate of asylum institutionalization was 3.38 per 1,000 people; since the deinstitutionalization movement, the disabled mentally ill are more likely to be in the community and receiving SSDI or SSI than in asylums. In 2003, the mental disability rate as measured by receipt of SSDI or SSI was 19.69 per 1,000, a nearly six fold increase;

- With minimal or no usage of neuroleptics, at least 40 percent of all people diagnosed with schizophrenia will not relapse after their first psychotic break, and 65 percent will function "fairly well" over the long term without medication (Bockoven & Sullivan, 1975);

- Three National Institutes of Mental Health studies (Bola & Mosher, 2003; Carpenter, McGlashan, & Strauss, 1977; Rappaport, et al. 1978) concluded that use of neuroleptics actually increases the long-term rate of relapse. This finding has been replicated in a number of subsequent studies;

- Neuroleptics produce changes in the brain;

- Those changes in the brain increase the biological vulnerability to psychosis, thus increasing the likelihood that users will become chronically mentally ill and permanently disabled;

- Therefore, psychiatry's drug-based paradigm for the treatment of schizophrenia is *increasing* rather than decreasing the nation's epidemic of severe mental illness.

Whether this argument is persuasive or not, the fact remains that the introduction of psychopharmaceuticals changed the practice of asylum medicine. It transformed asylum physicians from demigods whose epistemic gaze subdued the mad, from counselors who coaxed insight and reason out of them, from scientists who shocked and cut madness out of their brains, into technicians who dispensed pills.

The premises of this argument indeed are debatable—whether there is an "epidemic" of madness in this country and whether the indices cited actually support that contention are questionable; whether there is a biological vulnerability to madness is arguable. But there is another argument, this one sociological, that reaches the same conclusion. That argument goes like this:

- Psychopharmaceuticals are both the cause and the effect of the decontextualization of madness;

- The premise of decontextualization is that "it isn't overcrowding, aging, parenting, terrorism, global warming, recession, unemployment, or even the pressure of being a man or woman that is responsible for the epidemic of [madness] in this culture. It is the individual's failure to adequately respond to these challenges for reasons of emotional and/or psychological inadequacy" (Rubin, 2004, p. 219);

- That personal failure is recontextualized as illness;

- Illness demands a medical solution, and in a society where there is a "pill for every ill," the medical solution is the administration of psychopharmaceuticals;

- The administration of psychopharmaceuticals ignores the external factors that create the alleged illness, and thus "serves to reinforce and legitimize social attitudes and relations (such as sexism and alienating working conditions) which may actually contribute to the problems the [psychopharmaceuticals] target" (Kleinman & Cohen, 1991, p. 873);

- These social attitudes and relations continue unabated, thus producing more madness;

- Therefore, psychiatry's drug-based paradigm for the treatment of madness is *increasing* rather than decreasing the nation's epidemic of madness.

Conclusion

O! That way madness lies. — King Lear

THIS HAS BEEN A BOOK ABOUT MADNESS. Had it been about almost any other topic, that simple declarative sentence very well might have sufficed as a conclusion. But madness is not like most other topics. Perhaps by the time readers come to this final chapter of the book, the word "protean" will have seemed overused. But it is such a descriptive word that it can stand up to overuse, for it describes not only how the imagined line between sanity and madness — that line so often inscribed with the robust sociological variables of gender, race, socioeconomic class and sexual orientation — changes over time, but also how theories of madness, attitudes about it, and reactions to it, are historically variant as well.

If, indeed, the word "protean" has been overused, it is not with the intent of lulling readers into mind-numbing complacency; rather, it is with the intent of prodding readers to wonder why and how these changes occur. And that is where the sociological theory of social construction is particularly helpful. It draws attention to the social context and reveals the several ways in which madness is socially constructed (Church, 2004). Society can be said to construct madness:

- by first setting out the rules for rationality, sanity, normality, and order;
- by evaluating behaviors, thoughts and feelings against those rules to determine which are aberrant;

260

• and by grouping those aberrant behaviors, thoughts and feelings into types or, more formally, into syndromes and diagnoses of madness.

To say that "society" is responsible for the social construction is, of course, somewhat misleading. Here is where "the Majority," in poet Emily Dickinson's sense of the term, becomes relevant to analysis. Whether defined by gender, race, socioeconomic class, sexual orientation, or some other sociological variable, "the Majority" has the requisite social capital to initiate the social construction process and, it could be convincingly argued, the strongest vested interests in doing so. It would be a mistake, though, to overestimate the cohesion and single-mindedness of "the Majority." There was, and continues to be, considerable disagreement over theories of madness, as well as over diagnostic categories, not just between "the Majority" and the mad, but within "the Majority" as well. Thus, the politics of madness is more than worthy of critical analysis.

The disagreement is particularly fertile ground for the emergence of entrepreneurs whose claims discursively construct these theories and diagnoses. They are interesting figures in the history of madness, but their often larger-than-life personae should not distract from the task of dismantling their claims to better understand their grounds (data and facts), warrants (justifications based on evidence, emotion, and values), and qualifiers (indicators of the strength of the claims, usually assessed by words such as "most" or "sometimes") (Toulmin, 1969). The history of madness is a powerful reminder that claims do not have to be factual to be heard above the cacophony of disagreement. They just have to be persuasive; and the most persuasive claims are those that resonate best with the social and scientific contexts, or at least most people's understanding of and experience with them at that historical moment.

The overused word "protean," then, has great depth of meaning and is interpretatively linked to the sociological theory of social construction. The danger with that theory, though, is that it can reduce itself to the conclusion that there is nothing really "wrong" with the mad, that their "madness" is nothing more than a cobbled-together category, a socially convenient label that sticks with them for the rest of their lives (Hacking, 2000). That argument may sound familiar because it has been made before, sometimes by sociologists, other times by iconoclastic anti-psychiatrists, and even by those who have been labeled mad and who, for whatever reasons, reject the label. Their claims deserve careful consideration, if only because they invite a deeper analysis of protean politics, i.e., the social forces and the entrepreneurial discourses that give shape at any moment in history to the prevailing definition of madness.

These claims, though, have to be weighed against the experiences of the mad. After all, to say that there is nothing really "wrong" with the mad is to dismiss the suffering so many of them endure as insignificant, inconsequential. It is to ignore their subjectivity, the exercise of their agency as they manage their symptoms, negotiate their spoiled identities, and cope with the contingencies of institutionalization. For those reasons, the pathographies and asylum memoirs are treasure troves. These narratives reveal the selves beneath the labels. They often challenge the dominant cultural understanding of madness, sometimes even turning it on its head—but not always. Some of these narratives reiterate and reify exactly what "the Majority" thinks madness is, and what it imagines the mad are like. Some influential sociologists would argue in regard to the latter that in order for "the Majority's" understanding of madness to maintain its influence and thus maintain social order, those who are considered mad must not only be disciplined to the norm, but must also internalize the prevailing understanding of madness and then assess their own thoughts, feelings and behaviors against it (Fee, 2000; Foucault, 1965; Scull, 1989).

This book has relied upon published pathographies and asylum narratives, even while acknowledging that their authors are uniquely vested with the requisite social capital to have written and published their narratives in the first place. But it is important to note that the Internet has revitalized this time-honored tradition of storytelling by making it possible for unprecedented numbers of people to transform their private woes into public narratives. While both those narratives and the virtual communities that build up around them when website visitors leave comments, offer information and share their own experiences are being criticized for fragmentation, decontextualization, superficiality, and, often although not always, anonymity (Bowker & Tuffin, 2002; Jones, 2005; Stone, 2004), they are a rich vein to mine for first-person narratives of madness and institutionalization.

Both traditionally published and Internet-published

---

*Sample of Internet Sites
With First-Person Narratives of
Madness and/or Institutionalization*

BPD Sanctuary:
   http://www.mhsanctuary.com
Healthy Place:
   http://www.healthyplace.com
Incertus:
   http://www.incertus.imntb.com
Internet Mental Health:
   http://www.mentalhealth.com
Mind Freedom International:
   http://www.mindfreedom.org
Rethink:
   http://www.rethink.org
Wing of Madness:
   http://www.wingofmadness.com

narratives also give insight into experiences with therapeutic interventions, but few are up to the task of analyzing the social and scientific contexts of those interventions. They certainly can be forgiven for that, for to do so is to step into a veritable hornet's nest of debate between scholars, between practitioners, and between scholars and practitioners. At one extreme of the debate are those who see the history of therapeutic interventions as a long march toward scientific enlightenment, with each practitioner standing on the tall shoulders of all those who came before (Deutsch, 1937). At the other extreme, are those who evaluate therapeutic interventions as "bad science and bad medicine," which has resulted in the "enduring mistreatment of the mentally ill" (Whitaker, 2002).

This book has scrabbled to find a middle ground. It has treated science as socially contingent and therefore as—here is that word again—protean. Scientific knowledge changes and so do therapeutic interventions. And although there is plenty of reason to retrospectively judge them harshly, the fact is that they sometimes brought about stabilization, remission, recovery and cure. As an example, this book cites an 1812 report by psychiatric entrepreneur Benjamin Rush, who cured a young man by "copiously bleeding" him. Upon regaining consciousness, the young man felt completely relieved of his suicidal melancholy. A cure, perhaps? Rush thought so, and so did his patient. But the point is that "copious bleeding," were it administered to a depressed asylum patient today, would be unlikely to achieve the same result.

And why not? This book has argued that if society, science, institution, physician and patient share a set of beliefs about the relationship between the mind and the body, and between madness and sanity, and if the therapeutic practice is perceived to be a manifestation of that belief and is thus expected to be effective, it very well may be. When those beliefs change over time, so will the efficacy of the therapeutic intervention and so will judgment of it. There is no question that asylum therapeutics and many of their most ardent promoters and practitioners have experienced a hard fall from grace. That fall begins when ideas about the relationship between the mind and the body, between madness and sanity, between physician and patient, between patient and humanity start to shift. Throughout history they have; throughout the future they will.

This book began with a quote from an eminent scholar of madness: "Madness is a veritable Proteus! How infinite its varieties! How mercurial its qualities! How artfully can lunacy ape sanity! Is there not reason in madness; folly jumbled with reason?" (Porter, 2006, p.1). Quite aside from the rhapsodic language, the peppering of exclamation points is testimony to scholarly fascination with madness and with the mad. To study them is to study the unfamiliar; yet at the same time both hold a mirror to the familiar, requiring reflection upon it, as well. There are few subjects that are so doubly rewarding. Yet the study of madness and of the mad leave threads that cannot be woven into a well-knit narrative or, for that matter, into a tidy conclusion. Unanswered questions fringe any inquiry. And one of the most inflexible of the stray threads is the persistent question of what should be done for the mad.

In a recent essay titled "Iron Teeth," Michael Greenberg (2009) recounts his attempt to reconcile with the mad who attend a treatment program in his Upper West Side neighborhood in Manhattan. This is the same Michael Greenberg who wrote of his struggles in dealing with the "raw force of nature" that was his own daughter's madness. In this essay he contemplates the iron teeth fastened to the stone surround of his apartment building, put there to discourage the mad from sitting in front of the building. To prepare for an upcoming tenant's meeting where he intends to plead a case for the removal of the iron teeth, Greenberg visits the treatment center and interacts with the mad clients whose own desires, dreams and lives curiously parallel his own, "not least of which," he wryly observes, "is our dubious value to the gross national product" (p. 115). He is assured by the director that the program is a revival of moral treatment in that it nurtures personal attachments and encourages healthy aspirations. Coincidentally, the neighborhood once was known as Bloomingdale, where an asylum by the same name developed quite a reputation as a paragon of moral treatment. Buoyed by this information, and by his interactions with the program's mad clients, Greenberg rehearses his plea to the tenants' meeting:

> I'll open with a glowing description of the center. Our neighborhood used to be known as Bloomingdale, I might point out, after the Bloomingdale Lunatic Asylum, famous in its day for the enlightened treatment of the insane. This should have a positive impact on my neighbors: the mad, like the Indians, were here before we were. I rehearse Foucault's argument that the presence of madness on our doorstep is good for us, for it reminds us that the life we live is merely one among several human possibilities. Plato believed that insanity was essential to our nature and assumed that it held esoteric knowledge about who we are. We shouldn't be chasing these people away, we should be welcoming them, thanking them for forcing us into this debate with ourselves [p. 116].

He tries out this carefully practiced argument on a couple who live on the floor below. It is greeted with silence. Finally, his neighbor replies, "Not everyone has your superior moral fiber."

It may not require *superior* moral fiber to address the question about what to do for the mad. But it does require moral fiber. When the mad are invited in from the margins, when their subjectivity and agency are appreciated, when they are advocated for and when resources necessary for their decent care and humanitarian treatment are finally allocated, that moral fiber will at last be woven into a well-knit narrative.

Bibliography

Aarons, L.F. February 25, 1972. "Brain Surgery Is Tested on 3 California Convicts." *Washington Post,* pp. A1, A20.

Abbott, H. 1928. "An Expensive Luxury." In *2nd Annual Report of the Eugenics Survey of Vermont* (pp. 17–18), edited by H.F. Perkins. Burlington, VT: Eugenics Survey Office.

Abdy, E.S. 1835. *Journal of Residence and Tour in the United States of North America, from April, 1833 to October, 1834.* London: J. Murray.

Ackerman, N.W. 1958. *The Psychodynamics of Family Life: Diagnosis and Treatment of Family Relationships.* New York: Basic.

Acocella, J., ed. 1999. *The Diary of Vaslav Nijinsky.* New York: Farrar, Straus, and Giroux.

Adame, A.L., and G.A. Hornstein. 2006. "Representing Madness: How are Subjective Experiences of Emotional Distress Presented in First-Person Accounts?" *Humanistic Psychologist,* 34, 135–158.

Adams, C.E., G.Awad, J. Rathbone, and B. Thornley. 2007. "Chlorpromazine Versus Placebo for Schizophrenia." *Cochrane Data Base Systematic Review* 18. Retrieved on the World Wide Web. http://www.cochrane.org/reviews/en/ab000284.html.

"Address." May 30, 1821. *New York Evening Post,* 2.

Agnew, A. 1886. *From Under a Cloud, or Personal Reminiscences of Insanity.* Cincinnati: Robert Clark.

Alexander, G.H. 1953. "Electroconvulsive Therapy—A 5 Year Study of Results." *Journal of Nervous and Mental Disease,* 117, 244–250.

Alexander, L. 1953. *The Treatment of Mental Disorder.* Philadelphia: Saunders.

Alper, T.G. 1948. "Case Reports: 'An Electric Shock Patient Tells His Story.'" *Journal of Abnormal and Social Psychology,* 43, 201–210.

American Psychiatric Association. 1978. *Report of the Task Force on Electroconvulsive Therapy.* Washington, D.C.: American Psychiatric Association.

American Psychiatric Association. 2006. *Resolution Against Racism and Racial Discrimination and Their Adverse Impacts on Mental Health.* Washington, D.C.: American Psychiatric Association.

Anderson, E.L., and I.M. Retl. 2009. "ECT in Pregnancy." *Psychosomatic Medicine,* 71, 235–242.

Anderson, J.E. 2005. *Conjure in African-American Society.* Baton Rogue: Louisiana State University Press.

Andre, L. 2009. *Doctors of Deception: What They Don't Want You to Know About Shock Treatment.* Piscataway, NJ: Rutgers University Press.

Andy, O.J. 1966. "Neurosurgical Treatment

of Abnormal Behavior." *American Journal of Medical Sciences,* 252, 232–238.

Anonymous. March 23, 1793. "The Choleric Man." *Weekly Museum,* 5, 2.

Appel, K.E. 1954. "Presidential Address: 'The Present Challenge of Psychiatry.'" *American Journal of Psychiatry,* 111, 1–12.

Appleby, L., D.J. Luchins, and S. Freels. 2006. "Homeless Admissions and Immigration in a State Mental Hospital." *Psychiatric Services,* 57, 144.

Arieti, S. 1959. *American Handbook of Psychiatry.* New York: Basic.

Arika, A. 2007. *Passions and Tempers: A History of the Humours.* New York: HarperCollins.

Astbury, J. 1996. *Crazy for You: The Making of Women's Madness.* Oxford: Oxford University Press.

Aurthur, J. 2002. *The Angel and the Dragon: A Father's Search for Answers to His Son's Mental Illness and Suicide.* Deerfield Beach, FL: Health Communications.

Bainbridge, W.S. 1984. "Religious Insanity: The Official Nineteenth-Century Theory." *Sociological Analysis,* 45, 223–239.

Baker, J.H. 1987. *Mary Todd Lincoln: A Biography.* New York: W.W. Norton.

Ban, T.S. 2001. "Pharmacotherapy of Mental Illness: A Historical Analysis." *Progress in Neuro-psychopharmacology and Biological Psychiatry,* 25, 709–727.

Bancroft, C.P. 1908. "Presidential Address: 'Hopeful and Discouraging Aspects of the Psychiatric Outlook.'" *American Journal of Insanity,* 65, 1–16.

Barbier, J.M., G. Serra, G. Loas, and C.S. Breathnach. 1999. "Constance Pascal: Pioneer of French Psychiatry." *History of Psychiatry,* 10, 425–437.

Barnes, A. 2004. "Race, Schizophrenia, and Admission to State Psychiatric Hospitals." *Administration and Policy in Mental Health,* 31, 241–252.

Barr, E.S., and R.G. Barry. 1926. "The Effect of Producing Aseptic Meningitis Upon Dementia Praecox." *New York State Journal of Medicine,* 26, 89–92.

Basler, R.P., ed. 1953. *The Collected Works of Abraham Lincoln.* Vol. 5. New Brunswick, NJ: Rutgers University Press.

Bates, S.A., ed. 1886. *Records of the Town of Braintree, 1640–1793.* Randolph, MA: Daniel H. Huxford.

Bateson, G., D. Jackson, J. Haley, and J. Weakland. 1956. "Toward a Theory of Schizophrenia." *Behavioral Science,* 1, 251–264.

Bean, A. 2001. *Gracefully Insane: The Rise and Fall of America's Premier Mental Hospital.* New York: Public Offices.

Beard, G.M. 1869. "Neurasthenia, or Nervous Exhaustion." *Boston Medical and Surgical Journal,* 3, 217–220.

_____. 1879. "Other Symptoms of Neurasthenia." *Journal of Nervous and Mental Disease,* 6, 246–261.

_____. 1880. *A Practical Treatise on Nervous Exhaustion (Neurasthenia), Its Symptoms, Nature, Sequence and Treatment.* New York: William Wood.

_____. 1881. *American Nervousness, Its Causes and Consequences.* New York: G.P. Putnam and Sons.

Beaudreau, S.A., and S. Finger. 2006. "Medical Electricity and Madness in the 18th Century." *Perspectives in Biology and Medicine,* 49, 330–345.

Beck, J. March 30, 1958. "A Brighter Day for Mentally Ill." *Chicago Daily Tribune,* G16.

Beers, C.W. 1908. *A Mind That Found Itself.* New York: Longmans, Green.

Behrman, A. 2002. *Electroboy.* New York: Random House.

Bell, V., C. Maiden, A. Muñoz-Solomando, and V. Reddy. 1996. "'Mind Control' Experiences on the Internet: Implications for the Psychiatric Diagnosis of Delusions." *Psychopathology,* 39, 87–91.

Bender, L. 1947. "One Hundred Cases of Childhood Schizophrenia Cured with Electric Shock." *Transactions of the American Neurological Association,* 72, 165–169.

Bennett, A.E. 1938. "Convulsive Shock Therapy in Depressive Psychoses." *American Journal of Medical Sciences,* 196, 420–428.

_____. 1972. *Fifty Years in Neurology and Psychiatry.* New York: International Medical Book.

Benton, J.H. 1911. *Warning Out in New England.* Boston: W.B. Clarke.

Benzinger, B.F. 1969. *The Prison of My Mind.* New York: Walker.

Blackmar, F. 1897. "The Smoky Pilgrims." *American Journal of Sociology,* 2, 485–500.

Blanch, A.K., and J. Parrish. 1990. *Report on Round Table on Alternatives to Involuntary Treatment*. Rockville, MD: National Institutes of Mental Health.

Blanton, W.B. 1930. *Medicine in Virginia in the Seventeenth Century*. Richmond: William Byrd.

Block, J. 2008. "Issues for *DSM-V:* 'Internet Addiction.'" *American Journal of Psychiatry*, 165, 306–307.

Blumenthal, S.L. 1995. "'The Tempest in My Mind': Cultural Interfaces Between Psychiatry and Literature, 1844–1900." *Journal of the History of the Behavioral Sciences*, 31, 3–34.

Blumer, G.A. 1903. "Presidential Address." *American Journal of Insanity*, 60, 1–18.

Bly, N. 1887 .*Ten Days in a Madhouse*. New York: Ian L. Munro.

Bockoven, J., and H. Solomon. 1975. "Comparison of Two Five-year Follow-up Studies." *American Journal of Psychiatry*, 123, 796–801.

Bogdan, R. 2008. Postcard Collection. Retrieved on the World Wide Web <http://www. disabilitymuseum.org>

Boisen, A. 1960. *Out of the Depths: An Autobiographical Study of Mental Disorder and Religious Experience*. New York: Harper.

Bola, J., and L. Mosher. 2003. "Treatment of Acute Psychosis Without Neuroleptics: Two-year Outcomes from the Soteria Project." *Journal of Nervous and Mental Disorders*, 191, 219–229.

Bolden, L., and M.N. Wicks. 2005. "Length of Stay, Admission Types, Psychiatric Diagnoses, and the Implications of Stigma in African-Americans in the Nationwide Inpatient Sample." *Issues in Mental Health Nursing*, 26, 1043–1059.

Boodman, S.G. September 24, 1996."Shock Therapy: It's Back." *Washington Post*, 16–20.

Bourdon, K.H., D.S. Rae, W.E. Narrow, R.W. Manderschild and D.A. Regier. 1994. "National Prevalence and Treatment of Mental and Addictive Disorders." In *Mental Health: United States* (pp. 22–51), edited by R.W. Mandershild and A. Sonnenschein Washington, D.C.: Center for Mental Health Services.

Bourne, H. 1953. "The Insulin Myth." *Lancet*, 262, 964–988.

Bowes, A.H. 1956. "The Ataractic Drugs: The Present Position of Chlorpromazine, Frenqual, Pacatal, and Resperine in the Psychiatric Hospital." *American Journal of Psychiatry*, 115, 530–539.

Bowker, N., and K. Tuffin. 2002. "Disability Discourses for Online Identities." *Disability & Society*, 17, 327–344.

Boyer, P., and S. Nissenbaum. 1977. *The Salem Witchcraft Papers: Verbatim Transcripts of the Legal Documents of the Salem Witchcraft Outbreak of 1692*. New York: DaCapo. Retrieved on the World Wide Web <http://etext.lib.virginia.edu/salem/witchcraft>

Boyle. T.C. 1993. *The Road to Wellville*. New York: Viking.

Braslow, J. 1997. *Mental Ills and Bodily Cures*. Berkeley: University of California Press.

Brea, A. 1968. *Half a Lifetime*. New York: Vantage.

Breggin, P. 1970. *The Crazy from the Sane*. New York: Lyle Stuart.

_____. March 15, 1972. "Lobotomy—The Brain-Cutters Return." *Science and Government Report*, 2, 1–2, 4.

_____. 2007. *Brain Disabling Treatments in Psychiatry*. New York: Springer.

_____, and D. Greenberg. March 12, 1972. "Return of the Lobotomy." *Washington Post*, C1.

Brickell, J. 1737. *The Natural History of North-Carolina: With an Account of the Trade, Manners, and Customs of the Christian and Indian Inhabitants: Illustrated*. Dublin: James Carson.

Brinckle, A.P. 1887. "Life Among the Insane." *North American Review*, 144, 190–199.

"Bromide Sleep." 1900. *Merck Archives*, 110–111.

Broun, L. 1906. "A Preliminary Report of the Gynecological Surgery in the Manhattan State Hospital West." *American Journal of Insanity*, 62, 407–447.

Brown, D.L. July 12, 2009. "Through the Past, Darkly." *Washington Post*. Retrieved on the World Wide Web <http://washingtonpost.com/wp-dyn/content/article/2009/07/10/AR2009071000022.html>

Brown, E.M. 2000."Why Wagner-Jauregg Won the Nobel Prize for Discovering Malaria Therapy for General Paresis of the

In-sane." *History of Psychiatry*, 11, 371–382.

Brown, J.G. 2000. *Restraints and Seclusion: State Polices for Psychiatric Hospitals.* Washington, D.C.: Office of the Inspector General.

Brown, T.J. 1998. *Dorothea Dix: New England Reformer.* Cambridge, MA: Harvard University Press.

Brussel, J.A., and J. Schneider. 1951. "The B.E.S.T. in the Treatment and Control of Chronically Disturbed Mental Patients." *Psychiatric Quarterly*, 25, 55–59.

Buck v. Bell. 1927. 274 U.S. 200.

Bucke, R.M. 1900. "Two Hundred Operative Cases—Insane Women." In *Proceedings of the American Medico-Psychological Association Annual Meeting* (pp. 99–105). New York: American Medico-Psychological Association.

Bucknill, J.C. 1876. *Notes on Asylums for the Insane in America.* London: J & A Churchill.

Burroughs, W.S. 1959. *The Naked Lunch.* Paris: Olympia.

Butterfield, L.H., ed. 1951. *Letters of Benjamin Rush.* Vol. 2. Princeton, NJ: Princeton University Press.

Byrd, W.M., and L.A. Clayton. 2000. *American Health Dilemma: A Medical History of African-Americans and the Problem of Race.* New York: Routledge.

Calloway, E. 2007. *Asylum: A Mid-century Madhouse and Its Lessons About Our Mentally Ill Today.* Westport, CT: Praeger.

Cameron, D.E. 1956. "Psychic Driving." *American Journal of Psychiatry*, 112, 502–509.

Cameron, J.M. 1978. "Ideology and Policy Termination: Restructuring California's Mental Health System." *Public Policy*, 4 , 533–570.

Caminero-Santangelo, M. 2003. "Questions of Power: The Politics of Women's Madness Narratives." *Biography*, 26, 727–731.

Campbell, B. 2007. "The Making of 'American': Race and Nation in Neurasthenic Discourse." *History of Psychiatry*, 18, 157–178.

Caplan, E. 2001. *Mind Games.* Berkley: University of California Press.

Caplan, P.J. 1983. *The Myth of Women's Masochism.* New York: E.P. Dutton.

Carlson, B., J.D. Weingart, M. Guarnieri, and P.G. Fisher. 1997. "Third Ventricular Choroid Plexus Papilloma with Psychosis." *Journal of Neurosurgery*, 87, 103–105.

Carlson, E.A. 2001. *Unfit: A History of a Bad Idea.* Cold Spring Harbor, NY: Cold Spring Harbor Laboratory Press.

Carlson, E.T., and M.M. Simpson. 1963. "Opium as a Tranquilizer." *American Journal of Psychiatry*, 120, 112–117.

Carpenter, W., T. McGlashan, and J. Strauss. 1977. "The Treatment of Acute Schizophrenia Without Drugs." *American Journal of Psychiatry*, 134, 14–20.

Carroll, R.S. 1923. "Aseptic Meningitis in Combating Dementia Praecox Problem." *New York Medical Journal*, 68, 47–410.

_____, E.S. Barr, E.G. Barry, and D. Matzke. 1925. "Aseptic Meningitis in the Treatment of Dementia Praecox." *American Journal of Psychiatry*, 81, 673–703.

Carson, E.T., J.L. Wollock, and P.S. Noel. 1981. *Benjamin Rush's Lectures on the Mind.* Philadelphia: American Philosophical Society.

Cartwright, S.A. 1859. "Report on the Diseases and Physical Peculiarities of the Negro Race." *New Orleans Medical and Surgical Journal,* 7, 331–336.

Cayleff, S. 1988. "'Prisoners of Their Own Feebleness': Women, Nerves and Western Medicine—A Historical Overview." *Social Science and Medicine*, 26, 199–208.

Chavkins, S. 1980. *Mind Stealers.* Chicago: Lawrence Hill.

Chesler, P. 1973. *Women and Madness.* New York: Avon.

Chireau, Y.P. 2006. *Black Magic: Religion and the African-American Conjuring Tradition.* Berkeley: University of California Press.

Church, A. 1900. "The Treatment of the Opium Habit by the Bromide." *Illinois Medical Journal*, 50, 291–297.

Church, J. 2004. "Making Order Out of Disorder—On the Social Construction of Madness." In *The Philosophy of Psychiatry* (pp. 393–408), edited by J. Radden. New York: Oxford University Press.

Clardy, E.R., and Rumpf, E.M. 1954. "The Effect of Electric Shock Treatment on Children Having Schizophrenic Manifestations." *Psychiatric Quarterly*, 28, 616–623.

Clark, G.J. 1979. "In Defense of Deinstitutionalization." *Milbank Memorial Fund Quarterly*, 57, 461–479.

Clevenger, S.V. July 29, 1893. "Boodler Insane Asylums." *Chicago Times and Register*, 651–657.

Cline, S. 2002. *Zelda Fitzgerald: Her Voice in Paradise*. New York: Arcade.

Cloud, D. 1998. *Control and Consolation in American Culture and Politics*. Thousand Oaks, CA: Sage.

Colonial Connecticut Records. Vol. 4: August 1689–May 1706. Retrieved on the World Wide Web <http://www.colonialct.uconn.edu>

_____. Vol. 10: May 1751–February 1757. Retrieved on the World Wide Web <http://www.colonialct.uconn.edu>

_____. Vol. 11: May 1757–March 1762. Retrieved on the World Wide Web <http://www.colonialct.uconn.edu>

Cooley, T. 2001. *The Ivory Leg in the Ebony Cabinet: Madness, Race, and Gender in Victorian America*. Amherst: University of Massachusetts Press.

Coontz, S. 1992. *The Way We Never Were*. New York: Basic.

Cooper, D.G. 1967. *Psychiatry and Anti-Psychiatry*. London: Tavistock.

_____. 1978. *The Language of Madness*. London: Allen, Lane.

Cosgrove, L. 2000. "Crying Out Loud: Understanding Women's Emotional Distress as Both Lived Experience and Social Construction." *Feminism & Psychology*, 10, 247–268.

Cottington, F. 1941. "The Treatment of Childhood Schizophrenia by Metrazol Shock Modified by B-Erythroidin." *American Journal of Psychiatry*, 98, 397–400.

Cotton, H.A. 1923. "The Relation of Chronic Sepsis to the So-called Functional Mental Disorders." *Journal of Mental Science*, 69, 434–465.

_____. November 20, 1932. "Mental Cases Treated for Physical Defects." *New York Times*, Council of State Governments (1950). *The Mental Health Programs of the Forty-eight States*. Chicago: Author.

Cowles, E. 1896. "The Advancement of Psychiatry in America." *American Journal of Psychiatry*, 52, 364–386.

Cozanitis, D.A. 2004, "One Hundred Years of Barbiturates and Their Saint." *Journal of the Royal Society of Medicine*, 97, 594–599.

"The County—The Number and Character of Its Inmates." February 2, 1871. *Democrat* (Huntingdon, IN), 1.

Cranford, P.G. 1981, *But for the Grace of God: The Inside Story of the World's Largest Insane Asylum—Milledgeville!* Augusta, GA: Great Pyramid.

Culliton, B. 1976. "Psychosurgery—National Commission Issues Surprisingly Favorable Report." *Science*, 194, 299–301.

Culver, C.M., R.B. Ferrell, and R.M. Green. 1980. "ECT and Special Problems of Informed Consent." *American Journal of Psychiatry*, 137, 586–591.

Curran, L.K., C.J. Newschaffer, L. Li-Ching, S.O. Crawford, M.V. Johnston, and A.W. Zimmerman. 2007. "Behaviors Associated with Fever in Children with Autism Spectrum Disorders." *Pediatrics*, 120, 1386–1392.

Curwen, J., ed. 1875. *History of the Association of Medical Superintendents of American Asylums for the Insane*. Warren, PA: E. Cowen.

Cutbush, E. 1794. *An Inaugural Dissertation on Insanity*. Philadelphia: Zachariah Poulson, Jr.

Cutler, W.P., and J.P. Cutler. 1888. *Life, Journal and Correspondence of Rev. Manasseh Cutler*. Cincinnati: R. Clarke.

Dain, N. 1980. *Clifford W. Beers: Advocate for the Insane*. Pittsburgh: University of Pittsburgh Press.

_____. 1994. "Psychiatry and Anti-Psychiatry in the United States." In *Discovering the History of Psychiatry* (pp. 415–444), edited by M.S. Micale and R. Porter. New York: Oxford.

Dana, C. 1904. "The Partial Passing of Neurasthenia." *Boston Medical and Surgical Journal*, 150, 339–44.

Danielson, F.H., and C.B. Davenport. 1912. *The Hill Folk: Report on a Rural Community of Hereditary Defectives*. Lancaster, PA: New Era.

Dannecker, H.A. October 1942. "Psychosurgery Cured Me." *Coronet*, 12, 8–12.

Danquah, M.N. 1998. *Willow Weep for Me*. New York: W.W. Norton.

Davidson, L.M. 1841. "The Fear of Madness." In *Poetical Remains of the Late Lucretia Maria Davidson, Collected and Arranged by Her Mother* (p. 4). Philadelphia: Lea and Blanchard.

Davis, L.C. 1868. "A Modern Lettre de Cachet." *Atlantic Monthly*, 21, 588–603.

Davis, P. 1885. *Two Years and Three Months in the New York Lunatic Asylum at Utica.* Syracuse, NY: Author.

Dawkins, K., R.D. Ekstrom, M.A. Hill, D.L. Isaacs, and R.N. Golden. 2000. "Ethnicity and Seizure Threshold." *Progress in Neuro-Psychopharmacology and Biological Psychiatry,* 24, 1289–1298.

Dawson, J. 1961. *The Ha-Ha.* New York: Little, Brown.

Death Notice of Henry Cotton M.D. May 9, 1933.*Trenton* (NJ) *Evening Times,* 6.

Decker, W.A. 2008. *Asylum for the Insane: A History of the Kalamazoo State Hospital.* Traverse City, MI: Arbutus.

Delbourgo, J. 2006. *A Most Amazing Scene of Wonders: Electricity and Enlightenment in Early America.* Cambridge, MA: Harvard University Press.

Delgado, J. 1969. *Physical Control of the Mind.* New York: Harper.

"Dementia Praecox Curbed by Insulin." January 13, 1937. *New York Times,* 11.

Demos, J.P. 1982. *Entertaining Satan: Witchcraft and the Culture of Early New England.* New York: Oxford University Press.

"Dental Surgery for Treating the Insane." June 25, 1920. *Titusville* (FL) *Herald,* 7.

Department of the Interior. 1860. Census Office: "Instructions to U.S. Marshals." Washington, D.C.: Bowman.

Deutsch, A. 1936. "Dorothea Lynde Dix: Apostle of the Insane." *American Journal of Nursing,* 36, 987–997.

_____. 1937. *The Mentally Ill in America: A History of Their Care and Treatment from Colonial Times.* New York: Doubleday, Doran.

_____. 1948. *The Shame of the States.* New York: Harcourt, Brace.

Dhossche, D.M, and S. Stanfill. 2005. "Could ECT be Effective in Autism?" *Medical Hypotheses,* 64, 1070–1071.

Dickens, C. 1842. *American Notes.* Paris: Fain and Thunot.

Dickinson, Emily. 1891. *Poems.* Series 1. Ed. Mabel Loomis Todd and Thomas Wentworth Higginson. Boston: Roberts Brothers.

Diefenbach, G.J., D. Diefenbach, A. Baume-siter, and M. West. 1999. "Portrayal of Lobotomy in the Popular Press: 1935–1960." *Journal of the History of the Neurosciences,* 8, 60–69.

Digby, A. 1985. *Madness, Morality and Medicine: A Study of the York Retreat, 1796–1914.* Cambridge: Cambridge University Press.

Dillon, M. 1981. *A Little Original Sin: The Life and Work of Jane Bowles.* Berkeley: University of California Press.

"Doctor Cotton Is Improved." August 8, 1925. *New York Times,* 4.

"Dr. MacDonald's Case of Monomania." January 27, 1841. *Boston Medical and Surgical Journal,* 23, 25.

Doe, J. 1966. *Crazy.* New York: Hawthorn.

Doroshow, D.B. 2006. "Performing a Cure for Schizophrenia: Insulin Coma Therapy on the Wards." *Journal of the History of Medicine and Allied Sciences,* 62, 213–243.

Dow, G.F., ed. 1913. *Records and Files of the Quarterly Courts of Essex County.* Vol. 3. Salem, MA: Essex Institute.

_____. 1921. *Records and Files of the Quarterly Courts of Essex County.* Vol. 8. Salem, MA: Essex Institute.

Dowbiggen, I.R. 1997. *Keeping America Sane: Psychiatry and Eugenics in the United States and Canada 1880–1940.* Ithaca: Cornell University Press.

Dowell, D.A., and J.A. Ciarlo. 1989. "An Evaluative Overview of the Community Mental Health Center Program." In *Handbook on Mental Health Policy in the United States* (pp. 195–236), edited by D.A. Rochefort. Westport, CT: Greenwood.

Doyle, D. 2008. "'A Fine New Child': The Lafargue Mental Hygiene Clinic and Harlem's African-American Communities, 1946–1958." *Journal of the History of Medicine and Allied Sciences,* 64, 173–212.

Dugdale, R. 1877. *The Jukes: A Study in Crime, Pauperism, Disease, and Heredity.* New York: G.P. Putnam's Sons.

Dukakis, K., and L. Tye. 2006. *Shock.* New York: Avery.

Dully, H. 2007. *My Lobotomy.* New York: Crown.

Earle, P. 1848. *History, Description and Statistics of the Bloomingdale Asylum for the Insane.* New York: Egbert, Hovey & King.

_____. 1854. *An Examination of the Practice*

of Bloodletting. New York: Samuel S. & William Wood.

_____. 1887. *The Curability of Insanity: A Series of Studies.* Philadelphia: J.B. Lippincott.

Earley, P. 2006. *Crazy.* New York: Berkley.

Earnest, E. S. 1950. *Weir Mitchell, Novelist and Physician.* Philadelphia: University of Pennsylvania Press.

Eastabrook, A.H., and C.B. Davenport. 1912. *The Nam Family.* Cold Spring Harbor, NY: Eugenics Record Office.

"An Eccentric Man's Deed." May 15, 1891. *Philadelphia Inquirer,* 5.

Ehrenreich, B. 2009. *Bright-sided: How the Relentless Promotion of Positive Thinking Has Undermined America.* New York: Metropolitan.

Eldridge, L.D. 1996. "'Crazy-brained': Mental Illness in Colonial America." *Bulletin of the History of Medicine,* 70, 361–368.

El-Hai, J. 2005. *The Lobotomist.* Hoboken, NJ: John Wiley and Sons.

Ellis, G. April 18, 1009. "Mental Illness in the African-American Community." Retrieved on the World Wide Web <http://www.BlackPressUSA.com>

Ellison, R.W. 1952. *The Invisible Man.* New York: Random House.

Erfurth, A., and Hoff, P. 2000. "Mad Scenes in Early 19th Century Opera." *Acta Psychiatrica Scandinavica,* 102, 310–313.

Estroff, S.E. 1989. "Self, Identity and Subjective Experiences in Schizophrenia." *Schizophrenia Bulletin,* 15, 189–196.

_____. 2004. "Subject/Subjectivities in Dispute: The Poetics, Politics, and Performance of First-person Narratives of People with Schizophrenia." In *Schizophrenia, Culture and Subjectivity* (pp. 282–302), edited by J.H. Jenkins and R.J. Barrett. Cambridge: Cambridge University Press.

Evans, C. 1754. "A Relation of a Cure Performed by Electricity." *Medical Observations and Inquiries* 1, 83–86.

Evarts, A.B. 1914. "Dementia Praecox in the Colored Race." *Psychoanalytic Review,* 4, 388–403.

_____. 1916. "The Onotogenetic Against the Phylogenetic Elements in the Psychoses of the Colored Race." *Psychoanalytic Review,* 3, 327–387.

Eversley, S. 2001. "The Lunatic's Fancy and the Work of Art." *American Literary History,* 13, 445–468.

Ewald, F.R., W. Freeman, and J.W. Watts. 1947. "Psychosurgery: The Nursing Problem." *American Journal of Nursing,* 47, 210–213.

Ewalt, J.R. 1979. "The Mental Health Movement, 1949–1979." *Milbank Memorial Fund Quarterly,* 57, 507–515.

Exner, J.E., and Murillo, L.G. 1977. "A Long-term Follow-up of Schizophrenics Treated with Regressive ECT." *Diseases of the Nervous System,* 38, 162–168.

Fairley, J.W. 1991. "Patrick Watson-Williams and the Concept of Focal Sepsis in the Sinuses." *Journal of Laryngology and Otology,* 105, 1–6.

Falconbridge, A. 1788. *An Account of the Slave Trade on the Coast of Africa.* London: J. Phillips.

Farhall, J., K.M. Greenwood, and H.K. Jackson. 2007. "Coping with Hallucinated Voices in Schizophrenia." *Clinical Psychology Review,* 27, 476–493.

Farmer, F. 1972. *Will There Really Be a Morning?* New York: G.P. Putnam's Sons.

Farnham, A.M. 1887. "Uterine Disease in the Production of Insanity." *Alienist and Neurologist,* 8, 532–547.

Fee, D., ed. 2000. *Pathology and the Postmodern: Mental Illness as Discourse and Experience.* London: Sage.

Ferguson, J.T. 1957. "Neuropharmacological Agents in Rehabilitation of Patients with Chronic Mental Illness." *Journal of the American Medical Association,* 165, 1677–1682.

Fernández, I.C. 2001. "A Journey to Madness: Jane Bowles's Narrative and Schizophrenia." *Journal of Medical Humanities,* 22, 265–283.

Fine, G.A. 2003. "Crafting Authenticity: The Validation of Identity in Self-Taught Art." *Theory and Society,* 32, 153–180.

Fine, P. 1974. "Women and Shock Treatment." *Radical Therapy,* 2, 9–11.

Finlayson, A.W. 1916. *The Dack Family.* Cold Spring Harbor, NY: Eugenics Record Office.

Finn, R. 2004. "'Pathological Bias' Under Consideration for *DSM-V.*" *Internal Medicine News,* 37, 32.

Fisher, W.A. 1994. "Restraint and Seclusion: A Review of the Literature." *American Journal of Psychiatry,* 151, 1584–1591.

Fisher, W.H., P.J. Barreira, J.L. Geller, A.W. White, A.K. Lincoln, and M. Sudders. 2001. "Long-stay Patients in State Psychiatric Hospitals at the End of the 20th Century." *Psychiatric Services*, 52, 1051–1056.

Foley, H.A., and S.S. Sharfstein. 1983. *Madness and Government: Who Cares for the Mentally Ill?* Washington, D.C.: American Psychiatric Press.

Ford, W.C., ed. 1957. *The Diary of Cotton Mather.* Vol. 2. New York: F. Ungar.

Foucault, M. 1965. *Madness and Civilization.* New York: Pantheon.

"Fourth of July Among the Insane." July 22, 1843. *New York Observer and Chronicle*, 116.

Fouts, P.J., O.M. Helmer, S. Lepkovsky, and T.H. Jukes. 1937. "Treatment of Human Pellagra with Nicotinic Acid." *Proceedings of the Society of Experimental Biology and Medicine*, 37, 405–407

Francke, O.C. 1973. "William Hunter's 'Oral Sepsis' and American Odontology." *Bulletin of the History of Dentistry*, 21, 73–79.

Frank, L.R. *The History of Shock Treatment.* San Francisco: Author, 1978.

Frankel, F.H. 1973. "Electro-convulsive Therapy in Massachusetts: A Task Force Report." *Massachusetts Journal of Mental Health*, 3, 3–29.

Franklin, B. 1754. *Some Account of the Pennsylvania Hospital from Its First Rise, to the Beginning of the Fifth Month, Called May, 1754.* Philadelphia: B. Franklin & D. Hall.

Freeman, L. "Minnesota Raises Mental Care Rate." September 26, 1949. *New York Times*, 37.

Freeman, W. 1942/1950. *Psychosurgery in the Treatment of Mental Disorders and Intractable Pain.* Springfield, IL: Charles C. Thomas.

_____. 1949. "Transorbital Leucotomy: The Deep Frontal Cut." *Proceedings of the Royal Society of Medicine*, 42, 8–11.

_____. 1953. "Hazards of Lobotomy." *Journal of the American Medical Association*, 152, 487–491.

_____. 1962. "West Virginia Lobotomy Project: A Sequel." *Journal of the American Medical Association*, 181, 1134–1135.

_____, H.W. Davis, I.C. East, H.D. Tait, S.O. Johnson, and W.B. Rogers. 1954. "West Virginia Lobotomy Project." *Journal of the*

American Medical Association, 156, 939–943.

_____, and J. Watts. 1937. "Prefrontal Lobotomy in the Treatment of Mental Disorders." *Southern Medical Journal*, 30, 23–31.

Friedman, R., and K. Kutash. 1992. "Challenges for Child and Adolescent Mental Health." *Health Affairs*, 11, 129–130.

Friends Hospital. 2007. Retrieved on the World Wide Web <http://www.friendshospitalonline.org/History.htm>.

Fromm-Reichmann, F. 1948. "Notes on the Development of Treatment of Schizophrenics by Psychoanalysis and Psychotherapy." *Psychiatry*, 11, 263–273.

Furedi, F. 2004. *Therapy Culture.* London: Routledge.

Gale, T. 1802. *Electricity, or Ethereal Fire, Considered.* Troy, MI: Moffitt & Lyon.

Galt, J.M. 1848. *Report of the Physician and Superintendent of the Eastern Lunatic Asylum.* Williamsburg, VA: Author..

_____. 1855. "The Farm of St. Anne." *American Journal of Insanity*, 11, 352–357

Gambino, M. 2008. "'These Strangers Within Our Gates': Race, Psychiatry and Mental Illness Among Black Americans at St. Elizabeth's Hospital in Washington, DC, 1900–1940." *History of Psychiatry*, 19, 387–408.

Gamwell, L., and N. Tomes. 1995. *Madness in America: Cultural and Medical Perceptions of Mental Illness Before 1914.* Ithaca: Cornell University Press.

Garrett, E.S., and C.W. Mockbee. 1952. "New Hope for Far Advanced Schizophrenia: Intensive Regressive Electroconvulsive Therapy in the Treatment of Severely Regressed Schizophrenics." *Ohio State Medical Journal*, 48, 505–509.

Gazdag, G., I. Bitter, G.S. Ungvari, Baran, and M. Fink. 2009. "László Meduna's Pilot Studies with Camphor Inductions of Seizures: The First 11 Patients." *Journal of ECT*, 25, 3–11.

Geller, J. 1995. *Women of the Asylum.* New York: Anchor.

Gilman, C.P. 1899. *The Yellow Wallpaper.* Boston: Small and Maynard.

_____. 1935. *The Living of Charlotte Perkins Gilman: An Autobiography.* New York: Hawthorn.

Gilman, S. 1982. *Seeing the Insane.* New York: John Wiley & Sons.

_____. 1985. *Difference and Pathology: Stereotypes of Sexuality, Race and Madness.* Ithaca: Cornell University Press.

_____. 1991. *Disease and Representation.* Ithaca: Cornell University Press.

Glueck, B.C., H. Reiss, and L.E. Bernard. 1957. "Regressive Electric Shock Therapy: Preliminary Report on 100 Cases." *Psychiatry*, 31, 117–136.

Goddard, H.H. 1912. *The Kallikak Family: A Study in the Heredity of Feeblemindedness.* New York: Macmillan.

Goffman, E. 1961. *Asylums: Essays on the Social Situation of Mental Patients and Other Inmates.* Garden City, NY: Anchor.

_____. 1963. *Stigma: Notes on the Management of Spoiled Identity.* New York: Prentice Hall.

_____. 1969. "The Insanity of Place." *Psychiatry*, 32, 357–87.

Goldberg, C. June 13, 2008. "Mentally Ill Children Stuck in Hospital Limbo." *Boston Globe*, 1.

Goldstein, J. 1987. *Console and Classify: The French Psychiatric Profession in the Nineteenth Century.* Cambridge: Cambridge University Press.

Goodheart, L.B. 2002. "The Distinction Between Witchcraft and Madness in Colonial Connecticut." *History of Psychiatry*, 13, 433–444.

Gordon, H.L. 1948. "Fifty Shock Therapy Theories." *Military Surgeon*, 103, 397–401.

Gorman, M. 1946. "Misery Rules in State Shadowland." Series. *Daily Oklahoman.*

Gowran, C. October 17, 1944. "Describes U.S. Treatment of Battle Nerves." *Chicago Daily Tribune*, p. 3.

Grandbois, D. 2005. "Stigma of Mental Illness Among American Indians and Alaska Native Nations." *Issues in Mental Health Nursing*, 26, 1001–1024.

Granville, J.M. November 13, 1875. Letter to Editor. *Lancet*, 705–707.

Green, H. 1964. *I Never Promised You a Rose Garden.* New York: Macmillan.

Green, M.F. 2003. *Schizophrenia Revealed: From Neurons to Social Interactions.* New York: W.W. Norton.

Greenberg, M. 2008. *Hurry Down Sunshine.* New York: Other.

_____. 2009. "Iron Teeth." In *Beg, Borrow, Steal: A Writer's Life* (pp. 113–117), M. Greenberg. New York: Other.

Greene, R. August 25, 1960. "Old Folks Admitted to Mental Hospital to Die." *Post-Tribune*, 12.

Gregorie, A.K., ed. 1950. *Records of the Court of Chancery of South Carolina, 1671–1779.* Washington, D.C.: American Historical Society.

Gregory, J.N. 2007. *The Southern Diaspora.* Chapel Hill: University of North Carolina Press.

Grimes, J.M. 1934. *Institutional Care of Mental Patients in the United States.* Chicago: Author.

Grimshaw, A. 1969. *Racial Violence in the United States.* Chicago: Aldine.

Grinspoon, L., J. Ewalt, and R.I. Shader. 1972. *Schizophrenia: Pharmacotherapy and Psychotherapy.* Baltimore: Williams and Wilkins.

Grob, G.N. 1987. "The Forging of Mental Health Policy in America." *Journal of the History of Medicine and Allied Sciences*, 42, 410–446.

_____. 1983. *Mental Illness and American Society, 1875–1940.* Princeton, NJ: Princeton University Press.

_____. 1985. *The Inner World of American Psychiatry, 1890–1940.* New Brunswick, NJ: Rutgers University Press.

_____. 1984. *The Mad Among Us: A History of the Care of America's Mentally Ill.* Cambridge, MA: Harvard University Press.

_____. 1998. "Psychiatry's Holy Grail." *Bulletin of the History of Medicine*, 72, 189–219.

Grobe, J. 1995. *Beyond Bedlam: Contemporary Women Psychiatric Survivors Speak Out.* Chicago: Third Side.

Groneman, C. 2001. *Nymphomania: A History.* New York: W.W. Norton.

Gronfein, W. 1985. "Psychotropic Drugs and the Origins of Deinstitutionalization." *Social Problems*, 32, 437–454.

Gross, A.J. 2000. *Double Character: Slavery and Mastery in the Antebellum Southern Courtroom.* Princeton, NJ: Princeton University Press.

Hacking, I. 2000. *The Social Construction of What?* Cambridge, MA: Harvard University Press.

Hale, N.G. 1995. *The Rise and Crisis of Psychoanalysis in the United States.* New York: Oxford University Press.

Hall, M. 1986. "The Problem of Martín Ramírez: Folk Art Criticism as Cosmologies of Coercion." *Clairon*, 11, 58–59.

Haller, B., and R. Laresen. 2005. "Persuading Sanity: Magic Lantern Images and the 19th Century Moral Treatment in America." *Journal of American Culture*, 28, 259–272.

Haller, J. and Haller, R. 1974. *The Physician and Sexuality in Victorian America*. Carbondale: Southern Illinois University Press.

Hamel, P.B., and M.U. Chiltoskey. 1975. *Cherokee Plants and Their Use: A Four Hundred Year History*. Sylva, NC: Herald.

Hamilton, I. 1982. *Robert Lowell: A Biography*. New York: Random House.

Hampton, R. 1975. *The Far Side of Despair: A Personal Account of Depression*. Chicago: Nelson-Hall.

Hare, E. 1983. "Was Insanity on the Increase?" *British Journal of Psychiatry*, 142, 439–455.

Harrison, J.A. 1902. *The Complete Works of Edgar Allan Poe*. Vol. 4. New York: Crowell.

Haskell, E. 1869. *The Trial of Ebenezer Haskell*. Philadelphia: Author.

Haslam, J. 1810. *Illustrations, or Madness: Exhibiting a Singular Case of Insanity*. London: Rivingtons.

Haveliwala, Y.A. 1979. "Problems of Foreign Born Psychiatrists." *Psychiatric Quarterly*, 51, 307–311.

Hawthorne, N. 1837. "The Minister's Black Veil." In *Twice Told Tales*, N. Hawthorne (pp. 53–77). Boston: American Stationers, John B. Russell.

Hayden, R. 1996. *The Influencing Machine*. West Vancouver, B.C., Canada: Black Swan.

Health Care Finance Administration. 1999. "Medicare and Medicaid Programs; Hospital Conditions of Participation: Patients' Rights; Interim Final Rule." *Federal Register*, 64, 36069.

Healy, D. 2002. *The Creation of Psychopharmacology*. Cambridge, MA: Harvard University Press.

_____. 2008. *Mania: A Short History of Bipolar Disorder*. Baltimore: Johns Hopkins University Press.

Henry, O. 1910. *Let Me Feel Your Pulse*. New York: Doubleday.

Herzberg, D. 2009. *Happy Pills in America*. Baltimore: Johns Hopkins University Press.

Highland Hospital. 1943. *Highland Hospital, Asheville, North Carolina*. Asheville, NC: Highland Hospital.

Hilton, C. 2007. "An Exploration of the Patient's Experience of Electro-Convulsive Therapy in Mid-20th Century Creative Literature." *Journal of Affective Disorders*, 97, 5–12.

Hillyer, J. 1926. *Reluctantly Told*. New York: Macmillan.

Hirshbein, L., and S. Sarvananda. 2008. "History, Power and Electricity: American Popular Magazine Accounts of Electroconvulsive Therapy, 1940–2000." *Journal of the History of the Behavioral Sciences*, 44, 1–18.

Hoadly, C.J. 1870. *The Public Records of the Colony of Connecticut, from October 1706 to October 1716*. Vol. 5. Hartford, CT: Case, Lockwood.

_____. 1872. *The Public Records of the Colony of Connecticut, from May 1717 to October 1725*. Vol. 6. Hartford, CT: Case, Lockwood.

_____. 1885. *The Public Records of the Colony of Connecticut, from May 1768 to May 1772*. Vol. 13. Hartford, CT: Case, Lockwood & Brainard.

_____. 1895. *The Public Records of the State of Connecticut, from May 1778 to April 1780*. Vol. 2. Hartford, CT: Case, Lockwood & Brainard.

Hoffman, F. 1953. *The Twenties: American Writing in the Postwar Decades*. New York: Viking.

Hollingshead, A.B., and F.C. Redlich. 1958. *Social Class and Mental Illness*. New York: John Wiley and Sons.

Hollingshead, G. 2004. *Bedlam*. Toronto: HarperCollins.

Holmes, B.T. 1916. "Dementia Praecox Studies: The Treatment of the Toxemia of Dementia Praecox." *American Medicine*, 11, 702–704.

Holmes, E. 2001. "Vision for an Early Asylum." *Michigan Quarterly Review*, 40, 71–72.

Holmes, O.W. 1911. *Medical Essays, 1842–1882*. Boston: Houghton Mifflin.

Hornbacher, M. 2008. *Madness: A Bipolar Life*. Boston: Houghton Mifflin.

Hotchner, A.E. 1967. *Papa Hemingway*. New York: Bantam.

Hudson, C. 1976. *The Southeastern Indians*. Knoxville: University of Tennessee Press.

Hughes, J.S. 1993. "Labeling and Treating Black Mental Illness in Alabama, 1861–1910." *Journal of Southern History*, 58, 435–460.

Hunt, I. 1851. *Astounding Disclosure! Three Years in a Mad House*. Boston: Author.

Hunt, M. 1996. *Repossessing Ernestine*. New York: HarperCollins.

Hunter, M. 2007. "The Persistent Problem of Colorism: Skin Tone, Status and Inequality." *Sociology Compass*, 1, 237–254.

Hydén, L.C. 1997. "Illness and Narrative." *Sociology of Health and Illness*, 19, 48–69.

Impasto, D. 1960. "The Story of the First Electroshock Treatment." *American Journal of Psychiatry*, 116, 1113–1114.

Inmate [Woodson, M.M.], Ward 8. 1932. *Behind the Door of Delusion*. New York: Macmillan.

"Insanity Treated by Electric Shock." July 6, 1940. *New York Times*, 17.

Isaac, R.J., and V.C. Armat. 1990. *Madness in the Streets*. New York: Free Press.

Jackson, S.W. 1990. "The Use of the Passions in Psychological Healing." *Journal of the History of Medicine and Allied Sciences*, 45, 150–175.

Jackson, V. "Separate and Unequal: The Legacy of Racially Segregated Psychiatric Hospitals" (n.d.). Retrieved on the World Wide Web <http://www.patdeegan.com/documents/SeparateandUnequalCMHSFINAL.pdf>

Jackson, W.A. 2001. "A Short Guide to Humoural Medicine." *Trends in Pharmacological Sciences*, 22, 487–489.

Jamison, K.R. 1993. *Touched with Fire*. New York: Free Press.

Janis, I.L. 1948. "Memory Loss Following Electric Convulsive Treatments." *Journal of Personality*, 17, 29–32.

Jansson, B. October 12, 1998. "Controversial Psychosurgery Resulted in Nobel Prize." Retrieved on the World Wide Web <http://www.nobelprize.org/nobel_prizes/medicine/articles/moniz/index.html>

Jarvis, E. 1844. "Insanity Among the Coloured People of the Free States." *American Journal of the Medical Sciences*, 6, 71–83.

_____. 1855. *Report on Insanity and Idiocy in Massachusetts*. Massachusetts House Document No. 144. Boston: Author.

Jay, M. 2004. *The Air Loom Gang*. New York: Four Walls Eight Windows.

Jefferson, T. 1932. "The Letters of Thomas Jefferson to William Short." *William and Mary Quarterly* (2nd series), 12, 145–156.

Jimenez, M.A. 1987. *Changing Faces of Madness*. Hanover, NH: University Press of New England.

Johnson, H. 2001. *Angels in the Architecture*. Detroit: Wayne State University Press.

Jones, D.L. 1975. "The Strolling Poor: Transiency in Eighteenth Century Massachusetts." *Journal of Social History*, 8, 28–54.

Jones, E.P. 2006. "Root Worker." In *All Aunt Hagar's Children: Stories* (pp. 163–201), E.P. Jones. New York: HarperCollins.

Jones, R.A. 2005. "Identity Commitments in Personal Stories of Mental Illness on the Internet." *Narrative Inquiry*, 15, 293–322.

Jordanova, L. 1995. "The Social Construction of Medical Knowledge." *Social History of Medicine*, 8, 361–381.

Kaempffert, W. May 24, 1941. "Turning the Mind Inside Out." *Saturday Evening Post*, 18–19, 69, 71–72, 74.

Kaimowitz v. Department of Mental Health, July 10, 1973. Civ. No. 73–19434 AW (Circuit Court of Wayne County, MI).

Kaminer, W. 1993. *I'm Dysfunctional, You're Dysfunctional*. New York: Vantage.

Kant, J. 2008. *The Thought That Counts*. New York: Oxford University Press.

Kaplan, R.M. 2009. *Medical Murder*. Crows Nest, NSW, Australia: Allen & Unwin.

Kaye, H.L. 1993. "Why Freud Hated America." *Wilson Quarterly*, 17, 118–125.

Kaysen, S. 1993. *Girl, Interrupted*. New York: Vintage.

Kellogg, J.H. 1908. *Battle Creek Sanitarium*. Battle Creek, MI: Gage.

Kennedy, J.C.G. 1864. *Population of the United States in 1860*. Washington, D.C.: Government Printing Office.

Kerkhoff, J. 1952. *How Thin the Veil: A Newspaperman's Story of His Own Crackup and Recovery*. New York: Greenberg.

Kesey, K. 1962. *One Flew Over the Cuckoo's Nest*. New York: Viking.

Kinross-Wright, J.V. 1956. "The Intensive Chlorpromazine Treatment of Schizophrenics." In *Pharmacological Products Recently Introduced in the Treatment of Psychiatric Disorders* (pp. 53–62), edited by W.E. Lhamoen. Washington, D.C.: American Psychiatric Association.

"Kirkbride Buildings" 2008. Retrieved on the World Wide Web <http://www.kirk bridebuildings.com>

Kirkbride, T.S. 1842. *Annual Report of the Pennsylvania Hospital for the Insane.* Philadelphia: John C. Clark.

_____. 1880. *On the Construction, Organization, and General Arrangements of Hospitals for the Insane.* 2nd ed. Philadelphia: J.B. Lippincott.

Klein, N. 2007. *Shock Doctrine.* New York: Henry Holt.

Kleinman, D., and L. Cohen. 1991. "The Decontextualization of Mental Illness." *Social Science and Medicine,* 32, 867–874.

Klopp, H.I. 1932. "The Children's Institute of the Allentown State Hospital." *American Journal of Psychiatry,* 88, 1107–1118.

Kneeland, D.E. August 2, 1972. "Behind Eagleton's Withdrawal: A Tale of Confusion and Division." *New York Times,* 1, 20.

Kneeland, T.W., and C.A.B. Warren. 2002. *Pushbutton Psychiatry.* Westport, CT: Praeger.

Kolb, L. 1941. *Shock Therapy Survey.* U.S. Public Health Service Report. Washington, D.C.: U.S. Government Printing Office.

Kopeloff, N., and C.O. Cheney. 1922. "Studies in Focal Infection: Its Presence and Elimination in the Functional Psychoses." *American Journal of Psychiatry,* 79, 139–156.

Kopeloff, N., and Kirby. 1923. "Focal Infection and Mental Disease." *American Journal of Psychiatry,* 80, 149–187.

Kostir, M.S. 1916. *The Family of Sam Sixty.* Columbus: Ohio Board of Administration.

Kramer, M. 1953. "Long-range Studies of Mental Health Patients." *Milbank Quarterly,* 37, 253–266.

Krauch, E. 1937. *A Mind Restored: The Story of Jim Curran.* New York: G.P. Putnam's Sons.

Krim, S. 1961. "The Insanity Bit." In *Views of a Nearsighted Cannoneer* (pp. 112–129), S. Krim. New York: Excelsior.

Kroeger, B. 1994. *Nellie Bly: Daredevil, Reporter, Feminist.* New York: Random House.

Kutchins, H., and S.A. Kirk. 1997. *Making Us Crazy.* New York: Free Press.

Lachmund, J., and G. Stollberg, eds. 1992. *The Social Construction of Illness.* Stuttgart, Germany: Franz Steiner.

Laing, R.D. 1960. *The Divided Self.* Baltimore: Penguin.

_____. 1967. *The Politics of Experience.* London: Penguin.

Lamb, H.R. 1984. *The Homeless Mentally Ill: A Task Force Report of the American Psychiatric Association.* Washington, D.C.: American Psychiatric Association.

_____. 1981. "What Did We Really Expect from Deinstitutionalization?" *Hospital and Community Psychiatry,* 32, 105–109.

Lamb, P. 1956. "Suppressed Lobotomy: Commies' Secret for World Domination." *Suppressed,* 3, 34–35, 59.

Lando, H.A. 1976. "Being Sane in Insane Places: A Supplemental Report." *Professional Psychology,* 7, 47–52.

Lathrop, C.C. 1890. *A Secret Institution.* New York: Bryant.

"A Leaf from the Annals of Insanity." November 1847. *Knickerbocker* (New York City), 452–454.

Leon, S.C., N.D. Uziel-Miller, J.S. Lyons, and P. Tracy. 1999. "Psychiatric Service Utilization of Children and Adolescents in State Custody." *Journal of the American Academy of Child and Adolescent Psychiatry,* 38, 305–310.

Lerch, W. October 23, 1943. "Food for Mental Patients Revolting." *Cleveland* (Ohio) *Press,* 1.

_____. October 22, 1943. "Mental Patients Here Beaten and Shackled." *Cleveland* (Ohio) *Press,* 1, 2.

Lerman, P. 1985. "Deinstitutionalization and Welfare Policies." *Annals of the American Academy of Political and Social Science,* 479, 132–155.

Leudar, I., and P. Thomas. 2000. *Voice of Reason, Voices of Insanity.* London: Routledge.

Lewis, M. 2002. *Life Inside.* New York: Simon and Schuster.

Lichterman, P. 1992. "Self-help Reading as Thin Culture." *Media, Culture and Society,* 14, 421–447.

Lilienfeld, S.O., R.L. Spitzer, and M.B. Miller. 2005. "A Response to a Non-response to Criticisms of a Non-study."

Journal of Nervous and Mental Disease, 193, 745–746.

Longfellow, H.W. 1902. *Giles Corey of Salem Farms.* In *The Complete Poetical Works of Henry Wadsworth Longfellow* (pp. 495–522), H.W. Longfellow. Boston: Houghton Mifflin.

Lorenz, S.E. 1963. *And Always Tomorrow.* New York: Holt, Rinehart and Winston.

Loue, S., and M. Sajatovic. 2008. "Auditory and Visual Hallucinations in a Sample of Severely Mentally Ill Puerto Rican Women: An Examination of the Cultural Context." *Mental Health and Religion,* 11, 597–608.

Luchins, A.S. 1988. "The Rise and Decline of the American Asylum Movement in the 19th Century." *Journal of Psychology,* 122, 471–486.

"The Lunatics' Ball." January 24, 1874. *New York Times,* 15.

Lunt, A. 1871. *Behind Bars.* Boston: Lee & Shepard.

Lutes, J.M. 2002. "Into the Madhouse with Nellie Bly: Girl Stunt Reporting in Late Nineteenth Century America." *American Quarterly,* 54, 217–253.

Lutz, T. 1991. *American Nervousness, 1903: An Anecdotal History.* Ithaca: Cornell University Press.

Luxenberg, S. 2009. *Annie's Ghosts.* New York: Hyperion.

Lyden, J. 1999. *Daughter of the Queen of Sheba.* London: Virago.

Lydons, C. July 26, 1972. "Eagleton Tells of Shock Therapy on Two Occasions." *New York Times,* 1.

Lynn, D.J. 1993. "Freud's Analysis of A.B., a Psychotic Man, 1925–1930." *Journal of the American Academy of Psychoanalysis and Dynamic Psychiatry,* 21, 63–78.

Mabon, W., and W.L. Babcock. 1899. "Thyroid Extract." In *Proceedings of the American Medico-Legal Association,* pp. 281–301. New York: American Medico-Legal Association.

Macalpine, I., and R. Hunter. 1969. *George III and the Mad Business.* London: Allen Lane.

Macleod, N. 1900. "The Bromide Sleep: A New Departure in the Treatment of Acute Mania." *British Medical Journal,* 1, 134–136.

Maisel, A.Q. May 6, 1946. "Bedlam 1946." *Life,* 102–110, 112, 115–116, 118.

_____. November 12, 1951. "Scandal Results in Real Reforms." *Life,* 141–154.

Malzberg, B. 1939. "A Follow-up Study of Patients with Dementia Praecox Treated with Insulin in the New York State Civil State Hospitals." *Mental Hygiene,* 23, 641–651.

_____. 1934. *Mortality Among Patients with Mental Disease.* Utica, NY: State Hospitals Press.

_____. 1938. "Outcome of Insulin Treatment of One Thousand Patients with Dementia Praecox." *Psychiatric Quarterly,* 12, 528–553.

Manning, M. 1995. *Undercurrents.* New York: Harper.

Mannix, D.P. 1962. *Black Cargoes: A History of the Atlantic Slave Trade.* New York: Viking.

Mark, V.H., and F.R. Ervin. 1970. *Violence and the Brain.* New York: Harper.

Mark, V.H., W.H. Sweet, and F.R. Erwin. 1967. "The Role of Brain Disease in Riots and Urban Violence." *Journal of the American Medical Association,* 201, 895.

Mashour, G.A., E.E. Walker, and R.L. Martuza. 2005. "Psychosurgery: Past, Present, and Future." *Brain Research Review,* 48, 409–419.

Massachusetts Historical Society. 1862. Letter from Edward Stafford to Gov. John Winthrop. *Proceedings of the Massachusetts Historical Society.* Vol. 5. Boston: Massachusetts Historical Society.

Mather, C. 1972. *The Angel of Bethesda,* edited by G.W. Jones. Barre, MA: American Antiquarian Society.

Maw, J. April 1, 2008. "Revealing the Mind Bender General." BBC Radio 4. London: BBC. Retrieved on the World Wide Web <http://jb_speechification.s3.amazonaws.com/Revealing-the-Mind-Bender-General.mp3>

May, P. 1968. *Treatment of Schizophrenia.* New York: Science House.

Mayes, R., C. Bagwell, and J. Erkulwater. 2009. *Medicating Children.* Cambridge, MA: Harvard University Press.

McCandless, P. 1996. *Moonlight, Magnolias and Madness: Insanity in South Carolina from the Colonial Period to the Progressive Era.* Chapel Hill: University of North Carolina Press.

McCarthy, P. *The Twisted Mind: Madness in*

Herman Melville's Fiction. Iowa City: University of Iowa Press, 1990.

McCulloch, O.C. 1891. *The Tribe of Ishmael.* Buffalo, NY: Charity Organization Society.

McGarr, M.A. 1953. *And Lo, the STAR.* New York: Pageant.

McGovern, C.M. 1985. *Masters of Madness: Social Origins of the American Psychiatric Profession.* Hanover, NH: University of New England Press.

McKelway, B. October 28, 2009. "Patient Spared Solitary Death." Retrieved on the World Wide Web <http://www2.newsvirginian.com>

Mechanic, D. 1989. *Mental Health and Social Policy.* Englewood Cliffs, NJ: Prentice Hall.

_____, and Rochefort, D.A. 1990. "Deinstitutionalization: An Appraisal of Reform." *Annual Review of Sociology,* 16, 301–327.

"Medicine: Losing Nerves." June 30, 1947. *Time,* 45.

Meduna, L.J. 1950. *Carbon Dioxide Therapy: A Neurophysiological Treatment of Nervous Disorders.* Springfield, IL: Charles C. Thomas.

Meinke, P. 1977. "Cracking." In *The Night Train and the Golden Bird* (p. 54), P. Meinke. Pittsburgh: University of Pittsburgh Press.

Melville, H. 1924. *Billy Budd.* Cambridge, MA: Harvard University Press.

_____. 1851. *Moby Dick, or, the Whale.* New York: Harper & Brothers.

"Memorial of D.L. Dix, Praying a Grant of Land for the Relief and Support of the Indigent Curable and Incurable Insane in the United States." June 27, 1848. 30th Congress, 1st Session, Miscellaneous Senate Document No. 150.

Mersky, H. 1994. "Somatic Treatments, Ignorance, and the Historiography of Psychiatry." *History of Psychiatry,* 5, 387–391.

Metcalf, A. 1876. *Lunatic Asylums: And How I Became an Inmate of One.* Chicago: Ottaway & Colbert.

Metzl, J.M. 2003. *Prozac on the Couch.* Durham, NC: Duke University Press.

Micale, M. 1995. *Approaching Hysteria: Disease and Its Interpretations.* Princeton, NJ: Princeton University Press.

Miller, R.D. 1987. "Involuntary Civil Commitment of the Mentally Ill in the Post-Reform Era." Springfield, IL: Charles C. Thomas.

Millett, K. 1990. *The Loony-Bin Trip.* New York: Simon and Schuster.

Minsky, S., W. Vega, T. Miskimen, M. Gara, and J. Escobar. 2003. "Diagnostic Patterns in Latino, African American, and European Psychiatric Patients." *Archives of General Psychiatry,* 60, 637–644.

Mitchell, J., and A.D. Vierkant. 1989. "Delusions and Hallucinations as a Reflection of the Subcultural Milieu Among Psychotic Patients of the 1930s and 1980s." *Journal of Psychology,* 123, 269–274.

Mitchell, S.W. 1894. "Address Before the Fiftieth Annual Meeting of the American Medico-Psychological Association." *Journal of Nervous and Mental Disease,* 21, 413–437.

Mitchinson, W. 1982. "Gynecological Surgeries on Insane Women: London, Ontario, 1895–1901." *Journal of Social History,* 15, 467–484.

Moody, C.P. 1847. *Biographical Sketches of the Moody Family.* Boston: S.G. Drake.

Moody, R. 2003. *The Black Veil: A Memoir with Digressions.* Boston: Back Bay.

Moore, D. January 8, 2007. "Brainwashed 'Guinea Pig' Seeks More Damages." *Toronto Star,* 1.

Moore, W. 1955. *The Mind in Chains.* New York: Exposition.

Moran, M. 2009. "*DSM-V* Developers Weigh Adding Psychosis Risk." *Psychiatric News,* 44, 5.

Morris, C.E. 2001. "'Our Capital Aversion': Abigail Folsom, Madness, and Radical Anti-Slavery Praxis." *Women's Studies in Communication,* 24, 62–89.

Morrissey, J.P. 1989. "The Changing Role of the Public Mental Hospital." In *Handbook on Mental Health Policy in the United States* (pp. 311–338), edited by D.A. Rochefort. Westport, CT: Greenwood.

Morton, T.G., and F. Woodbury. 1973. *The History of the Pennsylvania Hospital.* New York: Arno.

Moskowitz, E. 2001. *In Therapy We Trust.* Baltimore: Johns Hopkins University Press.

Mossman, D. 1997. "Deinstitutionalization, Homelessness and the Myth of Psychiatric Abandonment: A Structural Anthropology

Perspective." *Social Science and Medicine,* 44, 71–83.

Moynihan, D.P. May 22, 1989. "Promise to the Mentally Ill Has Not Been Kept." Letter to the editor. *New York Times,* A16.

Murillo, L.G., and J.E. Exner. 1973. "The Effects of Regressive ECT with Process Schizophrenics." *American Journal of Psychiatry,* 130, 269–273.

"My Lobotomy." 2005. Retrieved on the World Wide Web <http://www.soundportraits.org/on-air/my_lobotomy/transcript.php>

Myrdal, G. 1944. *The American Dilemma: The Negro Problem and Modern Democracy.* New York: Pantheon.

Nasar, S. 1998. *A Beautiful Mind.* New York: Simon & Schuster.

Nash, G.B. 2004. "Poverty and Politics in Early American History." In *Down and Out in Early America* (pp. 1–37), edited by B.G. Smith. University Park: Pennsylvania State University Press.

Nash, John, Jr. "Autobiography" (n.d.). Retrieved on the World Wide Web <http://nobelprize.org/nobel_prizes/economics/laureates/1994/nash-autobio.html>

Neugeboren, J. 2003. *Imagining Robert: My Brother, Madness, Survival, a Memoir.* New Brunswick, NJ: Rutgers University Press.

"Neurosurgical Treatment of Certain Abnormal Mental States: Panel Discussion at Cleveland." 1941. *Journal of the American Medical Association,* 117, 517–527.

Nichols, C.H. 1855. "Proceedings of the Tenth Annual Meeting of the Association of Medical Superintendents of American Institutions for the Insane." *American Journal of Insanity,* 12, 39–101.

Nicolson, N., and J. Trautman, eds. 1975. *The Letters of Virginia Woolf.* Vol. 4. New York: Harcourt.

Nobles, M. 2000. *Shades of Citizenship: Race and Census in Modern Politics.* Stanford: Stanford University Press.

Noll, R. 2006. "Infectious Insanities, Surgical Solutions: Bayard Taylor Holmes, Dementia Praecox, and Laboratory Science in Early 20th Century America." *History of Psychiatry,* 17, 183–204.

Nordahl, B. 1994. "Unhinged Mind." Retrieved on the World Wide Web <http.www.mouthmag.com/snakepoem.htm>

O'Brien, D. 1993. "Haslam's Key." Unpublished play.

Okin, R.L. 1985. "Expand the Community Care System: Deinstitutionalization Can Work." *Hospital and Community Psychiatry,* 36, 742–745.

Oral Histories. 2005. "Sound Portraits." Retrieved on the World Wide Web <http://soundportraits.org/on-air/my_lobotomy/oralhistory.php>

O'Shea B., and A. McGennis. 1983. "ECT: Lay Attitudes and Experiences—A Pilot Study." *Irish Medical Journal* 76, 40–43.

Packard, E.P.W. 1866. *Marital Power Exemplified in Mrs. Packard's Trial, and Self-Defence from the Charge of Insanity.* Hartford, CT: Case, Lockwood.

_____. 1868. *The Prisoner's Hidden Life, or Insane Asylums Unveiled.* Chicago: Author.

Palmer, H.D., and A.L. Paine. 1932. "Prolonged Narcosis as Therapy in the Psychoses." *American Journal of Psychiatry,* 94, 37–57.

Parry-Jones, W. 1972. *The Trade in Lunacy.* London: Routledge and Kegan Paul.

"Pennsylvania Hospital." January 30, 1796. *Philadelphia General Advertiser,* 3.

Perrucci, R. 1974. *Circle of Madness: On Being Insane and Being Institutionalized in America.* Englewood Cliffs, NJ: Prentice-Hall.

"Personal Stories: Ted Chabasinski" (n.d.). Retrieved on the World Wide Web <http://www.mindfreedom.org/personal-stories/chabasisnskited>

Petit, C. December 30, 1974. "Shudders Over Shock Treatment." *San Francisco Chronicle,* 2.

Pfister, J. 1997. "On Conceptualizing the Cultural History of Emotional and Psychological Life in America." In *Inventing the Psychological* (pp. 17–59), edited by J. Pfister and N. Shnog. New Haven, CT: Yale University Press.

Pinel, P. 1806. *A Treatise on Insanity,* translated by D.D. Davis. London: Cadel & Davies.

Plath, S. 1963. *The Bell Jar.* New York: Bantam.

_____. 1952. "Johnny Panic." In *Johnny Panic and the Bible of Dreams and Other Prose Writings* (pp. 156–172), S. Plath. New York: HarperCollins.

Poe, E.A. 1845 "The System of Dr. Tarr and Prof. Fether." Retrieved on the World Wide Web <http://etext.virginia.edu/toc/mod eng/public/PoeTarr.html>

"Poem by George Clark Upon the Semicentennial Celebration of the Founding of the Hartford Retreat." January 7, 1873. *Hartford* (CT) *Daily Courant*, 2.

Politzer, W.S. 2005. *The Gullah People and Their African Heritage*. Athens: University of Georgia Press.

Porter, R. 1997. *The Greatest Benefit to Mankind: A Medical History of Humanity*. London: W.W. Norton.

_____. 2006. *Madmen: A Social History of Madhouses, Mad-doctors and Lunatics*. Stroud, UK: Tempus.

_____. 2002. *Madness: A Brief History*. Oxford: Oxford University Press.

_____. 1989. *A Social History of Madness*. New York: E.P. Dutton.

_____, ed. 1991. *The Faber Book of Madness*. London: Faber and Faber.

Porteus, S.D., and R.D. Kepner. 1944. "Mental Changes After Bilateral Prefrontal Lobotomy." *Genetic Psychology Monograph*, 29, 3–115.

Portman, T.A., and M.T. Garrett. 2006. "Native American Healing Traditions." *International Journal of Disability, Development and Education*, 53, 453–469.

Potter, D. January 6, 2009. "Mental Patients Isolated for Years Despite Laws." Associated Press. Retrieved on the World Wide Web <http://www.dailynewstranscript.com/archive>

Poussaint, A.F. 2002. "Is Extreme Racism a Mental Illness? Yes." *Western Journal of Medicine*, 176, 4.

Pressman, J.D. 1998. *Last Resort: Psychosurgery and the Limits of Medicine*. Cambridge: Cambridge University Press.

"Protection of Human Subjects." May 23, 1977. *Federal Register*, 42, 2–16.

"Psychosurgery" (n.d.). Retrieved on the World Wide Web <http://www.psychosurgery.org>

Pulver, S.E. 1961. "The First Electroconvulsive Treatment Given in the United States." *American Journal of Psychiatry*, 117, 845–846.

Rajakumar, K. 2000. "Pellagra in the United States." *Southern Medical Journal*, 93, 272–277.

Ramchandani, D. 2007. "Fooling Others or Oneself? A History of Therapeutic Fads and Its Current Relevance." *Psychiatric Quarterly*, 78, 287–293.

Rappaport, M., H. Hopkins, K. Hall, T. Belleza, and J. Silverman. 1978. "Are There Schizophrenics for Whom Drugs May Be Unnecessary or Contraindicated?" *International Pharmacopsychiatry*, 13, 100–111.

"Rat Bite Fever and Paresis." April 8, 1929. *Time*, 25.

Ratcliff, J.D. February 12, 1938. "Minds That Come Back." *Collier's*, 38.

Ray, I. 1863. "Doubtful Recoveries." *American Journal of Insanity*, 20, 26–44.

_____. 1868. "'A Modern Lettre de Cachet' Reviewed." *The Atlantic Monthly*, 22, 227–243.

Record Commissioners. 1887. *Boston Selectmen's Minutes, 1742–1743 Through 1753*. Westminster, MD: Heritage.

"Regulation of Electroconvulsive Therapy." 1976. *Michigan Law Review*, 75, 363–412.

Reich, R. 1973. "Care of the Chronically Mentally Ill: A National Disgrace." *American Journal of Psychiatry*, 130, 911–912.

Reilly, P. 1991. *The Surgical Solution: A History of Involuntary Sterilization in the United States*. Baltimore: Johns Hopkins University Press.

Reiss, B. 2005. "Bardolatry in Bedlam: Shakespeare, Psychiatry, and Cultural Authority in 19th Century America." *ELH*, 72, 769–797.

"Relation of Diseases of the Reproductive Organs in Women to Insanity." December 31, 1887. *Medical News*, 765–766.

Rensberger, B. "Psychiatrist Explains Medical Facts in Depression." July 29, 1972. *New York Times*, 11.

Reston, J. August 9, 1972. "Psychology and Politics." *New York Times*, 37.

Rieff, P. 1966. *The Triumph of the Therapeutic*. New York: Harper and Row.

Rinkel, M., and H.E. Himwich. 1959. *Insulin Treatment in Psychiatry*. New York: Philosophical Library.

Rivers, T.D., and E.D. Bond. 1941. "Follow-up Results in Insulin Shock Therapy After One to Three Years." *American Journal of Psychiatry*, 98, 382–384.

Roan, S. May 25, 2009. "Bitterness as Mental Illness?" *Los Angeles Times*. Retrieved on the World Wide Web <http://articles.la times.com/2009/may/25/health/hebitter ness25>

Robbins, S.L. 1987. "Samuel Willard and the Spectres of God's Wrathful Lion." *New England Quarterly*, 60, 596–603.

Robertson, L. 1979. *The Insanity of Mary Girard: A Drama in One Act*. New York: Samuel French.

Robitscher, J. 1975. "Implementing the Rights of the Mentally Disabled." In *Medical, Moral and Legal Issues in Mental Health Care* (pp. 13–156), edited by F. Ayd. Baltimore: Williams and Wilkins.

Rochefort, D.A. 1984. "Origins of the 'Third Psychiatric Revolution': The Community Mental Health Centers Act of 1963." *Journal of Health Politics, Policy and Law*, 9, 1–30.

Rohé, G.H. 1895. "Pelvic Disease in Women, and Insanity." *Journal of the American Medical Association*, 25, 624–626.

Rose, S.M. 1979. "Deciphering Deinstitutionalization: Complexities in Policy and Program Analysis." *Milbank Memorial Fund Quarterly*, 57, 429–460.

Rosen, S.R., D.E. Cameron, and J.B. Ziegler. 1941. "The Prevention of Metrazol Fractures by Beta-Erythroidin Hydrochloride." *Psychiatric Quarterly*, 14, 477–480.

Rosenberg, C.E. 1992. *Explaining Epidemics, and Other Studies in the History of Medicine*. New York: Cambridge University Press.

_____. 2002. "The Tyranny of Diagnosis: Specific Entities and Individual Experience." *Milbank Quarterly*, 80, 237–260.

Rosenhan, D. 1973. "On Being Sane in Insane Places." *Science*, 179, 250–258.

Roth, E.A., and L.H. Roth. 1984. "Children's Understanding of Psychiatric Hospitalization." *American Journal of Psychiatry*, 141, 1066–170.

Roth, M., ed. 1998. *Freud: Conflict and Culture*. New York: Knopf.

Rothman, D.J. 1990. *The Discovery of the Asylum*. Boston: Little, Brown.

Rothschild, D., D.J. VanGordon, and A. Varjabedian. 1951. "Regressive Shock Therapy in Schizophrenia." *Disease of the Nervous System*, 12, 147–150.

Rubin, L.B. 2007. "Sand Castles and Snake Pits: Homelessness, Public Policy, and the Law of Unintended Consequences." *Dissent*, 54, 51–56.

Rubin, L.C. 2004. "Merchandising Madness: Pills, Promises, and Better Living Through Chemistry." *Journal of Popular Culture*, 38, 369–383.

Rudin, D.O. 1980. "The Choroid Plexus and Systemic Disease in Mental Illness." *Biological Psychiatry*, 15, 517–539.

Rudolf, G.D.M. 1931. "Experimental Treatments of Schizophrenia." *Journal of Mental Science*, 77, 767–791.

Rush, B. 1784. *An Inquiry into the Effects of Ardent Spirits Upon the Human Body and Mind*. Philadelphia: Thomas Bradford.

_____. 1812. *Medical Inquiries and Observations Upon the Diseases of the Mind*. Philadelphia: Kimber and Richardson.

Russell, A.B. 1898. *A Plea for the Insane by Friends of the Living Dead*. Minneapolis: Roberts.

Saks, E.R. 2007. *The Center Cannot Hold*. New York: Hyperion.

Salinsky, E., and C. Loftus, C. 2007. "Shrinking Inpatient Psychiatric Capacity." National Health Policy Forum, Issue Brief No. 823. Washington, D.C.: George Washington University.

Sanborn, F.B., ed. 1885. *Life and Letters of John Brown*. Boston: Robert Brothers.

Sandyk, R. 1998. "Choroid Plexus Calcification as a Possible Marker of Hallucinations in Schizophrenia." *International Journal of Neuroscience*, 71, 87–92.

Sapinsley, B. 1991. *The Private War of Mrs. Packard*. New York: Paragon.

Sareyan, A. 1994. *The Turning Point: How Persons of Conscience Brought About Major Change in the Care of America's Mentally Ill*. Scottdale, PA: Herald.

Savitt, T.L. 1978. *Medicine and Slavery*. Urbana: University of Illinois Press.

Sayre, G.M. 1997. *Les Sauvages Américains: Representations of Native Americans in French and English Colonial Literature*. Chapel Hill: University of North Carolina Press.

Scharer, K., and D.S. Jones. 2004. "Child Psychiatric Hospitalization: The Last Resort." *Issues in Mental Health Nursing*, 25, 79–101.

Scheff, T.J. 1966. *Being Mentally Ill: A Sociological Theory*. Chicago: Aldine.

Schiller, L., and A. Bennett. 1994. *The Quiet Room.* New York: Warner, .

Schneider, D., and C.J. Schneider. 2007. *Slavery in America.* New York: Checkmate.

Scholinski, D. 1997. *The Last Time I Wore a Dress.* New York: Riverhead.

Scull, A.T. 1984. *Desegregation.* New Brunswick, NJ: Rutgers University Press.

_____. 2004. "The Insanity of Place." *History of Psychiatry,* 15, 417–436.

_____. 2005. *Madhouse: A Tragic Tale of Megalomania and Modern Medicine.* New Haven, CT: Yale University Press.

_____. 1977. "Madness and Segregative Control: The Rise of the Insane Asylum." *Social Problems,* 24, 337–351.

_____. 1995. Psychiatrists and Historical "Facts." *History of Psychiatry,* 6, 225–241.

_____. 1989. *Social Order/Mental Disorder.* Berkeley: University of California Press.

_____. 1984. "Somatic Treatments and the Historiography of Psychiatry." *History of Psychiatry,* 5, 1–12.

Sessions, M.A. 1917. "Feeblemindedness in Ohio." *Journal of Heredity,* 8, 291–298.

Sexton, A. 1982. *The Complete Poems: Anne Sexton.* New York: Mariner.

Shakespeare, William. 1984. *King Lear.* In *The Complete Works of William Shakespeare* (pp. 868–899), edited by J.D. Wilson. London: Octopus.

Sheehan, S. 1983. *Is There No Place on Earth for Me?* New York: Vantage.

Sherlock, R.K., R.F. Haykal, and R. Dresser. 1982. "Case Studies Saying 'No' to Electroshock." *Hastings Center Report,* 12, 18–20.

Shorter, E. 1997. *A History of Psychiatry: From the Era of the Asylum to the Age of Prozac.* New York: John Wiley & Sons.

_____, and D. Healy. 2007. *Shock Therapy: A History of Electroconvulsive Treatment in Mental Illness.* New Brunswick, NJ: Rutgers University Press.

Showalter, E. 1987. *The Female Malady.* New York: Virago.

_____. 1998. *Hystories.* New York: Columbia University Press.

Shrady, G.F. 1959. "Proceedings of the Fourteenth Annual Meeting of the Association of Medical Superintendents of American Institutions for the Insane." *American Journal of Insanity,* 16, 42–96.

Shurtleff, N.B. 1853–1854. *Records of the Governor and Company of the Massachusetts Bay in New England, 1628–1686.* Boston: William White.

Skinner v. State of Oklahoma, Ex. Rel. 1942. Williamson, 316 U.S. 535.

Slater, L. 1996. "Black Swans." *Missouri Review,* 19, 29–46.

_____. 2004. *Opening Skinner's Box: Great Psychological Experiments of the Twentieth Century.* New York: W.W. Norton.

_____. 2005. "Reply to Spitzer and Colleagues." *Journal of Nervous and Mental Disease,* 193, 734–739.

Smith, E.H. November 1, 1797. "Case of Mania Successfully Treated by Mercury." *Medical Repository of Original Essays and Intelligence,* 181–184.

Smith, J.M. May 5, 1844. "Protest Against Racism." *New York Tribune,* 1.

Smith, L.A. 1879. *Behind the Scene, or Life in an Insane Asylum.* Chicago: Culver, Page, Hoyne.

Smoak, G.E. 2006. *Ghost Dances and Identity: Prophetic Religion and American Indian Ethnogenesis in the Nineteenth Century.* Berkeley: University of California Press.

Snelders, S., C. Kaplan, and T. Pieters. 2006. "On Cannabis, Chloral Hydrate, and Career Cycles of Psychotropic Drugs in Medicine." *Bulletin of the History of Medicine,* 80, 95–114.

Snyder, K. 2007. *Me, Myself, and Them.* New York: Oxford University Press.

"The South: In Bill Moore's Footsteps." May 10, 1963. *Time,* 14.

"Southern Doctors." November 30, 1936. *Time,* 66–67.

Spaulding, J.M. 1986. "The Canton Asylum for Insane Indians: An Example of Institutional Neglect." *Hospital and Community Psychiatry,* 45, 1007–1011.

Spitka, E.C. 1878. "Reform in the Scientific Study of Psychiatry." *Journal of Nervous and Mental Disease,* 5, 201–229.

Spitzer, R.L. 1981. "The Diagnostic Status of Homosexuality in the *DSM-III:* A Reformulation of the Issues." *American Journal of Psychiatry,* 138, 210–215.

_____. 2008. "*DSM-V:* "Open and Transparent?" *Psychiatric Times,* 43, 26.

_____. 1976. "More on Pseudoscience and the Case for Psychiatric Diagnosis." *Archives of General Psychiatry,* 33, 459–470.

_____. 1975. "On Pseudoscience, Logic in Remission, and Psychiatric Diagnosis." *Journal of Abnormal Psychology*, 84, 442–452.

_____, S.O. Lilienfeld, and M.B. Miller. 2005. "Rosenhan Revisited: The Scientific Credibility of Lauren Slater's Pseudopatient Study." *Journal of Nervous and Mental Disease*, 193, 734–739.

Stafford, J. May 21, 1938. "The Shock That Cures." *Science News Letter*, 334–337.

Starks, H.A. 1938. "Subjective Experiences in Patients Incident to Insulin and Metrazoltherapy." *Psychiatric Quarterly*, 12, 699–709.

Starr, M. 1904. *Sane or Insane? or How I Regained My Liberty.* Baltimore: Fosnot.

Statement of Governor Luther W. Youngdahl at the Burning of the Restraints. October 31, 1949. Retrieved on the World Wide Web <http.www.mnddc.org/past/pdf/49-SGL-Youngdahl.pdf>

Stawicki, E. "A Haunting Legacy: Canton Insane Asylum." December 9, 1997. Retrieved on the World Wide Web <http://news.minnesota.publicradio.org/features/199712/09_stawickie_asylum>

Steele, E.E., and K. Hains. 2001. *Beauty Is Therapy: Memoirs of the Traverse City State Hospital.* Traverse City, MI: Denali.

Stefan, G. 1966/ *In Search of Sanity: The Journal of a Schizophrenic.* New Hyde Park, New York: University.

Stern, A.M. 2005b. *Eugenic Nation.* Berkeley: University of California Press.

_____. 2005a. "Eugenics and Historical Memory in America." *History Compass*, 3, 1–11.

Stoker, B. 1897. *Dracula.* London: Archibald Constable.

Stone, B. 2004. "Towards a Writing Without Power: Notes on the Narration of Madness." *Auto/Biography*, 12, 16–33.

Stone, E.T. 1842. *A Sketch of the Life of Elizabeth T. Stone, and of Her Persecution, with an Appendix of Her Treatment and Sufferings While in the Charleston McLean Asylum Where She Was Confined Under the Pretence of Insanity.* Boston: Author.

Strauss, J.R. 1989. "Subjective Experiences of Schizophrenia." *Schizophrenia Bulletin*, 15, 179–187.

Strecker, E.A., H.D. Palmer, and F.C. Grant.

1942. "A Study of Frontal Lobotomy." *American Journal of Psychiatry*, 98, 524–532.

Styron, W. 1990. *Darkness Visible.* New York: Random House.

Sullivan, H.C. 1958. "The American Psychiatric Association in Relation to American Psychiatry." *American Journal of Psychiatry*, 115, 1–9.

Susser, E.S., M. Cannon, and P.B. Jones. 2002. *Epidemiology of schizophrenia.* Cambridge: Cambridge University Press.

Sutton, J.R. 1991. "The Political Economy of Madness: The Expansion of the Asylum in Progressive America." *American Sociological Review*, 56, 665–678.

Swan, J. 1990. "The Slave Who Sued for Freedom." *American Heritage*, 42, 51–52, 54–55.

Swazey, J.P. 1974. *Chlorpromazine in Psychiatry: A Study in Therapeutic Innovation.* Cambridge: MIT Press.

Szajnberg, N.M., and A. Weiner. 1989. "Children's Conceptualization of Their Own Psychiatric Illness and Hospitalization." *Child Psychiatry and Human Development*, 20, 87–97.

_____, and _____. 1996. "The Child's Conception of Psychiatric Cure." *Child Psychiatry and Human Development*, 26, 247–254.

Szasz. T.S. 1970. *The Manufacture of Madness.* New York: Harper and Row.

_____. 1974. *The Myth of Mental Illness.* New York: Harper and Row.

_____. 1973. *The Second Sin.* Garden City, New York: Doubleday Anchor.

Theriot, N.M. 1993. "Women's Voices in 19th Century Medical Discourse." *Signs*, 19, 1–31.

Thompson, J., and J.D. Blaine. "Use of ECT in the United States in 1975, 1980 and 1986." *American Journal of Psychiatry*, 151 (1994): 1657–1661.

Thompson, T. 1995. *The Beast: A Reckoning with Depression.* NY: G.P. Putnam's Sons.

Thomson, R.G. 2000. "Seeing the Disabled: Visual Rhetorics of Disability in Popular Photography." In *The New Disability History: American Perspectives* (pp. 335–374), edited by P.K. Longmore and L. Umansky. New York: New York University Press.

Thomson S. 1834. *Learned Quackery Ex-*

posed, or Theory According to Art as Exemplified in the Practice of Fashionable Doctors of the Present Day. Boston: Author.

Tielkes, C.E.M., H.C. Comijs, E. Verwijk, and M.L. Stek. 2008. "The Effects of ECT on Cognitive Functioning in the Elderly: A Review." *International Journal of Geriatric Psychiatry*, 23, 789–795.

Tillotson, K.J., and W. Sulzbach. 1945. "A Comparative Study and Evaluation of Electric Shock Therapy in Depressive States." *American Journal of Psychiatry*, 101, 455–459.

Timberlake, W.H. 1955. "Neurosyphilis." *American Journal of Psychiatry*, 111, 524–527.

Tomes, N. 1994. *The Art of Asylum-Keeping: Thomas Kirkbride and the Origins of American Psychiatry.* Philadelphia: University of Pennsylvania Press.

_____. 1988. "The Great Restraint Controversy." In *The Anatomy of Madness.* Vol. 3, *The Asylum and Its Psychiatry* (pp. 190–225), edited by W.F. Bynum, R. Porter, and M. Sheperd. London: Routledge.

Tone, A. 2008. *The Age of Anxiety.* New York: Basic.

Torrey, E.F., and J. Miller. 2001. *The Invisible Plague: The Rise of Mental Illness from 1750 to the Present.* New Brunswick, NJ: Rutgers University Press.

Toulmin, S. 1969. *The Uses of Argument.* Cambridge: Cambridge University Press.

Trautman, R., and B. Trautman. 1892. *Wisconsin's Shame: Insane Asylums or the American Bastile! The Narrative of the Kidnapping of Misses Trautman, of Sauk City, Wisc., on a Sunday Afternoon, and Running Them into an Insane Asylum.* Chicago: Guiding Star.

"Treating the Insane." January 3, 1921. *Trenton Evening Times,* 6.

Tuke, S. 1813. *Description of the Retreat; an Institution Near York for Insane Persons of the Society of Friends.* Philadelphia: Isaac Peirce.

Turner, B.S., and C. Sampson. 1995. *Medical Power and Social Knowledge.* London: Sage.

Turner, T.H. 1992. "Schizophrenia as a Permanent Problem: Some Aspects of Historical Evidence in the Recency (New Disease) Hypothesis." *History of Psychiatry,* 3, 413–429.

U.S. Surgeon General. 2001. *Mental Health, Culture, Race and Ethnicity.* Washington, D.C.: U.S. Government Printing Office.

Unzicker, R.E. 1995. "From the Inside." In *Beyond Bedlam* (pp. 13–18), edited by J. Grobe. Chicago: Third Side.

Vallenstein, E.S. 1986. *Great and Desperate Cures.* New York: Basic.

van Waarde, J.A., J.J. Stolker, and R.C. van der Mast. 2001. "ECT in Mental Retardation: A Review." *Journal of ECT,* 4, 236–243.

Viets, H. 1935. "Some of the Features of the History of Medicine in Massachusetts During the Colonial Period, 1620–1770." *Isis,* 23, 389–405.

Vincent, N. 2008. *Voluntary Madness: My Year Lost and Found in the Loony Bin.* New York: Viking.

Viner, N. 1933. "A Case of Dementia Praecox Treated by Intraspinal Injections of Horse serum." *Canadian Medical Association Journal,* 48, 420–422.

"A Visit to the Philadelphia Alms House." August 11, 1832. *Liberator,* 2, 128.

Volkow, N.D., and C.P. O'Brien. 2007. "Issues for *DSM-V*: Should Obesity Be Included as a Brain Disorder?" *American Journal of Psychiatry,* 164, 708–710.

Vonnegut, M. 1975. *The Eden Express.* New York: Praeger.

Wahl, W. 1997. *Media Madness: Public Images of Mental Illness.* New Brunswick, NJ: Rutgers University Press.

Wallis, C., and Wilwerth, J. July 6, 1992. "Awakenings: A New Drug Brings Patients Back to Life." *Time,* 57.

Walter, G., A. McDonald, J.M. Rey, and A. Rosen. 2002. "Medical Student Knowledge and Attitudes Regarding ECT Prior to and After Viewing ECT Scenes from Movies." *Journal of ECT,* 18, 43–46.

Wang, P.S., O. Demler, and R.C. Kessler. 2002. "Adequacy of Treatment for Serious Mental Illness in the United States." *American Journal of Public Health,* 92, 92–98.

Warner, J.H. 1986. *The Therapeutic Perspective.* Cambridge, MA: Harvard University Press.

Warren, R.P. 1946. *All the King's Men.* New York: Harcourt, Brace.

Weickhardt, G.B. 1948. "Penicillin Therapy in General Paresis." *American Journal of Psychiatry,* 105, 63–67.

Weisman, R. 1984. *Witchcraft, Magic and Religion in 17th Century Massachusetts.* Amherst: University of Massachusetts Press.

Weiss, E.M. "Deadly Restraint." October 11, 1998. *Hartford* (CT) *Courant,* A-1-A-2.

Wells, S. "Ex-Mental Health Worker Recalls Time of Lobotomies." March 1, 2009. *Charleston* (WV) *Gazette.* Retrieved on the World Wide Web <http://wvgazette. com/News/200902280405>

Wesley, J. 1843. *Primitive Physic.* London: Barr.

Whaley, A.L., and P.A. Geller. 2003. "Ethnic/Racial Differences in Psychiatric Disorders: A Test of Four Hypotheses." *Ethnicity and Disease,* 13, 499–512.

Wharton, E. 1905. *House of Mirth.* New York: Charles Scribner's Sons.

Whitaker, R. 2005. "Anatomy of an Epidemic: Psychiatric Drugs and the Astonishing Rise of Mental Illness in America." *Ethical Human Psychology and Psychiatry,* 7, 23–35.

_____. 2002. *Mad in America: Bad Science, Bad Medicine, and the Enduring Mistreatment of the Mentally Ill.* Cambridge, MA: Perseus.

White, B., and E. Madara. 2009. American Self-Help Group Clearinghouse. Retrieved on the World Wide Web <http://www. mentalhelp.net/selfhelp>

Whitrow, M. 1990. "Wagner-Jauregg and Fever Therapy." *Medical History,* 34, 294–310.

Wiley, L. 1955. *Voices Calling.* Cedar Rapids, IA: Torch.

Willard, S. 1671. "A Briefe Account of a Strange & Unusuall Providence of God Befallen to Elizabeth Knap of Groton." In *Groton in the Witchcraft Times* (1883) (pp. 7–21), edited by S.A. Green. Cambridge, MA: John Wilson and Son.

Williams, E.Y. 1937. "The Incidence of Mental Disease in the Negro." *The Journal of Negro Education,* 6, 377–392.

Windholz, G., and L.H. Witherspoon. 1993. "Sleep as a Cure for Schizophrenia." *History of Psychiatry,* 4, 83–93.

Windolf, J. October 22, 1997. "A Nation of Nuts." *Wall Street Journal,* 6.

Wines, F.H. 1885. "The Law for the Commitment of Lunatics." *Journal of Social Science,* 20, 61–77.

Winkelman, N.W. 1954. "Chlorpromazine in the Treatment of Neuropsychiatric Disorders." *Journal of the American Medical Association,* 155, 8–21.

Winters, K. 2009. *Gender Madness in American Psychiatry.* Charleston, SC: Book-Surge.

Winthrop, J. 1825–1826. *The History of New England from 1630–1649.* Boston: Phelps and Farnham.

Wolfe, B. 1952. *Limbo.* New York: Ace.

Wood, M.E. 1994. *The Writing on the Wall: Women's Autobiography and the Asylum.* Springfield: University of Illinois Press.

Woodward, S.B. 1850. "Observations on the Medical Treatment of Insanity." *American Journal of Psychiatry,* 7, 1–34.

Woolley, J.T, and G. Peters. 2008. *The American Presidency Project.* Retrieved on the World Wide Web <http://www.presidency. ucsb.edu/ws/index.php?pid=9547>

Worthing, H.J., H. Brill, and H. Wigderson. 1949. "350 Cases of Prefrontal Lobotomy." *Psychiatric Quarterly,* 23, 617–656.

Wright, R. 1991. *Native Son.* New York: Perennial.

Wyatt, R.J., and E.G. DeRenzo. 1986. "Science-less to Homeless." *Science,* 234, 1309.

Wynne, L., I.M. Ryckoff, J. Day, and S.I. Hirsch. 1958. "Pseudo-Mutuality in the Family Relations of Schizophrenics." *Psychiatry,* 21, 205–220.

Yamada, A.M., C. Barrio, S.W. Morrison, D. Sewell, and D.P. Jeste. 2006. "Cross-Ethnic Evaluation of Psychotic Symptom Content in Hospitalized Middle-Aged and Older Adults." *General Hospital Psychiatry,* 28, 161–168.

Yamey, G., and P. Shaw. 2002. "Is Extreme Racism a Mental Illness? No." *Western Journal of Medicine,* 176, 5.

Youngberg v. Romeo. 1982. 457 U.S. 307.

Zetka, J.R. 2008. "Radical Logics and Their Carriers in Medicine: The Case of Psycho-pathology and American Obstetricians and Gynecologists." *Social Problems,* 55, 95–116.

Index

287